Asian/Oceanian Historical Dictionaries
Edited by Jon Woronoff

Asia

1. *Vietnam*, by William J. Duiker. 1989. *Out of print. See No. 27.*
2. *Bangladesh*, 2nd ed., by Craig Baxter and Syedur Rahman. 1996
3. *Pakistan*, by Shahid Javed Burki. 1991. *Out of print. See No. 33.*
4. *Jordan*, by Peter Gubser. 1991
5. *Afghanistan*, by Ludwig W. Adamec. 1991. *Out of print. See No. 29.*
6. *Laos*, by Martin Stuart-Fox and Mary Kooyman. 1992. *Out of print. See No. 35.*
7. *Singapore*, by K. Mulliner and Lian The-Mulliner. 1991
8. *Israel*, by Bernard Reich. 1992
9. *Indonesia*, by Robert Cribb. 1992
10. *Hong Kong and Macau*, by Elfed Vaughan Roberts, Sum Ngai Ling, and Peter Bradshaw. 1992
11. *Korea*, by Andrew C. Nahm. 1993
12. *Taiwan*, by John F. Copper. 1993. *Out of print. See No. 34.*
13. *Malaysia*, by Amarjit Kaur. 1993. *Out of print. See No. 36.*
14. *Saudi Arabia*, by J. E. Peterson. 1993. *Out of print. See No. 45.*
15. *Myanmar*, by Jan Becka. 1995
16. *Iran*, by John H. Lorentz. 1995
17. *Yemen*, by Robert D. Burrowes. 1995
18. *Thailand*, by May Kyi Win and Harold Smith. 1995
19. *Mongolia*, by Alan J. K. Sanders. 1996. *Out of print. See No. 42.*
20. *India*, by Surjit Mansingh. 1996
21. *Gulf Arab States*, by Malcolm C. Peck. 1996
22. *Syria*, by David Commins. 1996
23. *Palestine*, by Nafez Y. Nazzal and Laila A. Nazzal. 1997
24. *Philippines*, by Artemio R. Guillermo and May Kyi Win. 1997

Oceania

1. *Australia*, by James C. Docherty. 1992. *Out of print. See No. 32.*
2. *Polynesia*, by Robert D. Craig. 1993. *Out of print. See No. 39.*
3. *Guam and Micronesia*, by William Wuerch and Dirk Ballendorf. 1994
4. *Papua New Guinea*, by Ann Turner. 1994. *Out of print. See No. 37.*
5. *New Zealand*, by Keith Jackson and Alan McRobie. 1996

New Combined Series

25. *Brunei Darussalam*, by D. S. Ranjit Singh and Jatswan S. Sidhu. 1997
26. *Sri Lanka*, by S. W. R. de A. Samarasinghe and Vidyamali Samarasinghe. 1998
27. *Vietnam*, 2nd ed., by William J. Duiker. 1998
28. *People's Republic of China: 1949–1997*, by Lawrence R. Sullivan, with the assistance of Nancy Hearst. 1998
29. *Afghanistan*, 2nd ed., by Ludwig W. Adamec. 1997
30. *Lebanon*, by As'ad AbuKhalil. 1998
31. *Azerbaijan*, by Tadeusz Swietochowski and Brian C. Collins. 1999
32. *Australia*, 2nd ed., by James C. Docherty. 1999
33. *Pakistan*, 2nd ed., by Shahid Javed Burki. 1999
34. *Taiwan (Republic of China)*, 2nd ed., by John F. Copper. 2000
35. *Laos*, 2nd ed., by Martin Stuart-Fox. 2001
36. *Malaysia*, 2nd ed., by Amarjit Kaur. 2001
37. *Papua New Guinea*, 2nd ed., by Ann Turner. 2001
38. *Tajikistan*, by Kamoludin Abdullaev and Shahram Akbarzedeh. 2002
39. *Polynesia*, 2nd ed., by Robert D. Craig. 2002
40. *North Korea*, by Ilpyong J. Kim. 2003
41. *Armenia*, by Rouben Paul Adalian. 2002
42. *Mongolia*, 2nd ed., by Alan J. K. Sanders. 2003
43. *Cambodia*, by Justin Corfield and Laura Summers. 2003
44. *Iraq*, by Edmund A. Ghareeb. 2003
45. *Saudi Arabia*, 2nd ed., by J. E. Peterson. 2003

Historical Dictionary
of
Saudi Arabia

Second Edition

J. E. Peterson

Asian/Oceanian Historical Dictionaries, No. 45

The Scarecrow Press, Inc.
Lanham, Maryland, and Oxford
2003

SCARECROW PRESS, INC.

Published in the United States of America
by Scarecrow Press, Inc.
A Member of the Rowman & Littlefield Publishing Group
4501 Forbes Boulevard, Suite 200, Lanham, MD 20706
www.scarecrowpress.com

PO Box 317
Oxford
OX2 9RU, UK

British Library Cataloguing in Publication Information Available

Library of Congress Cataloging-in-Publication Data

Peterson, John, 1947–
  Historical dictionary of Saudi Arabia / J. E. Peterson.—2nd ed.
    p. cm. — (Asian/Oceanian historical dictionaries ; no. 45)
  Includes bibliographical references.
  ISBN 0-8108-4677-2
  1. Saudi Arabia—History—Dictionaries. I. Title. II. Series.
DS221.P48 2003
953.8'003—dc21   2002156346
First edition by J. E. Peterson, Asian Historical Dictionaries, No. 14,
Scarecrow Press, Metuchen, N.J., 1993   ISBN 0-8108-2780-8

CONTENTS

Maps	vii
Editor's Foreword *Jon Woronoff*	xi
Acknowledgements	xiii
Conventions and Spellings	xv
Acronyms and Abbreviations	xvii
Chronology	xix
Introduction	1
THE DICTIONARY	15
Appendix A: Rulers in the Al Sa'ud Dynasty	165
Appendix B: The Al Sa'ud: Relationship of Cadet Branches	166
Appendix C: Prominent Descendants of Imam 'Abd Al-Rahman bin Faysal	167
Appendix D: Prominent Descendants of King 'Abd Al-'Aziz bin 'Abd Al-Rahman	168
Appendix E: Al-Hashimi Sharifs of Makkah and Their Descendants	172
Appendix F: The Basic Law of Saudi Arabia	175
Appendix G: Statistical Tables	183
Selected Bibliography	205
General, Bibliography, and Collections	208
Oil	210
Economy and Finance	211
Exploration	218
Geography	219
History and Archaeology	220
General, Early, and Archaeology	220
18th and 19th Centuries: The First and Second Saudi States	222
20th Century: The Third Saudi State	223
Biography and Autobiography	228
Politics and Government	230
Law	237
Foreign Affairs and International Relations	238
Foreign Policy and General	238
Regional Relations	240
Relations with the United States	242
National and Regional Security	245
Society and Culture	248
Islam	254
Websites	255
About the Author	259

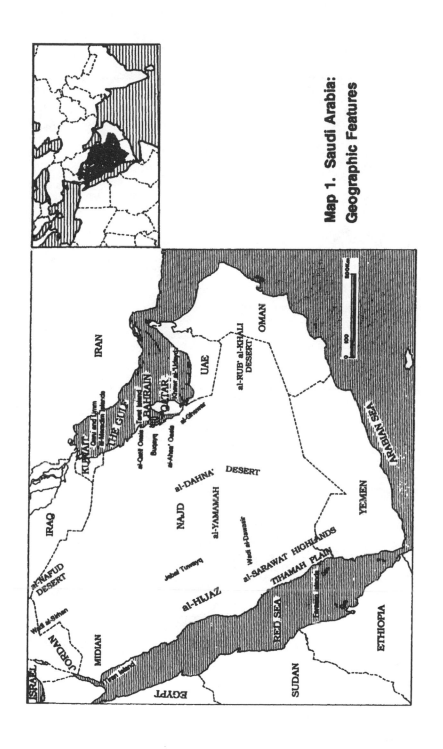

Map 1. Saudi Arabia: Geographic Features

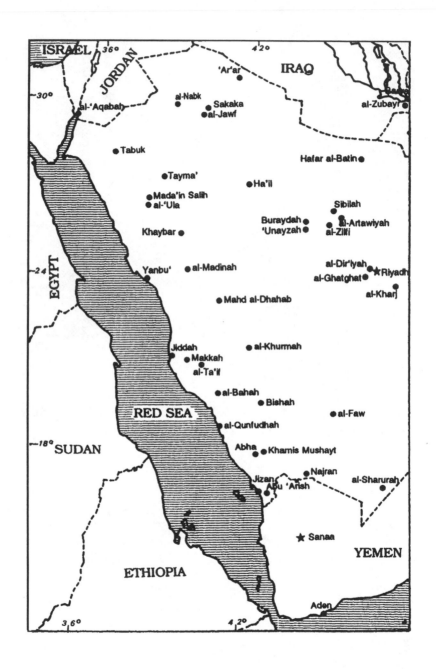

IRAN

KUWAIT

THE GULF

al-Khafji

al-Jubail

Thaj.

al-Qatif   Ra's Tanurah
            al-Khubar
al-Dammam
Dhahran   BAHRAIN
al-'Uqayr
al-Hufuf   QATAR

●Harad   ■Dubai

                    Abu Dhabi ●al-Buraymi
              UAE   Muscat

                    Umm al-Zamul

                          OMAN

ARABIAN SEA

0   100   500Km

Map 2. Saudi Arabia: Placenames

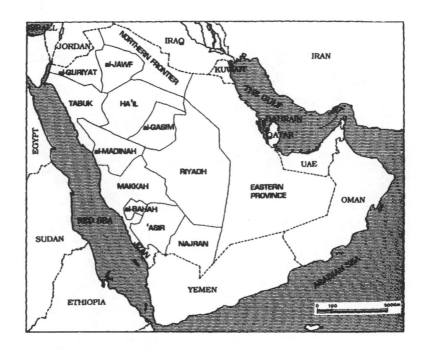

Map 3. Saudi Arabia: Administrative Divisions

International Border -------
Amirate Border   ---------

EDITOR'S FOREWORD

Not so long ago, indeed only a bit over a decade ago when the first edition of this volume was being written, it was necessary to stress that Saudi Arabia was more important than it appeared. For it was not as visible, or vociferous, as other countries in the region, exercising its considerable clout more quietly yet effectively. It was, among other things, instrumental in keeping the oil price relatively stable at all times and lower than otherwise in times of shortage or crisis. It could strongly influence the nearby Gulf States and, through its wealth, had a definite impact more broadly in the Arab and Muslim world. Nor should it ever be forgotten that it is the protector of Islam's holiest sites. But Saudi Arabia became more noticeable, and decisive, at the time of the Gulf War and thereafter and now, embarrassingly so, in the aftermath of September 11th.

With Saudi Arabia increasingly significant, it is clearly essential to know more about it. This knowledge should hopefully extend beyond the obvious. Oil, wealth and location are important. So is its help in any attempt to counter terrorism. But it is even more useful to know something about the state itself, how it is organized and run, not as easy to determine as elsewhere. Beyond this, to see how well it is progressing and where it is heading, it is necessary to consider its educational, social, defense and other policies. The key to much of this is its leaders, especially those in the ruling family which created and has directed the Saudi state for over two centuries. And even that must be set in the context of a civilization over 5,000 years old, a very rich culture and a pervasive religious heritage. All of these aspects, and many more, are amply covered in this *Historical Dictionary of Saudi Arabia*.

This second edition was written by J. E. Peterson who also wrote the first edition. He is thoroughly familiar with the Arabian Peninsula, having spent considerable time and traveled widely there over the years. Dr. Peterson has also done extensive research for, among others, the Foreign Policy Research Institute in Philadelphia, the Center for Strategic and International Studies in Washington, D.C., and the International Institute for Strategic Studies in London, and taught at Bowdoin College, the College of William and Mary, the University of Pennsylvania and Portland State University. Among the books he has written or edited are *Oman in the Twentieth Century, Yemen: The Search for a Modern State, The Politics of Middle Eastern Oil, Defending Arabia, The Arab Gulf States: Steps Towards Political Participation, Crosscurrents in the Gulf* and *Saudi Arabia: The Illusion of Security*. This historical dictionary is one more contribution, and a very welcome one, to our knowledge of a crucial region.

Jon Woronoff
Series Editor

ACKNOWLEDGEMENTS

First Edition

In many ways, this volume is the product of some 20 years of study of the Arabian Peninsula and Saudi Arabia. More directly, however, the pattern of my research in the last few years, focusing on a topic of comparative state building or historical and political change in the Arabian Peninsula, has provided the stimulus and the opportunity to gather much of the information presented in this dictionary.

I am grateful for the help provided by numerous Saudis and expatriates, both inside the kingdom and elsewhere, who have been very patient in answering questions and providing advice and information. Although I have been able to visit Saudi Arabia on various occasions over the years, two extended stays in 1988 were of particular value. For these opportunities, I would like to thank the Earhart Foundation and the government of the Kingdom of Saudi Arabia, particularly H.R.H. Prince Salman bin 'Abd al-'Aziz, the Ministries of Foreign Affairs and Information, and the Saudi Information Office in Washington, D.C.

In addition, several other people merit particular mention by name. Robin Lamb and 'Abdullah Muhammad al-Wuhaibi read an earlier draft of the manuscript and provided a multitude of knowledgeable comments. Dr. Monique Kervran provided assistance with sources for the archaeological entries and in preparing the maps. St. John Armitage and Dr. David E. Long were helpful in answering desperate queries in the final stages. Muhammad Said al-Wuhaibi very kindly checked the Arabic. Brenda Blackburn and Andrew T. Parasiliti supplied me with valuable research assistance, and the staff of the Middle East Institute Library were very helpful, as ever, in locating relevant sources.

Second Edition

This second edition corrects some scattered errors in the first edition, adds a number of new entries, and updates the chronology, many of the dictionary entries, and the bibliography. Additional information was acquired from many sources but a visit to Saudi Arabia in early 2001, as part of a delegation organized by the National Council on US-Arab Relations and hosted by the Saudi Committee for the Development of International Trade, was especially useful. I am grateful for very helpful responses to my queries by St. John Armitage (again) and Shaykh Abdulaziz O. Sager.

CONVENTIONS
AND SPELLINGS

1. Words and phrases in bold have their own entry in the dictionary.
2. Brackets ([..]) after an entry head include the complete transliteration with diacritics of Arabic words and phrases, the word or phrase in Arabic script, variant English spellings on occasion, and the geographical coordinates of places.
   a. While the full names of individuals and families are given in Arabic script, transliteration with diacritics is generally only partial:
      (i) only unusual given names for members of the Al Sa'ud are fully transliterated; and
      (ii) for other individuals, only the family name is transliterated, unless the given name or other elements are unusual.
   b. The vexing problem of spelling has been addressed by transliterating Arabic words according to the system employed by the Library of Congress, the British Library, and the *International Journal of Middle East Studies,* with a few anomalies. Words with variant spellings (*e.g.* eid for *'id*) are cross-referenced. A few place names (*e.g.* Riyadh) have retained their more common spelling, although Mecca has been spelled Makkah in line with Muslim sensitivities about the sometimes notorious connotation in the West (*e.g.* gambling institutions) that "Mecca" has acquired.
3. Use of the title "Imam" before a name indicates that the person was a head of the Al Sa'ud state.
4. It should be stressed that many dates, especially those before the 20th century, can be only approximate.
5. Geographical coordinates for most locations are taken from Husayn Hamzah Banduqji, *al-kharitah al jugrafiyah lil-mamlakah al-'arabiyah al-sa'udiyah* ["Geographical Map of the Kingdom of Saudi Arabia"] (Jiddah, 1404/1984).
6. An explanation of Arabic personal names may be useful. A standard Arabic name has four components, in the following order: [given name] ibn (son of) / bint (daughter of) [father's name] ibn [grandfather's name] [family or tribal name]. For example: Ahmad ibn Muhammad ibn Mahmud al-Shammari = Ahmad, son of Muhammad, who is the son of Mahmud, of the tribe of Shammar. "Ibn" is frequently pronounced "bin" and, in informal practice, the "ibn" or "bint" is often omitted. People are usually addressed by their given name, along with an honorific (if any). If the Ahmad of this example were the shaykh or head of a tribe, he would normally be called "Shaykh Ahmad." A parent will frequently be addressed informally as the father or mother of the child, *e.g.* "Abu Muhammad" or "Umm Muhammad." However, the use of "abu" in a name may also refer to an honorific for a respected figure or be part of a family name. Similarly, "ibn" was employed as an honorific for the leader of a community, *e.g.* Ibn Sa'ud or Ibn Rashid. Those Muslims

who have made the pilgrimage to Makkah dictated by Islam are entitled to use the honorific "Hajji." In a practice more common outside the Arabian Peninsula, the name of a grandfather may be adopted as a family name, *e.g.* someone called Ahmad M. ʿUthman in genealogical terms might actually be Ahmad ibn Musa ibn Muhammad ibn Ahmad ibn ʿUthman.

7. The placement of "A.D." with dates may appear inconsistent at first glance. As the letters are an abbreviation of Anno Domini, "in the year of our Lord," they properly should precede the date. Technically, it is nonsensical to apply the phrase to centuries, but this dictionary observes a common publishing compromise by placing A.D. following the mention of a century. A similar practice has been used for "A.H.," Anno Hegirae.

ACRONYMS AND ABBREVIATIONS

ARAMCO	Arabian American Oil Company
BCCI	Bank of Credit and Commerce International
b/d	barrels per day
c.	circa
CALTEX	Joint marketing company of SOCAL and TEXACO
CDLR	Committee for the Defense of Legitimate Rights
CPO	Central Planning Organization
CPSA	Communist Party of Saudi Arabia
d.	died
fem.	feminine
GCC	Gulf Cooperation Council
GDP	Gross Domestic Product
GIA	General Investment Authority
GPGE	General Presidency for Girls' Education
IBRD	International Bank for Reconstruction and Development (World Bank)
ICO	Islamic Conference Organization
IMF	International Monetary Fund
IPSA	Iraq Pipeline across Saudi Arabia
JECOR	US/Saudi Joint Economic Commission
KACST	King 'Abd al-'Aziz Center for Science and Technology
KSA	Kingdom of Saudi Arabia
MBC	Middle East Broadcasting Corporation
mbd	million barrels per day
mill.	millennium
MODA	Minister (or Ministry) of Defense and Aviation
MRL	Modified Riyadh Line
NCB	National Commercial Bank
NLF	National Liberation Front
OAPEC	Organization of Arab Petroleum Exporting Countries
OIC	Organization of the Islamic Conference
OIRAP	Organization of the Islamic Revolution in the Arabian Peninsula
OPEC	Organization of Petroleum Exporting Countries
PDF	Popular Democratic Front
PETROMIN	General Organization for Petroleum and Minerals
pl.	plural
PLO	Palestine Liberation Organization
PRPG	Political Resident in the Persian Gulf
r.	ruled
RSA	Royal Saudi Army
RSAF	Royal Saudi Air Force

RSN	Royal Saudi Navy
SABIC	Saudi Arabian Basic Industries Corporation
SAMA	Saudi Arabian Monetary Agency
SANG	Saudi Arabian National Guard
SFD	Saudi Fund for Development
sing.	singular
SOCAL	Standard Oil of California
SR	Saudi riyal
TAPLINE	Trans-Arabian Pipeline
UAE	United Arab Emirates
UPAP	Union of Peoples of the Arabian Peninsula
USMTM	US Military Training Mission
WTO	World Trade Organization

CHRONOLOGY

- B.C. -

4th mill. Settlements belonging to al-'Ubayd culture appear in eastern Arabia

3rd mill. Trading settlement established on Tarut Island in the Gulf

2nd mill. Middle: Walled town-complexes are built at al-Quriyat, Daydan (modern al-'Ula), Tayma' and Ha'il

1st mill. Dumat al-Jandal (modern al-Jawf) emerges as first known independent Arabian state

9th cent. Settlements established at Thaj and Najran; al-Faw flourishes until 2nd century B.C.

c. 750 Sabaean civilization of South Arabia appears and flourishes until c. 115 B.C.; Minaean civilization appears a few decades later and flourishes until 3rd century B.C.

1st mill. Middle: Mada'in Salih established as Minaean outpost

7th cent. Lihyanite civilization appears with its capital at Daydan (modern al-'Ula) and flourishes until 3rd century B.C.

4th cent. Early: Nabataeans establish a state with its capital at Petra and dominate northwestern Arabia for the next four centuries

c. 115 Himyaritic state supplants Sabaean and Minaean civilizations in South Arabia and flourishes until c. A.D. 300

24 Roman army under Aelius Gallus invades Arabia

- A.D. -

106 Petra becomes a Roman province

c. 500 Quraysh tribe establishes control over the trading center of Makkah

570 The Prophet Muhammad is born into Quraysh tribe at Makkah

622   **July 16:** Prophet Muhammad and his Muslim followers leave Makkah for Yathrib (now al-Madinah); this event (*hijrah*) marks beginning of Islamic calendar

624   Muslim forces of al-Madinah defeat superior army of Makkah at Battle of Badr

625   Makkan forces defeat Muslims at Battle of Uhud outside al-Madinah

630   Makkah submits to the Muslims

632   Prophet Muhammad makes his farewell *hajj* (pilgrimage) to Makkah and dies later that year

635   Jawatha Mosque established in al-Ahsa' oasis, making it the oldest mosque in eastern Arabia

8th cent. Pilgrims' way of Darb Zubaydah is built across the northern Arabian Peninsula to Makkah

899   al-Qaramitah (Carmathians) establish a state based on al-Hufuf

930   al-Qaramitah raid Makkah and bring the sacred Black Stone to al-Qatif; it is returned to Makkah in 951

c. 1446 Village of al-Dir'iyah is founded in southern Najd by Mani' bin Rabi'ah

1541   Portuguese attack Jiddah

c. 1541 Najdi town of Buraydah is founded

1550   Ottomans capture al-Hufuf during course of their expansion into perimeter of Arabian Peninsula

1669   Bani Khalid tribe ousts Ottoman forces from eastern Arabian Peninsula

1703   Islamic reformer Muhammad bin 'Abd al-Wahhab is born in al-'Uyaynah

1727   Muhammad bin Sa'ud bin Muqrin becomes first independent Saudi ruler of al-Dir'iyah

1744   Muhammad 'Abd al-Wahhab is forced to leave al-'Uyaynah and is welcomed at al-Dir'iyah by Imam Muhammad bin Sa'ud Al Sa'ud, who subsequently accepts Wahhabism

1762   Imam Muhammad bin Sa'ud Al Sa'ud dies and is succeeded by his son 'Abd al-'Aziz bin Sa'ud

1773   Forces of Al Sa'ud capture Riyadh

1792   Muhammad bin 'Abd al-Wahhab dies

1794   Al Sa'ud forces capture al-Ahsa'

1798   Saudi forces defeat Sharif Ghalib of Makkah near al-Khurmah

c. 1801   Saudi forces attack Karbala and strip tomb of Caliph al-Husayn; Saudi forces subsequently capture Makkah

1803   Imam 'Abd al-'Aziz bin Sa'ud Al Sa'ud is assassinated and is succeeded by his son Sa'ud bin 'Abd al-'Aziz

1805   Saudi forces capture al-Madinah

1814   Muhammad 'Ali, the Ottoman Viceroy of Egypt, captures al Hijaz from the Al Sa'ud

1814   Imam Sa'ud bin 'Abd al-'Aziz Al Sa'ud dies and is succeeded by his son 'Abdullah

1818   Muhammad 'Ali's son Ibrahim Pasha destroys Al Sa'ud capital at al-Dir'iyah; Imam 'Abdullah bin Sa'ud is taken to Istanbul where he is executed

1819   G. F. Sadleir becomes the first European to cross the Arabian Peninsula

1824   Turki bin Sa'ud, a cousin of previous Imam 'Abdullah, assumes leadership of Al Sa'ud and eventually recaptures Riyadh

1824   Al Khalifah of Bahrain seize al-Dammam and hold it for 17 years

c. 1830   Idrisi family settles in Sabya

1834   Imam Turki bin Sa'ud is assassinated; his son Faysal defeats the assassin and becomes Imam

1835   'Abdullah bin Rashid of 'Abdah Shammar tribe is appointed governor of Ha'il by Imam Faysal bin Turki Al Sa'ud, thus beginning Al Rashid dynasty

1838   Egyptian forces invade Najd a second time and take Imam Faysal to Cairo

1840   Direct Ottoman rule is reimposed on al-Hijaz

1843   Imam Faysal escapes from Cairo and regains control of Najd, thus marking beginning of Second Saudi State

1845   Saudi forces capture al-Buraymi oasis

1858   A massacre of Christians in Jiddah provokes a British naval bombardment

1864   Imam Faysal dies and dynastic squabbles ensue until 1889

1865   Col. Lewis Pelly, the senior British official in the Gulf, travels to Riyadh

1865   Saudi raids extend deep into Oman

1866   Anglo-Saudi agreement reached

1868   Appointment of Midhat Pasha as Governor-General of Baghdad generates Ottoman expansionist phase in Arabian Peninsula; Ottomans extend their control over eastern Arabia and capture 'Asir from local Al 'Ayid dynasty

1871   Muhammad bin Rashid Al Rashid captures al-Ahsa' from Al Sa'ud

1874   Imam Sa'ud bin Faysal Al Sa'ud dies of wounds received in battle and is succeeded briefly by his brother 'Abdullah

1884   Al Rashid dynasty of Ha'il consolidate their control over most of Najd and capture Riyadh

1889   'Abd al-Rahman bin Faysal, son of Imam Faysal, assumes uncontested leadership of Al Sa'ud and temporarily rejects Al Rashid control of Riyadh

1891   Muhammad bin Rashid Al Rashid captures Riyadh and Imam 'Abd al-Rahman is forced to flee, eventually settling in Kuwait

c. 1900   Idrisi family establishes independent dynasty in Sabya

1900   Work begins on al-Hijaz Railway, linking Syria with al-Madinah

1902   **January:** Imam 'Abd al-'Aziz bin 'Abd al-Rahman captures Riyadh from the Al Rashid, thus marking beginning of Third Saudi State

1905   A small Ottoman garrison is posted in al-Qasim

1908   Ottoman-built al-Hijaz railway reaches al-Madinah

1908   Husayn bin 'Ali al-Hashimi becomes Sharif of Makkah

c. 1908   Saudi sovereignty is extended over al-Qasim

1910   Captain W. H. I. Shakespear, the British Political Agent in Kuwait, becomes the first Englishman to meet Imam 'Abd al-'Aziz

1910 Sharif Husayn of Makkah sends an army to capture al-Qasim but is repulsed by Saudi forces

1912 First Ikhwan settlement is founded at al-Artawiyah

1913 Imam 'Abd al-'Aziz captures al-Ahsa'

1913 **29 July:** Anglo-Ottoman Convention establishes the "Blue Line" as the eastern Arabian boundary between the Ottoman and British empires

1914 **May:** Imam 'Abd al-'Aziz signs a treaty with the Ottomans

1915 Captain Shakespear is killed during the Battle of Jarrab between the Al Sa'ud and the Al Rashid

1915 **26 December:** Anglo-Saudi treaty provides British recognition of Imam 'Abd al-'Aziz bin 'Abd al-Rahman

1916 **5 June:** Sharif Husayn of Makkah proclaims the Arab Revolt

1916 **29 October:** Sharif Husayn of Makkah adopts the title of King of al-Hijaz

1916 **5 November:** Sharif Husayn of Makkah proclaims himself King of the Arabs

1918 **May:** Al-Khurmah is scene of first clash between forces of Imam 'Abd al-'Aziz Al Sa'ud and King Husayn al-Hashimi and the oasis falls to the Al Sa'ud in the following year

1920 The Al Sa'ud occupy mountainous areas of 'Asir

1920 Imam 'Abd al-'Aziz concludes Saudi-Rashidi agreement which places foreign relations of the Al Rashid amirate and control of Shammar tribe under Saudi control

1920 The Ikhwan under the leadership of Faysal al-Duwish rout Kuwaiti Shaykh Salim and his forces at al-Jahrah

1921 Imam 'Abd al-'Aziz annexes the Al Rashid amirate and becomes Sultan of Najd

1922 **5 May:** Representatives of Najd and Iraq sign Treaty of Muhammarah on common borders but the treaty is rejected by Imam 'Abd al-'Aziz

1922 **December:** Al-'Uqayr Protocol fixes Najdi-Iraqi and Najdi-Kuwaiti borders and creates Najdi-Iraqi and Najdi-Kuwaiti Neutral Zones

1923 Major Frank Holmes secures oil concession for al-Ahsa'

1923   Ikhwan raids into Transjordan and Iraq result in numerous deaths

1923   17 December: Kuwait Conference convenes to deal with Saudi-Hashimi border problems and to settle provisions of Treaty of Muhammarah; conference continues until April 1924

1924   3 March: Turkey abolishes Islamic caliphate and it is taken up by King Husayn of al-Hijaz on March 5

1924   August: Saudi forces invade al-Hijaz and Ikhwan capture of al-Ta'if degenerates into looting and a massacre

1924   3 October: King Husayn of al-Hijaz abdicates and leaves for al-'Aqabah; he is succeeded by his son 'Ali; Saudi forces enter Makkah unopposed less than a week later

1925   January: Saudi siege of Jiddah begins

1925   November: Sir Gilbert Clayton negotiates Haddah and Bahrah Agreements with Imam 'Abd al-'Aziz

1925   December: Al-Madinah and Yanbu' surrender to forces of Imam 'Abd al-'Aziz; Saudi army enters Jiddah on 19 December and ex-King 'Ali sails for Iraq on 22 December

1926   Tribal heads of the Ikhwan meet in al-Artawiyah to discuss their grievances against Imam 'Abd al-'Aziz

1926   8 January: Notables of al-Hijaz proclaim 'Abd al-'Aziz King of al-Hijaz and Sultan of Najd and Its Dependencies

1926   February: Britain recognizes 'Abd al-'Aziz as King of al-Hijaz

1926   October: King 'Abd al-'Aziz and Idrisi leader of 'Asir sign Treaty of Makkah

1927   Soviet Union recognizes Imam 'Abd al-'Aziz as King of al-Hijaz and Sultan of Najd and sends a minister to Jiddah

1927   20 May: Anglo-Saudi Treaty of Jiddah supersedes that of 1915; the British government recognizes full independence of Imam 'Abd al-'Aziz while the Saudi leader acknowledges the British treaty relationships with the shaykhdoms of the Gulf

1927   October: The Ikhwan massacre Iraqis at al-Busaya police post, which leads to hostilities between Britain and 'Abd al-'Aziz lasting into following year

1929 The Ikhwan kill an American missionary in his car on road between Basra and Kuwait

1929 **30 March:** King 'Abd al-'Aziz defeats the Ikhwan at the Battle of Sibilah

1929 **Late:** Bertram Thomas becomes the first European to cross al-Rub' al-Khali desert (the Empty Quarter), frustrating H. St. John B. Philby's ambition to be the first

1930 **January:** Imam 'Abd al-'Aziz breaks back of Ikhwan rebellion in Battle of Shu'ayb al- 'Awjah; Ikhwan leaders subsequently surrender in Kuwait and are turned over to 'Abd al-'Aziz

1930 **22 February:** Meeting between Imam 'Abd al-'Aziz and King Faysal of Iraq lays foundations for amicable relations between Al Sa'ud and al-Hashimi families

1930 First British minister arrives in Jiddah

1930 Ministry of Foreign Affairs is established

1930 **November:** King 'Abd al-'Aziz annexes 'Asir

1931 Council of Deputies is established for al-Hijaz

1931 **February:** Charles Crane visits King 'Abd al-'Aziz at Jiddah and sends Karl S. Twitchell to conduct the country's first geological survey

1932 Ministry of Finance is established

1932 **May:** Bin Rifadah, a tribal shaykh of northeastern Arabia, revolts against Imam 'Abd al-'Aziz

1932 **22 September:** Name of the country is changed to Saudi Arabia and 'Abd al-'Aziz adopts title of King of Saudi Arabia

1932 **October:** Idrisi Amir revolts against King 'Abd al-'Aziz

1933 **April:** King 'Abd al-'Aziz and King 'Abdullah of Transjordan recognize each other's regimes

1933 **May:** King 'Abd al-'Aziz grants al-Ahsa' oil concession to SOCAL

1934 **March-May:** Saudi-Yemeni war takes place; the two countries sign the Treaty of al-Ta'if (Yemen) in June

1935   **April:** King 'Abd al-'Aziz presents Britain with his "Red line" border proposal; Britain counters in November with the "Riyadh Line"

1936   Petroleum Concessions Ltd. receives al-Hijaz oil concession

1936   Saudi Arabia signs treaties with kingdoms of Iraq and Egypt

1936   Britain and Saudi Arabia agree to revised Treaty of Jiddah

1938   **March:** Oil discovered at Well No. 7 at Dammam Dome

1939   Oil pipeline is laid from Dhahran oil field to new oil terminal at Ra's Tanurah

1942   British government initiates war subsidy to Saudi Arabia of £3 million

1942   United States legation is established in Jiddah

1944   Californian Arabian Standard Oil Company is renamed Arabian American Oil Company (ARAMCO)

1945   First Saudi university graduates return from abroad

1945   **February:** King 'Abd al-'Aziz meets US President Franklin Roosevelt aboard the USS *Quincy* in the Suez Canal

1945   **March:** Saudi Arabia becomes a founding member of the League of Arab States

1946   Ministry of Defense is established

1946   American air base is established at Dhahran

1947   British Military Mission arrives at al-Ta'if

1948   ARAMCO discovers giant al-Ghawar oil field

1948   United States legation in Jiddah is upgraded to an embassy

1949   Saudi-Kuwait Neutral Zone oil concession is awarded to Getty Oil

1950   Deep-water port is opened at al-Dammam and TAPLINE oil pipeline is built from Eastern Province to Mediterranean ports

1951   Ministry of Interior is established

1951   Railroad is built between al-Dammam and Riyadh

1952 Capital of al-Ahsa' Province is moved to al-Dammam and province is renamed the Eastern Province

1952 Saudi Arabia and Britain discuss boundaries between the kingdom and the British-protected states of the Gulf at al-Dammam Conference, but without success

1952 **October:** Armed Saudi detachment occupies village of al-Hamasah in al-Buraymi oasis

1953 Ministries of Agriculture and Water, Communications, and Education are established

1953 First strike of ARAMCO workers takes place

1953 **9 October:** Royal decree establishes first Council of Ministers; but death of King 'Abd al-'Aziz delays council's first meeting until March 1954

1953 **November:** 'Abd al-'Aziz bin 'Abd al-Rahman (Bin Sa'ud) dies in Riyadh and is succeeded as King by his son Sa'ud bin 'Abd al-'Aziz

1954 Ministry of Health is established

1955 **11 September:** Al-Buraymi Arbitration Tribunal convenes in Geneva but is soon suspended

1955 **26 October:** The Trucial Oman Scouts expel the Saudi garrison from al-Buraymi oasis

1956 **June:** Strikes directed against King Sa'ud occur amongst ARAMCO workers

1956 **August:** King Sa'ud meets with the Soviet Ambassador to Iran in Tehran

1956 **November:** Arab-Israeli (Suez) War provokes demonstrations in Dhahran and Riyadh; Saudi Arabia breaks diplomatic relations with Britain and France

1957 King Sa'ud University, Saudi Arabia's first, opens in Riyadh

1957 King Sa'ud visits the United States and wins sympathy for plight of his polio-stricken young son

1958 **March:** King Sa'ud's plot to assassinate Egyptian President Jamal 'Abd al-Nasir is revealed by Syrian intelligence

1958 **24 March:** King Sa'ud hands over executive powers in foreign and internal affairs, including fiscal planning, to his half brother Faysal

1960   Ministry of Petroleum and Mineral Resources is established

1960   January: Oil production begins in Japan Oil Company concession offshore of Saudi-Kuwaiti Neutral Zone

1960   September: OPEC is formed with Saudi Arabia as a charter member

1960   December: King Saʻud regains control over government from Crown Prince Faysal

1961   Ministry of Labor and Social Affairs is established

1961   January: King Saʻud appoints a new Council of Ministers, including representatives of the "Liberal Princes"

1961   September: Saudi military units arrive in Kuwait as part of Arab League peacekeeping force to deter Iraqi invasion; they remain in Kuwait until January 1963

1961   September: King Saʻud's cabinet reshuffle sends "Liberal Princes" into exile

1962   Ministry of Hajj Affairs and Awqaf is established

1962   American air base at Dhahran reverts to Royal Saudi Air Force

1962   March: Prince Faysal is restored as Deputy Prime Minister and Foreign Minister to substitute for King Saʻud who is in the US for medical treatment

1962   September: Diplomatic relations are resumed with France, as a result of Evian accords which bring an end to Algerian war

1962   26 September: An attempted revolution in Yemen plunges that country into civil war; Egyptian support for the new republic provokes Saudi Arabia to support the ousted Yemeni Imam and his royalist followers

1962   October: The Al Saʻud family forces King Saʻud to appoint Crown Prince Faysal as Prime Minister again, and to appoint Faysal's half brother Khalid as Deputy Prime Minister

1962   November: Prince Faysal, as Prime Minister, announces a 10-point plan for reform, including promises to issue a constitution, establish local government, and form an independent judiciary

1963   Ministry of Information is established

1963   Diplomatic relations are reestablished with Britain

1964 **23 March:** *Fatwa* by *'ulama'* proclaims that King Sa'ud is unfit to rule

1964 **2 November:** A royal proclamation, signed by 68 princes, transfers power from King Sa'ud to Crown Prince Faysal; deposed as king, Sa'ud goes into exile in Greece; King Faysal's half brother Khalid becomes Heir Apparent

1965 Central Planning Organization is created

1966 **November to February 1967:** Underground opposition groups set off bombs inside Saudi Arabia

1967 **June:** Third Arab-Israeli War ends with Israeli occupation of Gaza Strip, the Sinai Peninsula, and Jerusalem and the West Bank; token Saudi forces participate in war while action by ARAMCO workers temporarily disrupts oil exports

1967 **August:** Khartoum summit of Arab leaders leads to settlement of Egyptian-Saudi differences over Yemen and commits Saudi Arabia and other Arab oil-producing states to provide financial subsidies to Arab frontline states

1969 **September:** Rapprochement is achieved with Egypt

1969 **September:** Discovery of putative plot against government sets off wave of arrests lasting into 1970

1970 Ministry of Justice is established

1970 First Five-Year Development Plan is inaugurated

1973 **October:** Fourth Arab-Israeli War begins with Egyptian forces crossing the Suez Canal; talks between OPEC states and oil company representatives in Vienna end inconclusively and are followed by unilateral price rises by Gulf producers; Arab oil producers, including Saudi Arabia, announce a mandatory cut in exports as result of the war and institute an embargo on exports to the United States and the Netherlands (later extended to Portugal, Rhodesia, and South Africa)

1974 **March:** Decision is taken to end Arab oil embargo against United States

1974 **June:** Visit of Second Deputy Prime Minister Fahd bin 'Abd al-'Aziz to Washington results in creation of Saudi-US joint commissions

1975 **25 March:** King Faysal bin 'Abd al-'Aziz is assassinated in Riyadh by his nephew, Prince Faysal bin Musa'id, who is subsequently beheaded; Faysal's half brother Khalid succeeds him as King; half brother Fahd is appointed Heir Apparent

1975   **October:** Council of Ministers is reorganized, with 20 ministries headed by ministers and three ministers without portfolio; King Khalid bin 'Abd al-'Aziz heads Council as Prime Minister, Heir Apparent Fahd bin 'Abd al-'Aziz becomes First Deputy Prime Minister, and 'Abdullah bin 'Abd al-'Aziz becomes Second Deputy Prime Minister

1975   Ministries of Higher Education, Industry and Electricity, Municipalities and Rural Affairs, Planning, Public Works and Housing, and Posts, Telephones, and Telegraphs are established after death of King Faysal

1976   **March:** Diplomatic relations established with South Yemen

1978   **May:** US Congress approves sale of F-15 combat aircraft to Saudi Arabia

1979   Antigovernment demonstrations by Shi'ah elements take place in Eastern Province, inspired by the Iranian revolution; more demonstrations occur in 1980

1979   **21 November:** Neo-Ikhwan group, led by Juhayman bin Muhammad al-'Utaybi seizes Great Mosque of Makkah; control is not regained until 5 December and after the loss of many lives; Juhayman and other surviving dissidents are subsequently executed

1980   ARAMCO becomes 100% Saudi-owned, with ownership backdated to 1976

1980   Carter Doctrine is announced, by which Washington signals its intention to intervene in the Gulf when necessary to protect oil supplies

1981   United States sells five AWACS radar-aircraft to Saudi Arabia after narrow vote of approval in US Congress

1981   **19 May:** Two bombs explode in Riyadh, killing one and wounding three

1981   **25 May:** Gulf Cooperation Council (GCC) is inaugurated in Abu Dhabi at summit of rulers of Saudi Arabia, Kuwait, Bahrain, Qatar, United Arab Emirates, and Oman

1982   King Khalid bin 'Abd al-'Aziz dies and is succeeded by his half brother Fahd: Fahd's half brother 'Abdullah is recognized as Heir Apparent and a full brother Sultan is recognized as next in line to the throne

1984   **June:** Royal Saudi Air Force shoots down an Iranian F-4 fighter invading Saudi airspace

1984   **April:** Minister of Health Ghazi al-Qusaybi is dismissed after he publishes a poem critical of the royal family

1985   Saudi Arabia places order for British Aerospace Tornado combat aircraft in al-Yamamah-I deal

1986   King Fahd Causeway is opened, connecting Eastern Province to Bahrain

1986   October: Minister of Oil and Mineral Resources Ahmad Zaki Yamani is dismissed

1987   31 July: Iranian demonstration in Makkah during *hajj* gets out of control and more than 400 people are killed in ensuing melee between demonstrators and Saudi police

1987   15 August: Explosion rips through natural gas plant in Eastern Province

1988   Saudi Arabia and Britain sign al-Yamamah-II deal for military equipment and construction of air bases

1988   March: United States government protests Saudi acquisition of Chinese ballistic missiles; in response, Riyadh declares US Ambassador Hume Horan persona non grata

1988   March: Explosions set off at refinery in Ra's Tanurah and at petrochemical plant in al-Jubayl; four Saudi Shi'i nationals are executed in September 1988 for the acts

1990   21 July: Diplomatic relations are established between Saudi Arabia and the People's Republic of China

1990   2 August: Iraq invades Kuwait, following the breakdown of talks over border and oil issues

1990   17 September: Saudi Arabia formally reestablishes diplomatic relations with the Soviet Union, suspended since 1938

1991   16 January: Operation Desert Storm air offensive begins against Iraq; on January 30-31, an Iraqi offensive against al-Khafji is contained; the Operation Desert Storm ground campaign begins against Iraq and occupied Kuwait on February 24; on February 27, Kuwaiti armed forces enter Kuwait City and a cease-fire in the war is announced on February 28

1991   26 March: Diplomatic relations between Saudi Arabia and Iran are reestablished; in June, Foreign Minister Sa'ud al-Faysal becomes first senior Saudi official to visit Tehran since Iranian revolution of 1979

1992   1 March: King Fahd announces institution of a Basic Law for the kingdom and establishment of a 60-member Majlis al-Shura (Consultative Council) within six months

1992   17 September: Justice Minister Muhammad bin Ibrahim bin Jubayr is appointed Speaker of proposed Majlis al-Shura

1992   30 September: Saudi forces attack a Qatari border post, killing at least one; Egypt's mediation defuses dispute in December and Qatar withdraws its threat to boycott the GCC summit

1992   21 December: King Fabd in speech criticizes religious extremists in Saudi Arabia and their foreign backers; this follows dismissal of seven members of the Supreme Authority of Senior 'Ulama'

1993   9 March: A riot in an Iraqi refugee camp inside Saudi Arabia's northern border results in 13 deaths

1993   13 May: Newly formed Committee for the Defense of Legitimate Rights is declared illegal and its members removed from their jobs

1993   11 July: Shaykh 'Abd al-'Aziz bin Baz is appointed Mufti of Saudi Arabia

1993   21 August: King Fahd appoints the 60 members of the long-promised Majlis al-Shura (Consultative Council)

1993   13 September: Lone gunman fires at gate of King Fahd's palace in Jiddah

1993   4 October: Saudi Arabia contributes $100 million to the $2 billion international fund for Palestinian development established after the Israeli-PLO accord

1994   17 May: Saudi diplomat Muhammad al-Khilawi defects to the United States and is granted political asylum; a second diplomat, Ahmad al-Zahrani, defects to Britain two months later

1994   September: Security forces arrest more than a hundred Islamic dissidents, many of them in the central region of al-Qasim; among them are Shaykh Salman al-'Awdah and Shaykh Safar al-Hawali

1995   2 January: As part of an austerity budget, the Saudi government announces prices increases for water, telephone charges, gasoline, and domestic air travel

1995   May: The flogging of an Egyptian schoolteacher in Saudi Arabia as punishment for an alleged crime provokes a brief crisis between Egypt and the kingdom

1995   **19 June:** Saudi Arabian Airlines announces the purchase of 61 commercial aircraft from US manufacturers Boeing and McDonnell Douglas in a deal worth more than $6 billion

1995   **5 July:** Details of the Sixth Five-Year Development Plan for 1995-2000 are published; the plan emphasizes austerity to match declining government revenues and economic diversification away from dependence on oil; nearly $258 billion is expended during the plan's life

1995   **2 August:** The most extensive reshuffling of the cabinet in two decades is announced, including new appointments for the ministries of petroleum and finance

1995   **13 November:** A car bomb explodes at a National Guard facility in Riyadh used by American military personnel; seven were killed and 60 were injured. Four Saudis confessed to the act on Saudi television on 22 April 1996, claiming they had been influenced by the Committee for the Defense of Legitimate Rights and Usamah bin Ladin; they were executed on 31 May 1996

1995   **22 November:** A powerful earthquake across the Middle East strikes the northwestern corner of Saudi Arabia, killing several

1996   **27 March:** Three Saudi tribesmen hijack an Egyptian aircraft to Libya

1996   **1 April:** The Saudi Ambassador to the United Kingdom, Dr. Ghazi al-Qusaybi, warns the British government that it must expel Saudi dissident Dr. Muhammad al-Mas'ari or risk losing millions of dollars in trade with the kingdom. A British court subsequently overturns the British government's deportation order

1996   **26 June:** A truck bomb at a US military housing complex in al-Khubar kills 19 Americans and injures nearly 400 individuals of various nationalities; the identity of the perpetrators remained unknown six years later but speculation focused on Saudi Shi'ah assisted by Iran

1996   **5 July:** French President Jacques Chirac visits Saudi Arabia and discusses payments for French arms sales to the kingdom

1996   **11 August:** King Husayn of Jordan meets King Fahd in Jiddah, the first time the rulers have met since 1990 because of Saudi displeasure with Jordan's apparent support for the Iraqi invasion of Kuwait

1996   **17 November:** Unexpected rainstorms and gale-force winds kill at least three people in southern Saudi Arabia and cause $24 million in damage

1997   **12 March:** Second Deputy Prime Minister and Minister of Defense and National Aviation Prince Sultan bin 'Abd al-'Aziz makes the first official visit to Britain by a senior Saudi official since 1989

1997   16 April: A cooking-gas cylinder ignites a fire in the pilgrims' camp during the annual *hajj* (pilgrimage) to Makkah, killing 343 pilgrims

1997   6 July: The Majlis al-Shura (Consultative Council) is reconstituted for a second term, with the retention of 30 members and the appointment of 60 new members

1997   7 September: Former Minister of Oil 'Abdullah al-Tariqi dies in Cairo

1997   10-11 December: Heir Apparent Prince 'Abdullah bin 'Abd al-'Aziz holds talks with Iranian President Muhammad Khatami during Prince 'Abdullah's presence at the Organization of the Islamic Conference summit in Tehran

1998   21 February: Former Iranian President Akbar Hashemi Rafsanjani begins a 10-day visit to Saudi Arabia, the first by a senior Iranian official since the 1979 revolution

1998   9 April: The official death toll from a stampede during the annual *hajj* (pilgrimage) to Makkah is put at 118 pilgrims

1998   13 May: King Fahd bin 'Abd al-'Aziz names his youngest son 'Abd al-'Aziz as a minister of state without portfolio; 'Abd al-'Aziz makes an official visit to the United States on his father's behalf two months later

1998   16 May: Iranian President Muhammad Khatami begins three-day visit to Saudi Arabia, the first by an Iranian leader since the 1979 revolution

1998   15 September: Heir Apparent Prince 'Abdullah bin 'Abd al-'Aziz starts a lengthy international tour by meeting British Prime Minister Tony Blair in London. Subsequent stops on his tour include France, the United States, and China

1998   22 September: Saudi Arabia announces it is recalling its chargé d'affaires from Afghanistan in response to the ruling Taliban government's failure to hand over Saudi-born dissident Usamah bin Ladin to the Saudi government

1998   26 September: Heir Apparent Prince 'Abdullah meets US oil company executives in Washington to invite US businesses to invest in Saudi Arabia's oil and gas industries

1998   15 October: Saudi Heir Apparent Prince 'Abdullah bin 'Abd al-'Aziz meets Chinese President Jiang Zemin in Beijing in first high-level Saudi visit to China. President Jiang Zemin returns visit in October-November 1999

1998   7-9 December: GCC summit in Muscat elects Jamil al-Hujaylan of Saudi Arabia to a three-year term as Secretary-General of the GCC, effective 1 April 1999

1999 **15 March:** As part of an accord among OPEC and other international oil exporters, Saudi Arabia agrees to cut its crude oil output by 585,000 barrels per day, dropping its total production below 8 million barrels per day for the first time in nearly a decade

1999 **13 May:** Shaykh 'Abd al-'Aziz bin 'Abdullah bin Baz, Mufti of Saudi Arabia, dies and is replaced by Shaykh 'Abd al-'Aziz bin 'Abdullah Al al-Shaykh

1999 **17 June:** The cabinet is reshuffled

1999 **29 July:** A fire engulfs a wedding-party tent in a village of the Eastern Province, killing at least 46 people

1999 **24 October:** New Pakistani ruler General Pervez Musharraf makes his first foreign trip as ruler to Saudi Arabia

1999 **29 October:** Kamal Adham, prominent businessman, brother-in-law of King Faysal, and former head of Saudi intelligence, dies in Egypt

2000 **28 February:** Japan's Arabian Oil Company loses its 40-year concession for the Saudi share of the Saudi-Kuwait Neutral Zone; operations are taken over by an ARAMCO subsidiary

2000 **17 March:** Shots fired from a moving car wound a guard at the Russian consulate in Jiddah; the Saudi government denies that the attack was because of Russia's campaign against Chechen rebels

2000 **17 April:** Higher Organization for Tourism is created as part of a policy of economic diversification, in conjunction with the issuing of guidelines for the country's first tourist visas

2000 **29 May:** Women are allowed to attend a session of the Majlis al-Shura (Consultative Council) for the first time

2000 **14 June:** Formation is announced of a council of the Royal Family composed of 18 senior princes with Heir Apparent 'Abdullah bin 'Abd al-'Aziz at its head; its purpose is apparently to bring the widespread family together and to arrange family affairs

2000 **28 August:** Ministry of Planning announces approval of the Seventh Five-Year Development Plan for 2001-2005, with spending set at $200 billion, concentrating on economic reforms, the diversification of income away from oil, and promotion of the private sector

2000 **14 October:** Four Saudi dissidents hijack a Saudi Arabian Airlines plane to Baghdad, where they were given sanctuary

2000   17 November: A British man is killed and his wife wounded when a bomb blows up their car in Riyadh. Subsequent explosions take place on 22 November and 15 December, all with British victims. Four Europeans confess on Saudi television on 4 February 2001 to the attacks, in what the Saudi government claims is a dispute over illegal alcohol smuggling in the kingdom. Questions regarding their guilt and punishment continue into 2002

2000   18 December: Saudi government announces a balanced budget for 2001, following a surplus for 2000, the first budget surplus in 19 years

2001   5 March: The second fatal stampede in three years during the annual *hajj* (pilgrimage) to Makkah kills 35 pilgrims

2001   17 April: Iran and Saudi Arabia sign a security pact intended to combat organized crime, terrorism, drug trafficking, and illegal immigration

2001   14 May: The Ministry of Health reports that an outbreak of Rift Valley fever in southern Saudi Arabia has killed 124 people since September 2000; dozens more die in adjoining regions of Yemen

2001   24 May: The membership of the Majlis al-Shura (Consultative Council) is expanded to 120 in preparation for its third four-year session; of these, 62 members are new

2001   8 September: Prince Turki al-Faysal, Director of General Intelligence since 1968, is replaced by his uncle, Prince Nawwaf bin 'Abd al-'Aziz

2001   11 September: Fifteen Saudis are among the 19 hijackers of four American domestic airliners, which are then used to destroy the World Trade Center in New York and damage the Pentagon in Washington; the Saudi government condemns the attacks and their presumed mastermind, Saudi-born dissident Usamah bin Ladin; US-Saudi relations are strained by American media attacks on the kingdom and perceived Saudi slowness to join US President George W. Bush's declared "war on terror"

2001   25 September: Saudi Arabia severs all diplomatic relations with Afghanistan's ruling Taliban government for its support of Usamah bin Ladin and al-Qa'idah organization

2002   18 January: Interim President of Afghanistan Hamid Karzai arrives in Saudi Arabia on his first trip abroad as president, seeking aid for his war-torn country; the kingdom provides $20 million in initial aid and pledges an additional $200 million at the Tokyo donors conference a few days later

2002   24 January: Shaykh Muhammad bin Ibrahim al-Jubayr, the Chairman of the Majlis al-Shura (Consultative Council) dies; he is replaced by Dr. Salih bin 'Abdullah bin Humayd

2002   February: Heir Apparent 'Abdullah bin 'Abd al-'Aziz announces his Arab-Israeli peace plan to a visiting journalist, proposing the normalization of Arab relations with Israel in exchange for Israel's withdrawal to its 1967 borders; the rough plan attracts international attention and is adopted in a more complete form by an Arab League summit on 28 March 2002

2002   11 March: At least 15 girls are killed during a fire at their school in Makkah, apparently because the *mutawwi'in* (religious police) prevented them from leaving the school because they are not properly dressed

2002   21 March: 'Abdullah bin 'Awad bin Ladin, head of the wealthy bin Ladin family and uncle of the estranged Usamah bin Ladin, dies in al-Madinah

2002   2 April: Amnesty International announces that Saudi Arabia executed at least 79 people in 2001, ranking it third in the world and slightly surpassing the United States

2002   5 April: Several thousand people demonstrate in Dhahran in protest against Israeli actions against West Bank towns. A subsequent Saudi telethon on 12-13 April raises more than $100 million for Palestinian relief

2002   12-15 April: Torrential rains and flash floods in western and southern Saudi Arabia kill more than 12 people

2002   25 April: Heir Apparent 'Abdullah bin 'Abd al-'Aziz visits US President George W. Bush at his Texas ranch in an attempt to mend bilateral relations after September 2001 and to ask for the US to exert pressure on Israel to stop its attacks on Palestinian towns; the visit follows the cancellation of an earlier visit scheduled for May 2001 because of Saudi objection to US support for Israel

2002   Early May: An empty missile tube from a Soviet-made SA-7 anti-aircraft missile launcher is discovered outside the Prince Sultan Air Base, used by United States aircraft enforcing the no-fly zone over Iraq; 13 men, including 11 Saudis, are arrested a few weeks later on charges of having been involved in the attempt on behalf of al-Qa'idah

2002   11 May: An Iraqi government minister attending an Arab meeting enters Saudi Arabia in the first such visit since the Kuwait War

2002   20 June: A British banker is killed by a car bomb explosion in Riyadh; bombs attached to the cars of two other expatriates are discovered a few days later

2002   Late June: A Saudi government team visits Guantánamo Bay in Cuba to check on the approximately 100 Saudi nationals being held there on suspicion of having links to terrorism

2002   5 July: Prominent Saudi businessman Sulayman al-'Ulayan dies

2002   23 July: Prince Ahmad bin Salman Al Sa'ud, son of Prince Salman bin 'Abd al-'Aziz, Governor of Riyadh Prince, dies of a heart attack six weeks after a horse he owned won the Kentucky Derby

2002   25-29 July: King Fahd bin 'Abd al-'Aziz undergoes two eye surgeries in Geneva amid concerns that his health was continuing to worsen

2002   19 September: The Saudi ambassador to the United Kingdom Ghazi al-Qusaybi is recalled to Riyadh and appointed Minister of Water

2002   30 September: A German employee of an electronics company is killed by a car bomb explosion in Riyadh

2002   1 October: The United States government introduces a policy of registration and fingerprinting of Saudi Arabian males entering the United States

2002   15 October: A Saudi unsuccessfully attempts to hijack a Saudi Arabian Airlines plane on a flight from Khartoum to Jiddah

2002   3 November: Foreign Minister Prince Sa'ud al-Faysal says that Saudi Arabia will not allow the United States to use its facilities for any attack against Iraq even if a strike was sanctioned by the United Nations. He clarifies his remarks on the following day to note that Saudi Arabia would be obligated to cooperate with the United Nations if Iraq refuses to implement UN resolutions but that it would not mean that the kingdom would join any fighting

2002   18 November: Saudi securities forces wound and apprehend a terrorist suspect in Riyadh

2002   20 November: Minister of Interior Prince Nayif bin 'Abd al-'Aziz says that Saudi Arabia holds more than 100 Saudi nationals on suspicion of ties to al-Qa'idah. On the same day, a gunman fires shots in an American fast-food restaurant in al-Kharj and is later arrested

2002   3 December: Saudi Arabia announces that former head of intelligence Prince Turki al-Faysal is to be appointed ambassador to the United Kingdom

INTRODUCTION

The Kingdom of Saudi Arabia now has been under the spotlight of Western curiosity for more than 50 years. With each succeeding year, it seems to encounter increasing scrutiny rather than less. Principally, of course, this is because of its oil: approximately one-quarter of the world's total oil reserves lie underneath Saudi Arabia and, in the early 1990s, the kingdom became the world's largest crude oil producer. Not surprisingly, a world highly dependent on oil regards the desert kingdom as an area of intense strategic concern, as reflected in the coalition of forces assembled on Saudi soil to oust Iraq from Kuwait in 1991.

But Saudi Arabia is of interest as well because of its intensely traditional society and strict adherence to Islamic legal principles, combined with a recent history of rapid economic growth and an enormous program of modernization. It is the birthplace of Islam and Islam's holiest sites are in Saudi Arabia, which gives the country a special responsibility. There is an inherently contradictory predicament between the forces of resistance and those of change. But the kingdom would appear to have handled these challenges far more capably than its critics give credit. The ruling family of Al Saʿud, who provide the country with its name, must preside over the panoply of economic transformation, the slow and almost imperceptible progress of political reform, the steady progression toward the center of Arab, Islamic, and world stages, and a succession of external threats from larger and avaricious neighbors.

Geography

The Kingdom of Saudi Arabia comprises the greater part of the Arabian Peninsula, occupying nearly 840,000 square miles (about one-fifth of the size of the United States). It has two coastlines: the Red Sea constitutes the western boundary and the Gulf (variously known as the Arabian Gulf or Persian Gulf) provides the eastern boundary. To the north, Saudi Arabia shares borders with Jordan, Iraq, and Kuwait. On the east, neighbors include Qatar, the United Arab Emirates, and Oman, while Yemen lies to the south (Bahrain, an island state, lies just off Saudi Arabia's east coast).

Generally speaking, the Arabian Peninsula is tilted from west to east. Thus Saudi Arabia displays a mountainous spine (al-Sarawat) paralleling the Red Sea and then gradually slopes down to low plains along the Gulf coast. Great deserts predominate to the north and south: al-Nafud lying across the northern boundaries and al-Rubʿ al-Khali across the southern frontiers. Most of the country is desert, including barren mountains and gravel plains as well as sand dunes. This means that herding and nomadism have provided the principal livelihood of much of the population, although the country is dotted with cultivated oases and the highlands of the southwest support intensive agriculture. The climate is generally very hot in summer, as well as humid along the coasts. Winters are mild, even cold in the interior.

The capital is Riyadh, which also constitutes one of the main cities, along with Jiddah, Makkah, al-Madinah in the west, and the Dhahran/al-Dammam/ al-Khubar conurbation on the east coast. The total population is unknown but it was estimated at 21.3 million in 1999, including 5.7 million expatriates. The population growth rate in that year was estimated at 2.6 percent. The indigenous people, known as Saudis (or less frequently, Saudi Arabians), are predominantly Arab, although there is more of an ethnic mixture in the Islamic holy cities. They are exclusively Muslim, mostly followers of the Wahhabi (or Muwahhidun) interpretation of Sunni (orthodox) Islam, apart from small communities of the Shi'ah sect of Islam in the east. Arabic is the official language, although English is widely spoken in the cities. The many expatriates, more than one-quarter of the total population, come from northern Arab countries, the Indian subcontinent, Southeast Asia, Europe, and the United States.

The country can be divided into four principal natural regions: Najd, al-Hijaz, the East, and the Southwest. (Administratively, however, Saudi Arabia is divided into 14 imarat or provinces.) The Najd (Nejd) comprises the central desert region and forms the cultural heartland of Saudi Arabia. It is home to many of the major tribes, the birthplace of the Wahhabi religious reform movement founded in the 18th century by Muhammad 'Abd al-Wahhab, and the home of the Al Sa'ud. This family spread the teachings of Muhammad 'Abd al-Wahhab throughout much of the Arabian Peninsula and grew into the ruling family and unifying force of modern Saudi Arabia. The principal settlements of the region are Riyadh (the capital and the country's largest city), the oasis town and military center of al-Kharj, the traditional entrepôts of Buraydah and 'Unayzah, and the ancient town and tribal center of Ha'il.

Equally important is the western region of al-Hijaz (Hejaz). A low coastal plain borders the Red Sea, behind which craggy mountains rise, and then the land gradually shades into the interior deserts of Najd. Formerly an Ottoman province and then a short-lived independent kingdom earlier in this century, al-Hijaz is best known as the birthplace of Islam. The Prophet Muhammad was born in the city of Makkah (Mecca) and the annual hajj (pilgrimage) of Muslims from around the world takes place there. Al-Madinah (Medina) is noteworthy as the location where the Prophet Muhammad established the first Islamic state and he is buried in the city's Great Mosque. The largest city in al-Hijaz is Jiddah (Jedda), site of the kingdom's commercial center, the country's largest seaport, and the airport through which the Muslim pilgrims make their way to Makkah. A second seaport is at Yanbu', site of a massive industrialization project.

On the opposite side of the country lies the Eastern Province, the source of all of Saudi Arabia's oil. The center of the oil industry is the new city of Dhahran, now joined by sister cities al-Dammam and al-Khubar, while Ra's Tanurah nearby is the world's largest petroleum port. The Eastern Province is also the site of millennia-old agricultural centers in the oases of al-Ahsa' (Hasa) and al-Qatif. Traditionally, its people have had close ties with the other states of the Gulf, including Iraq and Iran as well as nearby Kuwait, Bahrain, and Qatar.

The region of the extreme southwest was the last to be incorporated into the Saudi state, partly because of its rugged mountains and partly because of the area's close ties to neighboring Yemen. Prior to the 1930s, much of the area fell under Ottoman domination or was more or less independent. While Saudi Arabia gradually absorbed the northern parts, it gained sovereignty over the

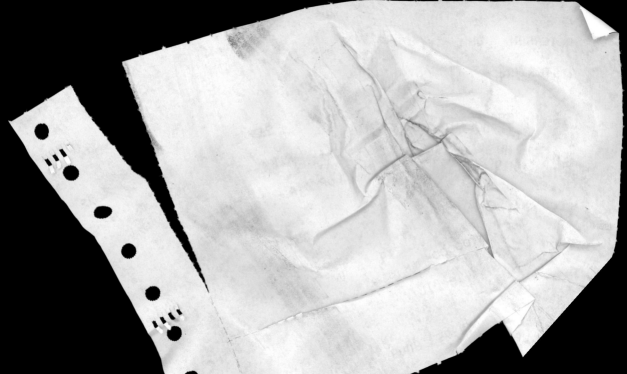

southernmost portions only as a result of the 1934 Saudi-Yemeni war. Topographically, the area resembles al-Hijaz to the north except that the mountains are higher and more complex and the region receives the highest rainfall of any part of the kingdom. The central mountainous spine (al-Sarawat) stretches from al-Bahah and the areas of Bani Ghamid and Zahran in the north to 'Asir in the south. Inland lies the oasis of Bishah and the ancient city of Najran on the Yemen border. Jizan is the principal settlement of the hot, dusty, coastal plain of the Tihamah.

Mention has already been made of the vast al-Nafud desert, which Saudi Arabia shares with Jordan, Syria, and Iraq. Several small provinces line the northern border, although the size of the population is tiny. The world's largest sand desert, al-Rub' al-Khali, lies in the southeast, providing an almost impenetrable barrier to passage to Oman and Yemen, except to the small badu (bedouin) tribes which routinely cross its vast expanse.

Society

All of Saudi Arabia's citizens are Muslims and most are Arab, resulting in a nearly homogenous society. But there are differences. Broadly speaking, Saudi citizens can be divided into tribal members and townspeople. In popular perception, Saudi Arabia's tribal identity is strongest in Najd, but important tribes range over the entire country. The badu (bedouin) tribes of Najd have long been a major element of Al Sa'ud power, providing the backbone of the Saudi armies which forged the modern state. Because of the Al Sa'ud's origins in Najd, the tribes and their shaykhs (tribal leaders) continue to receive close attention. Najdi tribesmen dominate the National Guard, which serves as a counterweight to the Royal Saudi Army and owes its loyalty directly to the royal family. In some areas, particularly the south, tribes were never nomadic but have always been cultivators. While tribal identity remains strong in the modern state, the traditional nomadism and pastoral occupations have come under increasing economic threat and many tribal people have settled in and around the towns and cities.

It is often forgotten that much of Saudi Arabia's indigenous population derives from urban roots. This is true not only for the older cities of the west, such as Makkah, al-Madinah, Jiddah, and al-Ta'if, but also traditional Najdi entrepôts like 'Unayzah and Buraydah, seaports like Yanbu', Lith, Jizan, and al-'Uqayr, and oases and trading centers such as Bishah, al-Khurmah, Tayma', and Tabuk. A variety of other occupations and lifestyles have always been present in the kingdom. The fertile oases of al-Ahsa' and al-Qatif in the east have been the scene of peasant cultivation, while the seacoasts have been the home of fishermen.

Because it is the location of Islam's holiest sites and hosts the annual hajj (pilgrimage) to Makkah, the western region of the kingdom has attracted an enormous variety of immigrants over the centuries. Today, the population of Makkah, al-Ta'if, Jiddah, and al-Madinah includes Saudi citizens of South Asian, Central Asian, Iranian, and African origin. A disproportionate number of merchants trace their ancestors to the Hadramawt region of southern Yemen, and other prominent Saudis are descended from Ottoman officials who resided in the Hijaz before 1918.

More recently, the oil boom has resulted in the influx of approximately 5.7 million expatriates. They exhibit all ranges and levels of skills and fill jobs right across the spectrum from technical consultants and managers to sweepers. In part, the low standards of education in Saudi Arabia at the beginning of the oil boom required expatriates to assume newly created positions for which there were no qualified Saudis, but this has changed with the government's emphasis on education. In recent years, the continued high dependence on foreign manpower reflects the enormous pace of development and economic change as well as the limited numbers of qualified Saudi nationals.

Not surprisingly, a large proportion of foreign workers in the kingdom have been Arabs, because of both their ability to communicate in Arabic and their cultural affinity with Saudis. The large numbers of Egyptians, Jordanians, and Sudanese reflect both their countries' poverty as well as a relative abundance of educators, doctors, and bureaucrats at home. Lebanese and Syrians dot the commercial sector while Yemenis have been ubiquitous in many roles but especially as small shopkeepers.

But the Saudi government has also deliberately sought to encourage labor migration from non-Arab and even non-Muslim countries to reduce the risk of cultural dilution and political intrigue. While Pakistanis and Indian Muslims are present in large numbers, even more workers hail from non-Muslim India, Sri Lanka, Thailand, and the Philippines. The largest Western community comes from the United States but there are also many British, French, and other Europeans. The number of Westerners declined with the drop in oil income in the mid-1980s but it is not certain whether the totals of unskilled and semiskilled workers from Asia has diminished.

Most Saudis belong to the Wahhabi movement within Sunni or orthodox Islam, although there is a sizeable Shi'ah minority in the Eastern Province. The conservative nature of Wahhabism has produced an insular traditional society, leading some elements to strongly resist the introduction of modern innovations. The strength of the religious leadership means that Islamic prohibitions, such as bans on alcohol and pork, are enforced much more strictly than in most other Islamic countries; similarly, the Islamic requirement for prayer at five stipulated intervals during the day means all offices and shops must close at those times. Conservatives' insistence on the modesty of women has meant that women must cover themselves almost completely, are unable to hold jobs in which they have contact with men, and are prevented from driving vehicles. The opposition of some conservatives has produced muted religious grievances with the government and may have been behind al-Qa'idah's recruitment of the Saudi hijackers of 11 September 2001.

But the coming of oil and the Saudi leadership's unwavering determination to use oil wealth to develop the country has resulted in undeniable social change and brought about a certain degree of tension between traditionalist and modernist elements in the population. A small but growing element of educated, liberal Saudis chafes against the myriad of restrictions. Although the Saudi government consistently has legitimized a series of economic and social changes over the last half century, it has done so cautiously and at a glacial pace. A recent example of the inherent tensions was the 1990 convoy of women drivers through Riyadh's streets in a challenge to the custom against women driving. The women who staged the protest were reprimanded and laws were enacted to change the informal custom into formal prohibition. The deaths of 15 girls in a fire at a school in Makkah in early 2002, allegedly because the mutawwi'in (religious police) forced them to remain in the building because they were not properly dressed, enabled the government to transfer jurisdiction over girls' education away from the religious establishment to the Ministry of Education.

The change fed by oil has also introduced, or intensified, social stratification. Besides holding political power, the royal family has enjoyed a growth in social privileges and many members have taken advantage of their status, connections, and official positions to build prosperous businesses. Despite the persistence of many seemingly egalitarian customs from more traditional times (such as the majlis or gatherings held by many family members and open to all citizens), the gulf between the royal family and commoners has grown wider and become more rigid.

The classical rivalry between the hadar (settled or urban people) and the badu (tribal or nomadic people) was kept in traditional balance by a symbiotic relationship. The oil era appears to have tilted this balance strongly in favor of hadar culture. Career advancement, social standing, and economic prosperity increasingly depend on qualifications and lifestyles found in an urban (*i.e.* modern) environment. At the same time, it must be remembered that social standing is closely linked to lineage. A poor and uneducated Saudi of impeccable tribal origins will always consider himself superior to a wealthy government minister or merchant of mixed (or non-tribal) blood.

Another aspect of recent social change has been the emergence of an amorphous middle class, bumping up against the elite strata of royal family, wealthy merchants, and senior government officials. In addition, explosive population growth, estimated at 4.5 percent per annum in 1990 but reduced to about 2.6 percent at the end of that decade, has produced a youthful demographic profile with more than half of all Saudis under the age of 18. As a result, recent years have seen about 175,000 secondary-school graduates flood annually into the job market, where there is little employment to be had. One consequence is the beginning signs of alienation and inappropriate public behavior by some male youths.

History

Arabia Before the Saudi State

Pre-Islamic History. By history and tradition, the Arabs are divided into South and North Arabs. In the interior of present-day Yemen, the southern Arabs fashioned a series of advanced civilizations which emerged in the last half of the second millennium B.C. and finally collapsed about the third or fourth century after Christ. The prosperity of these states was based on control of frankincense and other trade along routes north to the Mediterranean and their northern colonies provide some of the earliest archaeological sites in Saudi Arabia. Meanwhile, the northern Arabs were mostly nomadic and, apart from city-states such as Petra and Palmyra (now in Jordan and Syria respectively), left little trace of a sedentary culture. Still, there were important settlements at Mada'in Salih, Tayma', al-Jawf, and Ha'il. These too declined early in the Christian era, ushering in the Age of al-Jahiliyah, or ignorance, as the Muslims later would describe it. Mesopotamia, Persia, and Rome periodically threatened the north while Abyssinia and Persia did the same in the south.

Few of the centers of early Arab civilization had been located within the boundaries of present-day Saudi Arabia. After the decline of the South Arabian civilizations, the most prominent city undoubtedly was Makkah, an important intermediate point on the caravan routes between South Arabia and the Mediterranean and which the Quraysh tribe had come to dominate. Makkah was also a sacred precinct which experienced a proliferation of idols installed in the vicinity of a small building called the Ka'bah. At the same time, Najran, al-Faw, and Thaj formed key links in a secondary trade route running across modern Saudi Arabia from southwest to northeast.

Islamic History. The future prophet of Islam, Muhammad, was born in Makkah in A.D. 570, according to tradition. Orphaned at an early age, he was raised by an uncle and, as a young man, married a wealthy widow named Khadijah. Given to extensive meditation, Muhammad eventually began preaching on a theme given to him by the Angel Gabriel, *viz.* that earlier divine messages given in the form of Judaism and Christianity had become corrupted, thus requiring a new attempt to return mankind to the right path in the form of Islam. Muhammad converted a small band of followers to be the first Muslims, largely drawn from Makkah's poor and dispossessed, but aroused the antipathy of the city's elite because of the egalitarianism of his teaching. By 622, the Muslims were forced out of Makkah and accepted the hospitality of Yathrib to the northeast which subsequently became known as al-Madinah. This move, or *hijrah*, marks the beginning of the Islamic calendar (generally abbreviated to A.H. for Anno Hegirae). After a series of battles between the Makkans and the Muslims, a peace was arranged and Muhammad was able to undertake the hajj (pilgrimage) to Makkah shortly before his death in 632.

The entire Arabian Peninsula was converted to Islam during the Prophet's lifetime, although it seems that some conversions were only superficial and Muhammad's successors (known as *khalifah*s, commonly spelled caliphs) found it necessary to wage the Wars of the Riddah (Wars of Apostasy) to return many areas to the Islamic fold. The office of the fourth of these successors, the Prophet's son-in-law 'Ali, was usurped by another Makkan clan which moved the Islamic capital to Damascus. This inaugurated the Umayyad dynasty, which extended the territories of Islam across North Africa, to the gates of Constantinople, and into Persia. It lasted about a century before being replaced by the 'Abbasid dynasty with its capital in Baghdad. Thus the locus of power in the Islamic world soon passed out of Arabia, never to return. The holy cities of Makkah and al-Madinah were held by a series of Islamic monarchs until absorbed, at least fitfully, into the Ottoman Empire in the 16th century. Most of the rest of what was to become Saudi Arabia remained politically fragmented as largely autonomous tribes and towns until the 20th century. Occasionally, a tribally based family would hurl up strong leadership and expand over its neighbors. One of these was the Al Sa'ud.

Arabia Under the Al Sa'ud

The First Saudi State (1744-1818). An alliance begun in 1744 between Muhammad bin Sa'ud, the head of the small village of al-Dir'iyah in southern Najd, and an Islamic reformer named Muhammad bin 'Abd al-Wahhab soon resulted in the expansion of the Wahhabi doctrine throughout much of Arabia and the establishment of the Al Sa'ud dynasty. By the time of Muhammad bin Sa'ud's death in 1765, most of Najd was under Saudi control, and the young state had expanded to eastern Arabia by the end of the 18th century. The Ottoman Empire began to regard the movement as a serious threat after the holy city of Karbala (site of an important Shi'ah shrine in present-day Iraq) was invaded and Damascus was threatened in 1802, followed by the capture of Makkah in 1803. The Ottoman response was to ask Muhammad 'Ali, the Viceroy of Egypt, to attack the Wahhabis. An Egyptian army recaptured Makkah and al-Madinah in about 1811. The death of Muhammad bin Sa'ud's grandson Sa'ud in 1814 opened the way for an Egyptian advance across Arabia: in 1818, Ibrahim Pasha (son of Muhammad 'Ali) captured the Saudi capital of al-Dir'iyah and sent the Al Sa'ud imam ('Abdullah bin Sa'ud) to Istanbul where he was beheaded.

The Second Saudi State (1843-1891). Following Ibrahim Pasha's withdrawal, the Al Sa'ud established a new headquarters in Riyadh, not far from al-Dir'iyah. Succeeding Saudi imams were able to exert their jurisdiction over much of Najd and parts of eastern Arabia until a second Egyptian invasion in 1838 ended with the capture of the imam at the time. However, this imam, Faysal bin Turki, was able to escape from Egypt and by 1843 had reasserted himself at the head of the Al Sa'ud. Under his capable leadership, the second Saudi State soon incorporated al-Qasim (central Najd) and exercised influence over Ha'il and Shammar (northern Najd), thus regaining most of the territories of the first state with the exception of al-Hijaz (Makkah and al-Madinah). But Faysal's death in 1865 marked a return to civil war within the family. By 1884, the Al Rashid family of Ha'il were able to replace Saudi rule with their own over much of Najd, and by 1891 Faysal's youngest son 'Abd al-Rahman was forced into exile in Kuwait.

The Third Saudi State (1902-present). It was left to 'Abd al-Rahman's son 'Abd al-'Aziz to restore the family's prestige. The construction of the Third Saudi State began in a modest way when 'Abd al-'Aziz left Kuwait with a small group of followers and, slipping into Riyadh, killed the Al Rashid governor and captured the city. In just a couple of years, 'Abd al-'Aziz had managed to capture most of Najd. His overtures to the British received a mostly frosty response and he was forced to accept nominal Ottoman suzerainty. But in 1913, following Ottoman setbacks in Europe, 'Abd al-'Aziz captured the Ottoman garrisons in al-Ahsa' and al-Qatif in eastern Arabia. Although this obliged the Government of India to conclude a treaty with him, the effect of which principally was to encourage the Al Sa'ud to attack the Al Rashid, who remained Turkish allies, 'Abd al-'Aziz still did not have British favor. The Arab Bureau in Cairo championed Sharif Husayn bin 'Ali al-Hashimi of Makkah as the preferred leader of the "Arab Revolt" against the Ottomans and recognized his declaration of an independent Kingdom of al-Hijaz in 1916.

Following the end of the war, 'Abd al-'Aziz resumed his expansionist policies, conquering his arch rivals, the Al Rashid of Ha'il, in 1921. In the same year, he dropped the traditional Al Sa'ud title of imam and adopted the secular title of Sultan of Najd. His designs on al-Hijaz, forestalled by British intervention during the war, grew more transparent as the Hijazi kingdom's weaknesses became apparent. British concern was provoked when the first major Saudi conquest in al-Hijaz, the city of al-Ta'if in 1924, was accompanied by a massacre perpetrated by the Wahhabi fanatics in the Ikhwan, 'Abd al-'Aziz's tribal levies. Makkah surrendered without a struggle soon afterwards, al-Madinah in 1925, and Jiddah fell at the end of 1925 after a siege. With the flight of the Hashimi family, the Hijazi notables recognized 'Abd al-'Aziz as their sovereign and he combined the titles of Sultan of Najd and King of al-Hijaz. 'Abd al-'Aziz continued to probe to the south and his sovereignty over 'Asir, Najran, and the northern Tihamah plain was recognized by his Yemeni rival, Imam Yahya, after Saudi victory in the Saudi-Yemeni War of 1934. Further expansion to the north was blocked by the British-backed Hashimi monarchies of Transjordan and Iraq, and similar obstacles were encountered on the Gulf littoral because of the British-protected shaykhdoms in Kuwait, Bahrain, Qatar, and Abu Dhabi. In 1932, 'Abd al-'Aziz adopted as the official name of his country the Kingdom of Saudi Arabia.

Subsequently, 'Abd al-'Aziz turned his attention to transforming a fragile rule in Najd, based on tribal alliances, into a central state, and then to gradually integrating al-Hijaz and Najd. A principal step in this process had occurred in the late 1920s when the Ikhwan rebellion was finally put down. A long series of negotiations with the British over boundaries in eastern Arabia ended in stalemate when the Saudi king rejected the British "Red Line" and London rejected his "Riyadh Line." A third major concern was over the lack of finances. The signature bonus to the oil concession granted to the Standard Oil of California (SOCAL) in 1933 saved 'Abd al-'Aziz from poverty. Although oil was discovered at Dhahran in 1935 and production started in 1938, the first significant impact of oil came after the Second World War when exports began in large quantities. It was perhaps unfortunate that the rush of oil income should occur in 'Abd al-'Aziz's declining years. Although attempts were made to create a more rational infrastructure, to expand the government and establish social welfare programs, much of the early wealth was squandered by members of the Al Sa'ud royal family.

King Sa'ud (r. 1953-1964). This situation became even worse on the death of 'Abd al-'Aziz in 1953 and succession by his son Sa'ud. Sa'ud's essentially weak personality led to a loss of effective control over his relatives. In foreign policy, he flirted with Egyptian revolutionary president Jamal 'Abd al-Nasir (Nasser) until the latter's intervention in the Yemeni civil war (1962-1970) brought the Arab radical threat uncomfortably close to the Saudi borders. Sa'ud's reign was also marked by an intense rivalry with his younger half brother Faysal. Faysal had proven himself to be a capable Viceroy of al-Hijaz under his father, but he accepted his father's decision to make Sa'ud his successor. Sa'ud was forced to relinquish much of his decision-making power to Faysal in March 1958, but he managed to regain control in December 1960. The royal family again forced Sa'ud to accept Faysal as Prime Minister in October 1962 but relations between the two continued to smolder. Finally, in March 1964, the *'ulama'* (religious leaders) and inner circle of the family stripped Sa'ud of all but his title. His deposition came in November 1964 and Faysal was named King.

King Faysal (r. 1964-1975). It was undoubtedly fortunate for Saudi Arabia that Faysal proved to be as strong and capable as his father (or, indeed, as his 19th-century namesake). Faysal had proved himself as a military commander during the early years of conquest and then had gained considerable administrative experience as the semiautonomous Viceroy of al-Hijaz. In internal affairs, King Faysal had to establish the foundations of a political and economic infrastructure that could cope with the growing wealth of the country and expectations of its population. Under Faysal, Saudi Arabia's horizons seemed to expand beyond the Arabian Peninsula for the first time. The kingdom participated more fully in Arab councils and instituted an extensive aid program to fellow Arab states, as well as other Islamic and Third World recipients. Not surprisingly, Saudi Arabia was drawn into the arena of the Arab-Israeli conflict because of the "oil weapon," and Faysal adhered to the Arab oil boycott of 1973-1974 despite his close relations with the United States. Saudi Arabia had been a founding member of the Organization of Petroleum Exporting Countries (OPEC) and, under Oil Minister Ahmad Zaki Yamani, the kingdom played an increasingly pivotal role in OPEC pricing decisions.

King Khalid (r. 1975-1982) and King Fahd (r. 1982-present). Many of the basic directions in Saudi development and policy had been set out by Faysal before his assassination in 1975. This was a considerable blessing for the future since his successor, half brother Khalid, did not have as forceful a personality nor the same keen attention to detail and incisiveness of action. The country was also fortunate in that Khalid's reign roughly coincided with the oil boom, when opportunities for many seemed limitless. Soon after another half brother Fahd inherited the throne, the oil boom was replaced by recession and regional threats grew more intimidating.

Although the Iranian Revolution of 1979 produced a barrage of verbal assaults on the Al Sa'ud, the direct impact was limited to antigovernment demonstrations among the Shi'ah population of the Eastern Province in 1979 and 1980. But as Baghdad's initial successes in the Iran-Iraq War (1980-1988) were checkmated and reversed, the possibility of a direct threat from Iran grew. In 1981, Saudi Arabia and its smaller neighbors in the Gulf (Kuwait, Bahrain, Qatar, the United Arab Emirates, and Oman) banded together in the Gulf Cooperation Council (GCC). In 1984, an Iranian F-4 Phantom invaded Saudi airspace over the Eastern Province and was shot down by the Royal Saudi Air Force. The emergence of the Palestinian *intifadah* (uprising) also embarrassed the Saudi government for having such close ties to Israel's principal supporter, the United States. The subsidence of the Communist threat, in the shape of the demise of the Soviet Union (however, not before diplomatic relations had been reestablished between Moscow and Riyadh in 1990) and the folding of the Marxist government of neighboring South Yemen into a unified Yemeni republic in 1990, provided only a brief respite.

The most serious threat to the Saudi state since the early 1960s came from an unexpected direction. Iraq's President Saddam Husayn, enraged over Kuwaiti intransigence on oil matters and the amirate's refusal to discuss conflicting border claims, ordered his armed forces to invade his smaller neighbor on 2 August 1990. King Fahd invited the United States and other Western powers, in combination with Saudi and other Arab forces (particularly those of Egypt and Syria) to use the kingdom as a platform from which to liberate Kuwait. Following months of preparation ("Operation Desert Shield"), the war against Iraq ("Operation Desert Storm") began in January 1991 with an intensive aerial assault. Saudi Arabia, along with Israel, was a target of attacks by Iraqi Scud missiles, with several landing in Riyadh and Dhahran. Six weeks of intensive bombardment resulted in a relatively quick ground campaign that freed Kuwait by 28 February.

As King Fahd's health declined through the 1990s, Heir Apparent 'Abdullah bin 'Abd al-'Aziz took over increasing responsibility for running the state. The decade saw the settlement of long-standing border disputes with Oman and Yemen and an improvement in relations with Iran, as well as with the Arab states that had backed Iraq in 1990-1991. Riyadh continued to support international sanctions against Iraq and permitted the basing of Western air force detachments in the kingdom to enforce the no-fly zones in southern Iraq. Like the rest of the Arab world, Saudi Arabia was deeply concerned by the Israeli-Palestinian violence as a result of the second Palestinian *intifadah* (uprising) from September 2000. Nevertheless, 'Abdullah advanced his peace plan in 2002, calling for full Arab recognition of Israel in exchange for the return of all the territories occupied since 1967.

The kingdom was shocked by the involvement of 15 Saudis among the 19 suicide hijackers of American civil aircraft which were used to crash into the World Trade Center in New York and the Pentagon in Washington and the Saudi government backed the consequent American campaign in Afghanistan against the Taliban government there and the Islamic extremist movement known as al-Qa'idah and headed by Saudi-born Usamah bin Ladin. Nevertheless, official relations between the United States and Saudi Arabia were strained in the aftermath of the attacks and the demands made by President Bush's administration in its "war on terror." The relationship was further eroded through 2002 by the Israeli reoccupation of parts of Palestinian autonomous territory and the American threat to launch a war against Iraq.

Government

Saudi Arabia is an absolute monarchy under the Al Sa'ud family. Since the death of King 'Abd al-'Aziz bin 'Abd al-Rahman in 1953, accession to the throne has passed through his sons: Sa'ud (r. 1953-1964), Faysal (r. 1964-1973), Khalid (r. 1973-1982), and Fahd (r. 1982-present). The family has agreed upon another son 'Abdullah as the successor to Fahd and apparently yet another son Sultan as his successor. King Fahd also serves as Prime Minister with 'Abdullah and Sultan as First Deputy and Second Deputy Prime Ministers respectively. There is no written constitution and the government asserts that the legal system is based on the shari'ah or Islamic law. The King makes all major decisions, after consultation with the Al Sa'ud royal family and sounding out the *'ulama'* (religious scholars), senior government officials, tribal shaykhs, and prominent merchants.

The highest formal organ of government is the Council of Ministers, and individual ministers are appointed by and answerable only to the King. There is no parliament or similar legislative body with popular representation.

On 1 March 1992, King Fahd announced the institution of a Basic Law and the establishment of an appointed Majlis al-Shura (Consultative Council). Among the dictates of the Basic Law were rules for succession (involving consultation among the sons and grandsons of King 'Abd al-'Aziz bin 'Abd al-Rahman), provisions for the privacy of individuals, an indication of the responsibilities of the state regarding the social and economic welfare of its people, the stipulation of an independent judiciary, and reforms for local and regional administration. Although Justice Minister Muhammad bin Ibrahim bin Jubayr was named Speaker of the new Majlis al-Shura in 1992, its 60 members, prohibited from being government officials or company directors, were not appointed until 1993. At the end of the four-year term, the council was expanded to 90 members and the 2001-2005 council was again expanded to 120 members. Political parties are prohibited, although a few minor dissident groups exist outside the country.

When 'Abd al-'Aziz founded the Third Saudi State in 1902, he was simply restoring a tribal state that had little more need of formal institutions than a single dominant ruler. 'Abd al-'Aziz consolidated his control over the nucleus of Central Arabia by forging alliances with the principal tribes (often through marrying daughters of tribal *shaykh*s) and soliciting the allegiance and financial support of the townspeople and merchants. The situation became more complicated when 'Abd al-'Aziz conquered the western Arabian Kingdom of al-Hijaz in the mid-1920s. Its more cosmopolitan population and relatively sophisticated government led to a bifurcation between the tribal system used in central and eastern Arabia and a continuation of the existing system of government in the Hijaz. The latter had included, as early as 1916, a council of ministers under a prime minister, as well as a senate, although the Hashimi King continued to wield real authority. Despite unification (the present name of the Kingdom of Saudi Arabia was adopted in 1932), Najd (central Arabia) and al-Hijaz were administered separately until the 1950s. 'Abd al-'Aziz's son Faysal served as the Viceroy of al-Hijaz and a Council of Deputies was established in 1931 only for that province.

The income generated by oil and the dilemma over how to distribute its benefits added to the strains on the rickety structure and the King relied increasingly on a small coterie of Hijazis and expatriate Arabs to administer his fledgling state. Initial efforts were made to centralize the administration in the early 1940s, and a variety of new ministries was established in the early 1950s to complement the Ministries of Foreign Affairs (1930), Finance (1932), and Defense (1944). The final step in unification was the creation of a Council of Ministers for the entire country in 1953, which differed from the now-defunct Hijazi Council of Deputies by having its decisions routed through the King for approval.

Adding to the original three ministries, a number of service and regulatory ministries were created between 1951 and 1954, including interior, education, agriculture, communications, commerce and industry, and health. The key Ministry of Petroleum and Minerals was established in the 1960s, as were social affairs and labor, and information. While most Arab countries have a Ministry of Islamic Affairs and Awqaf (religious endowments), Saudi Arabia's equivalent, the Ministry of Hajj and Awqaf (also established in the early 1960s) has the unique responsibility of organizing and administering the annual hajj (pilgrimage) to Makkah of Muslims from around the world. The Ministry of Justice came into existence in 1970, its existence complicated by the strong role of the *'ulama'* in the kingdom's political and public life. Another six ministries were created in October 1975: public works and housing; municipal and rural affairs; higher education; industry and electricity; posts, telegraphs and telephones; and planning. The last cabinet reshuffle occurred in 1999 when four ministers were replaced. Other members of the Council of Ministers are eight ministers of state, and the presidents of the Seaports Authority, the Central Auditing Bureau, the Investigation and Control Board, the Higher Council of 'Ulama', and the Governor of the Saudi Arabian Monetary Agency.

The work of the government is carried out through other agencies besides ministries. There are three principal executive offices associated with the King: the King's Office [al-dīwān al-mālikī; الديوان المالكي], which handles functions pertaining to the King's role as head of state (such as communications with other states, and preparing royal decrees, as well as handling royal family affairs); the Office of the Presidency of the Council of Ministers [dīwān ri'āsat majlis al-wuzarā'; ديوان رئاسة مجلس الوزراء], which deals with matters relating to the King as head of government or Prime Minister, and whose head, Muhammad al-Nu'aysir, is also head of the King's Office; and Royal Protocol (which deals with the King directly and not through the head of his offices). Other offices around the King include his Private Office, the Crown Prince's Office, the Office of Bedouin Affairs, and the Experts' Division (legal affairs).

Other key independent agencies include the Seaports Authority, the Institute of Public Administration, the Civil Service Bureau, the General Presidency for Youth Welfare, the Supreme Board for Saudi ARAMCO, and the Royal Commission for al-Jubayl and Yanbu'. Given the country's conservative Islamic character, religious bodies figure prominently in the government structure. Among these are the Directorate of Religious Research, Legal Opinions, Islamic Propagation and Guidance [idārat al-buhūth al-'ilmīyah wal-iftā' wal-da'wah wal-irshād; إدارة البحوث العلمية والافتاء والدعوة والارشاد] (headed for many years by Shaykh 'Abd al-'Aziz bin Baz, the senior religious figure in the country until his death in 1999), the Committees for Commanding the Good and Forbidding Evil (which comprise the *mutawwi 'in* or so-called religious police), and the General Presidency for Girls' Education (the religious establishment that supervised nearly all female education until 2002). There are also a number of public corporations, such as Saudi Arabian Airlines and the Saudi Arabian Monetary Agency (SAMA), which serves as the country's central bank.

Although the three major divisions of the country are al-Hijaz, Najd, and the Eastern Province, only the last is an administrative entity. Formally, the kingdom is divided into 14 imarat (provinces; sing. imarah), each headed by an amir (governor). The most important of these are Riyadh (which covers most of the Saudi heartland of Najd), the Eastern Province (including the oases of al-Ahsa' and al-Qatif, as well as the oil center and urban hub around Dhahran and al-Dammam), Makkah (including the cities of Jiddah and al-Ta'if), and al-Madinah. The remaining imarat consist of al-Qasim and Ha'il in Najd; Tabuk, al-Jawf, al-Quriyat, and Northern Frontier in the north; and al-Bahah, 'Asir, Najran, and Jizan in the south. Somewhat confusingly, there is a plethora of smaller subunits also known as imarat but whose amirs report to the Deputy Minister of the Interior rather than direct to the Minister or the King.

Economy

Prior to oil, much of Saudi Arabia's economic life revolved around pastoralism. Given the sparseness of vegetation and the country's badu (bedouin) heritage, it is not surprising that perhaps a majority of the population was nomadic, herding camels, goats, and sheep within ancient tribal grazing areas. At the same time, however, the traditional economy contained other important elements as well. Farming has long taken place in most regions of Saudi Arabia. It is particularly important in the relatively well-watered highlands of al-Sarawat in the southwest, but such oases as al-Ahsa' and al-Qatif in the east have been major agricultural hubs for centuries. Even in Najd, old farming settlements existed around Buraydah, 'Unayzah, and many other locations. Date-palm cultivation was most important but wheat and other cereals were also grown.

Previously, trade, both local and long distance, was vital to economic life. Camel caravans crisscrossed the Arabian Peninsula and extended into present-day Iraq and Syria; the tradition dates back thousands of years to the utilization of frankincense routes from southern Arabia to the Mediterranean. At the same time, many small settlements were founded around weekly markets. Seaports such as Jiddah developed into commercial centers supplying extensive hinterlands. Along the Gulf and Red Sea coasts, fishing has been important since prehistoric times, both for subsistence and for sale inland and to urban centers. Pearldiving was another mainstay in the Gulf until its devastation by the economic depression of the 1930s and the introduction of Japanese cultured pearls. Traditionally, the economy of al-Hijaz, especially Makkah and Jiddah, depended greatly on income from the hajj, the annual pilgrimage to Makkah. Before oil, the hajj provided the single greatest source of income for King 'Abd al-'Aziz and the decline in the number of pilgrims because of the depression in the 1930s and the Second World War placed his state in a perilous financial situation.

The discovery of oil in the 1930s and the steady growth of oil exports in the late 1940s and the 1950s struck hard at the traditional economy. Many of the farmers in the Eastern Province were lured to well-paying jobs in the oil industry and the importation of foodstuffs harmed cultivators elsewhere. Handicrafts also suffered, with the weaving industry displaced by mass-produced textile imports and local manufacture of silver and gold was undercut by cheap competition from the Indian subcontinent. Only the big merchant families prospered and their ranks were swelled by new entrepreneurs. At first concentrating on new ranges and volumes of imports, Saudi merchants soon expanded into providing services for the rapidly swelling government and creating import-substitution industries.

As mineral resources belong to the state in Saudi Arabia, all oil income accrued to the government, which then became responsible for developing the country and distributing the new wealth to its citizenry. At first, development spending consisted largely of identifying a need on an ad hoc basis, for which expenditure was then allocated. Unfortunately, that was the basis for all spending, especially by the King and the royal family, and, by the late 1950s, the result was financial chaos. Draconian measures instituted by Crown Prince (later King) Faysal bin 'Abd al-'Aziz in 1958 were necessary to restore economic health. In 1970, the first of a series of five-year plans marked the kingdom's commitment to development planning. Successive plans emphasized sectoral developments such as manpower training, economic diversification to reduce dependence on oil, and the creation of indigenous industry.

The rush to development, particularly in the latter half of the 1970s and the first half of the 1980s, produced a tremendous construction boom and an equally tremendous thirst for manpower. The Saudi population was neither plentiful nor educated enough to satisfy this demand and so several million expatriates were engaged in nearly all occupations, from managers and experts to construction workers and domestic help. Saudi Arabia's stress on education has produced welcome results but the flow of young, educated Saudis unfortunately has coincided with stagnant oil revenues and lack of job opportunities.

The decline in oil prices during the late 1980s and 1990s led to 16 years of budget deficits. It was not until 2000 that the government recorded a surplus of SR 23 billion or about $6 billion (*see* APPENDIX G, Table 3). The deficits were financed by drawing down reserves, delaying government payments and domestic borrowing. Although the government did contract some international loans, it has sought to avoid this route.

The fundamental question is whether economic development can create a viable non-oil-dependent economy. In some ways, this is not an immediate problem, as Saudi Arabia's oil reserves are the largest in the world and the kingdom enjoys more spare productive capacity than any other producer. However, the oil industry is capital intensive and will not provide new jobs for the burgeoning Saudi population. Furthermore, increasing demands on government expenditure are not being met from oil revenues and the government is actively seeking to privatize many government-owned corporations and services.

THE DICTIONARY

ABA AL-KHAYL, MUHAMMAD BIN 'ALI. (1935-) [abā al-khayl; محمد بن علي ابا الخيل] A Saudi government official and Minister of Finance and National Economy from 1975 until 1995. Born in **Buraydah** (Najd) in 1935, he received a BA from Cairo University and returned home to join the Ministry of Communications. He established the Institute of Public Administration in 1962, became Deputy Minister of State for Finance and National Economy in 1970, and was appointed Minister in King **Khalid's** first cabinet.

'ABD AL-'AZIZ BIN 'ABD AL-RAHMAN AL SA'UD. (1880-1953) [عبد العزيز بن عبد الرحمن آل سعود] The 16th leader of the **Al Sa'ud** state and the son of **'Abd al-Rahman bin Faysal**, the 15th imam, 'Abd al-'Aziz was born in **Riyadh** but was forced to flee to **Kuwait** with his father when the rival **Al Rashid** family captured Riyadh in 1891. From there, he launched a daring infiltration of Riyadh in 1902 and succeeded in killing the Rashidi governor and capturing **al-Musmak** fort. With Riyadh regained, 'Abd al-'Aziz was able gradually to extend his control over southern **Najd**. Perpetually constrained by lack of funds and the paramount **British** influence in most of the surrounding territory, 'Abd al-'Aziz was forced to wait for favorable opportunities to extend his realm to the frontiers of his forebears. **Ottoman** setbacks in Europe allowed him to capture **al-Ahsa'** in the east in 1913. A British subsidy helped him to vanquish the Al Rashid in northern Najd and take over their capital at **Ha'il** in 1921. The subsequent elimination of the subsidy left him free to conquer **al-Hijaz** during 1925-1927. The weakness of local rulers in the south and a brief border war with **Yemen** in 1934 resulted in the annexation of the provinces of **'Asir, Jizan**, and **Najran**. 'Abd al-'Aziz adopted the title of King of Saudi Arabia in 1932 as well, marking the end of the expansionist phase of the Third Saudi State.

Even more remarkable than the military prowess of 'Abd al-'Aziz was his skill in transforming an ephemeral tribal entity of the Najdi interior into a permanent and cohesive nation-state. Admittedly the discovery of oil in 1938 and the beginning of large-scale crude oil exports after the Second World War helped immensely in binding together the disparate regions of the country. But even before that, 'Abd al-'Aziz had succeeded in imposing central authority and law on the great **badu** (bedouin) tribes, subordinating the warriors of the **Ikhwan** movement to his power, and gaining the confidence of the townspeople and merchants. Much of the success of modern Saudi Arabia can be traced to the personality of King 'Abd al-'Aziz: his prowess as a military tactician, his skills in creating an effective coalition of tribes and townspeople, his capability in dealing with outside powers, and his farsightedness in knitting together his conquests into a single state. At the same time, however, the socioeconomic changes put in train by oil wealth in his latter years created new challenges. The reckless spending and pervasive

15

corruption seemed beyond his power to control. It was also perhaps unfortunate that he had insisted that his son Sa'ud succeed him, instead of the more capable but younger Faysal. King 'Abd al-'Aziz had more than 40 sons, four of whom have followed in his footsteps as King: **Sa'ud b. 'Abd al-'Aziz** (r. 1953-1964), **Faysal b. 'Abd al-'Aziz** (r. 1964-1975), **Khalid b. 'Abd al-'Aziz** (r. 1975-1982), and **Fahd b. 'Abd al-'Aziz** (r. 1982-present). A fifth son, **'Abdullah bin 'Abd al-'Aziz** is the Heir Apparent.

'ABD AL-'AZIZ BIN FAHD BIN 'ABD AL-'AZIZ AL SA'UD. (c. 1974-)
[عبد العزيز بن فهد بن عبد العزيز آل سعود] The only son of King **Fahd** by his second wife, Jawharah bint Ibrahim al-Ibrahim. From an early age, 'Abd al-'Aziz was clearly his father's favorite and even accompanied him to summit meetings. He was appointed Minister of State without Portfolio in 1998. A few months later, he represented his father on an official trip to the United States and then added to his public profile by opening Saudi-financed mosques in various European countries.

'ABD AL-'AZIZ BIN MUHAMMAD AL SA'UD. (r. 1765-1803)
[عبد العزيز بن محمد آل سعود] Succeeded his father **Muhammad bin Sa'ud** as the second leader of the Al Sa'ud state. Close to **Muhammad bin 'Abd al-Wahhab**, the founder of the **Wahhabi** movement, 'Abd al-'Aziz waged war on towns and regions which remained opposed to the Wahhabi message. Under his leadership, Saudi control was extended over **al-Ahsa'**, **al-Qatif**, **al-Buraymi**, and temporarily over **Makkah** in 1804. 'Abd al-'Aziz was assassinated, possibly by a **Shi'i** from Karbala (a prominent holy Shi'i city in present-day Iraq) in 1803. He was succeeded by his son **Sa'ud**.

'ABD AL-MAJID BIN 'ABD AL-'AZIZ AL SA'UD. (1941-)
[عبد المجيد بن عبد العزيز آل سعود] A son of King **'Abd al-'Aziz** by a **Sudayri** mother. 'Abd al-Majid was appointed Amir of Tabuk in 1980 and then Amir of al-Madinah in 1986. In 1999, he replaced his brother Majid as Amir of Makkah.

'ABD AL-MUHSIN BIN 'ABD AL-'AZIZ AL SA'UD. (1925-)
[عبد المحسن بن عبد العزيز آل سعود] A son of King **'Abd al-'Aziz** by a **Sudayri** mother, 'Abd al-Muhsin was associated with the **"Liberal Princes"** of the 1960s. Appointed Minister of the Interior by King **Sa'ud** in the new cabinet of 1960, he joined his half brother **Talal** in exile a few months later. Following his return to Saudi Arabia, he was made Amir of al-Madinah by King **Faysal** in 1965.

'ABD AL-RAHMAN BIN 'ABD AL-'AZIZ AL SA'UD. (1931-)
[عبد الرحمن بن عبد العزيز آل سعود] A son of King **'Abd al-'Aziz** and one of the so-called **"Sudayri Seven"** (seven sons by the same Sudayri mother), thus a full brother of King **Fahd**. 'Abd al-Rahman was the first of King 'Abd al-'Aziz's sons to study abroad, receiving a BA from the University of California. He was appointed Deputy Minister of Defense and National

Aviation, under his full brother **Sultan**, in 1983, and also has extensive business interests.

'ABD AL-RAHMAN BIN FAYSAL AL SA'UD. (r. 1875 and 1889-1891) [عبدالرحمن بن فيصل آل سعود] The 13th and 15th leader of the **Wahhabi Al Sa'ud** state. Caught in the rivalry of his two older brothers **'Abdullah bin Faysal** and **Sa'ud bin Faysal** for leadership of the Saudi state after their father's death, 'Abd al-Rahman appeared to have aligned himself with the more liberal Sa'ud. Once Sa'ud had ousted 'Abdullah from the capital **Riyadh**, 'Abd al-Rahman was sent to Baghdad to negotiate with the **Ottomans** for the return of **al-Ahsa'** in eastern Arabia (which had been captured with the help of the ousted brother 'Abdullah). After two years of unsuccessful talks, 'Abd al-Rahman returned to Riyadh, stopping on the way to unsuccessfully attack al-Ahsa'.

When Sa'ud died in the summer of 1874, 'Abd al-Rahman was recognized as successor by the people of Riyadh. A year later, however, his elder brother 'Abdullah managed to take Riyadh and force 'Abd al-Rahman to abdicate. But when, in 1887, 'Abdullah was captured by the sons of Sa'ud bin Faysal, the **Al Rashid**, the family's rivals, forced 'Abdullah's release. Their price, however, was to take both 'Abdullah and 'Abd al-Rahman to their capital at **Ha'il** and to appoint their own governor of al-Riyadh. In 1890, 'Abd al-Rahman was permitted to accompany his ailing brother 'Abdullah back to Riyadh. 'Abdullah died the day after their arrival and 'Abd al-Rahman, not willing to live in Riyadh under Al Rashid rule, rose in revolt and successfully defended Riyadh against a Rashidi army. His attempt to extend his control to **al-Qasim** in central **Najd** ended in disaster, though, and 'Abd al-Rahman was forced to retreat to al-Ahsa'. A brief recapture of Riyadh was followed by 'Abd al-Rahman's flight back to al-Ahsa' in 1891 and then on to Kuwait. There he remained until his son **'Abd al-'Aziz** managed to recapture Riyadh in 1902 and establish the Third Saudi State. 'Abd al-Rahman subsequently abdicated his rights to leadership of the Al Sa'ud to this son.

'ABDULLAH AL-FAYSAL (OR 'ABDULLAH BIN FAYSAL) BIN 'ABD AL-'AZIZ AL SA'UD. (1921-) [عبدالله الفيصل بن عبدالعزيز آل سعود] The eldest son of King **Faysal**. A deputy to his father when Faysal governed **al-Hijaz** as viceroy, 'Abdullah served as Minister of Health (1951-1954) and also Minister of the Interior (1951-1959) until dismissed as a consequence of the growing rivalry between King **Sa'ud** and Faysal. Since then, 'Abdullah has concentrated on his business interests.

'ABDULLAH BIN 'ABD AL-'AZIZ AL SA'UD. (1923-) [عبد الله بن عبد العزيز آل سعود] Sixth son of King **'Abd al-'Aziz**, by al-Fahdah bint 'Asi of the Shammar tribe (her only son). His early career is obscure but he was appointed Commander of the National Guard in 1964 by his half brother, King **Faysal**, following King **Sa'ud**'s abdication. He became Crown Prince and First Deputy Prime Minister after the death of King **Khalid** (1982). As the recognized successor to King **Fahd**, he would be the fifth son of King 'Abd al-'Aziz to rule. 'Abdullah's strengths are regarded as his leadership of the National Guard, his ties to the **badu** (bedouin) tribes and conservatives, and his closeness to other Arab states, notably Syria. However, he has not held any administrative position apart from the Guard, unlike previous Kings, and he has neither full brothers on which to rely nor any sons in prominent positions. Perhaps most importantly, it is generally believed that he faces strong opposition from within the family by the so-called **"Sudayri Seven"** or Al Fahd, the seven full brothers headed by King Fahd and including Defense Minister **Sultan**, Interior Minister **Nayif**, and Governor of Riyadh **Salman**. At the time of writing, it was entirely possible that he might not succeed as he is only three years younger than King Fahd, who continues to rule despite increasingly bad health.

Because of King Fahd's increasingly poor condition, 'Abdullah gradually became de facto ruler of Saudi Arabia and began to put his own stamp on Saudi politics, with prominent statements against corruption and warnings that the kingdom faces prolonged economic austerity. He pushed for economic rationalization and the privatization of many government-owned entities, and invited international **oil** companies to participate in the development of the kingdom's extensive **natural gas** reserves. He also became active internationally with a number of highly publicized trips abroad, including to Europe and the US. In early 2002, he advanced his own peace plan for the **Arab-Israeli conflict** which was hailed in the West and by some in Israel.

'ABDULLAH BIN FAYSAL AL SA'UD. (r. 1865-1871 and 1875-1889) [عبد الله بن فيصل آل سعود] The 11th and fourteenth leader of the **Al Sa'ud** state. While his father **Faysal** still ruled, 'Abdullah became embroiled in serious rivalry with his brother **Sa'ud**: 'Abdullah was noted as the leader of the fanatically religious group while Sa'ud became the champion of the moderate or liberal party. Although 'Abdullah had been made heir by his father Faysal, 'Abdullah proved to be a poor administrator and statesman, causing many to abandon loyalty to him. Northern **Najd** fell under the influence of the **Al Rashid** family of **Ha'il** and soon only the environs of the capital **Riyadh** and some southern districts of Najd were totally secure. Less than a year after his father's death, Sa'ud began to gather supporters among the tribes and shaykhs of **al-Ahsa'** in the east and, capturing al-Ahsa', defended it successfully against 'Abdullah's forces. Sa'ud captured Riyadh in 1870, causing 'Abdullah to flee to the tribes of the north, where he established an alliance with the **Ottomans** which allowed them to take over al-Ahsa'. Estranging the population of Najd by his reliance on tribal allies from eastern Arabia, Sa'ud was expelled from Riyadh in 1871. Although he managed to recover the capital in the following year, he was wounded in a battle against other tribes and died in Riyadh in 1874. **'Abd al-Rahman** was acclaimed as the new leader but a year later 'Abdullah forced his younger brother to abdicate. In 1887, 'Abdullah was captured by the sons of his other brother Sa'ud but was released by the Al Rashid of Ha'il, who took both 'Abdullah and 'Abd al-Rahman to their capital and appointed their own governor of Riyadh. Finally in 1890, the Al Rashid allowed 'Abdullah, by then old and in failing health, to return to Riyadh but he died the day after his arrival.

'ABDULLAH BIN FAYSAL BIN TURKI BIN 'ABD AL-'AZIZ AL SA'UD.
[عبد الله بن فيصل بن تركي بن عبد العزيز آل سعود] (-1946) Secretary-General of the
Royal Commission for Yanbu' and al-Jubayl from its founding in 1985 and
then named as the first head of the General Investment Authority, formed
in 2000 to manage foreign investment in the kingdom. 'Abdullah's father
Faysal is a well-known businessman from the **Sa'ud al-Kabir** branch of
the **Al Sa'ud**.

'ABDULLAH BIN HUSAYN AL-HASHIMI. (1880-1951)
[عبد الله بن حسين الهاشمي] A son of **Husayn bin 'Ali** (the Sharif of **Makkah**
and subsequently King of al-Hijaz [1916-1924]), 'Abdullah represented
Makkah in the **Ottoman** parliament before the First World War. During
the Arab Revolt declared in 1916 by his father, 'Abdullah led the army that
captured the city of **al-Ta'if**, and later served as Foreign Minister of the
Kingdom of al-Hijaz. After the war, the **British** made him king of the new
state of Transjordan (later Jordan). Assassinated in Jerusalem by a Palestinian
subject in 1951 because of his contacts with Israeli leaders, he was succeeded
briefly by his son Talal and then by his grandson Husayn and great grandson
'Abdullah, the present King of Jordan.

'ABDULLAH BIN SA'UD AL SA'UD. (r. 1814-1818) [عبد الله بن سعود آل سعود]
Succeeded his father **Sa'ud bin 'Abd al-'Aziz** as the fourth leader of the
Al Sa'ud state in 1814. 'Abdullah's first task of overcoming opposition from
his uncle 'Abdullah paled before the threat posed by Muhammad 'Ali and
the **Egyptian** forces invading **al-Hijaz**. An inferior warrior and leader
compared to his father, 'Abdullah concluded a truce with the Egyptians soon
after he came to power, which enabled them to regroup. He then foolishly
confronted the superior Egyptian army in open battle instead of utilizing
guerrilla tactics. 'Abdullah also inherited the unpopularity of his father and
consequently his opponents in the **Najd** heartland of his state began treating
with the Egyptians, thus allowing Egyptian general Ibrahim Pasha to invade
Najd and lay waste to the Sa'udi capital at **al-Dir'iyah**. 'Abdullah was sent
as a prisoner to Istanbul and executed there, thus bringing the First Saudi
State to an ignominious end. The Al Sa'ud mantle subsequently fell to his
uncle **Turki bin 'Abdullah** (after a brief attempt to rule by 'Abdullah's brother
Mishari bin Sa'ud).

'ABDULLAH BIN THUNAYAN AL SA'UD. (r. 1841-1843)
[عبد الله بن ثنيان آل سعود] The ninth leader of the **Al Sa'ud** state, 'Abdullah
rebelled against the **Ottoman**-imposed **Khalid bin Sa'ud** and gradually
forced Khalid out of Arabia. Soon after 'Abdullah's victory, however, former
Imam **Faysal bin Turki** escaped from his exile in Egypt and reappeared
in **Najd**, causing the tribal leaders to switch their allegiance from 'Abdullah
to Faysal.

ABHA. [abhā; ابها; 42 30 - 18 13] A medium-sized city in the highlands of southern
Saudi Arabia, sitting on the edge of the escarpment leading to the **Tihamah**
coastal plain, and the capital of the province of **'Asir**. Abha's history before

the last two centuries is obscure. About 1800, it apparently fell under the sway of the **Al Sa'ud** and at least some of its population became **Wahhabis**. It was occupied briefly by Egyptian forces in 1834. Subsequently, Abha was ruled by the **Al 'Ayid** clan of the Bani Mughayd tribe until conquered by the **Ottomans** in 1871. Presumably because of its central location at the hub of a regional road network and its pleasant climate, the Ottomans made Abha an administrative center. Following the demise of the Ottoman Empire in the aftermath of World War I, the Al 'Ayid regained control of Abha, only to be challenged first by Muhammad **al-Idrisi** and then by the Al Sa'ud. The city fell into Saudi hands in 1922 and was made the seat of the Saudi province of 'Asir following the Idrisi defeat in 1926. The striking stone fortress of Shada served as the office of the **amir** (governor) until recent years.

ABQAYQ. *See* BUQAYQ.

ABU. [abū; ابو; sometimes spelled bu or aba] Father. It may be used as part of a place-name (*e.g.* Abu 'Arish, Abu Dhabi) or as part of a family name (*e.g.* Muhammad Aba al-Khayl). *See also* UMM (mother) and BIN (son).

ABU 'ARISH. [abū 'arīsh; ابو عريش; 42 50- 16 58] A town in **Jizan** province, about 20 miles inland from the capital of Jizan. First settled in the 13th century, Abu 'Arish was controlled by the Zaydi imams of **Yemen** during the 17th century. Later, a local family of ashraf (sing. **sharif**, *i.e.* descendants of the Prophet **Muhammad**) ruled the town independently for several hundred years, apart from brief occupations by **Wahhabi** and **Egyptian** forces. The **Ottoman** occupation of 'Asir in the 1870s put an end to Abu 'Arish's independent status. Following World War I, and after a brief period under **Idrisi** control, it was absorbed into the Saudi state.

ADHAM, KAMAL. (1920-1999) [adham; ادهم] Born in **Jiddah**, Kamal served as an Adviser to the Court of Heir Apparent **Faysal bin 'Abd al-'Aziz** and was then appointed Special Adviser to the King when Faysal succeeded to the throne in 1964. Of Turkish origins, his half sister was Faysal's wife **'Iffat**. He subsequently held the position of Head of Intelligence until replaced by his nephew, **Turki al-Faysal**, in 1978. Subsequently, he was a prominent businessman with investments said to include members of the royal family as silent partners. In 1992, he was fined $105 million by the United States government for his role in helping BCCI (Bank of Credit and Commerce International) illegally purchase an American bank.

AFGHANISTAN AND SAUDI ARABIA. A dry, mountainous, and landlocked state in central Asia, Afghanistan exhibits an ethnically and linguistically mixed population. Most Afghanis are **Sunnis**. Following the deposition of Afghanistan's king in 1973, the country has endured a long period of turbulence. A Soviet invasion in 1979 was thwarted a year later by popular opposition and foreign assistance. Among the latter were thousands of *mujahidin* (freedom fighters) from many Islamic countries. Many of these returned to their own countries imbued with a radical antigovernment Islamic ideology, among them Saudi Arabia's **Usamah bin Ladin**.

The extremist Taliban movement, born in Pakistani archconservative seminaries allegedly funded in part by sympathetic Saudi **Wahhabis** and apparently supported by **Pakistan**'s Inter-Service Intelligence (ISI), restored a rough order in much of Afghanistan during the mid-1990s. Although it wrested control of more than 90 percent of the country from opponents, notably the Northern Alliance, the movement was refused Afghanistan's seat in the **United Nations** and was recognized by only three countries: Pakistan, Saudi Arabia, and the **United Arab Emirates**.

Saudi Arabia gave active support to the *mujahidin* in their struggle against the Soviet occupiers and attempted to mediate between Afghanistan's warring factions both before and after the Soviet occupation. Riyadh downgraded its diplomatic relations with the Taliban in 1998 after the latter reneged on their agreement to deport Usamah bin Ladin, by then resident in Afghanistan, to Saudi Arabia. The kingdom severed all relations with the Taliban on 25 September 2001, condemning the attacks on the United States and providing guarded support to Washington in its campaign to destroy **al-Qa'idah** and capture or kill Usamah bin Ladin. After the collapse of the Taliban under American firepower in late 2001 and establishment of an interim government headed by Hamid Karzai, Saudi Arabia was Karzai's first destination in his search for financial aid to rebuild the country. Riyadh provided $20 million in initial aid and pledged $100 million at a donors conference a few days later in January 2002.

AGRICULTURE. Pastoralism played a pivotal role in Saudi Arabia's traditional economy but agriculture was also important. Farming has been particularly important in the relatively well-watered highlands of **al-Sarawat** in the southwest but such oases as **al-Ahsa'** and **al-Qatif** in the east have been major agricultural hubs for centuries. Even in **Najd**, old farming settlements existed around **Buraydah**, **'Unayzah**, and many other locations. Date-palm cultivation has been most important but agricultural production also includes wheat, barley, tomatoes, melons, dates, citrus, mutton, chickens, eggs, and milk. Along with other traditional industries, agriculture has declined markedly in importance during the **oil** era. Only a small and declining proportion of the kingdom's population is employed in agriculture. Since the 1970s, the government has sought to ensure food security by heavily subsidizing certain crops. Substantial subsidies led to a serious overproduction of wheat on many agroindustrial complexes throughout the kingdom; subsequently, barley production increased exponentially as subsidies were switched to that crop.

A.H. *See* HIJRAH.

AHMAD BIN 'ABD AL-'AZIZ AL SA'UD. (1941-) [احمد بن عبد العزيز آل سعود]
The youngest of the so-called **"Sudayri Seven,"** the sons born to King **'Abd al-'Aziz** by a Sudayri mother, and thus a full brother of King **Fahd**. One of only two of the seven brothers to be educated abroad (receiving a BA from the University of the Redlands), Ahmad's first government appointment

was as Deputy Amir of **Makkah** in 1971. He has been Deputy Minister of the Interior under full brother **Nayif** since 1975.

AHSA', AL-. [al-aḥsā'; الإحسا; also spelled Hasa; 49 30 to 49 50 - 25 20 to 25 40] An oasis complex in the **Eastern Province** of Saudi Arabia, often called al-Hasa. Its population is estimated at 200,000, with about half the total located in the principal towns of **al-Hufuf** and **Mubarraz**. Thanks to the plentiful artesian wells, the oasis is the largest in the kingdom and has been an agricultural center for several millennia. It also sits astride the old caravan routes between **al-'Uqayr** on the Gulf and **Najd** in the interior. These factors have produced a racially mixed population which, except for the **badu** (bedouin) who have settled more recently on the periphery, is not organized into tribes. About half the Hasawis are **Sunni**, with the rest being **Shi'ah**, a similar composition to the nearby oasis of **al-Qatif** and also the state of **Bahrain**.

Al-Ahsa' (also known in earlier times as al-Hajar) has a long recorded history and was the center of the violent movement of **al-Qaramitah** (Carmathians) in the ninth century A.D. The Portuguese ruled the oasis in the early 16th century before the **Ottomans** established control in 1550. They were displaced by the **Bani Khalid** tribe in 1673. The **Al Sa'ud** captured the oasis in 1797 but it regained its independence several decades later. Incorporated into an Ottoman sanjak (district) in 1872, al-Ahsa' was recaptured by Imam **'Abd al-'Aziz bin 'Abd al-Rahman** in 1913 and integrated into the present Saudi kingdom. Al-Hufuf served as the capital of al-Ahsa' Province until 1952, when the province was renamed the Eastern Province and the capital was moved to **al-Dammam**. The Jawatha [jawāthā; جواثا] Mosque, located in the oasis, was founded about A.D. 635 and is the earliest mosque in Eastern Arabia; only a few arches remain although they probably date from the ninth century.

Al-Ahsa' is famous for its dates and also produces wheat and rice. Sand encroachment is a constant problem, forcing the occasional relocation of settlements. Agriculture suffered in the 1950s when many Hasawi men left for employment with the oil company in nearby **Dhahran**. The subsequent rise in standards of living lessened the competitiveness of al-Ahsa's produce with packaged imports. At the same time, the introduction of electric water pumps, combined with poor drainage, reduced production levels, requiring government intervention to control water use and to construct drainage channels.

'AJMAN, AL-. [al-'ajmān; sing. 'ajmī; also spelled 'ujmān; العجمان؛ عجمي] An important tribe of the Samman plateau and **al-Dahna'** region of **Najd**, as well as along the Gulf coast and around **al-Ahsa'** oasis in the **Eastern Province**. The tribe is mostly **badu** (bedouin) and considered to be of "pure lineage." It is related to the **Qahtan** tribe and traditionally was on bad terms with the **Al Murrah** tribe. The 'Ajman revolted against Imam **'Abd al-'Aziz Al Sa'ud** soon after he occupied al-Ahsa' in 1913 and the Saudi leader waged several battles against the 'Ajman in the following years, driving them temporarily into **Kuwait**. The shaykh of the tribe, **Daydan al-Hithlayn** (or

Bin Hithlayn), served as one of the leaders of the **Ikhwan**; when he was treacherously murdered by one of 'Abd al-'Aziz's lieutenants in 1929, the tribe rose in revolt again. There is no connection between the 'Ajman tribe and the State of 'Ajman, one of the smaller member states of the **United Arab Emirates**.

AL AND AL-. Although spelled the same in English, these are two entirely different words in Arabic. "Al" [āl; آل] means family and is often used in conjunction with family names (*e.g.* Al Sa'ud, the ruling family of Saudi Arabia). On the other hand, "al-" is the equivalent of the article "the," and is affixed to the following word (*e.g.* the region of al-Hijaz). American and British geographical usage sometimes confuses the two words, *e.g.* Al Hijaz. Words or phrases in this dictionary beginning with either "Al" or "al-" are alphabetized according to the main element of the first word (*e.g.* "Sa'ud, Al" or "Hijaz, al-"). (Confusingly, the sons of the late King **Faysal** style themselves "al-Faysal," *e.g.* Sa'ud al-Faysal rather than Sa'ud Al Faysal.)

'ALI, ANWAR. [انور علي] A **Pakistani banking** expert loaned to the Saudi government in 1954, where he became responsible for initiating a number of reforms in the **Saudi Arabian Monetary Agency** (SAMA). His work was so impressive that he was invited to remain on the SAMA board of governors until his health failed in 1971. He died in 1974.

'ALI BIN HUSAYN AL-HASHIMI. (1879-1935) [علي بن حسين الهاشمي] A son of **Husayn bin 'Ali** (the Sharif of **Makkah** and King of **al-Hijaz** [1916-1924]), 'Ali was placed in charge of Hashimi forces in the northern al-Hijaz during the Arab Revolt of the First World War and subsequently represented his father at **al-Madinah**. When Husayn abdicated in 1924, following the disastrous losses of **al-Ta'if** and Makkah to the invading Saudi forces, 'Ali succeeded him as King of al-Hijaz. But his throne seemed doomed from the beginning and he was forced by the advancing Saudis to leave **Jiddah** for exile in **Iraq** in 1926. His son 'Abd al-Ilah served as Regent of Iraq during the period 1935-1953.

'ALI RIDA. ['alī ridā; علي رضا; also spelled Alireza] An important merchant family of **al-Hijaz**, founded by Hajji Zaynal (d. 1929), who came to **Jiddah** in 1884 from Persia as a domestic servant and started his business career as a peddler. His younger brother 'Abdullah 'Ali (d. 1932) took care of family interests in India for many years; in the 1920s, he was appointed Qa'im-maqam (mayor) of Jiddah by King **Husayn bin' Ali al-Hashimi** and played an important mediatory role during the Saudi siege of Jiddah. Zaynal's eldest son Qasim (d. 1927) served as a deputy in the **Ottoman** parliament and two other sons became government ministers during the 1950s (Muhammad as Minister of Commerce and 'Ali as Minister of State). A fourth son Yusuf (d. 1960) eventually took charge of the family business. Several grandsons have served as ambassadors and in other senior government positions. The family business interests are concentrated in the Haaco Company and Xenel industries. A separate branch of the family, headed by 'Abdullah 'Abd al-Ghaffar 'Ali Rida and his son Taymur, owns a separate business known as Rezayat Trading.

'ALIM. *See* 'ULAMA'.

ALIREZA. *See* 'ALI RIDA.

ALWALEED BIN TALAL. *See* WALID, AL-, BIN TALAL BIN 'ABD AL-'AZIZ AL SA'UD.

AMARAH. *See* IMARAH.

AMIR. [amīr, pl. umarā', fem. amīrah; أمير؛أمراء؛أميرة; sometimes spelled "emir"] Prince or governor; member of **Al Sa'ud** ruling family. In Saudi Arabia, amir is the title of the governor of a province (imarah) or a smaller governorate. Amir is also employed as the title of the rulers of the smaller Arab Gulf states.

AMIRATE. [imārah; إمارة; also spelled emirate] The territory governed by an **amir.** *See* IMARAH.

'ANAIZAH. *See* 'UNAYZAH.

'ANAZAH. ['anazah, sing. 'anazī; عنزة؛عنزي] One of the largest Arab tribes, or group of tribes, and considered to be of "pure lineage." In Saudi Arabia, the 'Anazah are located both in **Najd** and **al-Hijaz.** Their territory stretches from the Hijazi oases of **Khaybar** and **Tayma'** up through **al-Jawf** and **Wadi Sirhan** into Syria and Jordan. The 'Anazah's traditional rivals were the equally large and widespread **Shammar.** As the 'Anazah were almost all nomadic, they remained outside the control of the **Ottomans** and then remained semiautonomous of successor governments in Jordan and Syria. Best known amongst the Syrian branches is the **Ruwala** while the Al Sabah ruling family of **Kuwait** and the Al Khalifah ruling family of **Bahrain** are also from the 'Anazah. In Najd, the **Al Sa'ud** royal family is traditionally considered to be descended from an 'Anazi subdivision, although there is some opinion that it derives from the Bani Hanifah.

'ANQARI, IBRAHIM BIN 'ABDULLAH AL-. ['anqarī; إبراهيم بن عبدالله العنقري] A government official educated in Cairo and married to King **Faysal**'s sister. Deputy Minister of the Interior before his appointment as Minister of Information in 1970, he was shifted to Minister of Labor and Social Affairs in 1975 and then to Minister of Municipalities and Rural Affairs in 1983. In 1989, he was replaced as minister by a cousin, Khalid bin Muhammad al-'Anqari, and named Private Adviser to the King with the rank of minister.

ARAB-ISRAELI CONFLICT AND SAUDI ARABIA. In a direct sense, Saudi Arabia has not played a strong role in this long-running confrontation. Nevertheless, it has been extremely concerned about Arab-Israeli developments for a variety of reasons, including: the close emotional ties between Saudis and other Arabs; the kingdom's emphasis on its special role as the protector of the Islamic holy places (Jerusalem contains the third holiest site in Islam); the kingdom's close ties with the **United States**, which in turn has close ties with Israel; and the potential threat Israel poses to Saudi Arabia itself (due to the near contiguity of the two countries and occasional Israeli air force overflights of Saudi territory). The depth of Saudi concern has been manifest at least since King **'Abd al-'Aziz bin 'Abd al-Rahman**'s meeting with US President Franklin Roosevelt in 1945. The 1956 Suez War, in which Israel invaded Egypt's Sinai Peninsula in conjunction with **Britain** and **France**, provided an excuse for the severing of relations with the United Kingdom.

Saudi Arabia contributed token military units to the Arab front during the June 1967 and October 1973 wars. The real Saudi contribution to the Arab cause, however, was the **oil** boycott of 1973-1974, imposed expressly against the United States, Portugal, the Netherlands, and South Africa, but which affected nearly every oil-importing country.

Saudi Arabia's fundamental position on the Arab-Israeli conflict, as on other pan-Arab issues, has been a search for Arab consensus. As a result of the Arab summit at Khartoum after the 1967 war, Riyadh accepted the responsibility (along with the other Arab oil producers) of providing financial aid to the "confrontation states" (**Egypt, Jordan**, Syria, and **Lebanon**). Saudi Arabia has adhered as well to the decision taken at the 1974 Rabat summit to recognize the Palestine Liberation Organization (PLO) as the sole representative of the Palestinian people, and has long supported the PLO financially (apart from the interregnum caused by the PLO's support for **Iraq** after the invasion of **Kuwait** in 1990).

The search for an Arab consensus also led Saudi Arabia, along with all but a few of the other members of the Arab League, to suspend diplomatic relations with Egypt when Anwar al-Sadat signed a separate peace treaty with Israel. In 1981, King **Fahd bin 'Abd al-'Aziz** presented his own plan for Arab-Israeli peace, which seemed implicitly to recognize Israel. Following the war for Kuwait (1991), the Saudis appeared to be active in pushing the Arab confrontation states to pursue American-backed negotiations with Israel. In early 2002, Heir Apparent **'Abdullah bin 'Abd al-'Aziz** attracted international attention with the disclosure of his peace plan proposing full Arab recognition for Israel in exchange for the return of all occupied Palestinian territories.

ARAB LEAGUE. Officially known as the League of Arab States, the Arab League was established in March 1945 to strengthen ties and coordinate policies amongst the independent Arab states. It has grown to a membership of 21, including the Palestine. Saudi Arabia under King **'Abd al-'Aziz bin 'Abd al-Rahman** was instrumental in the creation of the organization, although it later was dominated by the "progressive" Arab republics, particularly **Egypt** under President Nasir (Nasser). In conformity with a majority of the league's members, Riyadh supported the expulsion of Egypt because of its separate peace treaty with Israel in 1979 and the move of the Arab League's headquarters from Cairo to Tunis. The kingdom subsequently and wholeheartedly supported the return of the headquarters to Cairo when Egypt was reinstated in 1982. The kingdom participates fully in the league's subunits and it complies with the league's boycott of Israel. Saudi Arabia enjoined other members to contribute to an Arab League defensive force in **Kuwait** when Iraq threatened in 1961 and King **Fahd bin 'Abd al-'Aziz** was instrumental in mediation in Lebanon's civil war, including engineering the creation of an Arab League peacekeeping force in Lebanon in 1976 and calling for subsequent Arab League meetings on the problem. The kingdom also welcomed the inclusion of Egyptian and Syrian troops during **Operation Desert Storm**, although this was not under the auspices of the Arab League.

ARABIAN GULF. *See* GULF, THE.

ARABIAN PENINSULA. [al-jazīrah al-'arabīyah or jazīrat al-'arab; جزيرة العرب؛ الجزيرة العربية؛] A roughly rectangular peninsula about 1,300 miles long and about 1,200 miles wide at its greatest points. The peninsula is bounded on the west and southwest by the **Red Sea**, on the south and southeast by the Arabian Sea and Gulf of Oman (both extensions of the Indian Ocean), and on the east and northeast by the **Gulf** (also known as the Arabian or Persian Gulf). The artificial land boundaries of the peninsula to the north and northwest are formed by frontiers with **Jordan** and **Iraq**. Saudi Arabia is the largest of the seven states contained on the Arabian Peninsula; the others are **Kuwait**, **Bahrain**, **Qatar**, and the **United Arab Emirates** (UAE) (all located on the Gulf); **Oman** (on the Gulf of Oman and the Arabian Sea); and the Republic of **Yemen** (on the Arabian Sea and the Red Sea). Saudi Arabia has common land boundaries with all of these except Bahrain, which is composed entirely of an island archipelago. Border disputes were problematic between most of the peninsula's countries for most of the 20th century but most of these have been solved—including the most prominent and vexatious of those existing between Saudi Arabia and Oman (1990), Saudi Arabia and Yemen (1995), and Bahrain and Qatar (2001)

'ARAFAT. ['arafāt; عرفات] A small plain about 12 miles southwest of **Makkah**. A stop in 'Arafat is the main requirement of the **hajj**, the annual pilgrimage of Muslims to Makkah.

'ARA'IF, AL-. [al-'arā'if; العرائف] Descendants of Imam **Sa'ud bin Faysal** (r. 1871-1875), who was supplanted by his brother **'Abd al-Rahman bin Faysal**, father of Imam (later King) **'Abd al-'Aziz** (r. 1902-1953). Thus constituting a senior branch of the **Al Sa'ud** but denied the throne, the 'Ara'if joined forces with the **'Ajman** tribe in rebellion against 'Abd al-'Aziz about 1910 and, when defeated, fled to Sharif **Husayn bin 'Ali al-Hashimi** in **al-Hijaz** and to **Bahrain**. Some members later reconciled with 'Abd al-'Aziz, hence the name (which is used by the **badu** [bedouin] to signify camels that were lost in a raid but later recovered). The branch is more commonly known as Al Sa'ud al-Kabir. *See also* SA'UD, AL.

ARAMCO, Arabian American Oil Company. [sharikat al-bitrūl al-'arabīyah al-amrīkīyah; شركة البترول العربية الامريكية] The predominant oil-producing company in Saudi Arabia, based in **Dhahran**, properly known since nationalization as Saudi ARAMCO. The company was formed as a result of a 60-year concession (later extended to 66 years) for the **Eastern Province** granted to Standard Oil of California (SOCAL) in 1933. SOCAL sold half interest the following year to the Texas Company (TEXACO). A well drilled in Dhahran found oil in 1935 and production began in 1938, although most production was delayed until after the Second World War. In 1948, three other companies bought into ARAMCO, resulting in an ownership divided among SOCAL (30%), TEXACO (30%), Standard Oil of New Jersey (later Exxon [now ExxonMobil], 30%), and Socony Vacuum (later Mobil [now ExxonMobil], 10%). In 1950, a 50-50 profit-sharing agreement with the Saudi government was introduced, as well as payment of Saudi income taxes above the modest royalties on every barrel of oil produced.

Two years later, ARAMCO agreed to Saudi participation in the company's policy deliberations and in 1959 two Saudis were elected to the company's board of directors. The Saudi Arabian government took a stake of 25 percent in ARAMCO in 1973, and increased it to 60 percent the following year. By 1980, the assets of ARAMCO had become 100 percent Saudi-owned, but with effect from 1976. The Saudi Arabian government in 1988 established a national oil company, known as Saudi ARAMCO, to manage the nationalized assets of ARAMCO and to expand downstream activities abroad (internal refining and marketing is handled by **PETROMIN**). The first major acquisition by the new company was the $1.28 billion purchase in 1988 of a 50 percent interest in TEXACO's refining and marketing system in 23 eastern and southern US states.

ARAMCO has served as a primary instrument in forging strong Saudi-US ties, arranging for some of the first Saudi students to be educated in the **United States** and promoting early development in Saudi Arabia's Eastern Province. In recent years, some 85 percent of its 55,000 employees have been Saudi.

'AR'AR. ['ar'ar; عرعر; 41 02 - 30 59] A settlement of about 30,000 in the extreme north, near the Iraqi and Jordanian frontiers. The town dates from the establishment of a **TAPLINE** station about 1950: the wells drilled for the **badu** (bedouin) sparked the development of a *suq* (market) and a settlement which quickly grew to several thousand. By the 1970s, 'Ar'ar had so grown in importance that it was removed from the control of the older regional center of **al-Jawf** and made the capital of the **Northern Frontier Province**.

'ARID, AL-. [al-'āriḍ; العارض] The central district of southern **Najd**, bounded by the districts of **Sudayr** on the north and al-Hawtah on the south, and stretching from **al-Dahna'** desert on the east to **Jabal Tuwayq** in the west. It includes the Saudi capital of **Riyadh**.

ARMED FORCES. *See* MILITARY AND DEFENSE.

ARTAWIYAH, AL-. [al-arṭawīyah; الارطوية; 45 20 - 26 31] An oasis in northern **Najd**, founded by King **'Abd al-'Aziz bin 'Abd al-Rahman** in 1912 as an **Ikhwan** settlement. Settled mostly by **Mutayri** tribesmen, its population may have reached as much as 35,000 at its peak in the 1920s. As the home of **Faysal al-Duwish**, one of the principal leaders of the 1928-1930 Ikhwan rebellion against 'Abd al-'Aziz, it was destroyed in 1929. Later rebuilt, its population was estimated at 16,000 in the early 1970s, with an additional 24,000 **badu** (bedouin) inhabitants in the summer.

ARTS AND CULTURE. The development of arts in Saudi Arabia has been slower and more restricted than in most parts of the world, partly because of its historical isolation and poverty and partly because of widespread Islamic reluctance to portray living creatures, combined with conservative **Wahhabi** disapproval of music, dancing, theater, and cinema. There are, however, various traditional tribal dances. As a consequence, literature has been one of the most strongly established art forms in the kingdom. In part, this is due to the traditional Arab love of poetry: some famous poems date to the pre-Islamic era. Composers of poems range from **badu** (bedouins) in the desert to intellectuals in the cities. The former Saudi ambassador to London and recently named Minister of Water **Ghazi al-Qusaybi**, has long been well known for his poetry.

The kingdom has sought to maintain traditional arts and handicrafts, such as jewelry, weaving, and basketry, but with considerable difficulty as the kingdom's consumers have chosen to purchase imported goods.

The Saudi government officially encourages the arts. The General Presidency of Youth Welfare organizes regular competitions and exhibitions at home and abroad. In addition, the Saudi Arabian Society for Culture and Arts was created in 1972 to raise artistic standards and to sponsor young talent. The society is responsible for the King Fahd Cultural Center in Riyadh, which contains display areas, a theater, and a library. The National Guard organizes the annual Janadriyah Heritage and Cultural Festival outside **Riyadh**, which includes a camel race, performances of traditional music, and folkloric dances during its two weeks.

'ASIR. ['asīr; عسير] A southern province of Saudi Arabia, with its capital at **Abha**. From west to east, a cross section of the province rises dramatically from the hot, dry, coastal plain of the **Tihamah** up to the cool and fertile highlands of **al-Sarawat**, and then gradually descends into an eastern desert plateau. With peaks rising over 9,000 feet, the highlands receive ample rainfall and are able to support more cultivation and a higher population density than the rest of the country. The population of 'Asir is thought to be in excess of one million, with **Khamis Mushayt** and Abha being the largest towns. Because of its proximity to **Yemen**, much of the 'Asiri countryside and architecture appears more Yemeni than Hijazi or Najdi. The name 'Asir seems to have referred originally to a tribe of Abha and its use as a provincial name dates only from the **Ottoman** occupation in the 19th century.

'ATIYAH, BANI. [banī 'atīyah; بني عطية] A tribe of **al-Hijaz**, with elements extending from south of **al-Ta'if** to the border with **Jordan**. An old tribe said to be closely related to the **'Anazah**, the Bani 'Atiyah are close to the **Huwaytat** tribe.

'AWAZIM, AL-. [al-'awāzim; sing. 'āzimī; العوازم؛ عازمي] A tribe of mean origins, not related to the "pure" **badu** (bedouin) tribes. Partly located in the **Eastern Province**, north of **al-Ahsa'** up to **al-Khafji** and **Kuwait**, as well as in **Khaybar** and **al-Jawf** districts of **al-Hijaz**. The 'Awazim were early supporters of Imam **'Abd al-'Aziz bin 'Abd al-Rahman** (r. 1902-1953), who freed them from their inferior status vis-à-vis the **'Ajman** tribe. Although the tribe is officially recognized as being under the sovereignty of Saudi Arabia, a number of 'Awazim have been employed as personal retainers by the Amir of Kuwait.

'AWDAH, SALMAN BIN FAHD AL-. (1955-) [salmān al-'awdah; سلمان بن فهد العودة] A dissident religious figure born near the town of **Buraydah** in **al-Qasim** region of central Arabia. After attending an Islamic institute in Buraydah, he studied at **Imam Muhammad bin Sa'ud University** in **Riyadh** and returned to Buraydah to teach in the university's branch there. He opposed the presence of American troops in the kingdom during and after the **Kuwait** War. The popularity of his sermons, distributed via cassette tapes, led to demonstrations in 1994 and his arrest. He was not released until 1999. *See also* OPPOSITION GROUPS.

'AYID, AL. [āl 'āyiḍ; آل عايض] A clan of the Bani Mughayd tribe of **'Asir**, who rose to prominence in the early 19th century when they made the town of **Abha** their base from which they ruled 'Asir until the **Ottoman** conquest of 1871. The clan regained their independence in the aftermath of the First World War but were defeated by the **Al Sa'ud** in 1922.

'AYN. ['ayn; pl. 'uyūn; عين؛ عيون] The Arabic word for eye or spring, it is often used as part of geographical place-names, especially desert water holes. It is also the name of a consonant in the Arabic alphabet, for which there is no English equivalent and is represented in transliteration by the symbol " ' ".

'AZZAM, 'ABD AL-RAHMAN AL-. (1893-1976) [al-'azzām; عبدالرحمن العزام] An Egyptian politician of the old régime and former Secretary-General of the **Arab League**, driven into exile by Jamal 'Abd al-Nasir's (Nasser) revolutionary government of 1954. In subsequent years, he represented Saudi Arabia in the **al-Buraymi** dispute and later served in the Saudi Mission to the **United Nations** in New York. His daughter married King **Faysal's** son **Muhammad**.

- B -

B. AND IBN. Abbreviation for and variation of **bin**, "son of. "

BADR. [badr; بدر; 38 46 - 23 44] Site in **al-Hijaz**, about 90 miles south of **al-Madinah**, of the first major battle between the **Muslims** of al-Madinah and an army from **Makkah** in A.H. 623. The much smaller Muslim force gained a surprising victory over the Makkans, although the latter amassed a stronger battalion and defeated the Muslims in the subsequent Battle of **Uhud**.

BADR BIN 'ABD AL-'AZIZ AL SA'UD. (1933-) [بدر بن عبد العزيز آل سعود] One of the sons of King **'Abd al-'Aziz** by a **Sudayri** mother. As one of the **"Liberal Princes"** under the leadership of his half brother **Talal**, Badr was appointed Minister of Communications in King Sa'ud's cabinet of 1960 but joined Talal in exile a few months later. After making his peace later with **King Faysal**, he was named Deputy Commander of the National Guard in the late 1960s, a position he still holds.

BADU. [badū, sing. badawī; بدو؛بدوي; often spelled bedu or bedouin] The Arabic term for nomads, often used in contrast with hadar [ḥaḍar; حضر] (the settled population). Regarding themselves as the only pure Arabs, badu tribes exist in most parts of Saudi Arabia. For much of history, the badu were feared for their attacks upon towns and camel caravans. Early in the 20th century, however, King **'Abd al-'Aziz bin 'Abd al-Rahman** enlisted the help of the badu in spreading his authority and the teachings of **Wahhabism**, giving birth to the badu settlements of the **Ikhwan**. By the early 1930s, the badu were brought firmly under the control of the **Al Sa'ud** and today remain among the royal family's most loyal supporters. Changes in legislation abolishing communal tribal lands (the **dirah** and hima), as well as the assertion of private and state ownership of tribal lands, also have contributed to the decline of nomadism. The number of badu who remain nomadic increasingly grows smaller because of the economic hardships of nomadic life and the lure of better opportunities in the city. But large-scale attempts to settle them (*see* SIRHAN, WADI; HARAD) were not particularly successful. Badu are said to predominate in the National Guard.

BAHAH, AL-. [al-bāḥah; الباحة; 41 40 - 20 00] A small city located in **al-Sarawat** highlands midway between **al-Ta'if** and **Abha**. It is the capital of a small province of the same name.

BAHARINAH, AL-. [al-bahārinah; sing. bahrānī; البحارنة؛بحراني] The indigenous Arab **Shi'ah** of the **Gulf** region, especially in **al-Qatif** and **al-Ahsa'** oases of the **Eastern Province** and in the state of **Bahrain** where they form the majority of the population.

BAHARNA. *See* BAHARINAH.

BAHRAIN AND SAUDI ARABIA. An archipelago of 30 islands, Bahrain has been a fully independent state since 1971. It was the site of the first discovery of oil in the Arab Gulf states and production began in 1932. The producing company, CALTEX (composed of Standard of California and TEXACO), also acquired the concession for Saudi Arabia; with the addition of later partners, this became known as **ARAMCO**. However, Bahrain's modest reserves have nearly all been depleted and its refinery mainly processes crude oil brought in from Saudi Arabia by underwater pipeline. The Al Khalifah, the Bahraini ruling family, trace their origin to **Najd** and after wandering along the Arab littoral for several centuries, they conquered Bahrain in the 18th century, accompanied by fellow tribes of Najdi origin. In the 20th century, Bahrain constituted a window on the outside world for Najd: the (British) Political Agent in Bahrain was the means by which the **Al Sa'ud** communicated with the British Government; and many imports to Najd and the **Eastern Province** came through Bahrain. A Bahraini merchant, **'Abd al-'Aziz al-Qusaybi** (Gosaibi) served as King **'Abd al-'Aziz bin 'Abd al-Rahman**'s purchasing agent and unofficial ambassador in the 1930s and 1940s. Bahrain, relatively more open and cosmopolitan than the kingdom, has attracted Saudi visitors for a number of years for its hotels, shopping, and nightclubs. The opening of the King Fahd Causeway in 1986, which connects Bahrain with **al-Dammam**, intensified the number of weekend visitors.

BANDAR BIN SULTAN BIN 'ABD AL-'AZIZ AL SA'UD. (1949-)

[بندر بن سلطان بن عبدالعزيز آل سعود] The fourth son of the Defense Minister **Sultan**, Bandar was trained in **Britain** as an air force pilot. He early caught the eye of then-King **Faysal**, who married him to one of his daughters. A capable and charismatic spokesman, Bandar has been ambassador to the **United States** since 1983 (and eventually Dean of the Diplomatic Corps) but King **Fahd** has entrusted him with many important duties and missions which range well beyond his official position. He was given ministerial rank in 1995.

BANKING. Saudi Arabia has a vibrant banking sector with 11 commercial banks and total banking deposits of over $70 billion as of 2000. The oldest bank is the National Commercial Bank (NCB), established by the **bin Mahfuz** family in **Jiddah** in 1938 and the kingdom's sole bank until the 1950s. It remained the largest bank until running into trouble in the early 1990s when its chairman, Khalid bin Mahfuz, was implicated in the international scandal and collapse of the Bank of Credit and Commerce International (BCCI). NCB was bought out in 1999 by the Saudi government. The Saudi-American Bank was established in Jiddah in 1955 as a branch of Citibank; its first **Riyadh** branch opened in 1966. It merged with the United Saudi Bank in 1999. In accordance with Saudi laws adopted in the mid-1970s, Saudi nationals acquired majority interest in the bank and it took its present name. The laws affected all foreign-owned banks, such as the Saudi British Bank and al-Bank al-Saudi al-Hollandi. The Riyadh Bank, established in 1957, is the oldest publicly held bank in the kingdom and is one of three banks that are 100 percent Saudi owned. Al-Rajhi Banking Investment Corporation was created in 1988 from al-Rajhi Company for Currency Exchange and Commerce, established by four **Rajihi** brothers from **al-Qasim** and for many years the largest money-exchange operation in the kingdom. The new bank was the first and still the only Islamic bank in Saudi Arabia. The kingdom enacted a new anti-money laundering law as a result of the 11 September attacks.

BANU OR BANI. *See* BIN.

BASIC LAW. The Saudi state created by King **'Abd al-'Aziz bin 'Abd al-Rahman** was based fundamentally on the practical quality of his personal leadership and on the legal basis of the **shari'ah**, the corpus of Islamic law that governs most Muslim behavior. As the government grew, assumed many new functions, and confronted the need for some popular participation in its policies, so the necessity of a new constitutional framework became clear. After much delay, King **Fahd bin 'Abd al-'Aziz** announced the promulgation of a Basic Law on 1 March 1992, along with the imminent establishment of an appointed **Majlis al-Shura** (Consultative Council). Although not officially termed a constitution, the Basic Law serves as the constitutional basis of the state. It spells out the country's system of government and its powers and responsibilities, economic principles, rights and duties of its citizens, and the state's financial organization. The Basic Law was noteworthy for establishing basic rules for succession (involving consultation among the sons and grandsons of King 'Abd al-'Aziz bin 'Abd al-Rahman), setting out provisions for the privacy of individuals, stipulating an independent judiciary, and enunciating reforms for local and regional administration. The kingdom's adoption of the Basic Law places it on similar constitutional footing with its fellow members in the **Gulf Cooperation Council**. *See* APPENDIX F for the complete text.

BATIN, AL-. *See* HAFAR AL-BATIN.

BAZ, 'ABD AL-'AZIZ BIN 'ABDULLAH BIN 'ABD AL-RAHMAN BIN. (1912-1999) [عبد العزيز بن عبد الله بن عبد الرحمن بن باز] The senior religious figure of Saudi Arabia until his death in 1999. Born in **Riyadh** in 1912, he served as a **qadi** (religious judge) in **al-Kharj**, and taught at the Religious Institute in Riyadh and then in the Faculty of Shari'ah at **Imam Muhammad bin Sa'ud University**. Shaykh 'Abd al-'Aziz was Rector of the **Islamic University** in **al-Madinah** before being appointed President of the Islamic Research, Legal Opinions, Islamic Propagation, and Guidance Department (one of the two supreme religious councils of Saudi Arabia). He was appointed Grand Mufti in 1993 and held the position until his death. Also known as Shaykh bin Baz, the blind religious leader was noted for his ultra-conservative religious and social views. On the other hand, he was careful to support the government with **fatwa**s approving the entry of Western troops in 1990 to defend the kingdom against Iraq and the Arab-Israeli peace process.

BEDOUIN. *See* BADU.

BIDA', AL-. [al-bida'; البدع; 35 06 -28 30] Located in the extreme northwestern corner of the kingdom, on the eastern coast of the Gulf of al-'Aqabah, al-Bida' is the site of ancient Maghayir Shu'ayb, whose inhabitants were known to the author of the "**Periplus of the Erythraean Sea**" (first century A.D.) as the people of "Bethmuni." Nearby are substantial ruins, including **Nabataean** tombs with Nabataean and **Lihyanite** inscriptions. The modern port of Haql (25 miles to the northeast) is the ancient port of Maqna.

BIJAD, BIN. *See* SULTAN BIN BIJAD BIN HUMAYD.

BILHARITH. [bilḥarith; بلحرث] A tribe of the **Tihamah** coast of '**Asir** province, living between **Jizan** and Midi on the border of **Yemen**.

BIN. [bin; correctly, ibn; pl. banū or banī; بن؛ ابن؛ بنو؛ بني] Son; used in the construction of proper names, *e.g.* Muhammad bin Ahmad (Muhammad the son of Ahmad). Sometimes used as an honorific for the leader of a tribe or community (as in Bin Saʻud or Ibn Saʻud). In the plural, banu (formally correct) or bani (more commonly used) often forms part of a tribal name (*e.g.* Bani Khalid). Bin (used in this dictionary) is more formally spelled "ibn" and may be abbreviated to "b." *See also* BINT (daughter).

BIN SAʻUD. [or Ibn Saʻud; ابن سعود] A traditional honorific for each succeeding head of the **Al Saʻud** family. In this century, the phrase is most closely associated with the founder of the Third Saudi State, '**Abd al-ʻAziz bin ʻAbd al-Rahman** Al Saʻud.

BINT. [bint; pl. banāt; بنت؛ بنات] Daughter or girl. The word for son is **bin**.

BIRKAT AL-KHURABAH. *See* DARB ZUBAYDAH.

BISHAH. [bīshah; بيشة; 42 60 - 20 05] An oasis in the northern part of the province of '**Asir**; Nimran and al-Rawshan are its two most important settlements. Bishah derives its importance from its central location on the caravan routes between 'Asir and **Yemen** to the south, **al-Hijaz** to the northwest, and **Najd** to the northeast. The town fell under the control of the **Al ʻAyid** family of 'Asir until the **Ottoman** occupation of 'Asir about 1871. It was absorbed into the Saudi kingdom with the rest of 'Asir in the 1920s.

"BLUE" LINE. The cartographic line established by the Anglo-Ottoman convention of 29 July 1913, which delineated the eastern limits of the Ottoman sanjak (province) of **Najd**, and thus the eastern boundary of the Ottoman Empire in Arabia. The line was drawn on a north-south axis from a point near Zakhuniyah Island (now part of Saudi Arabia) through the Jafura desert and ending in **al-Rubʻ al-Khali** desert. It definitively established that **Qatar** was not an Ottoman possession and formed the first tentative boundary in what was to be a long dispute between Saudi Arabia (the successor to the Ottoman Najd) and the British-protected littoral states of the Gulf. In 1935, King '**Abd al-ʻAziz bin ʻAbd al-Rahman** presented his counter-boundary, which came to be known as the "**Red**" **Line**.

BLUNT, WILFRID SCAWEN, AND LADY ANNE. English diplomat and poet (1840-1922) and his wife (1837-1917), both of whom gained fame as Arabian travellers and breeders of Arabian horses. Wilfrid, introduced to Arabian affairs by Sir **Richard Burton**, became a passionate advocate of Arab nationalism. Lady Anne, the granddaughter of the poet Byron, wrote *A Pilgrimage to Nejd* (1879).

BRITAIN AND SAUDI ARABIA. Britain has experienced probably the longest sustained contact with the **Al Sa'ud** state of any country. Nevertheless, it has often been a troubled relationship, shifting from an affinity of interests and mutual understanding to hostile recriminations and the disruption of official relations, and back. British relations with the Al Sa'ud came quite late as the First and Second Saudi States were, generally speaking, confined to the interior of Arabia and therefore did not pose a threat to British interests. An exception to this was Al Sa'ud support given to fellow **Wahhabis** al-Qawasim, the maritime house of the Oman Coast (later Trucial Coast, now **United Arab Emirates**), who were engaged in a naval war with British and other European vessels during the first several decades of the 19th century. This may have been a factor in prompting the dispatch in 1819 of the first British official to meet an Al Sa'ud imam. **G. F. Sadleir**'s pursuit of the Saudi leader led him to become the first European to cross the Arabian Peninsula. Still, such instances of direct contact were largely spasmodic until the beginning of the 20th century.

There were several contacts during the reign of Imam **Faysal bin Turki** (r. 1834-1838, 1843-1865), particularly when the Wahhabi forces began to threaten **al-Buraymi** oasis in the 1840s. More friction followed in the ensuing years as the Al Sa'ud probed at **Bahrain**, **Qatar**, the Trucial Coast, and northern **Oman**, all areas considered by Britain to lie within its sphere of influence. In spring 1865, Col. **Lewis Pelly**, the (British) Political Resident in the Persian Gulf (PRPG), journeyed to **Riyadh** to protest Saudi intrigues in Oman. But Imam Faysal's death soon after brought renewed Wahhabi raids on Oman's town of Sur and Batinah Coast. In 1866, an agreement was reached with the new Saudi Imam **'Abdullah bin Faysal**, which was regarded by Britain as tantamount to a treaty, and further Saudi provocations ceased. In large part, however, this may have been due to the contraction of Saudi ambitions because of their gradual eclipse by the **Al Rashid** of **Ha'il**, and relations with Britain were practically nonexistent until the beginning of the 20th century.

Not until after Imam **'Abd al-'Aziz bin 'Abd al-Rahman** recaptured Riyadh (1902) and founded the Third Saudi State was there any occasion to reestablish contact. As early as 1903, 'Abd al-'Aziz had requested that he be incorporated into the British trucial system in order to protect his fragile new state from the Al Rashid and the **Ottomans**. But Britain was not particularly interested and instead pushed the Saudi leader into an ambiguous vassal relationship with Istanbul. In part, Britain's attitude was the consequence of differing outlooks between the Foreign Office in London, which was reluctant to upset relations with Istanbul over what seemed a trivial matter, and the Government of India, which was responsible for British relations with the Gulf states through the PRPG and his subordinate Political Agents along the littoral.

By 1910, 'Abd al-'Aziz had begun to assert himself in central Arabia: he had held his own against the Al Rashid and clashed for the first time with the **Hashimi** rulers of **al-Hijaz**. Opinion grew more divided within the British bureaucracy on how to deal with him. The Political Agent in **Kuwait**, Captain **W. H. I. Shakespear**, was tasked with opening discussions, at which 'Abd al-'Aziz proposed an alliance to oust the Ottomans from Eastern Arabia. Still, Britain, engaged in Anglo-Ottoman negotiations, declined to back Riyadh. 'Abd al-'Aziz, taking advantage of Ottoman setbacks elsewhere, quickly seized the Eastern Arabian oases of **al-Ahsa'** and **al-Qatif** in 1914. But continued British refusal to recognize him forced 'Abd al-'Aziz to deter an Ottoman attack by accepting status as their Wali (governor) of **Najd**. Only after the outbreak of the First World War was Shakespear sent on a mission to 'Abd al-'Aziz; tragically, he was killed when trapped behind Saudi lines during a battle with the Al Rashid.

War aims prodded Britain to act quickly to overcome the setback of Shakespear's death. Essentially, London was concerned that 'Abd al-'Aziz focus his attention on harrying Ottoman allies such as the Al Rashid while refraining from attacking British allies such as the Hashimis. The Anglo-Saudi Treaty of 26 December 1915 provided British recognition of 'Abd al-'Aziz in return for his promise to accept British advice and renounce other foreign relations.

The small Saudi state of Najd remained a sideshow for Britain, even in Arabia. London was far more concerned about the impact on its Indian Muslims of the possibility of the Ottoman sultan, who also held the Islamic religious title of caliph, declaring a jihad or holy war against his enemies. Consequently, at the urging of the Foreign and Colonial Offices and the Arab Bureau in Cairo, **Husayn bin 'Ali al-Hashimi**, the Sharif of **Makkah**, was encouraged to declare his independence of Istanbul. As a descendant of the Prophet **Muhammad** and the traditional guardian of the two holiest places in **Islam**, it was felt that Sharif Husayn would prove a far more important client than 'Abd al-'Aziz. The opinion of the Government of India and the India Office in London, regarding 'Abd al-'Aziz as a more capable and dynamic leader, was disregarded until proven correct years later.

Britain continued to recognize 'Abd al-'Aziz's benefit as a minor nuisance to the Ottomans and half heartedly encouraged his offensive against the Al Rashid. But the Hashimi-Saudi clash over ownership of the oasis of **al-Khurmah** (on the dividing line between al-Hijaz and Najd) put London in a quandary. At the end of the war, London was still sympathetic to the Hashimis: it had recognized Husayn as King of al-Hijaz, and had made one of his sons King of Syria (later transferred to Iraq when **France** took over Damascus) while creating another throne in Transjordan for another son. Britain also feared the excesses of a Wahhabi invasion of the Hijaz, but found itself with little means of constraint over an expansionist Saudi state intention expanding to the frontiers of its 19th-century predecessor.

Between 1920 and 1922, 'Abd al-'Aziz extended his control over the southern territory of **'Asir**, conquered the Al Rashid and Ha'il, and moved north into **al-Jawf**. Now he found himself confronting British-backed Hashimi states in al-Hijaz, Transjordan, and Iraq, as well as the Al Sabah in Kuwait, across ill-defined and unrecognized boundaries.

The drawing of borders across the ancient migratory routes of the great nomadic tribes was to prove a troubling aspect of Saudi-British relations for years to come. The difficulty was compounded by cross-border raids by the **Ikhwan**, 'Abd al-'Aziz's uncontrollable and fanatic Wahhabi tribal forces. These often resulted in horrendous massacres. To put an end to them, Britain prevailed upon 'Abd al-'Aziz to settle boundaries with Iraq through the Treaty of Muhammarah (5 May 1922), but eventually he rejected the draft treaty. The agreement at **al-'Uqayr** (November 1922) was more successful, principally because Sir **Percy Cox**, High Commissioner in Iraq, handed over to Iraq wide swathes of Najdi-claimed terrritory and compensated by giving Najd about two-thirds of Kuwait in return.

While al-'Uqayr settled the Saudi-Kuwaiti frontier, there still remained problems with the Hashimi neighbors. The stumbling block on the Transjordan border was the **Wadi Sirhan**, sovereignty of which had implications for both trade routes and control over wide-ranging nomadic tribes. The seasonal movements of the **badu** (even when their allegiances were sorted out) also bedeviled the Saudi-Iraqi frontier. A further worrying element throughout the 1920s was Ikhwan raids across the border, which scuppered the 1923-1924 Kuwait conference.

Agreement between 'Abd al-'Aziz and his Hashimi neighbors was not reached until Sir **Gilbert Clayton** brokered the Haddah and Bahrah Agreements of 1925. These notably did not include al-Hijaz, the conquest of which 'Abd al-'Aziz completed that same year. Clayton also negotiated the Treaty of **Jiddah** (1927) with 'Abd al-'Aziz, which replaced the treaty of 1915. By its terms Britain recognized the absolute independence of the Al Sa'ud in return for 'Abd al-'Aziz's acceptance of the existence of the Trucial States, the suppression of slavery, and protection for British subjects during the **hajj** (pilgrimage).

The final impediment of the 1920s to correct relations between 'Abd al-'Aziz and the British clients in the region was the Ikhwan rebellion. The major Ikhwan leaders, who were also **shaykh**s of important tribes, had been restless since 'Abd al-'Aziz reined them in during the conquest of al-Hijaz and pointedly refused to appoint them to high positions. They also objected to 'Abd al-'Aziz's treating with the non-Muslim British. Ikhwan cross-border raids had been a problem since 1921 and caused Britain to employ the Royal Air Force in the defense of its Hashimi client states; whether these raids were undertaken at the initiative, or even with the knowledge, of 'Abd al-'Aziz still remains unclear. However, it is certain that by 1926 the Ikhwan leaders were poised on the edge of revolt and an unprovoked massacre at an Iraqi police post in 1927 pushed them over the edge. 'Abd al-'Aziz was able to deliver a crushing blow at the Battle of **Sibilah** (March 1929) but the final capitulation did not come until the remaining leaders and their followers were forced to surrender to the British in Kuwait at the beginning of 1930. They were subsequently turned over to 'Abd al-'Aziz and the leaders imprisoned in Riyadh.

Although 'Abd al-'Aziz's victories in al-Ahsa', 'Asir, and al-Hijaz had enabled him to declare the Kingdom of Saudi Arabia in 1932, relations with Britain remained troubled. The Saudi King chafed at being regarded as the equal of the minor Trucial shaykhs, particularly as he continued to manifest designs on their territory. A series of talks involving competing lines drawn across the desert (*see* entries for BLUE, RED, and RIYADH LINES) continued throughout the 1930s. But the failure of Britain to establish a commanding position in Saudi Arabia was even more the consequence of losing what was to be the world's most important oil concession to American companies (*see* OIL; ARAMCO). Although Britain undertook in 1942 to pay Saudi Arabia a subsidy to compensate the financially strapped kingdom for the loss of hajj revenues because of the war, cost-saving measures the following year led to a joint Anglo-American subsidy and supply efforts. The loss of influence was compounded by Britain's reluctance during the war to allow the US Army Air Force to establish facilities in Bahrain; the Americans consequently persuaded 'Abd al-'Aziz to let them build a base at **Dhahran**. As a consequence, the **United States** supplanted British influence in the two most significant areas of oil and defense, which London has never been able to regain.

Some ground was recovered following the Second World War when a British Military Mission and a Civil Air Training Mission were provided for the kingdom, but more calamities were in store. The boundaries between Saudi Arabia and the Trucial States and Oman had never been settled and Riyadh continued to claim large tracts of territory on the basis of intermittent occupation in the 19th century. In October 1952, Saudi Arabia occupied one of the villages of al-Buraymi oasis, setting off a fresh crisis in Anglo-Saudi relations. The possibility of oil underlay this boundary dispute, with American oil companies in Saudi Arabia and British rivals on the other side. The Buraymi presence also provided Saudi Arabia and radical **Egypt** with a channel to provide support to tribesmen fighting in the interior of Oman against the British-backed government. Although the Buraymi dispute was referred to an arbitration tribunal, the British accused the Saudi member of the tribunal of attempting to bribe the witnesses and withdrew. The Saudi garrison was ousted in October 1955 by units of the British-officered Trucial Oman Scouts.

This action undoubtedly contributed to the Saudi decision to cut off diplomatic relations when Britain joined with **France** and Israel to invade Egypt during the November 1956 Suez War. Relations were not restored until after King **Sa'ud**, who had aligned himself with Egypt's Jamal 'Abd al-Nasir (Nasser), had been replaced by his half brother **Faysal** in 1964.

Undoubtedly the decline of Britain's position in the Middle East, marked in the Arabian Peninsula by the retreat from Aden in 1967 and withdrawal from the Gulf in 1971, contributed to the improvement of relations between London and Riyadh. With the boom after the 1974 explosion in oil prices, Britain was well placed to offer technical assistance, and British companies contracted for a large share of the kingdom's development projects and took advantage of expanding trade opportunities. Britain found itself in the forefront of Saudi efforts to diversify from overreliance on American suppliers. The growing British interest in Saudi Arabia easily survived several temporary blips: the showing on British television of "The Death of a Princess," a documentary about the tragic consequences of adultery within the Saudi royal family; and the publication of a leaked final dispatch by a British ambassador who described the situation in Saudi Arabia in unflattering terms.

When the Saudi government encountered resistance from the US Congress over arms sales already agreed with the American administration, Britain was the first source to which Riyadh turned. In a 1985 accord, Riyadh placed orders for 72 British Aerospace tornado combat aircraft and 60 other aircraft; the cost of $5 billion to $7 billion was to be financed by oil deliveries to Britain. Known as Yamamah-I, this deal was designed as an "offset" program, in which Britain undertook to invest some of the proceeds from the sale in Saudi industrialization projects. Three years later, Yamamah-II was born out of identical Saudi frustration with a hostile US Congress: in one of the largest arms deals ever (press reports put the total amount between $12 billion and $25 billion), the Saudi government ordered up to 50 Tornado fighters, 60 Hawk trainer aircraft, 50 Blackhawk helicopters, and six minesweepers, and approved the construction of several expensive air bases. However, part of the order was cancelled in the following years when Saudi oil income fell drastically. The friendship between the two states was emphasized when King **Fahd** made an official visit to the United Kingdom in 1987, reciprocating Queen Elizabeth's visit to Saudi Arabia in 1979.

Given Kuwait's status as a formerly British-protected state, it is not surprising that London was quick to participate in "Operation Desert Shield," the buildup of Western and Arab armed forces in Saudi Arabia and the Gulf following the Iraqi invasion of Kuwait on 2 August 1990. British Prime Minister Margaret Thatcher, who was visiting the US at the time, was quick to urge US President George Bush to act firmly against Baghdad's aggression. In early 1991, Britain's most concentrated force since the Second World War, including 30,000 British troops, an armored division, Special Air Service (SAS) teams, combat and bomber aircraft, and Royal Naval vessels, played a prominent role in the war to liberate Kuwait (code-named **"Operation Desert Storm"**).

Anglo-Saudi relations continued to be strong after the Kuwait War. Saudi Arabia purchased additional British-made Tornado combat aircraft in the early 1990s. A visit to Britain by Prince **Sultan bin 'Abd al-'Aziz**, the Minister of Defense and Aviation in 1997, the first high-level visit since 1989, was followed by a state visit by Heir Apparent **'Abdullah bin 'Abd al-'Aziz** in 1998. Troubling elements in the bilateral ties included Saudi wrath at Britain's granting of asylum to Saudi dissident **Muhammad al-Mas'ari** in 1996 and the arrest in 2001 of five British subjects on charges of smuggling alcohol and setting off car bombs against their expatriate enemies in the kingdom.

BULLARD, READER (WILLIAM). [Sir] (1885-1956) British diplomat who spent most of his career in the Middle East. He served as British Agent and Consul in **Jiddah** during 1923-1925 and returned as minister to Saudi Arabia from 1936 to 1939. He retired in 1946 after a long stretch as Ambassador to Iran but was called upon to be a member of the **al-Buraymi** Arbitration Tribunal in 1954-1955. His autobiography is *Camels Must Go* (1961).

BUQAYQ. [buqayq; also spelled Abqayq; بقيق; 49 46 - 18 09] An oil field of the **Eastern Province**, located about halfway between **Dhahran** and **al-Hufuf**. At one point, Buqayq was the world's largest producing oil field, with production reaching a peak of 600,000 barrels a day (b/d) in 1951. Although the resultant settlement of Buqayq now boasts a sizeable population, it was uninhabited before the discovery of **oil**. In the environs of Buqayq are located thousands of tumuli dating back to the third millennium B.C.

BURAIMI. *See* BURAYMI, AL-.

BURAYDAH. [buraydah; بريدة; 26 20 - 4358] The capital of the province of **al-Qasim** in central **Najd**, located on the left bank of the Wadi al-Rummah. About half its population traditionally lived in the surrounding agricultural settlements of al-Khubub. The settled population is a mixture of the tribes of **Harb, 'Anazah, Mutayr, 'Utaybah,** and **Bani Tamim**. Even more important than agriculture for Buraydah was its reputation as a trading center, and its citizens maintained ties with and even resided in **al-Hijaz**, Damascus, Basra, and India. The town was probably founded in the 16th century and was generally engaged in a fierce competition with its traditional rival **'Unayzah**, about 15 miles to the south. Like the rest of al-Qasim, Buraydah was caught between the **Al Rashid** of **Ha'il** and the **Al Sa'ud** of **Riyadh** in their struggle for domination of Najd, and it frequently switched sides. A small **Ottoman** garrison was briefly established in the town in 1905 but Buraydah fell under the permanent control of the Al Sa'ud about 1909. The extension of Saudi authority over the ports of both the **Gulf** coast and the **Red Sea** caused Buraydah's decline as an entrepôt.

BURAYMI, AL-. [al-buraymī; البريمي; also spelled Buraimi; 24 14 - 53 46] An oasis formerly consisting of nine villages, of which six belonged to Abu Dhabi (now part of the **United Arab Emirates** [UAE]) and three to Oman. The oasis recently has become heavily urbanized, and the larger Abu Dhabi portion is invariably referred to as al-'Ayn. The Second Saudi State held control of the oasis for several years in the 1860s and subsequent Al Sa'ud claims to retain the loyalty of the region's tribes led the Third Saudi State to occupy one of the villages (al-Hamasa) in October 1952. **Britain**, acting on behalf of Abu Dhabi and Oman, protested this action to Riyadh, and both sides agreed in 1954 to submit the dispute to a tribunal. In preparation, each side compiled an exhaustive memorandum, consisting primarily of background on the tribes in the area, their supposed allegiances, and the history of **zakat** (Islamic alms tax) payments.

The tribunal, composed of a Belgian chairman and **Pakistani** and Cuban members, as well as supposedly independent Saudi and British judges, did not meet until September 1955. However, it did not meet long and never rendered judgment, as Britain withdrew after charging that the Saudi member, **Yusuf Yasin**, was attempting to direct the witnesses and that the Saudi government was distributing bribes in the Buraymi area of up to £30 million. In October 1955, units of the British-officered Trucial Oman Scouts ejected the Saudi detachment from the oasis. Saudi Arabia's dormant claims appeared to have been dropped when the kingdom reached agreements on its borders with the UAE in 1974 and with Oman in 1991.

The significance of the dispute went beyond frontiers, however. At the heart of the Saudi action, and the reason for the spirited British objection, was the possibility of oil in the area. **ARAMCO** held the concession for Saudi Arabia, while a largely British firm, the Iraq Petroleum Company, held the concessions in Abu Dhabi and Oman. Consequently, London and Washington found themselves arrayed on opposing sides and American and British individuals prepared the detailed memorials presented by each side.

BURCKHARDT, JOHANN LUDWIG. (1784-1817) An Arabian explorer of the early 19th century. Burckhardt was born in Lausanne and was educated at the University of Cambridge. He began his travels in North Africa and the Middle East in 1809 under the sponsorship of the Association for Promoting the Discovery of the Interior Parts of Africa, and died in Cairo while preparing to cross the Sahara Desert. He is credited with the European rediscovery of the **Nabataean** city of Petra (now in **Jordan**) and the ancient Egyptian temple at Abu Simbel. Among his books are *Travels in Arabia* (1829) and *Notes on the Bedouins and Wahabys* (1830).

BURTON, RICHARD F. [Sir] (1821-1890) Undoubtedly the most famous of the 19th-century European explorers and a prolific author (publishing over 40 books) and linguist (mastering some 25 languages). Although born in Devon, Burton was raised in **France** and Italy. He studied at Trinity College, Oxford, but, after being expelled in 1842, he joined a regiment of the Bombay Native Infantry. His Pilgrimage to *El-Medinah and Mecca* (1855-56) describes his participation in the **hajj** (Islamic pilgrimage). From 1856 until his death, he served as British consul in Fernando Po, Brazil, Damascus, and Trieste. Outside of Arabia, his exploits embraced extensive explorations of Africa (including the European discovery of Lake Tanganyika) and manifold translations (including the Arabian Nights and the Kama Sutra).

- C -

CARMATHIANS. *See* QARAMITAH, AL-.

CHINA AND SAUDI ARABIA. Saudi Arabia long regarded the People's Republic of China with suspicion because of its Communist régime and maintained close political, military, and economic ties with Taiwan instead. Nevertheless, trading ties between Riyadh and Beijing began to appear in the mid-1980s and the kingdom secretly purchased a number of Chinese-made CSS-2 "East Wind" ballistic missiles in 1988. The two countries opened trade offices in each other's capital in 1989 and full diplomatic relations were established on 21 July 1990. Heir Apparent **'Abdullah bin 'Abd al-'Aziz** made the first Saudi high-level visit to China in October 1998 and Chinese

President Jiang Zemin met King **Fahd** and Prince 'Abdullah in Saudi Arabia in November 1999.

CLAYTON, GILBERT F. [1875-1929] Originally a British Army officer, Clayton served in the Egyptian Army and the Sudan government before becoming Director of Intelligence in Egypt and then Chief Political Officer to the Egyptian Expeditionary Force during the First World War. Following the war, he served as Adviser to the Egyptian Ministry of the Interior and Chief Secretary of the Government of Palestine. As a Special Envoy to al-Hijaz and Najd, he negotiated the Bahrah and **Haddah** Agreements with Imam 'Abd al-'Aziz Al Sa'ud, as well as the Anglo-Saudi Treaty of **Jiddah** (1927). His memoirs were published posthumously as *An Arabian Diary* (1969).

COMMITTEE FOR THE DEFENSE OF LEGITIMATE RIGHTS. *See* OPPOSITION GROUPS.

CONSULTATIVE COUNCIL. *See* MAJLIS AL-SHURA.

COX, PERCY Z. [Sir] (1864-1937) A Government of India official with extensive service in the **Gulf**. In his capacity as Political Resident in the Persian Gulf (1904-1913), Cox was an early champion of Imam **'Abd al-'Aziz bin 'Abd al-Rahman Al Sa'ud** and advocated that the **British** government support the nascent **Al Sa'ud** state in **Najd** as a counter to the **Ottoman** Empire. He was overruled by his superiors in London, who chose to support the **al-Hashimi** family of **al-Hijaz**. In a later capacity as High Commissioner for Mesopotamia (1920-1923), Cox played a key role in negotiating the frontiers between Saudi Arabia, **Iraq**, and **Kuwait**.

CRANE, CHARLES R. (1858-1939) An American businessman and philanthropist who first experienced the Middle East as a member of the King-Crane Commission of 1919, charged by US President Woodrow Wilson with investigating the wishes of the inhabitants of former **Ottoman** territories in the Middle East on their preferred political status. In later years, Crane arranged for water and agricultural assistance for **Yemen** and the short-lived Kingdom of **al-Hijaz**. He was invited to **Jiddah** in 1931 to meet King **'Abd al-'Aziz** and made arrangements to provide a free geological survey of the country, led by **Karl S. Twitchell**.

- D -

DABBAGH, AL-. [al-dabbāgh; الدباغ] A **Makkah** family of North African origin with connections in South Yemen. After the Saudi conquest of **al-Hijaz** in the mid-1920s, some of al-Dabbagh were active in a Hijazi nationalist party opposed to **Al Sa'ud** rule and helped organize an abortive uprising in 1932.

DAHNA', AL-. [al-dahnā'; الدهنا.] A narrow sand desert, varying in width between six and 50 miles and over 600 miles long, curving around the eastern side of central Arabia and connecting the two great deserts of **al-Rub' al-Khali** in the south with **al-Nafud** in the north. It divides the central region of **Najd** from **al-Ahsa'** and the **Gulf** coast. Al-Dahna' itself is mainly the territory (or **dirah**) of the **Mutayr** tribe. In the far past, al-Dahna' marked the boundary between the coastal region of al-Bahrayn and the interior of **al-Yamamah**. In the present kingdom, it informally demarcates the provinces of **Najd** and the **Eastern Province**.

DAMLUJI, 'ABDULLAH. [damlūjī; عبد الله دملوجي] Apparently an officer of Iraqi origin in the **Ottoman** army in **al-Ahsa'** when it was captured by the **Al Sa'ud** in 1913 who transferred his allegiance to Imam **'Abd al-'Aziz bin 'Abd al-Rahman**. His sophistication (he was educated in Istanbul and had spent some time in Paris) made him useful as an intermediary with Europeans. Consequently, he served as the Saudi representative to the treaty conferences of **al-'Uqayr** in 1922 and **Jiddah** in 1927. Later, he became a business associate of **H. St. John B. Philby**.

DAMMAM, AL-. [al-dammām; الدمام; 50 06- 26 26] A medium-sized city of the **Eastern Province** and the largest Saudi port on the **Gulf**. Al-Dammam was the site of a fort allegedly built by the 19th-century buccaneer Rahmah bin Jabir of the Jalahimah. He was killed by the Al Khalifah of **Bahrain** in 1826 who took control of the site until it was overrun by the **Al Sa'ud** in 1844. In 1852, a branch of the Al Khalifah settled there but their attempted invasion of Bahrain resulted in **British** attacks on al-Dammam in 1861 and 1866. After **Ottoman** seizure in 1871, al-Dammam gradually decayed until a group of **al-Dawasir** tribesmen fleeing Bahrain built a small fishing settlement. It was not until the discovery of oil at nearby **Dhahran** that al-Dammam gained new life: a deep-water port was built in 1950 and it became the capital of the **Eastern Province** in 1952. The growth of housing for the oil company's local workers transformed the village into a city and it also became the terminus of the **railroad** from **Riyadh**. In 1952, al-Dammam hosted a conference at which then-Crown Prince (and later King) **Faysal bin 'Abd al-'Aziz** and the (British) Political Resident in the Persian Gulf, Sir Rupert Hay, unsuccessfully attempted to sort out the Saudi-**Qatar** and Saudi-Abu Dhabi frontiers. Later in the 1950s, al-Dammam hosted an army of Omani dissidents fighting against the **Omani** government in Muscat.

DARB ZUBAYDAH. [darb zubaydah; درب زبيدة] The ancient pilgrims' route from Baghdad to Makkah, much of which ran through present-day Saudi Arabia and was built by Zubaydah, wife of the 'Abbasid caliph, Harun al-Rashid. It continued to be used until recently by Iranian pilgrims. One of its most impressive remains is Birkat al-Khurabah (birkat al-khurābah; الخرابة بركة), 60 miles northeast of **al-Ta'if**, which is a circular pool 20 feet deep and 130 feet in diameter and presumably dates from the 'Abbasid period like the other stations of the Darb. Approximately 125 miles east of **al-Madinah**, impressive ruins remain of al-Rabadah, a city of pilgrimage on the Darb Zubaydah, as well as a religious and intellectual center, founded by the third caliph in Islam, 'Umar bin al-Khattab, and abandoned in the 11th century A.D.

DARIN. *See* TARUT ISLAND.

DAWASIR, AL-. [al-dawāsir; dawsirī; الدواسر؛ دوسري; also spelled Doasir and Dosari] A major nomadic tribe of "pure lineage" inhabiting southern **Najd**, especially the Wadi al-Dawasir and around al-Aflaj. Some elements are sedentarized. The Dawasir are remarkably widespread. Branches are found in the Najdi districts of **al-Kharj, al-'Arid**, and **Sudayr**. The well-known Sudayri family, which has become closely connected to the **Al Sa'ud**, is of Dawsiri origins. Some of the tribe settled in **Bahrain** in the mid-19th century, where they are probably second in importance only to the ruling family, and offshoots of this branch are to be found in **Qatar** and **Kuwait**, as well as on the **Iranian** side of the **Gulf**. Other branches are to be found in **Iraq**, especially around al-Zubayr. Subunits of al-Dawasir in Bahrain also founded the **Eastern Province** towns of **al-Dammam** and **al-Khubar**. The Wadi al-Dawasir has been one of the most isolated parts of Saudi Arabia; **Philby** in 1918 was the first Westerner to visit it. In ancient times, an important trading route ran through the wadi, connecting Yemen with Mesopotamia, and the ruins of the pre-Islamic city of **al-Faw** are located there. Wadi al-Dawasir's traditional coffee trade was diverted to **Bishah** earlier in the 20th century and the country's oil wealth has been slow to trickle down to the area.

DAWSIRIYAH, AL-. *See* JUBAYL, AL-.

DAYDAN. *See* 'ULA, AL-.

DEDAN. *See* 'ULA, AL-.

DESERT STORM, OPERATION. Code name for the war launched in 1991 against Iraqi forces occupying **Kuwait**. In July 1990, **Iraq** backed up its complaints about Kuwaiti overproduction of oil (as well as claims to the portion of al-Rumaylah oil field in Kuwaiti territory and the islands of Warbah and Bubiyan) by moving troops into position along the Iraqi-Kuwaiti border. A conference arranged in **Jiddah** on 1 August between Iraq and Kuwait was acrimonious and broke up amid insults. Early the next morning, Iraqi forces moved across the border and, brushing aside scattered resistance, occupied all of Kuwait. Saudi fears that Iraq would continue to move down the coast toward Saudi oil fields prompted King **Fahd** to request US military assistance and within a week the first American soldiers, aircraft, and naval vessels were in the vicinity.

When Iraq refused to comply with **United Nations** Security Council resolutions demanding its withdrawal and instead increased its forces in Kuwait and proclaimed it as its 19th province, the decision was made to go to war to liberate the amirate. Operation Desert Shield put together 700,000 allied military personnel in Saudi Arabia, its GCC neighbors, and on the waters of the **Gulf**. When Iraq failed to comply with a 15 January 1991 deadline for withdrawal, a massive air bombing campaign was begun in the early hours of 16 January. This was followed by a ground offensive on 24 February, in which a frontal attack on occupied Kuwait served as a deception for the main thrust through the Iraqi desert, flanking the defenses around Kuwait and driving to the Euphrates River. One hundred hours after the ground campaign began, Iraq signalled its acceptance of the resolutions and a cease-fire was instituted.

While Western armed forces were placed under the command of the head of the US Central Command, the joint Arab and Islamic troops were headed by Lt. Gen. **Khalid bin Sultan Al Sa'ud**. Saudi Arabia suffered 29 deaths, the majority coming during the disastrous Iraqi offensive against the Saudi border town of **al-Khafji** on 30-31 January.

DEVELOPMENT PLANNING. Even after the state began receiving oil revenues, new projects were initiated in haphazard fashion, one at a time. The absence of any clear projection of eventual costs, combined with growing demands and commitments, the expansion of the government, and the profligacy associated with King **Sa'ud** brought the kingdom to the brink of financial ruin in the late 1950s and early 1960s.

Clearly, more rational development goals and formulation were required. An emphasis on project planning came with the creation of a Development Committee in 1958, making economic growth an objective along with infrastructural development. Later, the establishment of the Central Planning Organization (CPO) in 1965 laid the basis for the formulation of the first five-year development plan, although the plan appeared to be consistently underspent.

The explosion of oil income after 1973-1974 meant that the first plan (1970-1975) was eclipsed nearly 10 times by the second plan (1975-1980). In addition to infrastructural improvements, the $142 billion plan placed heavy emphasis on defense and the immense industrialization projects at **al-Jubayl** and **Yanbu'**. With the third plan (1980-1985), greater consideration was given to increasing production, especially in agriculture. This trend was accelerated under the fourth plan (1985-1990), with a primary target being industrialization in the private sector.

The fifth plan (1990-1995) was formulated in a period of tighter constraints on spending while deteriorating regional security meant that a larger share of government expenditures went to **military** programs. The sixth plan (1995-2000) also sought to cut back on public spending and subsidies while emphasizing the role of the private sector and efforts to reduce dependence on oil. The seventh plan (2000-2005) further sought to shift state expenditures to the private sector with increased foreign and domestic investment. *See also* NAZIR, HISHAM BIN MUHYI AL-DIN AL-.

DHAFIR, AL-. [al-ẓafīr; ẓafīrī; الظفير؛ ظفيري] The only one of the great Central Arabian tribes to remain fully nomadic, with a territory (**dirah**) traditionally ranging across northern **al-Hijaz** and northern **Najd** and into **Iraq** as far as the Euphrates River. Assigned to the sovereignty of Iraq in 1920 and given responsibility for patrolling the Iraqi-Saudi border against incursions of the fanatical **Ikhwan**, the Dhafir defected to Imam **'Abd al-'Aziz bin 'Abd al-Rahman** after continued raids against Iraqi settlements resulted in their punishment by the Iraqi government.

DHAHRAN. [al-ẓahrān; الظهران] An urban center of the **Eastern Province**, located just off the **Gulf** coast near **al-Dammam**. There was no settlement before Saudi Arabia's first oil strike was made at Dhahran in 1935. Since then, Dhahran has grown to include the headquarters of the Saudi **ARAMCO** oil company, the residential quarters for ARAMCO employees, and the site of the **King Fahd University of Petroleum and Minerals**. A major air force base at Dhahran was operated by the **United States** from 1946 to 1962 and since then by the Royal Saudi Air Force. Dhahran also boasts one of Saudi Arabia's three international airports, with a large new terminal completed in 1999.

DIRAH. [dīrah, pl. diyār; ديرة،ديار] Arabic term for territory generally occupied by, or acknowledged to belong to, a particular tribe. The term normally applies to **badu** (bedouin) tribes. A badu tribe's dirah, therefore, will usually encompass rights to grazing and water usage within a specified area. As part of his consolidation of authority, King **'Abd al-'Aziz bin 'Abd al-Rahman** abolished the tribal dirah in Saudi Arabia.

DIR'IYAH, AL-. [al-dir'īyah; الدرعية; also spelled al-Dar'iyah; 46 35 - 24 44] A village in **al-'Arid** district of southern **Najd**, located on the Wadi Hanifah about 9 miles west of **Riyadh**. It was founded in the mid-15th century by Mani' bin Rabi'ah al-Muraydi who apparently emigrated from **al-Qatif** and is considered to have been from the **'Anazah** tribe. His descendant Muhammad bin Sa'ud bin Muqrin threw off **Bani Khalid** rule in about 1727 and, after having welcomed the Islamic reformer **Muhammad bin 'Abd al-Wahhab** to al-Dir'iyah in 1744, founded the **Al Sa'ud** dynasty. Subsequent Saudi expansion alarmed the **Ottoman** Empire and an invading **Egyptian** army destroyed the settlement in 1818. The Al Sa'ud then transferred their headquarters to Riyadh. A new village was built nearby in the mid-19th century by elements of **Bani Tamim** and **al-Dawasir**. The name is also given to the new Diplomatic Quarter on the edge of Riyadh closest to al-Dir'iyah.

DIYAH. [diyāh; ضياح] "Blood money." In the case of death or injury, the payment of diyah may be accepted by the victim or his or her family in lieu of demanding the death of, or a corresponding injury to, the responsible individual.

DOSARI. *See* DAWASIR, AL-.

DOUGHTY, CHARLES M. (1843-1926) A 19th-century Arabian explorer and poet. Doughty was born in Suffolk and educated at the universities of London and Cambridge. He is best known for his *Travels in Arabia Deserta* (1888, although reprinted frequently), generally regarded as the most literary of Arabian travel accounts and which detail his journeys between Damascus and **Makkah**, via **Ha'il** and **'Unayzah** in **Najd**. His first visit to the **Arabian Peninsula** in 1876 included a period at the ancient site of **Mada'in Salih**. He died in Kent in 1926.

DUMAH. *See* JAWF, AL-.

DUWISH, FAYSAL BIN SULTAN AL-. [al-duwīsh; فيصل بن سلطان الدويش] The paramount shaykh of **al-Mutayr** tribe in the first quarter of the 20th century. An enemy of the **Al Rashid** family of **Ha'il**, Faysal joined the camp of Imam **'Abd al-'Aziz Al Sa'ud** and then became one of the principal leaders of the **Ikhwan**, the extremist **Wahhabi** forces of nomadic tribesmen used by 'Abd al-'Aziz in his conquests. By the late 1920s, Faysal was one of the prime instigators in the rebellion of the Ikhwan against 'Abd al-'Aziz and was badly wounded in the Ikhwan defeat at the Battle of **Sibilah** in 1929 and left to die. He recovered, only to suffer another disastrous defeat a year later, which left him with no choice but to take his tribe into **Kuwait** and surrender to the **British**. He was subsequently turned over to 'Abd al-'Aziz and languished in a **Riyadh** prison until his death in October 1931.

- E -

EASTERN AND GENERAL SYNDICATE. A London investment group which, through the efforts of its agent, Major **Frank Holmes**, acquired Saudi Arabia's first oil concession in 1923 by agreeing to pay Imam **'Abd al-'Aziz bin 'Abd al-Rahman** £2,000 per year. Unable to resell the concession to an oil company, the syndicate soon lapsed on its rent payments and its concession was revoked in 1928.

EASTERN PROVINCE. [al-minṭaqah al-sharqīyah; المنطقة الشرقية] Saudi Arabia's largest province in area, extending from the Iraqi frontiers in the north to **al-Rub' al-Khali** desert in the south, which it encompasses apart from the southern fringes within **Yemen** and **Oman**. All of the kingdom's territory on the **Gulf**, running between **Kuwait** and **Qatar**, belongs to the province. Inland, it extends to **al-Dahna'** desert, where it abuts the province of **Najd**. The population exceeds several million, much of it concentrated in the older settlements of **al-Hufuf** and **al-Qatif** and their agricultural suburbs, as well as the newer towns of **Dhahran**, **al-Dammam**, **al-Khubar**, and the industrial city at **al-Jubayl**. The great majority of the kingdom's oil reserves are located in the province, especially in the area around Dhahran, which serves as center of operations for **ARAMCO**. Most of the crude oil is exported from **Ra's Tanurah**.

The province also boasts two of Saudi Arabia's largest and richest oases: **al-Ahsa'** (about 60 miles inland, of which al-Hufuf is the principal settlement) and al-Qatif, on the Gulf itself. These contain the region's oldest settlements and their many centuries of cultivation has produced largely non-tribal populations with large elements of **Shi'ah**, analogous to the pattern in nearby **Bahrain**. The present province largely corresponds to the medieval area known as al-Bahrayn. In the ninth century, al-Ahsa' served as a center of the extremist al-**Qaramitah** (Carmathian) movement. The area was largely untouched, at least directly, by the European penetration of the Gulf.

It fell under the influence of the First Saudi State in the late 18th century and the Second Saudi State in the mid-19th century. The **Ottomans** installed a number of garrisons in the 1870s, which remained until driven out by Imam **'Abd al-'Aziz bin 'Abd al-Rahman** about 1913.

The latter organized the area into al-Ahsa' Province under the governorship of a cousin, **Bin Jiluwi**. Al-Hufuf served as the provincial capital until 1952 when it was moved to al-Dammam in recognition of the oil industry's importance; at the same time, the name was changed to Eastern Province.

ECONOMY. Despite sustained efforts for economic diversification, **oil** continues to account for nearly 70 percent of total government income and over 50 percent of the country's gross domestic product (GDP) of $90 billion (1999). About 35 percent of GDP derives from the private sector. As a consequence, the primary determinants in the health of the Saudi economy remain the twin factors of level of oil production and the international price for oil. When the price of oil tumbled in 1986 and Saudi production levels were cut sharply (as part of **OPEC** strategy to keep supply in tandem with demand), the Saudi budget recorded deficits on the order of $1 billion per month and the country's financial reserves were seriously depleted. From a high of $145 billion in 1982, foreign assets fell to under $60 billion in early 1990.

Although government finances improved slightly in the late 1990s, falling oil prices in 1999 nearly halved government revenues and dramatically increased the budget deficit. The rise in oil prices in 2000 gave the kingdom its first budget surplus in nearly two decades but the budget slipped back into the red in the following year. The 2002 budget was prepared with the expectation of expenditures of $54 billion but revenues of only $42 billion, thus leaving a projected deficit of $12 billion. The largest sectors in the budget were **education** ($14.7 billion), health services and social development ($6.2 billion), municipal services and water authorities ($2.6 billion), transportation and communications ($700 million), and $2.7 billion for the rest of infrastructure, including **industry** and **agriculture**. New projects were budgeted at $7.6 billion. Salaries of state employees accounted for more than 55 percent of the budget. Acting conservatively, the Saudi government based its revenue projections on a price of about $17 a barrel of crude oil when prices in early 2002 fluctuated between $20 and $25. So many years of budget deficits have produced $170 billion in domestic public debt, which takes 15 percent of total expenditure to service.

Gross national product per capita has been shrinking for two decades. It reached a high of slightly more than $14,000 in 1980 but had shrunk to only $5,650 in 1988. The preliminary figure for 2000 was a little less than $8,000.

Apart from the petroleum sector, industrial production is modest. While agricultural production, particularly that of wheat, has increased markedly over the years, thanks to heavy subsidies, its contribution to national product remains minimal. Considerable emphasis has been devoted recently to building up the petrochemical industry, and Saudi Arabia has led the **Gulf Cooperation Council** in negotiations with the European Community for favorable access to European markets.

Oil and oil products constitute 85 percent of exports, while imports consist largely of manufactured goods and foodstuffs, as well as construction materials. The country remains heavily dependent on several million foreign workers, ranging from professionals, technical consultants and commercial managers to skilled and unskilled labor. The northern Arab countries, the Indian subcontinent, Southeast Asia, Europe, and the United States are represented by substantial numbers. The expulsion of up to one million Yemeni workers following the **Iraqi** invasion of **Kuwait** (because of **Yemen**'s failure to condemn the invasion) caused severe dislocations. *See also* BANKING, DEVELOPMENT PLANNING, SAUDI ARABIAN MONETARY AGENCY, SAUDI FUND FOR DEVELOPMENT, TRADE, APPENDIX G (STATISTICAL TABLES).

EDUCATION. Before oil revenues began, nearly all education in Saudi Arabia was of a traditional nature. Children, mostly boys, generally received only instruction in the **Qur'an** (Koran) and many Saudis were illiterate. King **'Abd al-'Aziz bin 'Abd al-Rahman** established the first primary schools in the 1930s. Early oil income enabled the expansion of schools in the late 1940s and the Ministry of Education was created in 1954 with Prince **Fahd bin 'Abd al-'Aziz** (later king) as the first minister.

In 1948, there were only 182 primary schools with a total enrollment of 21,000. Four years later, however, the number of students had nearly doubled. By 1970, there were more than 3,000 schools and by 2000 the number had multiplied to more than 22,000. The number of students at all levels grew proportionately, from 547,000 in 1970 to 4,774,000 in 2000. While less than a third of these students were female in 1970, the proportion of male to female had become nearly equal by 2000.

The first schools for girls opened in **Jiddah** in the late 1950s. An attempt in 1960 to open a girls' school in **Buraydah**, in probably the most conservative part of the kingdom, provoked active opposition. The state was able to keep its commitment to female education only by reaching a compromise with the religious authorities whereby the General Presidency for Girls' Education (GPGE) controlled all girls' and women's education instead of the Ministry of Education. A fire at a girls' school in **Makkah** in early 2002, when 15 girls were killed because of the apparent refusal of the **mutawwi'in** (religious police) to allow them to exit because they were not properly dressed, resulted in the merger of the GPGE with the Ministry of Education.

The first four Saudi university graduates returned from Egypt in 1945, followed by a few others from **Britain** and the **United States** in the early 1950s. Higher education in the kingdom began with **shari'ah** (Islamic law) colleges in Jiddah (1949) and **Riyadh** (1953). **King Sa'ud University**, established in Riyadh in 1957, was the kingdom's first. During the 1970s and the 1980s, Saudi Arabia sent many students abroad on full scholarship for higher education; more than 15,000 Saudi students were enrolled in

American institutions at the peak in the late 1970s and early 1980s. But the number of scholarships abroad shrank as the kingdom built new and larger **universities** at home (the number of students in the US declined to less than 2,000). There are now eight Saudi universities.

Until 1974, there were only five female Ph.D.s, but postgraduate education for **women** boomed in the following decades. In addition to separate women's branches at most of the secular universities, there are about a dozen colleges of education spread throughout the country, which primarily produce schoolteachers. The latter are popular choices for many women because they do not have to travel or live away from home.

In addition to the universities, higher education in the kingdom includes a number of colleges of education, and industrial, commercial, and technical schools. One of the most respected institutions in the country is the Institute of Public Administration, founded in Riyadh in 1961. The institute is noteworthy for its large, public library and government documentation project.

EGYPT AND SAUDI ARABIA. Egyptian involvement with Arabia is of great antiquity. Egypt was one of the principal destinations for South Arabia's frankincense and myrrh, much of which was transported through **Makkah** by caravan and thus made the Makkans rich. Egypt was one of the early conquests of the Islamic state in the seventh century, and later Islamic dynasties in Egypt, especially the Mamluks (13th-16th centuries), often exercised control over **al-Hijaz** and the holy cities of Makkah and **al-Madinah**. At the beginning of the 19th century, the **Ottoman** Empire grew increasingly worried about the growing power of the First Saudi State in **Najd**, whose **Wahhabi** warriors had raided the holy **Shi'ah** city of Karbala (in present-day **Iraq**), threatened Damascus, and captured Makkah. In response, the Ottoman court ordered its Viceroy of Egypt, Muhammad 'Ali, to attack the Wahhabis. Egyptian forces captured Makkah and al-Madinah and eventually made their way across Arabia, razing the Saudi capital of **al-Dir'iyah** in 1818. A recrudescence of Saudi power brought a repeat Egyptian invasion in 1838.

The Egyptian revolution in 1952 marked a change in Egyptian-Saudi relations from friendly ties between fellow monarchs to the acrimonious period of the "Arab cold war," which pitted the progressive Arab republics against the conservative Arab monarchies. At first, King **Sa'ud** (r. 1953-1964) was on good terms with Egyptian President Jamal 'Abd al-Nasir (Nasser), providing Egypt with financial aid for its struggle against Israel and forwarding Egyptian assistance to the dissident movement in **Oman**'s interior. But Egypt's involvement in the **Yemeni** revolution of 1962 and subsequent dispatch of troops to support the new Yemen Arab Republic shattered ties with Saudi Arabia, which provided the Yemeni royalists with sanctuary and financial and logistical assistance. The Egyptian air force even carried out a few attacks on Saudi border towns. Ironically, following his deposition in 1964, King Sa'ud spent some time in self-imposed exile in Egypt.

The June 1967 **Arab-Israeli** War marked a turning point in Saudi-Egyptian relations. First, the outbreak of war forced Egypt to withdraw its troops from Yemen (leading eventually to an end to the civil war there). A few months after the disastrous Arab defeat, the Arab summit conference at al-Khartoum (Sudan) defined the role of the oil-rich Arab states in the common Arab struggle against Israel as providing financial assistance to the Arab frontline states; Saudi Arabia subsequently initiated subsidies for Egypt, as well as **Jordan**, Syria, and **Lebanon**. After the death of Jamal 'Abd al-Nasir in 1970, the Saudis warmed to his successor Anwar al-Sadat and King **Faysal bin 'Abd al-'Aziz** instituted the oil boycott in support of Egypt and other frontline states during the October 1973 Arab-Israeli War. Political, economic, and security ties continued to flourish through the 1970s, including the partnership of Egyptian technical expertise and Saudi money in the Arab Military Industrialization Corporation.

But Saudi-Egyptian relations were shattered a second time in 1979 when al-Sadat signed a separate peace treaty with Israel and the kingdom followed the lead of most Arab states in breaking off diplomatic relations. Al-Sadat's assassination the following year and his succession by Husni Mubarak brought a restoration of relations. Both countries backed **Iraq** during the Iran-Iraq war and Egypt was one of the first Arab states to throw its support behind Saudi Arabia and **Kuwait** after Iraq's invasion of the latter in 1990: Egypt provided the largest contingent of non-Gulf Cooperation Council (GCC) Arab troops during **Operation Desert Storm**. But postwar plans to involve Egypt and Syria in an Arab security scheme for the GCC states were never fully realized.

EID. *See* 'ID.

EMIR. *See* AMIR.

- F -

FADL. [fadl; فضل] A family originally from **'Unayzah** in **al-Qasim** but later settled in **al-Hijaz** as important merchants. The family also had strong commercial ties with India, where it served as the agent of Imam (later King) **'Abd al-'Aziz bin 'Abd al-Rahman** until1930 when an intra-family squabble caused the business to collapse. A prominent member of the family was 'Abdullah bin Muhammad al-Fadl (b. about 1883) who became 'Abd al-'Aziz's **Jiddah** agent when al-Hijaz was still under the rule of the **Hashimi** family. 'Abd al-'Aziz later employed him on missions to the Italians in Eritrea and to the **British**. A later post was Vice-President of the Consultative Council and he eventually rose to become Assistant to the Viceroy of al-Hijaz (Crown Prince **Faysal**).

FAHD BIN 'ABD AL-'AZIZ AL SA'UD. (1921-)
[فهد بن عبد العزيز آل سعود] King of Saudi Arabia from 1982 to present, Fahd is the 20th Saudi leader as well as the fourth son of King **'Abd al-'Aziz bin 'Abd al-Rahman** (r. 1902-1953) to rule. The eldest son of Hussah bint Ahmad al-Sudayri, his full brothers (the so-called **"Sudayri Seven"** or Al Fahd) include Defense Minister **Sultan**, Interior Minister **Nayif**, and Governor of Riyadh **Salman**. Earlier in his career, Fahd served as Governor of **al-Jawf** (1949-1953), the first Minister of Education (1953-1962), and the Minister

of the Interior (1962-1975). He become Second Deputy Prime Minister when his half brother **Faysal** acceded in 1964 and then Heir Apparent and First Deputy Prime Minister when his half brother **Khalid** became King. Fahd came to the throne when Khalid died of natural causes, but he also has long been in chronically poor health.

Although generally regarded as a more diligent and efficient administrator than Khalid bin 'Abd al-'Aziz, Fahd has also faced greater challenges which have made his reign more difficult. The end of the **oil** boom in the 1980s forced him to seek austerity measures which dampened his popularity. His inability to cut back newfound standards of living led to a hemorrhaging of the state's financial reserves by as much as $1 billion a month at the end of the 1980s. At the same time, Saudi Arabia has been imperilled by increasingly dangerous external threats, notably the hostility of **Iran** at the time of its 1979 revolution and in the latter part of the Iran-Iraq war (1980-1988), as well as the **Iraqi** invasion of **Kuwait** in 1990. His heavy reliance on the **United States**, perceived as Israel's strongest supporter, has been criticized both outside and inside the kingdom. While regarded as more progressive than his predecessors, he was hampered in introducing a measure of liberalization into the system by a widespread social conservatism after the oil boom and his own playboy image of earlier years.

A half brother **'Abdullah bin 'Abd al-'Aziz** has been selected to succeed him. King Fahd's first wife, and mother of five of his sons, al-Anud bint 'Abd al-'Aziz Al Jiluwi, died in 1999. King Fahd appointed one of these sons, **Muhammad bin Fahd**, as **Amir** (governor) of the **Eastern Province** in 1985 (Muhammad is regarded as one of the most aggressive businessmen in the royal family) and another son Sa'ud as Deputy Director-General of Intelligence. His eldest son **Faysal bin Fahd** was head of the General Presidency of Youth Welfare until his death in 1999, while another son Sultan was an army officer before being named deputy to his brother Faysal at Youth Welfare in 1992. King Fahd's second wife, Jawharah bint Ibrahim al-Ibrahim, bore him one son, **'Abd al-'Aziz bin Fahd** (born about 1974), who is clearly his father's favorite and even accompanied him to summit meetings. 'Abd al-'Aziz was appointed Minister of State without Portfolio in 1998. King Fahd was declared the world's third richest person with a net worth of $30 billion by an American magazine in 2000. Diabetic, arthritic, and hampered by bad knees and loss of memory, King Fahd underwent eye surgery in Switzerland in mid-2002, sparking unfounded rumors of his imminent demise.

FAHD BIN 'ABDULLAH BIN SA'UD AL-KABIR AL SA'UD.

[فهد بن عبد الله بن سعود الكبير آل سعود] A career officer in the Royal Saudi Air Force and descended from the **Sa'ud al-Kabir** collateral branch of the royal family. A highly respected Director of Operations for the Air Force, he was appointed Assistant Minister (*wakil*) of National Defense and Aviation in 1984, allegedly to put **Saudi Arabian Airlines** back on its feet and to manage the huge Peace Shield and **al-Yamamah** arms offset programs.

FAHD BIN SA'UD BIN 'ABD AL-'AZIZ AL SA'UD. (1923-)
[فهد بن سعود بن عبد العزيز آل سعود] The eldest son of King **Sa'ud**, Fahd served
as Head of Diwan (1953-1956) and as Minister of Defense (1956-1960).
Since then, he has concentrated on his business interests.

FAISALIAH, AL-. *See* KING FAYSAL FOUNDATION.

FAQIH, SA'D AL-. (1958-) [sa'd al-faqīh; سعد الفقيح] Born in **Iraq** in a family
of **Najdi** origin, his family moved to Saudi Arabia when Sa'd was a teenager
and, after medical school in **Riyadh**, he became a surgeon and professor
at **King Sa'ud University**. Influenced by the Muslim Brotherhood from
his youth, he became a founding member of the Saudi **opposition group**,
the Committee for the Defense of Legitimate Rights (CDLR), in the early
1990s. He joined the group's spokesman **Muhammad al-Mas'ari** in London
in 1994, but broke with Mas'ari two years later and formed his own Movement
for Islamic Reform in Arabia, which he claimed remained the true voice
of Islamic dissent within the kingdom.

FARA'AWN, GHAYTH BIN RASHAD. [fara'awn; غيث بن رشاد فرعون; also
spelled Pharaon] A successful Saudi businessman born in **Riyadh** in 1940.
His father Rashad was born in Syria and served first as King **'Abd al-'Aziz**'s
personal physician and then as a trusted adviser and Minister of Health. Ghayth
received an MBA from Harvard University and is one of the founders of
the firm Tihamah for Advertising, Public Relations and Marketing. His chief
business interests are concentrated under the roof of REDEC (Saudi Research
and Development Corporation). In 1997, the US Federal Reserve Bank fined
him $37 million and permanently barred him from the US banking industry
for his role in illegal bank purchases by the troubled Bank of Credit and
Commerce International (BCCI).

FARASAN ISLANDS. [farasān; فرسان; 42 00- 16 45] A small archipelago off
Saudi Arabia's **Red Sea** coast, nearly opposite the port of **Jizan**. Prior to
the First World War, sovereignty was held by the **Ottoman** Empire and
the islands were briefly occupied by British forces in 1916-1917, who
subsequently recognized the claim of the **Idrisi amir** of **'Asir** to the islands.
They were absorbed into the new Saudi state in the 1920s along with the
rest of the Idrisi amirate.

FARHAN, AL. [āl farhān; آل فرحان] One of the cadet branches of the royal family.
See SA'UD, AL.

FATWA. [fatwā; فتوى] An opinion on a matter of Islamic law or doctrine given
by a religious authority or authorities, such as a body of **'ulama'**.

FAW, AL-. [al-fāw; also known as Qaryat al-Faw; الفاو; قرية الفاو; 45 08 -19 52]
An important archaeological site located in the **Wadi al-Dawasir** region
of southern Saudi Arabia. It occupied a strategic location on the ancient trade
routes crossing the **Arabian Peninsula** from **Najran** in the southwest to

Thaj in the northeast. Al-Faw reached prominence under Selucid influence during the ninth to second centuries B.C. and was abandoned by the fourth century A.D. It may have been the center of the Kingdom of Kinda, the earliest identifiable political entity in the Arabian heartland. It should not be confused with the city of the same name in Iraq.

FAWWAZ BIN 'ABD AL-'AZIZ AL SA'UD. (1943-) [فواز بن عبد العزيز آل سعود]
A son of King **'Abd al-'Aziz** who joined half brother **Talal** as one of the "**Liberal Princes.**" King **Sa'ud** appointed him **Amir** of **Riyadh** in 1960 but he joined Talal and the others in exile soon after. On his return to Saudi Arabia, he was named Deputy Amir of **Makkah** in 1969 and promoted to Amir in 1971. Removed from his position as a result of the 1979 seizure of the Great Mosque of Makkah, he has since been in business.

FAYD. *See* HA'IL.

FAYSAL BIN 'ABD AL-'AZIZ AL SA'UD. (r. 1964-1975)
[فيصل بن عبد العزيز آل سعود] The 18th ruler in the **Al Sa'ud** dynasty. Faysal, born in 1904, was the only son of a mother from the **Al al-Shaykh** family. He proved his worth to his father in the conquests of **'Asir** and **al-Hijaz** during the early 1920s and so was appointed Viceroy of al-Hijaz, a position in which he was given considerable independent responsibility. In 1953, with his father's death and the succession of half brother **Sa'ud** to the throne, Faysal became Crown Prince and also assumed the portfolio of Foreign Minister (which he held with a single break, 1960-1962, until his death in 1975). Other cabinet positions held by Faysal during Sa'ud's reign included Interior, Defense, Finance, and Commerce. King Sa'ud's profligacy and foreign-policy misadventures provoked the royal family to force him to accept Faysal as Prime Minister in October 1962. Following a renewed attempt by Sa'ud to regain control of the state, the royal family felt forced to act once again. In 1964, Sa'ud was deposed and Faysal proclaimed King.

Faysal's reign marked a period of considerable change within Saudi Arabia fuelled by oil wealth and rising expectations. It also covered the Arab Israeli wars of 1967 and 1973. While Faysal, a deeply religious man and imbued with deep concern over the future of Jerusalem, held aloof from Arab calls to institute an oil boycott of the West during the June 1967 war, he was forced to bow to pressure during the October 1973 war and joined an Arab boycott specifically imposed against the **United States** and several other countries for their support of Israel. Despite this, a bedrock of Faysal's foreign policy remained close political, economic, and military ties to the United States, even as he sought to work for an Arab consensus on Arab-Israeli matters.

On 25 March 1975, King Faysal was assassinated by a nephew, **Faysal bin Musa'id bin 'Abd al-'Aziz,** during a *majlis* (an audience open to all comers). He was succeeded by his half brother **Khalid.** Faysal had three wives, best known of which was **'Iffat** (popularly regarded as "Queen" during Faysal's reign). Among his very capable sons are **Khalid al-Faysal** (Amir of 'Asir Province), **Muhammad al-Faysal** (involved in Islamic banking),

Sa'ud al-Faysal (Foreign Minister), and **Turki al-Faysal** (Director-General of Intelligence up to 2001).

FAYSAL BIN FAHD BIN 'ABD AL-'AZIZ AL SA'UD. (1946-1999)
[فيصل بن فهد بن عبدالعزيز آل سعود] The eldest son of King **Fahd bin 'Abd al-'Aziz**, Faysal received a degree in economics from the **United States** and was appointed Director-General of Youth Welfare in 1972. He made several prominent visits abroad during the 1980s, especially when he held talks with Soviet Foreign Ministry officials in Moscow during the period before diplomatic relations were established and when he met President François Mitterand and Prime Minister Jacques Chirac in **France**. A football enthusiast, he became head of the Arab Sports Federation and the Arab Football Association prior to his death of a heart attack in 1999.

FAYSAL BIN HUSAYN AL-HASHIMI. (1885-1933) [فيصل بن حسين الهاشمي]
A son of the Sharif of **Makkah**, **Husayn bin 'Ali**, Faysal served as a deputy for **al-Hijaz** in the **Ottoman** parliament in 1915. Following the announcement of the Arab Revolt by his father, who also declared himself King of al-Hijaz, Faysal commanded the Hashimi forces along the Hijaz **railroad** and then served as Minister of the Interior. Championed by British officials in the Arab Bureau in Cairo, including **T. E. Lawrence**, Faysal assumed the title of King of Syria in 1920 but was forced out of Damascus by the French a few months later. The British then installed him as King of **Iraq** in 1921. He successfully guided Iraq to independence in 1930 and died in 1933. He was succeeded by his son Ghazi (r. 1933-1939) and then by his grandson Faysal (r. 1939-1958), who was killed in the Iraqi Revolution of 1958.

FAYSAL BIN MUSA'ID BIN 'ABD AL-'AZIZ AL SA'UD. (c. 1957-1975)
[فيصل بن مساعد بن عبد العزيز آل سعود] A grandson of King **'Abd al-'Aziz**, he assassinated his uncle, King **Faysal**, in 1975 and was subsequently beheaded. While his motives for the killing are still not clear, it may have been related to the death of his brother Khalid in 1965 during a religious protest over the establishment of **Riyadh**'s first television station.

FAYSAL BIN TURKI AL SA'UD. (r. 1834-1838 and 1843-1865)
[فيصل بن تركي آل سعود] The seventh and 10th leader of the **Wahhabi Al Sa'ud** state. Faysal had been captured with other members of the Al Sa'ud during the Egyptian sack of **al-Dir'iyah** in 1818 and remained a prisoner in **Egypt** for a number of years. After his father **Turki** (who had established the Second Saudi State) was assassinated through the machinations of a cousin in 1834, Faysal returned from eastern Arabia and successfully besieged **Riyadh**, killing the pretender and succeeding his father. Faysal's success in retaking many territories held by previous Al Sa'ud rulers worried the **Ottomans** and Egyptians and another campaign was dispatched to Arabia, accompanied by their pretender to Al Sa'ud leadership, **Khalid bin Sa'ud**. In 1838, Faysal was forced to surrender and accept exile in Egypt. For the next five years, civil war raged in **Najd** but Faysal was able to escape to Najd and regain the allegiance of the tribal **shaykh**s. From this start, Faysal once again rebuilt

the Saudi state, failing only to reconquer **al-Hijaz**. Faysal grew weak in his later years and was unable to prevent a deadly rivalry from springing up between his sons **'Abdullah** and **Sa'ud**, which had severe implications for the future of the state following Faysal's death in 1865.

FAYSAL BIN TURKI BIN 'ABD AL-'AZIZ AL SA'UD. (1920-)
[فيصل بن تركي بن عبدالعزيز آل سعود] The posthumous son of King **'Abd al-'Aziz's** eldest son Turki, Faysal was raised by his uncle (and later King) **Sa'ud**. Not surprisingly he supported King Sa'ud in his struggle against Crown Prince (later King) **Faysal**. Sa'ud appointed him Minister of Labor and Social Affairs (1961-1962) and Minister of the Interior (1962).

FOREIGN AFFAIRS. Not surprisingly, most of Saudi Arabia's strongest relations are with its neighbors. On the **Gulf** side, a multitude of similarities have drawn the kingdom and the smaller Gulf states together. A rising tide of threats to their security prompted them in 1981 to formalize their security, political, and economic relations under the umbrella of the **Gulf Cooperation Council (GCC)**. Besides Saudi Arabia, the Council's membership includes **Kuwait, Bahrain, Qatar**, the **United Arab Emirates**, and **Oman**.

Elsewhere, Saudi Arabia's neighbors are perceived more as threats than allies. **Iraq** to the northeast has been viewed with suspicion since its creation following the First World War. Iraq's **al-Hashimi** kings naturally opposed the **Al Sa'ud** who had driven the family from **Makkah**. The Iraqi revolution in 1958 advanced the radical Arab threat to the kingdom's borders and brought attempted subversion within Saudi Arabia and its Gulf neighbors. Most recently, Iraq invaded Saudi ally Kuwait in 1990 and appeared poised to move into Saudi Arabia. Riyadh spearheaded the coalition behind **Operation Desert Storm** which liberated Kuwait and provided facilities for Western air forces engaged in enforcing the prohibition against Iraqi air activities in southern Iraq.

The invasion of Kuwait also demonstrated the kingdom's ambivalence towards its northwestern neighbor, **Jordan**. Like Iraq, Jordan (known as Transjordan until 1948) was forged by the British with a Hashimi king and included territory and tribes that King **'Abd al-'Aziz** regarded as his. Later, however, Jordan provided an important buffer against Israel and the Arab radical threat. For these reasons, Riyadh provided Jordan with regular subsidies. The failure of Jordanian King Husayn to condemn the invasion of Kuwait provoked Saudi Arabia to expel Jordanian diplomats and cut off its subsidies. It was well into the 1990s before relations returned to normal.

To the south, the two **Yemeni** states have always worried the Saudis. North Yemen (the Yemen Arab Republic) was the first republic in the **Arabian Peninsula** and the Yemeni civil war (1962-1970) posed a direct threat because of the **Egyptian** military presence. After the civil war ended, Riyadh sought to keep the North Yemeni state weak but also propped it up because of the greater threat from more radical South Yemen. The latter, the People's Democratic Republic of Yemen, was the only Marxist state in the Arab world and provided the **Soviet Union** with military facilities. The Republic of Yemen, formed from a merger of the two states in 1990, quickly ran afoul of Riyadh by not condemning the Iraqi invasion of Kuwait. Not only were its diplomats expelled and subsidies terminated, as happened to Jordan, but hundreds of thousands of Yemenis working in the kingdom were forced to leave. This was one reason why Saudi Arabia gave tacit support to the southern Yemeni leadership when it unsuccessfully sought to secede in 1994. After the southerners were defeated in a traumatic civil war, Riyadh continued to improve its relations with Yemen. A comprehensive border settlement was reached in 1995, which put an end to more than 60 years of acrimony.

With its growing wealth, traditionally isolationist Saudi Arabia gradually has assumed a higher profile on Arab concerns. Foremost has been the **Arab-Israeli Conflict**. Although token Saudi military contingents fought in the 1967 and 1973 wars, the Saudi contribution has been more financial, with subsidies to the Arab frontline states, including the Palestine Liberation Organization (PLO), since 1967. Riyadh also joined the Arab **oil** boycott during the 1973 war to protest American support of Israel and has complied with the **Arab League** boycott of Israel. King Fahd advanced an Arab-Israeli peace plan in 1981 and Heir Apparent **'Abdullah bin 'Abd al-'Aziz** reiterated a similar plan in 2002. Generally, the Saudi approach in inter-Arab affairs has been to seek an Arab consensus, just as consensus is the goal of the kingdom's internal politics. This conciliatory method never recovered fully from the Iraqi invasion of Kuwait, although the kingdom gradually restored normal relations with all Arab countries except Iraq.

Across the Gulf, **Iran** has long been regarded with suspicion, because of the ethnic divisions between Arabs and Persians, religious distinctions between **Sunnis** and **Shi'ah**, and because of Arab suspicions of Iranian desires for regional hegemony. Relations with the Shah (deposed in 1979) were correct but frosty. Under the Islamic Republic of Iran, relations frequently have been hostile but were placed on a better footing in the late 1990s and the two countries signed a security cooperation agreement in 2001.

Saudi Arabia's position as the protector of the Holy Cities of **Islam** has led it to assume a special interest in international Islamic affairs. It hosts the secretariat of the **Organization of the Islamic Conference** (OIC) and conducts a worldwide program of mosque building and distribution of **Qur'an**s (Korans). Riyadh also distributes considerable foreign aid to Islamic countries, as well as to Arab and other Third World recipients. Another important tie to the Third World is the several million expatriate workers in the kingdom. Although many are Arab and some are Western, large numbers come from **Pakistan**, **India**, Sri Lanka, Bangladesh, Thailand, and the Philippines.

Saudi Arabia has sought special relationships over the course of the 20th century with two Western powers. For most of the first half of the century, the strongest foreign influence on Saudi Arabia was exercised by **Britain**. From almost the very beginning of his struggle to rebuild the Saudi state, **'Abd al-'Aziz bin 'Abd al-Rahman** sought a treaty relationship with Britain, similar to that of the Gulf shaykhdoms. Failing that, he made do with a subsidy and arms for confronting the **Ottomans**, especially their clients, the **Al Rashid** of **Ha'il**. The expansion of the Saudi state in most directions was constrained by encircling spheres of British influence: Transjordan to the northwest, Iraq to the northeast, and the shaykhdoms of the Gulf on the east. In the west,

British pressure dissuaded 'Abd al-'Aziz from attacking the Hashimi Kingdom in **al-Hijaz** until the subsidy was terminated.

In the end, the Anglo-Saudi Treaty of **Jiddah** (1927) conferred full independent status on 'Abd al-'Aziz. Anglo-Saudi relations were further bedevilled in the 1920s by **Ikhwan** raids against Transjordan, Iraq, and Kuwait, and then in the 1930s by border disagreements along the Gulf littoral (*see* BLUE LINE; RIYADH LINE). Beginning with the awarding of the oil concession to an American partnership, British influence in Saudi Arabia steadily waned in favor of the **United States**. The clash over **al-Buraymi** oasis in the early 1950s was followed by Riyadh's disruption of diplomatic relations after the Anglo-Franco-Israeli invasion of the Sinai in 1956. Relations improved in the 1970s and 1980s and the kingdom has turned to Britain to provide combat aircraft and other military equipment which it could not get from the US. Political and military cooperation continued through the 1990s into the early 2000s, as the Heir Apparent and the Minister of Defense both paid official visits to the UK. Disputes over British sanctuary for Saudi dissidents and British concern over the treatment of British nationals charged with murder in the kingdom did not seriously disrupt relations. Relations with other Western European countries have been close and **France** has played a substantial role in arms sales and military training.

The United States provided modest military assistance through the 1940s and 1950s and the oil concessionaire **ARAMCO** played a major role in early development efforts. But the Saudi-American special relationship really took root with the oil boom. Saudi development owes much to American consultants, the thousands of Saudis trained in the US, and the predominance of American firms in Saudi Arabia's trade and contracting patterns. The security relationship remains of prime importance, as illustrated by Riyadh's cooperation with the US in encouraging opposition to the Soviet occupation of **Afghanistan** and later in **Operation Desert Storm**. However, the attacks on the US on 11 September 2001, apparently organized by Saudi-born **Usamah bin Ladin** and carried out by a number of Saudis, severely damaged US-Saudi relations. The kingdom gave qualified support to the US campaign against **al-Qa'idah** in Afghanistan but there was further dispute over whether Saudi Arabia would support the United States in an attack on Iraq as the year 2002 ended.

FOREIGN AID. For many years, Saudi Arabia has contributed foreign aid to a multitude of countries by various methods for different purposes. Some of this aid has had a decidedly political aspect. Direct subventions to Arab neighbors such as Jordan, Yemen, and Palestine not only have constituted vital subsidies for economic needs but have also strengthened the capacity of these states to govern. The kingdom has provided sizeable donations to other countries in order to influence policies and enhance the international standing of Saudi Arabia. It can also be argued that a strong motivation behind Saudi Arabia's commitment to foreign aid has been the principle of **zakat** (the Islamic alms tax).

The kingdom has been strongly committed to development assistance. The $4.8 billion the kingdom gave to developing countries between 1975 and 1987 was second only to the **United States** in the value of aid contributions and averaged 4.2 percent of GNP over this period. However, the kingdom's disbursements in 1990 were only one-third of the total in 1989, thus indicating the country's response to the economic stringencies caused by the **Iraqi** invasion of **Kuwait**, and they remained at roughly the same level through the end of the century. Much of Saudi aid is disbursed through regional institutions and United Nations organizations. Principal recipients of Saudi contributions have been the Arab Fund for Economic and Social Development, the Arab Bank for Economic Development in Africa, the Islamic Bank for Development, the OPEC Fund for International Development, the United Nations Development Program and other UN agencies, and the World Bank and International Monetary Fund. In addition, the kingdom channels aid through its own institutions, principally the **Saudi Fund for Development** (SFD). By 2001, the SFD had loaned a total of nearly $6 billion to 63 countries on four continents.

FOREIGN INVESTMENT. *See* INDUSTRY.

FRANCE AND SAUDI ARABIA. The kingdom's ties with France have been excellent throughout Saudi Arabia's existence but never as close as those with the **United States** and **Britain**. Although France is the kingdom's sixth biggest trading partner, the relationship has centered on French arms sales and military assistance. The French have been particularly instrumental in the development of the Saudi navy and the Saudis have bought French naval vessels, tanks, surface-to-air missiles, and other military hardware. French aircraft were also stationed in the kingdom after the **Kuwait** War to participate in Southern Watch (the enforcement of prohibitions on Iraqi air movements in the southern part of Iraq). Saudi Heir Apparent **'Abdullah bin 'Abd al-'Aziz** met with French President Jacques Chirac in Paris in 1998 and 2001.

- G -

GALLUS, AELIUS. The Roman Prefect of **Egypt** who led a Roman army down the Arabian coast of the **Red Sea** coast in 24 B.C., reaching the region of **Najran** before being forced to retreat. His expedition constituted the deepest Roman penetration of Arabia.

GAS, NATURAL. *See* NATURAL GAS.

GCC. *See* GULF COOPERATION COUNCIL.

GHAMID, BANI. [banī ghāmid, sing. ghāmidī; غامد بني ;غامدي] Large and important tribe of **al-Sarawat** highlands of southern **al-Hijaz** and northern **'Asir**. The tribe has both settled and nomadic sections. Under the suzerainty alternatively of the **Ottomans** and the Sharif of **Makkah** until the 1920s, the Bani Ghamid have been combined into a single district with the **Zahran** tribe to the north with an administrative center at **al-Bahah**.

GHATGHAT, AL-. [al-ghatghat; الغطغط; 46 19 - 24 30] One of the first two settlements (**hijrah**) of the **Ikhwan** forces to be established about 1912. Principally occupied by the '**Utaybah** tribe, the 'Utaybi paramount shaykh, **Sultan bin Bijad bin Humayd**, settled there in 1914 and al-Ghatghat became the center of Ikhwan activities for the surrounding region and its population grew to approximately 10,000. After Saudi Imam '**Abd al-'Aziz**'s crushing victory over the rebellious Ikhwan, including Shaykh Sultan, at **Sibilah** in 1929, he ordered al-Ghatghat to be completely razed. Resettlement on the site was permitted only in 1956.

GHAWAR, AL-. [al-ghawār; الغوار; 49 23- 25 22] A hilly area of the **Eastern Province** about 20 miles south of **al-Hufuf**, and the site of one of the world's largest oil fields, discovered by **ARAMCO** in 1948.

GHAZWAH. [ghazwah; pl. ghazawāt; غزوات ؛غزوة] A desert raid and, by extension, battle or war. By tradition and necessity, most **badu** (bedouin) tribes of Arabia have always engaged in raids against other tribes, camel caravans, and settlements. In the early 20th century, Imam '**Abd al-'Aziz bin 'Abd al-Rahman Al Sa'ud** sought to harness the potential of these raids for his own expansionist purposes by organizing the badu tribes of **Najd** into the **Ikhwan**, the warriors of the **Wahhabi** movement. When he had established the foundations of the Third Saudi State, 'Abd al-'Aziz faced opposition from these same tribes, in part because he forbade the practice of ghazwah for any purpose.

GIZAN. *See* JIZAN.

GOLD. *See* MAHD AL-DHAHAB.

GOSAIBI. *See* QUSAYBI, AL-.

GOVERNMENT. Saudi Arabia is a monarchy, headed by King **Fahd bin 'Abd al-'Aziz Al Sa'ud**, who succeeded to the throne in 1982. His half brother '**Abdullah bin 'Abd al-'Aziz**, now head of the National Guard, has been designated heir apparent and another half brother **Sultan bin 'Abd al-'Aziz**, at present Minister of Defense and Aviation, is the likely choice to follow 'Abdullah. The present state is the third under **Al Sa'ud** leadership and dates from 1902 although the present name of the country was adopted only in 1932. There is no formal system of representation and political parties are not allowed. The **shari'ah**, the corpus of Islamic law, remains the basis of the legal system. **Oil** continues to be the mainstay of the **economy**, and the government has spent enormous sums on the physical development of the country, as well as on **military** expenditures, a reflection of the kingdom's vulnerable position in the region. The emphasis on socioeconomic development has resulted in dramatic improvements in health standards, life expectancy, **educational** levels, and personal income.

    The government of Saudi Arabia is highly centralized, with all authority flowing down through the ministries and independent agencies (nearly all of which are located in the capital at **Riyadh**), via the Council of Ministers, from the King. Not only does the inner circle of the royal family function like a supreme council above the formal government structure, but its members also hold the key positions. As mentioned before, the King is also the Prime Minister, while the Heir Apparent, 'Abdullah, holds the title of First Deputy Prime Minister, in addition to being head of the National Guard. Prince Sultan, next in line to the throne, is the second Deputy Prime Minister, as well as Minister of Defense and National Aviation. Other family members hold the portfolios of interior (**Nayif bin 'Abd al-'Aziz**), foreign affairs (**Sa'ud al-Faysal**), and public works and housing (Mu'tib bin 'Abd al-'Aziz). In addition, **Salman bin 'Abd al-'Aziz** is Governor of Riyadh, **Nawwaf bin 'Abd al-'Aziz** is Director-General of Intelligence, and others hold ministerial rank as governors of other provinces and deputy ministers. However, the proportion of senior posts held by the royal family is far less than the near monopoly enjoyed up to the 1950s.

Technically, the present government dates from the date of King Fahd's accession, as the King also serves as the Prime Minister. However, major reshuffles took place on 2 August 1995, when 18 new ministers were appointed, and on 16 June 1999, when four ministers were replaced, the Ministry of Civil Service was created, and several new ministers of state without portfolio were added. These reshuffles, especially the one of 1995, were a result of reforms announced by King Fahd at the time of his introduction of the kingdom's **Basic Law** in 1992. New blood was to be introduced into the government by the appointment of ministers for fixed terms; nearly all the senior Al Sa'ud have retained their government positions, however. *See also* INTRODUCTION; APPENDIX F (BASIC LAW).

GULF, THE. The body of water separating the **Arabian Peninsula** from the southwest Asian mainland, also known as the Arabian Gulf or Persian Gulf. Its northern source is the Shatt al-'Arab (formed by the merger of the Tigris and Euphrates Rivers) in **Iraq** and it empties into the Gulf of Oman at the Strait of Hormuz. The Gulf lies in a northwesterly-southeasterly direction and is approximately 570 miles long and from 125 to 275 miles wide. There are eight littoral states: **Iran** along the northern coast, Iraq at the top, and **Kuwait**, Saudi Arabia, **Bahrain**, **Qatar**, the **United Arab Emirates**, and **Oman** along the southern coast. The waterway, which is very shallow and reaches a maximum depth of approximately 500 feet, is noted for its variety of sea life, its pearling banks and underwater petroleum deposits, and its role as one of the most strategically important maritime arteries in the world. About two-thirds of the world's oil deposits are held by the littoral countries, and the majority of oil exports must pass through the Strait of Hormuz. The discharge of millions of barrels of crude oil into the Gulf by Iraqi troops retreating from Kuwait in 1991 created an environmental disaster (*see* DESERT STORM, OPERATION). Saudi Arabia's coastline on the Gulf stretches from Kuwait in the north to the base of the Qatar peninsula, and the King Fahd Causeway connects the **Eastern Province** to Bahrain. The kingdom's principal ports on the Gulf include **al-Jubayl**, **Ra's Tanurah**, and **al-Dammam**.

The Dictionary

GULF COOPERATION COUNCIL (GCC). [majlis al-ta'āwun li-duwal al-khalīj al-'arabī; مجلس التعاون لدول الخليج العربي] Properly, the Cooperation Council for the States of the Arab Gulf, the GCC was founded in 1981 with six members: Saudi Arabia, **Kuwait, Bahrain, Qatar**, the **United Arab Emirates (UAE)**, and **Oman**. Although the stated aims at the time of establishment were to provide a framework for cooperation in the economic, social, cultural, political, and security spheres, the threat from the Iran-Iraq War (1980-1988) ensured that priority was placed on regional security concerns. A series of bilateral agreements for cooperation on internal security was signed and joint military exercises were accompanied by the creation of the Peninsula Shield Force, a putative quick reaction force with elements from all six members (although Saudi troops were in the majority), based at **Hafar al-Batin** in northeast Saudi Arabia. This force formed the nucleus of the GCC military units contributing to the recovery of Kuwait during **Operation Desert Storm** in 1991. The Unified Economic Agreement provided for the free movement of citizens, capital, and investment, but it has not been fully implemented and so further efforts to integrate the six economies have been stymied. A summit of the six heads of state is held annually in December, rotating through the six capitals. The host ruler at each summit serves as the President of the GCC until the following summit. In recent years, there have also been several other summits held midway between the December ones.

GULF WAR. Media term for the 1991 war to liberate **Kuwait** following the **Iraqi** invasion in 1990 (*see* DESERT STORM, OPERATION). Confusingly, the same term was also used by the media to refer to the Iran-Iraq War (1980-1988).

- H -

HADDAH AGREEMENT. [haddah; حدة] Sir **Gilbert Clayton** and Imam **'Abd al-'Aziz bin 'Abd al-Rahman Al Sa'ud** signed an Anglo-Saudi agreement on 2 November 1925 at Haddah, a suburb of **al-Ta'if**. Most of the agreement dealt with Saudi relations with the new **Hashimi** state of Transjordan: in return for an undertaking to spare Transjordan from raids by his **Ikhwan**, 'Abd al-'Aziz was guaranteed free transit for his trade with Syria. The agreement also set the borders between Transjordan and **Najd** by giving most of **Wadi Sirhan** to 'Abd al-'Aziz in return for inclusion of the port of al-'Aqabah and the inland town of Ma'an within Transjordan.

HADITH. [hadīth; حديث] A source of Islamic law based on the traditions of the Prophet **Muhammad**'s words and actions, as related by his companions and later codified by Islamic scholars. These traditions constitute the **Sunnah**, the primary source of Islamic law after the **Qur'an** (Koran).

HAFAR AL-BATIN. [hafar al-bāṭin; حفر الباطن; 45 55 - 28 28] The only settlement in Wadi al-Batin, at the extreme northeastern corner of Saudi Arabia and adjacent to the **Iraqi** and **Kuwaiti** borders. The **wadi** was once part of Wadi al-Rummah of **al-Qasim** but later became cut off by the sands of **al-Dahna'** desert. A major military installation, known as King Khalid Military City, has been built at Hafar al-Batin and Peninsula Shield, the **Gulf Cooperation Council** 's rapid deployment force, was based there. It also figured in **Operation Desert Storm**, the 1991 war to liberate Kuwait from Iraqi occupation.

HA'IL. [hā'il; حائل; also spelled Hayil or Hail; 41 46 - 27 33] The principal town of the Jabal **Shammar** district of northern **Najd**. Ha'il's origins date back to the appearance of the first walled town in the second millennium B.C. This settlement, known as "Are Kome" in later Greek sources, grew rapidly during the first millennium B.C. as a result of its strategic location at the convergence of the trade routes connecting the South Arabian civilizations with those of both Mesopotamia and the Levant. Early Arabian tradition maintains that nearby Fayd was the oldest settlement in northern Najd, probably dating from 3,000 to 2,500 years ago. Other nearby sites contain inscriptions and graffiti ranging from **Thamudic** and Palmyrene times through the early Islamic period. In the 19th and early 20th centuries, Ha'il was the capital of the **Al Rashid** amirate until conquered by the arch-rival **Al Sa'ud** in 1921. It is now the capital of a Saudi province of the same name.

HAJJ. [hajj; حج] The pilgrimage to **Makkah** is one of the Five Pillars (basic requirements of Islam) and is required of all **Muslims** once in their lifetime, provided they are physically and financially able to undertake it. One who has performed the hajj is entitled to use the title al-haj or hajji before his name. The elaborate ritual associated with the hajj includes circumambulation of the **Ka'bah** (inside the Great Mosque of Makkah) and visits to several sites just outside Makkah. Some hajjis, especially the **Shi'ah**, also visit the mosque of the Prophet **Muhammad** in **al-Madinah**, although this is not a requirement. The hajj takes place during the first part of the Islamic month of Dhu al-Hijjah. Since the Islamic year is lunar, the hajj can occur during any season, making it quite difficult when it falls in the hot summer. The circumambulation of the Great Mosque, known as the **'umrah**, may be made at any other time during the Islamic year, but then it is considered a lesser pilgrimage and is voluntary. Before **oil**, the hajj was one of the principal sources of income for **al-Hijaz**. With the advent of air travel and the expansion of facilities by the Saudi government, the number of hajjis has increased to approximately two million each year.

HAMZAH, FU'AD. (c. 1900-1950) [فؤاد همزة] Saudi government official of Syrian (Lebanese) Druze origin. He attended university in Beirut and taught school in Palestine before arriving in **al-Hijaz** in 1926. He eventually secured an appointment in the Saudi Foreign Ministry through fellow Syrian **Yusuf Yasin** and was made ambassador to **France** in 1939.

HANBALI SCHOOL OF ISLAMIC LAW. [hanbalī; حنبلي] Generally regarded as the most conservative of the four schools of law or jurisprudence within **Sunni** (or orthodox) **Islam** (the other schools are the Hanafi, Maliki, and

Shafi'i). It stems from the ideas of Ahmad bin Hanbal (d. A.D. 855), who argued for a return to the purity of the early Islamic community and a reliance on the fundamental sources of religious doctrine: the **Qur'an** (Koran, the book of revelations of God) and the **Sunnah** (the words and deeds attributed to the Prophet **Muhammad**). The school predominates in Saudi Arabia and **Qatar** because of adherence in those countries to **Wahhabism** (**Muhammad bin 'Abd al-Wahhab** was trained in Hanbali jurisprudence); it is also followed in parts of the **United Arab Emirates (UAE)**.

HARAD. [harad; حرض; 49 11 - 23 14] Located in the Wadi al-Sahbah of the **Eastern Province** and site of the King Faysal Settlement Project, Harad was the kingdom's most extensive attempt to settle **badu** (bedouin) tribes, in this case primarily the **Al Murrah**. Physical development of the project was begun in 1971 but few badu were actually settled and the project was eventually transformed into an agricultural enterprise.

HARB. [harb; sing. harbī; حرب؛ حربي] An important tribe, or confederation of tribes, of **al-Hijaz**, with territory ranging along the **Tihamah** shores of the **Red Sea** from **Yanbu'** in the north to **al-Qunfudhah** in the south, as well as in the mountains along the road between **Makkah** and **al-Madinah**. Other branches have moved into **Najd** around **Ha'il** and **al-Qasim**. In the first part of the 20th century, the western Harb came under the authority of the Sharif of Makkah while the eastern Harb owed allegiance to the **Al Rashid** rulers of Ha'il; they were particularly noted for attacks on caravans. One section near al-Madinah is **Shi'ah**.

HARIRI, RAFIQ. [harīrī; رفيق حريري] A Lebanese who went to Saudi Arabia in 1965 as a teacher but quickly entered business and eventually became a billionaire. Although a Saudi citizen since 1978, he has maintained a close interest in Lebanon and has made the rebuilding of Beirut a personal ambition. He became Prime Minister of Lebanon in October 1992.

HASA, AL-. *See* AHSA', AL-.

HASHIMI, AL-, OR AL-HAWASHIM. [al-hāshimī, pl. al-hawāshim; الهاشمي؛ الهواشم] The dynasty controlling the city of **Makkah** from the 10th century until the early 20th century. As descendants of the Prophet **Muhammad** (taking their dynastic name from the great-grandfather of Muhammad, Hashim bin 'Abd al-Manaf), the Hawashim were entitled to use the title of **sharif**. For much of the period of their rule over Makkah, they were surbordinate to the Mamluks of **Egypt** or the **Ottomans** of Istanbul. But in 1916, Sharif **Husayn bin 'Ali al-Hashimi**, with **British** encouragement, declared the Arab Revolt against the Ottomans and proclaimed himself the independent King of **al-Hijaz**. In return for Hashimi services and in recognition of the family's presumed widespread legitimacy (due to their status as sharifs and holders of the keys to the holiest sites in Islam), Britain helped establish Sharif Husayn's son **Faysal** briefly as the King of Syria (1920) and then subsequently as the King of **Iraq** (1921-1933). His descendants continued to rule Iraq until the revolution of 1958. A second son of Sharif Husayn, **'Abdullah**, was installed as the King of Transjordan (later **Jordan**); his great-grandson 'Abdullah is the present king.

For the duration of the First World War, the **Al Sa'ud** leader, **'Abd al-'Aziz bin 'Abd al-Rahman**, was dissuaded by the British from attacking the weak Hijazi kingdom and the long-simmering dispute over ownership of the oasis of **al-Khurmah** was kept in abeyance. After the war, however, the Hashimi-Saudi rivalry heated up, as 'Abd al-'Aziz's **Ikhwan** warriors raided the new Hashimi states in Iraq and Jordan, facing retaliation from British Royal Air Force aircraft. Apart from the disastrous Hashimi defeat at al-Khurmah and nearby Turabah in 1919, Hashimi-Saudi hostilities in Arabia itself were postponed until 1924. 'Abd al-'Aziz was provoked to renew his pressure on al-Hijaz as a result of the termination of the British subsidy to the **Al Sa'ud** and Sharif Husayn's assumption of the Islamic title of *khalifah* or caliph when the Turkish Republic abolished it as an Ottoman title. (Theoretically, the title denoted succession to the Prophet Muhammad as head of the entire Islamic community but it had been largely meaningless for centuries.)

Using al-Khurmah as a base, the Saudi armies easily captured **al-Ta'if**. Uncontrolled, the Ikhwan massacred many of the city's inhabitants, causing much of the population of nearby Makkah to flee to the port of **Jiddah** and the notables of al-Hijaz to demand the abdication of King Husayn. He was succeeded by his son **'Ali** but the Hashimi position was untenable. A few weeks after the fall of al-Ta'if, the Saudi forces occupied Makkah without opposition. British concern and international Muslim disquiet over the actions of the Ikhwan at al-Ta'if led 'Abd al-'Aziz to move to al-Hijaz in December 1924 to supervise personally the siege of Jiddah. At the beginning of December 1925, **al-Madinah** and **Yanbu'** both fell, leaving only Jiddah in Hashimi hands. On 21 December 1925, Jiddah formally surrendered and King 'Ali embarked for exile in Iraq. On 8 January 1926, 'Abd al-'Aziz was proclaimed as King of al-Hijaz, in addition to his capacity as Sultan of Najd, and a thousand years of Hashimi politics in al-Hijaz came to an end. (*See* Appendix E for a dynastic list of al-Hawashim.)

HAWALI, SAFAR BIN 'ABD AL-RAHMAN AL-. (1950-) [safar al-ḥawālī; (سفر الحوالي)] A dissident religious figure born in **al-Bahah** province and a member of the **Ghamidi** tribe. He studied at the **Islamic University** in **al-Madinah** and then received his M.A. and Ph.D. at **Umm al-Qura University** in **Makkah**, where he subsequently joined the faculty. Noted for his conservative religious stance, he opposed the presence of American troops in the kingdom during and after the **Kuwait** War. The popularity of his sermons, distributed via cassette tapes, led to demonstrations in 1994 and his arrest. He was not released until 1999. *See also* OPPOSITION GROUPS.

HAWASHIM, AL-. *See* HASHIMI, AL-.

HEGELAN, AL-. *See* HUJAYLAN, AL-.

HIJAZ, AL-. [al-ḥijāz; الحجاز] The western quarter of Saudi Arabia and, along with **Najd** and the **Eastern Province**, one of the three most important regions of the kingdom. The region's **Tihamah** coastal plain, adjoining the **Red Sea**, includes the country's principal port of **Jiddah** and the new industrial city at **Yanbu'**. The southern plain also includes the seaside towns of Lith and **al-Qunfudhah**. Inland, a north-south range of mountains separates the coastal plain from the inner desert plateaux leading to Najd. The two holiest cities of Islam, **Makkah** and **al-Madinah**, are located in this belt, as well as other important sites of early Islamic history such as **'Ukaz**, **Badr**, **Uhud**, and **Khaybar**, as is **al-Ta'if** with its nearby summer resorts. Administratively, al-Hijaz is divided into the provinces of Makkah and al-Madinah, although **Tabuk** and **al-Bahah** provinces may be said to fall within the region as well. The name is taken to mean barrier, possibly as a reference to the mountains separating the Tihamah from Najd or as an obstacle between Syria and Yemen.

Once the center of the Islamic state, the region now known as al-Hijaz became a subordinate part of first the Umayyad and then the 'Abbasid Empires, eventually falling under the influence of the Mamluk dynasty of **Egypt**. From the 16th century, it was a vilayet (province) of the **Ottoman** Empire but the Sharifs of Makkah, provided by **al-Hawashim**, a family descended from the Prophet, exercised considerable autonomy. In the early 19th century, the **Wahhabis** of Najd invaded al-Hijaz and provoked an Egyptian occupation, which was replaced in 1840 by reimposition of direct Ottoman rule. Once again, the Sharifs of Makkah regained their importance. In 1916, with **British** encouragement, Sharif **Husayn bin 'Ali al-Hashimi** declared his independence of Istanbul and named himself King of al-Hijaz. But his kingdom was increasingly threatened by the revival of **Al Sa'ud** power in Najd. In 1924, the Saudis captured al-Ta'if and Makkah, followed by al-Madinah and Jiddah in 1925. In early January 1926, **'Abd al-'Aziz bin 'Abd al-Rahman Al Sa'ud** was proclaimed King of al-Hijaz in addition to his title of Sultan of Najd. Despite its long history, al-Hijaz served as the name of an independent state for only the eight years of 1916-1924.

HIJR, AL-. *See* MADA'IN SALIH.

HIJRAH. [hijrah; هجرة; sometimes spelled hegira] Literally meaning migration, the term specifically refers to the move in September A.D. 622 of the Prophet **Muhammad** with a small group of early Muslims from hostile **Makkah** to Yathrib (later **al-Madinah**), where they were invited to settle. Since it resulted in the first Islamic state, the Islamic calendar begins with this event. The abbreviation A.H. (Anno Hegirae) is used to distinguish Islamic dates from the Christian calendar. The term can also mean place or settlement and hijrah [pl. hijrāt; هجرات] is used for a settlement established in the early 20th century for **badu** (bedouin) who had become **Ikhwan**.

HIMYAR, HIMYARITIC. *See* SOUTH ARABIAN CIVILIZATIONS.

HINA, AL-. [al-ḥinā; الحنا; 48 50 - 26 56] Site near **al-Jubayl** on the **Gulf** of a substantial settlement of the **Seleucid** period, rivaling in size that of **Thaj**

(which lies nine miles to the southwest). The location was reutilized for the settlement of the **badu** by the early Saudi government.

HITHLAYN, AL-. [al-ḥithlayn; الحثلين] The paramount **shaykhs** of the **'Ajman** tribe of **Najd** and eastern Arabia. Although the 'Ajman had opposed Saudi rule since the occupation of **al-Ahsa'** in 1913, Shaykh Daydan al-Hithlayn (or Bin Hithlayn) had been persuaded by Saudi Imam **'Abd al-'Aziz bin 'Abd al-Rahman** not to join the rebellious **Ikhwan** at the Battle of **Sibilah** in March 1929. However, he was killed by the son of the Saudi governor of al-Ahsa' in May 1929 despite a safe conduct, thus provoking the 'Ajman to rise up once again.

HOGARTH, DAVID GEORGE. (1862-1927) An Oxford archaeologist and Orientalist, instrumental in the Arab Bureau in Cairo in encouraging the Arab Revolt during the First World War, and in introducing **T. E. Lawrence** to the Middle East. Among his books are the *Penetration of Arabia: A Record of the Development of Western Knowledge Concerning the Arabian Peninsula* (1904) and *Hejaz Before World War I: A Handbook* (1917).

HOLMES, FRANK. [Major] A New Zealand mining engineer and businessman who appeared at **al-'Uqayr** border conference between **Iraq** and Saudi Arabia in 1922 and a few months later in 1923 persuaded **Al Sa'ud Imam 'Abd al-'Aziz bin 'Abd al-Rahman** to sign the first Saudi **oil** concession with **Eastern and General Syndicate**, which Holmes represented, in return for payment of £2,000 a year. However, as Eastern and General was unable to survey the concession area properly or to resell it to an oil company and so defaulted on its rent payments, Imam 'Abd al-'Aziz revoked the concession in 1928. Fortunately for Holmes, he had managed to secure a similar concession for **Bahrain**, which he was able to resell to SOCAL (Standard Oil of California) who discovered oil there in 1932.

HUFUF, AL-. [al-hufūf; الهفوف; the older form is al-Hufhūf; الهفهوف; 49 34 -25 22] The principal town of the extensive **al-Ahsa'** oasis in the **Eastern Province**. Most of its population of nearly 100,000 has become homogenized over the centuries and is not organized into tribes. As many as 40 percent of the inhabitants are **Shi'ah**. Al-Hufuf was the residence of the **Ottoman** governor of al-Ahsa' during 1871-1913 and then it served as the capital of the Eastern Province until 1952. There are several old buildings in the town: al-Jabri [al-jabrī; الجبري] mosque, dated about A.D. 1450, and Qasr Ibrahim [qaṣr ibrāhīm; قصر ابراهيم], originally dating from A.D. 1558 and subsequently used as an Ottoman fort. Another palace, Qasr Khazzam [qaṣr khazzām; قصر خزام] was built about A.D. 1800 and also was used as an Ottoman fort.

HUJAYLAN, FAYSAL BIN 'ABD AL-'AZIZ AL-. (1929-) [al-ḥujaylān; فيصل بن عبدالعزيز الحجيلان] A Saudi diplomat educated in Cairo. He was appointed as a royal adviser to King **Sa'ud** in 1961 but the King was forced by Prince **Talal** to send him abroad as ambassador. Subsequent ambassadorial posts included Venezuela and Argentina, Denmark, the United Kingdom, and the United States. He became Minister of Health in the early 1980s but was dropped from the cabinet in 1995.

HUJAYLAN, JAMIL BIN IBRAHIM AL-. [جميل بن ابراهيم الحجيلان] A Saudi government official who received his law degree from Cairo University in 1950 and became the country's first Minister of Information in 1963. He subsequently served as Minister of Health until appointed as ambassador to **France** in 1976. In 1995, he was appointed Secretary-General of the **Gulf Cooperation Council**, and held the position until 2002.

HUMAYD, 'UTHMAN AL-. (c. 1923-) [عثمان الحميد] A long-serving officer of the Royal Saudi Army, with service dating back to the 1940s. General al-Humayd was Chief of the General Staff before being named Assistant Minister for Military Affairs in the Ministry of Defense and Aviation about 1981.

HURGRONJE, C. (CHRISTIAAN) SNOUCK. (1857-1936) A Dutch Orientalist whose thesis for Leiden University was on the **hajj** (pilgrimage to **Makkah**) and whose career began as an instructor at an institute for Dutch East Indies colonial administrators. He spent much of 1885 carrying out research in Makkah, which was incorporated into his exhaustive two-volume work, published in German in 1888-1889 and translated as *Mekka in the Latter Part of the Nineteenth Century* (1931). This was followed by another period at the colonial institute and work in the Dutch East Indies (1889-1906) before becoming professor at Leiden University until his death.

HUSAYN BIN 'ALI AL-HASHIMI. (1852-1931) [حسين بن علي الهاشمي] Sharif of **Makkah** (r. 1908-1916) and King of **al-Hijaz** (r. 1916-1924). Grandson of the first **al-Hashimi sharif** from the 'Abadilah clan, Husayn was regarded as a threat by his uncle 'Awn al-Rafiq, the Sharif of Makkah (r. 1882-1905), and so was sent to Istanbul in the early 1890s. Three years after 'Awn al-Rafiq's death, a compromise choice between rival Hashimi clans saw Husayn become Sharif of Makkah. At first an **Ottoman** ally, as shown by his action in support of Istanbul against the **Idrisi** ruler of **'Asir**, Husayn later established common cause with the **British** against Istanbul. On 5 June 1916, he announced the "Arab Revolt" and made himself the independent King of al-Hijaz (expanding his title in November 1916 to "King of the Arabs"). Within a few months, he had captured all the major cities of al-Hijaz and only **al-Madinah** eluded him (its garrison did not surrender until the end of the war). But Husayn's ambitions were rivalled by Imam **'Abd al-'Aziz bin 'Abd al-Rahman** and the nascent **Al Sa'ud** state in **Najd**. The two men had clashed in 1910 when Husayn had sent an army to wrest **al-Qasim** (central Najd) from the Al Sa'ud but failed. While the British restrained both sides from fighting each other during the First World War, 'Abd al-'Aziz responded afterwards by capturing the strategic oasis of **al-Khurmah** in about 1919. British pressure kept the two rulers apart during the early 1920s but Husayn's weakness invited 'Abd al-'Aziz to return to the attack. Husayn was forced to abdicate in favor of his son **'Ali** after the fall of **al-Ta'if** and Makkah to

Saudi forces in 1924. He remained in exile in Cyprus until permitted to spend his last few days in 'Amman with another son **'Abdullah**, the King of Transjordan (r. 1920-1951), where he died on 4 July 1931. Another son **Faysal** served briefly as King of Syria (r. 1920) and then as King of Iraq (r. 1921-1933).

HUSAYNI, JAMAL AL-. (1894-?) [جمال الحسيني] Born to a prominent Palestinian family, he was active in Arab and anti-British politics until arriving in Riyadh in 1950, where he was appointed a royal counsellor to King **'Abd al-'Aziz**. He apparently had left the kingdom for Damascus before the end of King **Sa'ud**'s reign (r. 1953-1964).

HUWAYTAT, AL-. [al-huwaytāt; sing. huwaytī; الحويطات؛ حويطي] One of the biggest tribes of **al-Hijaz**, stretching from **Tayma'** in the south to the Saudi border with **Jordan**, and inland from the **Red Sea** to deep into **al-Nafud** desert. The Huwaytat are prominent throughout the southern half of Jordan and branches are also located in the Sinai Peninsula and elsewhere in Egypt. They claim to be descendants of the Prophet but there is some speculation that they are descended from the ancient **Nabataeans**.

- I -

IBN. *See* BIN.

IBRAHIM, WALID AL-. Saudi businessman and a principal owner of the Middle East Broadcasting Corporation, which he cofounded with **Salih Kamil**. He studied business in Oregon and is the brother of one of King **Fahd**'s wives (the mother of **'Abd al-'Aziz bin Fahd**).

'ID. ['īd; عيد; sometimes spelled eid] The Arabic word for feast or festival. The most important feast in Islam is 'Id al-Adha (or 'Id al-Kabir, the "big feast"), which falls on the 10th of Dhu al-Hijjah. It marks the culmination of the **hajj** or pilgrimage, and commemorates the near-sacrifice by Ibrahim (Abraham) of his son Isma'il (Ishmael). Next in importance is 'Id al-Fitr (or 'Id al-Saghir, the "little feast"), which marks the breaking of the fast after **Ramadan**.

IDRISI, AL-. [al-idrīsī; الادريسي] A short-lived dynasty at the beginning of the 20th century in the southern province of **'Asir**. Ahmad al-Idrisi, a descendant of Idris bin 'Abdullah, the founder of an independent state in North Africa during the eighth century A.D., left Fez in Morocco for **Makkah** in the early 19th century, where he became a religious teacher. About 1830, he moved to Sabya on the **Tihamah** coast of 'Asir (about 20 miles inland from **Jizan**), where he died a few years later. His great-grandson, Muhammad bin 'Ali, was able to supplant the Sharifs of **Abu 'Arish** as the ruler of the coastal plain of Tihamat 'Asir in about 1900. A few years later, he made an abortive attack on the **Ottomans** at their capital in highland **Abha**. Originally allied with Italy, Muhammad accepted British assistance in fighting the Ottomans during the First World War in return for recognition as an independent ruler. On his death in 1923, Muhammad was succeeded by his son 'Ali, who faced dissent within his family and lost al-Hudaydah on the Yemeni Tihamah to the **Imam** of Yemen. In 1926, he was overthrown by his uncle and Muhammad's brother Hasan. But in the same year, Hasan was forced to recognize the suzerainty of '**Abd al-'Aziz bin 'Abd al-Rahman Al Sa'ud** and in 1931 'Asir was effectively annexed. An Idrisi rebellion the following year was unsuccessful. The Sanusi dynasty of Libya was founded by a disciple of Ahmad al-Idrisi and the two families were closely connected through intermarriage.

'**IFFAT BINT AHMAD AL THUNAYAN.** [عفة بنت احمد آل ثنيان] Wife of King **Faysal bin 'Abd al-'Aziz** and mother of **Sa'ud al-Faysal** (Minister of Foreign Affairs) and **Turki al-Faysal** (Head of Saudi Intelligence). From Istanbul, her father was from the **Al Thunayan** branch of **Al Sa'ud**, which had gone into exile early in the 19th century, and her mother was Turkish. **Kamal Adham** was a half brother. The appellation of "Queen" during the period of King Faysal's reign was purely unofficial.

IJMA'. [ijmā'; اجماع] The principle of consensus in **shari'ah** (Islamic law). It is based on the **hadith** (the saying of the Prophet **Muhammad**) that "my people will never agree on an error." Where the established sources of Islamic doctrine (the **Qur'an** [Koran] and the **Sunnah**) do not cover a particular question of law, a consensus, or majority, of the **'ulama'** (religious scholars) can produce a legitimate decision.

IKHWAN. [ikhwān; اخوان; from sing. akh, اخ, "brother"; thus literally, "the Brotherhood"] The Ikhwan movement of the first few decades of the 20th century resulted from the encouragement given by the Al Sa'ud Imam (later King) '**Abd al-'Aziz** of an **Islamic** revival, with emphasis on **Wahhabi** tenets, among the **badu** (bedouin). Tied to this was an active policy of sedentarization in order to bring the badu more closely under his control. By 1920, the Ikhwan ranks comprised an estimated 150,000 fighting men in more than 200 settlements. They provided the Saudi leader with an extremely mobile, tough and dedicated striking force. The military skills of the Ikhwan and the fear they inspired in their opponents were important elements in 'Abd al-'Aziz's capture of '**Asir** in 1920, Ha'il in 1921, **al-Jawf** in 1922, and al-Hijaz in 1924-1925.

But the same religious fervor responsible for their creation ultimately made the Ikhwan uncontrollable. The political necessity incumbent on a head of state to accept compromise, *e.g.* in the matter of boundaries with the British-influenced Arab states to the north, was denounced by Ikhwan leaders such as **Faysal al-Duwish** of the **Mutayr** tribe and **Sultan bin Bijad** of the '**Utaybah**. As a consequence, they led attacks during 1920-1922, probably without the approval of 'Abd al-'Aziz, on **Kuwait**, **Iraq**, and even up to the outskirts of 'Amman, where they were routed by British airplanes and armored cars. 'Abd al-'Aziz's failure to give the Ikhwan leaders key positions in newly conquered al-Hijaz led to a convening of the tribes in

1926, resulting in the drawing up of a list of grievances against the **imam** and a resolve to oppose him.

An Ikhwan raid against an Iraqi policy post in 1927 and resultant massacre brought British wrath against 'Abd al-'Aziz and forced him to move against his former subordinates. As a consequence, the Ikhwan directly confronted 'Abd al-'Aziz in battle in 1928. Their defeat at the Battle of **Sibilah** (1929) permanently broke the power of the Ikhwan but it was not until January 1930, when 'Abd al-'Aziz led warriors in the field for the last time and won, that they were finally subdued. Trapped between 'Abd al-'Aziz and the British in Iraq and Kuwait, the rebel leaders were forced to surrender to the British. Turned over to the Saudi leader, they spent the remainder of their days in a **Riyadh** prison.

IMAM. [imām; pl. a'immah; ائمة؛امام] An Arabic word meaning leader, originally applied only to the one who leads the prayers required by **Islam** five times daily (the noun derives from the preposition *imama*, "in front of"). Later, it acquired a second meaning of a religious leader who also heads an Islamic state. Until recently, **Yemen** and **Oman** boasted imamates or states headed by imams. The title of imam was used by the **Al Sa'ud** until the time of '**Abd al-'Aziz bin 'Abd al-Rahman** (r. 1902-1953), who styled himself Sultan of Najd and King of al-Hijaz from 1926 and then King of Saudi Arabia from 1932. (Use of the title Imam before a name in this dictionary indicates that the individual was one of the leaders of the Al Sa'ud state.)

IMAM MUHAMMAD BIN SA'UD UNIVERSITY. Established in **Riyadh** in 1953 as an institute for **shari'ah** (Islamic law) and Islamic studies, it became a university in 1974 and specializes in training **'ulama'** (religious scholars), Islamic preachers, *shari'ah* judges, and schoolteachers in the subjects of Arabic and Islam. It is the best known and by far the largest of the kingdom's three "Islamic" universities. Its branch in the southern province of 'Asir was absorbed by the new **King Khalid University**.

IMARAH. [imārah, pl. imārāt; امارات؛امارة] The territory governed by an **amir**. The word designates a province in Saudi Arabia but is used elsewhere in the **Gulf** to refer to independent states. *See* GOVERNMENT.

INDIA AND SAUDI ARABIA. Relations between Saudi Arabia and India have never been very close. In part, this was due to Cold War alliances when **Riyadh** was close to the **United States** and India was supported by the **Soviet Union**. More importantly, Saudi Arabia has always been close to **Pakistan** which has warred and feuded with India since the two countries became independent in 1947. Still, India is one of the kingdom's major trading partners, ranking fifth in imports from Saudi Arabia and 10th in exports to the kingdom in 2000. The **Saudi Fund for Development** provided India with $175 million in loans during the period 1975-2001.

INDUSTRY. The most important industry is the production of crude **oil** and **natural gas**, which still constitutes over 50 percent of gross domestic product

(GDP) and provides nearly 70 percent of government revenues. Oil and gas exploitation is entirely operated by the government. However, the kingdom has invested heavily since the 1970s in industrial development in order to diversify the economy away from oil and to provide employment for its burgeoning population. At the same time, traditional industries such as weaving, handicrafts, agriculture, and pastoralism have declined rapidly in importance.

Most industrial development in the private sector has been in the field of import substitution, as a consequence of the development of the country's major companies from family-owned import or construction firms. In 1999, the largest non-oil sector was construction, followed by trade. Therefore, the state was forced to take a leading role in identifying, creating, and developing most new industries. The creation of the **Saudi Arabian Basic Industries Corporation** (SABIC) in 1976 marked a major step in creating new petrochemical and steel industries, particularly in the massive new industrial cities of **al-Jubayl** and **Yanbu'**. All of SABIC's equity in these industries was eventually sold to the Saudi public. While encouraging the expansion of manufacturing companies and light industrial workshops, the government has placed emphasis on high-technology industries which will require fewer expatriate workers.

Chronic budgetary problems, the impetus of economic diversification, and Saudi Arabia's application for membership in the World Trade Organization (WTO) have driven the kingdom's recent decision to seek foreign investment in the country. The economic need for foreign investment, as well as repatriation of capital held abroad by Saudi citizens (estimated at $400-$800 billion), was announced by Heir Apparent **'Abdullah bin 'Abd al-'Aziz** in an interview with the Saudi papers *'Ukaz* and *Saudi Gazette* in 1998 and formed a major goal in his subsequent tour of Asia, Europe, and the United States. The General Investment Authority (GIA) was created in 2000 to manage and encourage this investment and new legislation in 2001 promised to cut red tape, permitted full foreign ownership of projects and reduced the profits tax rate on foreign-owned operations; and foreign ownership of real estate property was thought to be under consideration. Plans were under way in the early 2000s for the participation of a number of major international energy companies in Saudi upstream natural gas exploration. In April 2002, a GIA statement said that it had granted foreign investors a total of 784 licenses for projects worth $10.2 billion, with more than half of these solely owned by foreign investors.

IPSA-1 AND IPSA-2. *See* PIPELINES.

IRAN AND SAUDI ARABIA. Iranian-Arab relations in the **Gulf** traditionally have been characterized by mutual suspicion and animosity, despite the mixture of the two races along all Gulf littorals. Iranians have tended to look down on Arabs as little more than rustics, and Arabs regard Iranians as arrogant and rude. Furthermore, the Arab side of the Gulf instinctively fears Iranian hegemony, as realized by various invasions in both the distant and relatively recent past and indicated by the massive military buildup under

Shah Muhammad Reza Pahlavi (r. 1941-1979). Animosity is also stoked by religious differences, as most Iranians are **Shi'ah** and the great majority of Saudis are **Sunni**.

The Iranian revolution of 1979 exacerbated existing tensions and added new ones. As had happened with the Iraqi revolution in 1958, the revolutionary fervor of the new régime in Tehran threatened existing governments in the Gulf, especially the monarchies. In addition, Iran's message of Islamic revolution posed a direct challenge to Saudi Arabia because of the latter's role as protector of the Holy Places of **Islam**. The Islamic Republic of Iran directed its subversive activities at the indigenous Shi'ah populations of the Arab littoral and undoubtedly contributed to the demonstrations in Saudi Arabia's **al-Qatif** oasis in 1979-1980.

In response, Riyadh heavily backed **Iraq** during the 1980-1988 Iran-Iraq War. Iran continued and even intensified its provocative behavior against Saudi Arabia as the war wound on: shipping to and from Saudi Gulf ports was interfered with, an Iranian F-4 Phantom was intercepted over Saudi airspace and shot down in 1984, and Saudi-bound oil tankers were attacked with Exocet missiles. The culmination of these hostilities came during the 1987 **hajj** (Islamic pilgrimage to **Makkah**), when an Iranian political demonstration on 31 July 1987 erupted out of control. In the ensuing mêlée, over 400 people, the majority of them Iranians, were killed and more than 600 injured. Mobs occupied the Saudi and **Kuwaiti** embassies in Tehran and a Saudi diplomat died of injuries suffered.

This affair was followed by an intensified war of words and further incidents. In October 1987, an Iranian speedboat attack on a Saudi offshore oil field was thwarted, and, in April 1988, Saudi Arabia cut off diplomatic relations after an increase in Iranian attacks on its oil tankers. Iran charged that this was a pretext for preventing Iranian pilgrims from making the hajj and, rejecting Saudi demands that the size of the Iranian delegation be reduced in the same proportion as other countries' delegations, Iran announced a boycott of the hajj. During the 1989 hajj, three bombs were exploded and Saudi Arabia subsequently beheaded 16 Kuwaiti Shi'ah who were allegedly supplied with explosives by the Iranian Embassy in Kuwait. Shortly afterwards, Islamic Jihad took credit for assassinating the sole Saudi diplomat in Beirut. Several other Saudi diplomats were killed during this period, amid indications that Iran was responsible.

The extreme hostility shown by the Iranian régime toward the kingdom, as well as toward much of the world in general, moderated somewhat following the death of Ayatollah Khomeini and indirect contacts between Riyadh and Iranian President Rafsanjani were made through several **Gulf Cooperation Council** (GCC) states. These did not bear fruit, however, until after the **Iraqi** invasion of **Kuwait** in 1990. While condemning the presence of foreign military forces in the Gulf, Tehran kept a strict neutrality during the ensuing war against Iraq and Saudi-Iranian diplomatic relations were reestablished on 26 March 1991. In June 1991, Saudi Foreign Minister **Sa'ud al-Faysal** became the first senior Saudi official to visit Tehran since the 1979 revolution. As part of the rapprochement, agreement was reached on a return to Iranian participation in the hajj, and the 1991 and 1992 hajjs passed without incident.

However, low-key tensions resurfaced during the period between 1993 and 1996 over the number of Iranians allowed to proceed on hajj, differences in oil strategy, Saudi backing for the **United Arab Emirates**' claim to three islands in the Gulf disputed with Iran, and accusations of Iranian involvement in a 1995 bombing at the US Military Training Mission in **Riyadh** and the 1996 bombing of an American air force residence at **al-Khubar**.

But relations began to improve in 1997 when Iranian Foreign Minister 'Ali Akbar Velayati visited Saudi Arabia for the first time in four years, Iran Air began its first flights to the kingdom since 1979, and Heir Apparent **'Abdullah bin 'Abd al-'Aziz** held talks with new Iranian President Muhammad Khatami in December during the **Organization of the Islamic Conference** (OIC) summit in Tehran. In early 1998, Khatami's predecessor, Akbar Hashemi Rafsanjani, became the highest ranking official of the Islamic Republic of Iran to visit the kingdom and an Iranian warship put into **Jiddah** for the first time since the 1979 revolution.

The following years witnessed an increasing exchange of bilateral visits by senior officials and agreements for cooperation on **oil**, industry, culture, and sports, despite continuing disputes over Iranian protests during the hajj. The 2001 signing in Tehran of a mutual security agreement to combat crime, drug trafficking, and illegal immigration by Prince **Nayif bin 'Abd al-'Aziz**, the Saudi Minister of the Interior, and his Iranian counterpart put a positive stamp on the rapprochement.

IRAQ AND SAUDI ARABIA. Ties between the two geographical regions now comprising Iraq and Saudi Arabia are ancient. In the seventh century A.D., the Islamic armies poured out of **al-Hijaz** into Iraq and beyond into Iran. Little more than a century later, the 'Abbasid dynasty was established in Baghdad, although its sway over Arabia was minimal. Still, routes for the Islamic pilgrimage (**hajj**) crossed Arabia from Iraq to **Makkah** and the Iraqi city of Basra traded with **Najd**, especially the entrepôts of **Buraydah** and **'Unayzah**. The **Shi'ah** of the **Eastern Province** still maintain ties with their fellow sectarians of southern Iraq and make pilgrimages to the Shi'ah holy cities of Najaf and Karbala, now in Iraq. In the days before oil, a number of Saudi families settled, for either economic or political reasons, in the Iraqi town of al-Zubayr.

The modern state of Iraq was created by the British, who installed **Faysal bin Husayn al-Hashimi** as its first king (r. 1921-1933), just as they installed another of the Sharif of Makkah's sons as the King of Transjordan. Efforts to define a boundary between Iraq and the Saudi state in the 1920s (such as the Treaty of **al-'Uqayr** in 1922) were hampered by the animosity between the **Al Sa'ud** and the Hashimi family as a result of the Saudi advances on the Hashimi Kingdom of al-Hijaz, as well as by ferocious and frequent raids into Iraq by the **Ikhwan**, **Wahhabi** tribesmen imbued with religious fervor. With the development of the "Arab cold war" of the 1950s, the monarchies of Saudi Arabia and Iraq drew closer together for protection against the attacks of the radical republics, but the connection was abruptly shattered by the Iraqi revolution of 1958 in which many royal family members were killed.

For nearly two decades, increasingly radical régimes in Baghdad verbally assaulted Saudi Arabia and its smaller **Gulf** neighbors and supported subversive activities against them. But with the **Iranian** revolution of 1979, Baghdad and Riyadh once again drew closer because of a common enemy. Agreement was reached in 1980 to divide equally the diamond-shaped **Neutral Zone** between the two countries, created by the 1920s border treaties and regularized in 1939. During the Iran-Iraq War (1980-1988), Saudi Arabia provided billions of dollars for the Iraqi war chest and brokered the resumption of diplomatic relations between Iraq and the **United States** (broken off during the June 1967 Arab-Israeli War). The income from **oil** production in the Saudi-Kuwaiti Neutral Zone was handed over to Baghdad and Iraq was permitted to build two oil **pipelines** across Saudi Arabia to the **Red Sea**, to make up for the loss of its oil port at al-Faw and the closure of the pipeline across Syria.

All this went by the boards when President Saddam Husayn of Iraq invaded **Kuwait** on 2 August 1990 and appeared to be poised to enter Saudi Arabia. In response, the Saudi government sought the military protection of the United States, and then invited the US and other Western and Arab countries to use the kingdom as a platform for the liberation of Kuwait, which was accomplished in late February 1991. *See also* DESERT STORM, OPERATION.

The following decade was marked by Saudi cooperation in the sanctions régime against Iraq, including allowing American, British, and—for a time—French combat aircraft employed in the enforcement of the southern no-fly zone in Iraq to be based in the kingdom. This cooperation was maintained into the 2000s even though much of the Saudi public came to oppose the sanctions régime because of its negative impact on the Iraqi population. Although the Saudi government still remained staunchly opposed to Saddam Husayn, it also warned it would not support American ideas of attacking Iraq (which seemed to grow stronger after the events of 11 September 2001) in order to remove the Iraqi leader. There were also scattered incidents along the Saudi-Iraqi border throughout this period and two Saudis hijacked a **Saudi Arabian Airlines** jet to Baghdad in 2000. Although minor border confrontations and Saudi opposition to the régime in Baghdad continued into the 2000s, there were some steps toward better relations. Heir Apparent **'Abdullah bin 'Abd al-'Aziz** embraced the head of the Iraqi delegation at the March 2002 Arab summit, the first visit to Saudi Arabia by an Iraqi minister since the Kuwait War occurred in May 2002 (to attend an Arab meeting), and the two countries reached agreement on opening the border post at **'Ar'ar** in June 2002.

ISLAM. [islām; اسلام]. Literally meaning "surrender," and deriving from the same root as *salam* (peace or salvation), Islam is the name of the religion revealed to the Prophet **Muhammad** in western Arabia in the early seventh century A.D. All the prophets of Judaism are found in Islam, as is Jesus Christ (although he is not regarded as divine). During Muhammad's lifetime, the entire **Arabian Peninsula** became converted to Islam and in the succeeding centuries, the sway of Islam was extended to the rest of the Middle East and beyond to Central Asia in the north, China and Southeast Asia in the east, eastern Africa in the south, and Europe in the west. There are over 1 billion Muslims throughout the world today. One who believes in Islam is a **Muslim**, and one becomes a Muslim by publicly affirming one's belief in Islam and adhering to the "Five Pillars," or fundamental requirements, of Islam: ① *shahadah*, the affirmation that there is no god but God (Allah) and that Muhammad is the Messenger of God; ② *salat*, the five daily prayers at fixed times; ③ *zakat*, the giving of alms to the poor; ④ *sawm*, fasting during the Islamic month of **Ramadan**; and ⑤ *hajj*, the pilgrimage to **Makkah** during the month of Dhu al-Hijjah. Over the centuries, a comprehensive legal system known as the **shari'ah** has been developed within Islam. The two principal sects of Islam are the **Sunni** and the **Shi'ah**. The holiest sites in Islam are located in Makkah, **al-Madinah** (where Muhammad is buried), and Jerusalem [al-Quds in Arabic; القدس].

ISLAMIC RADICALISM. *See* OPPOSITION GROUPS.

ISLAMIC UNIVERSITY. Founded in **al-Madinah** in 1961 as a small international institute of Islamic theology on the model of the famous al-Azhar University of Cairo. By regulation, the majority of its students are non-Saudi citizens.

ISRAEL AND SAUDI ARABIA. *See* ARAB-ISRAELI CONFLICT AND SAUDI ARABIA.

- J -

JABAL. [jabal; pl. jibāl; جبل؛ جبال] Arabic for hill or mountain.

JABRIN. [jabrīn; جبرين] An oasis 150 miles south of **al-Ahsa'**, near the northern edge of **al-Rub' al-Khali** desert. The majority of its inhabitants are from the **Al Murrah** tribe, although there are ruins dating from at least the 12th century A.D. The first Western visitor was R. E. Cheesman in 1923-1924.

JAHILIYAH, AL-. [al-jāhilīyah; الجاهلية] The age of "ignorance," *i.e.* the period immediately before the rise of **Islam**.

JAMMAMIL. [jammāmīl; sing. jammāl; جماميل؛ جمال] The organizers of camel caravans to carry out long-distance trade, not only within regions of Saudi Arabia, but also between regions (*e.g.* **Najd** and **al-Hijaz**) and to entrepôts elsewhere, such as **Kuwait, Iraq**, and Syria. The name derives from camel [jamal in Arabic].

JARASH. [jarash; جرش; 43 00 - 18 00 approx.] Ruins of a substantial pre-Islamic settlement between **Najran** and **Abha** in southwestern Saudi Arabia. The site was contemporaneous with the flourishing of Najran. A nearby outcrop contains South Arabian inscriptions and rock drawings. It should not be confused with the ruins of the Roman city with the same name in northern Jordan.

JAWAN. *See* RA'S TANURAH.

JAWF, AL-. [al-jawf; الجوف; 39 50 - 29 48] A town and province of north central Saudi Arabia at the southern end of the **Wadi Sirhan**. It is the site of one of the earliest recorded settlements in north Arabia (mid-to-late second millennium B.C.), known in ancient times as Dumat al-Jandal, or the Dumah mentioned in the Old Testament. Its favorable location in the Wadi Sirhan caused it to expand considerably during the first millennium B.C. as a trading center between the South Arabian civilizations and those of the Levant and Mesopotamia. Eventually it was able to dominate all of central and northern Arabia as the first known independent Arabian state. Dumat al-Jandal was later incorporated into the **Nabataean** kingdom. The most important ruins in the area are: Qasr Marid [qasr mārid; قصر مارد; also known as Qasr al-Ukaydir], a fortress originally dating to the third century B.C. but rebuilt many times; the ancient stone mosque of 'Umar, with foundations believed to date to the reign of the Caliph 'Umar (A.D. 634-644); and inscribed stones in **Minaean**, one of the old South Arabian languages.

First conquered by the **Al Sa'ud** in 1794, al-Jawf fell under the sway of the **Al Rashid** of **Ha'il** during the latter half of the 19th century. Captured by Nuri al-Sha'lan of the **Ruwala** tribe in 1909, the district was fought over by arch rivals Ruwala and **Shammar** (to which the Al Rashid belong) until captured in 1922 in the name of the Al Sa'ud by the **Ikhwan**. The town of al-Jawf, an important market center in the past for the surrounding **badu** tribes, has been eclipsed in importance by **Sakaka**, the new capital of the province. The name al-Jawf is derived from an Arabic geographical term for a concave plain or bowl; similar areas in Yemen and Oman are also named al-Jawf; the term jaww may also be used for jawf.

JEBEL. *See* JABAL.

JEDDA. *See* JIDDAH.

JIDDAH. [jiddah; جدة; also spelled Jedda or, classically, Juddah; 39 12 -21 29] The second largest city of Saudi Arabia, with a population estimated at one-and-a-half million, and the largest city of **al-Hijaz**. Traditionally, an important trading center on the **Red Sea**, Jiddah is regarded as the most cosmopolitan of Saudi Arabia's cities, not least because of the centuries-old immigration of **Muslims** from around the world: many of its citizens are of Bukhari, Yemeni, and Hadrami descent, as well as from the indigenous **Harb** tribe. Its history dates from pre-Islamic times but its prosperity began when chosen by the Caliph 'Uthman, an early successor to the Prophet **Muhammad**, to replace al-Shu'aybah as the port of the Islamic capital of **Makkah**, 45 miles inland. Having fallen under the sway of the Egyptian Mamluk dynasty, it was attacked unsuccessfully by the Portuguese in 1541. The diversion of transit trade away from the Red Sea in the 17th century caused it to decline

and it was occupied by the **Wahhabi** forces of the **Al Sa'ud** in the early
19th century. Muhammad 'Ali of **Egypt** restored it to nominal **Ottoman**
authority in 1811 and Istanbul took direct control in 1840. It was bombarded
by a British naval vessel in 1858 after a massacre of Christians.

Jiddah was the first city of al-Hijaz to be liberated by Sharif **Husayn
bin 'Ali al-Hashimi** after he declared the "Arab Revolt" against the Turks
in 1916. It was also the last city in the Hashimi Kingdom of al-Hijaz to resist
the Al Sa'ud, finally surrendering after a long siege in 1925. Two years later,
the British signed the Treaty of Jiddah, recognizing for the first time the
absolute independence of the Saudi state. The city walls, erected in 1511
as protection against the Portuguese, were demolished in 1946-1947. Jiddah
has retained its importance during the Al Sa'ud era and the **oil** boom due
to its role as the commercial and **banking** center of the country, the
development of Saudi Arabia's largest port, the Islamic Port of Jiddah, and
the expansion of King 'Abd al-'Aziz Airport, through which most of the
pilgrims pass during the annual **hajj** (pilgrimage).

JILUWI, AL. [āl jiluwī; آل جلوي] A cadet branch of the **Al Sa'ud** royal family,
descended from Jiluwi bin Turki bin 'Abdullah, a brother of **Faysal bin
Turki** (great-grandfather of present King **Fahd**). Members of the Al Jiluwi
have been prominent in service to the Saudi leaders as governors of various
localities and provinces. The only governors the Eastern Province knew
from 1913 until 1985 were 'Abdullah bin Jiluwi (until his death in 1941),
frequently known as Bin Jiluwi, his son Sa'ud (until his death in 1968), and
another son 'Abd al-Muhsin (replaced by King Fahd's son **Muhammad**
in 1985).

JINNA ISLAND. [jinnā; جنا; 49 53 - 2722] An island in the **Gulf**, east of **al-
Jubayl** and north of **al-Qatif**. It contains the remains of prehistoric and third
millennium B.C. settlements, as well as a 19th-century fort.

JIZAN. [jīzān; جيزان; also spelled Jayzan, Gizan, or, classically, Jāzān; جازان;
42 32 - 16 54] A port and capital of the province of the same name along
the **Red Sea** coast of southern Saudi Arabia. Pearling and salt mining were
important in earlier times, and the Wadi Jizan has agricultural potential.
The region, also known as al-Mikhlaf or Tihamat 'Asir, came under **Ottoman**
control in the 16th century and then under the influence of the Zaydi rulers
of **Yemen** until the indigenous Khayrat family made it independent in the
18th century. In the 19th and early 20th centuries, the **Al Sa'ud**, the
Egyptians, the Ottomans, the Khayrat family, and the **Idrisi** family all held
the area successively until it was incorporated into the Saudi realm in the
1920s. The capital, for the first time, was moved to Jizan town from **Abu
'Arish**.

JORDAN AND SAUDI ARABIA. Saudi Arabia has always been ambivalent
in its policy toward Jordan, ever since Transjordan was created in 1920 for
'Abdullah bin Husayn al-Hashimi. 'Abdullah's family, the Hawashim,
had been the titular leaders of **Makkah** for a thousand years but in the 20th

century they had also become deadly rivals of the **Al Sa'ud** for control of Arabia. Although Saudi leader **'Abd al-'Aziz bin 'Abd al-Rahman** was able to conquer Makkah and the Hashimi Kingdom of **al-Hijaz** by 1926, the **British** placement of Hashimis on the thrones of Transjordan and Iraq frustrated Saudi expansion in the north. In the first half of the 1920s, this frustration showed in raids by the **Ikhwan**, 'Abd al-'Aziz's tribal warriors, across the Transjordanian frontier. By the Haddah Agreement of 1925, 'Abd al-'Aziz accepted the inclusion of al-'Aqabah and Ma'an in Transjordan and in return received most of the important **Wadi Sirhan**.

By the 1950s, relations between the two countries had gradually improved. At the end of the Palestinian mandate, King 'Abdullah absorbed Jerusalem and the West Bank into his territories and changed the name of his country from Transjordan to Jordan. **Riyadh** realized that a viable Jordan was in its interest, first as a buffer against Israel and then as a fellow monarchy in a sea of increasingly hostile radical Arab republics. With the **Iraqi** revolution of 1958, Jordan became the last Hashimi kingdom. Following the disastrous June 1967 **Arab-Israeli War**, in which Jordan lost Jerusalem and the West Bank to Israel, Saudi Arabia joined fellow Arab **oil** states in accepting responsibility for subsidies to Jordan and other "frontline" states. In 1992, the total amount given to Jordan was stated by the Saudi government to have been in excess of $6.5 billion.

The two countries' affinity was also aided by their shared closeness to the **United States** and the West. At the same time, however, Jordan's geographical position, bordering Israel, Syria, and **Iraq**, as well as its heavily Palestinian population, placed the Hashimi kingdom directly within the maelstrom of Arab politics. Inevitably, its foreign policy became less conservative than that of Riyadh and this caused some friction. Jordan became a close ally of Iraq during its war with **Iran** (1980-1988), receiving oil and financial aid in return for providing a corridor for Iraqi supplies from the **Red Sea** port of al-'Aqabah.

When Iraq invaded **Kuwait** in August 1990, Jordan's King Husayn (grandson of 'Abdullah bin Husayn) was caught in the middle. Unable to denounce the invasion, King Husayn suffered the wrath of Saudi Arabia, which cut off its financial aid and oil supplies, and expelled most Jordanian diplomats. King Husayn did not meet King Fahd again until 1996. Husayn was succeeded as king by his son 'Abdullah on his death in 1999.

JUBAYL, AL-. [al-jubayl; الجبيل; 49 41- 27 01] A small port on the **Gulf** coast of Saudi Arabia traditionally serving the **Najd** hinterland, especially **al-Qasim** district. The kingdom's Second Five-Year Development Plan (1975-1980) teamed al-Jubayl with **Yanbu'** on the Red Sea coast in an ambitious industrial development scheme, involving crude **oil** refining, petrochemical complexes and steel manufacturing industries, linked by trans-Saudi Arabian oil and gas **pipelines**. The development of the two sites was envisaged as taking 10 years and costing in excess of $70 billion. Al-Jubayl was to be the bigger of the two, with three petroleum refineries, six petrochemical plants, an aluminum smelter and a steel mill, as well as support industries, an industrial port, and a city of 100,000 inhabitants. Al-Dawsiriyah, a few miles south of al-Jubayl, contains ruins of a settlement from the period of al-'Ubayd culture of southern Mesopotamia and Arabia (about 4000 B.C.).

JUBAYR, MUHAMMAD BIN IBRAHIM BIN. (1929-2002) [jubayr; محمد بن ابراهيم بن جبير] Saudi judge and government minister. After receiving a degree in Islamic law from **Umm al-Qura University** in **Makkah**, he served as a judge in Makkah and **Riyadh** and was eventually appointed Minister of Justice in 1989. In 1992, he was appointed as the first Speaker of the new **Majlis al-Shura** (Consultative Council), a position he held until his death in early 2002.

JUBBAH. [jubbah; جبة; 40 56 - 28 02] Sandstone cliffs some 60 miles northeast of **Ha'il**, on which are drawn the finest Neolithic rock art in Arabia, dating perhaps to 11,000 years ago.

JUFFALI, AL-. [al-juffālī; الجفالي] A wealthy merchant family with origins in **Najd**. Although the family business began with the supply of electricity in **al-Ta'if** and **Riyadh** in the 1950s, its biggest source of income has been the agency for Mercedes. The group is also involved in heavy equipment, electronics and telecommunications, tires, and air-conditioning, as well as industrial concerns and real estate. A recent estimate put the family fortune at more than $1 billion.

JUHAYMAN BIN MUHAMMAD BIN SAYF AL-'UTAYBI. *See* 'UTAYBI, JUHAYMAN BIN MUHAMMAD BIN SAYF AL-.

JUHAYNAH. [juhaynah; sing. juhanī; جهينة؛ جهني] A large tribe of **al-Hijaz** with both nomadic and settled sections. Its paramount **shaykh** in the past was drawn from a clan of **sharifs** (descendants of the Prophet **Muhammad**). Juhani territory ranges along the **Red Sea** coast from just south of **Yanbu'** to Wadi Hamd and inland to the line of the old Hijaz Railway.

- K -

KA'BAH. [ka'bah; كعبة] A small rectangular building in the center of the Great Mosque of **Makkah**, the age of which is uncertain but antedates **Islam** by some centuries. Previous to Islam, it housed various idols which made Makkah a renowned religious center. With the coming of Islam, the idols were removed and the building was rebuilt several times, last in A.D. 782. In one corner of the Ka'bah is set the venerated Black Stone, marking the starting point for the circumambulation of the Great Mosque which each pilgrim must make during the annual **hajj** (pilgrimage).

KAF. *See* QURIYAT, AL-.

KAMIL, SALIH BIN 'ABDULLAH. [kāmil; صالح بن عبدالله كامل] Prominent Saudi businessman, owner of the Dallah and al-Barakah companies, involved in Islamic **banking**, and founder of Arab Radio Television and cofounder with

Walid al-Ibrahim of the Middle East Broadcasting Corporation (MBC), although he has divested his holdings in the latter. Salih was born in **Makkah** in 1940 and received a degree in commerce from **King Saʻud University**. His net worth has been estimated at $1.9 billion.

KHADIJAH BINT KHUWAYLID. (A.D. ca. 555-619) [khadījah bint khuwaylid; خديجة بنت خويلد] Wife of **Muhammad** the Prophet. The widow of a wealthy merchant from the **Quraysh** tribe, she was about 15 years older than Muhammad and bore him a number of children, of whom only a daughter survived her father. This daughter, Fatimah, married the caliph 'Ali.

KHAFJI, AL-. [al-khafjī; الخفجي; 48 59- 28 23] A town at the northeastern corner of Saudi Arabia, on the Gulf coast and next to the **Kuwait** border. It is inside the former Saudi-Kuwaiti **Neutral Zone** and the name is also given to an offshore **oil** field. Al-Khafji serves as the headquarters for Saudi Arabia's onshore concession operated by Getty Oil Company and was the terminal for crude oil exports of Japan's Arabian Oil Company from the Neutral Zone until 2000. It figured momentarily during the 1991 war to liberate Kuwait from Iraqi occupation when **Iraq** made its only ground offensive move of the war by briefly occupying the town. Saudi and **Qatari** troops mounted a counter offensive and, after a day of hard fighting, the Iraqis were forced out of al-Khafji. A small oil refinery at al-Khafji was destroyed during the war.

KHALID, BANI. [banī khālid; sing. khālidī; بني خالد؛ خالدي] One of the oldest and historically most important tribes of Arabia. The Bani Khalid ousted the **Ottomans** from eastern Arabia in the mid-17th century and ruled much of the **Gulf** littoral until superseded in **Kuwait** by the Al Sabah in the 18th century and in **al-Ahsa'** by the **Al Saʻud** in the 19th century. Most remnants today are nomads along the Gulf coast, although there are settled elements in **al-Qatif, al-Hufuf**, and in **al-Qasim** in **Najd**.

KHALID AL-FAYSAL (OR KHALID BIN FAYSAL) AL SAʻUD. (1941-) [خالد الفيصل آل سعود] A son of King **Faysal bin ʻAbd al-ʻAziz**, Khalid was educated in the United States and at Oxford. He has been **Amir** (Governor) of the province of ʻ**Asir** since 1971 and is a leading proponent of the charitable **King Faysal Foundation**, established after King Faysal's death in 1975. Khalid's half brothers are **Saʻud al-Faysal** (the Minister of Foreign Affairs) and **Turki al-Faysal** (the former Director-General of Intelligence), but his mother was from the **Al Jiluwi** collateral branch of the **Al Saʻud**. He was named to the new Ruling Family council on its creation in 2000.

KHALID BIN ʻABD AL-ʻAZIZ AL SAʻUD. (r. 1975-1982) [خالد بن عبد العزيز آل سعود] The 19th ruler in the **Al Saʻud** dynasty, born in 1912, Khalid was the third of King **ʻAbd al-ʻAziz** 's sons to succeed their father as King of Saudi Arabia. After having commanded one of the two Saudi armies during the Saudi-Yemen war (1934), Khalid often served as a deputy to his older brother **Faysal**. Appointed First Deputy Prime Minister in 1964 and Heir Apparent in 1965, Khalid acceded to the throne upon Faysal's assassination in 1975, simultaneously adopting the position of Prime Minster. However, he was frequently in poor health while King and much of the day-to-day governing was left to his half brother **Fahd**, who succeeded Khalid upon the latter's death in 1982 from natural causes.

KHALID BIN SA'UD AL SA'UD. (r. 1839-1841) [خالد بن سعود آل سعود] The eighth ruler of the **Al Sa'ud** state. With **Ottoman** support, Khalid defeated his cousin **Faysal bin Turki** and made himself **Imam** of **Najd**. However, he was soon challenged by another cousin, **'Abdullah bin Thunayan**, who began a campaign to rid Najd of all Ottoman forces. Khalid was eventually forced into exile in **Makkah**, where he died.

KHALID BIN SULTAN BIN 'ABD AL-'AZIZ AL SA'UD. [خالد بن سلطان بن عبد العزيز آل سعود] Son of Defense Minister **Sultan bin 'Abd al-'Aziz**, Khalid is a graduate of the Royal Military Academy at Sandhurst (UK) and has a master's degree from Auburn University. As a major-general and the most senior uniformed member of the **Al Sa'ud**, he was appointed Commander of the Air Defense Forces (a separate service in Saudi Arabia) in May 1986, and later promoted to lieutenant-general. After the **Iraqi** invasion of **Kuwait** in August 1990, he was named commander of all Arab and Muslim forces in Saudi Arabia, which gave him enormous public exposure. It was speculated that this, along with his concentration on his extensive business interests and a supposed demand to the King to be appointed Chief of the General Staff, led to his dismissal in September 1991. He subsequently published *Desert Warrior* (1994), his account of the war along with many autobiographical details. He also owns the prominent pan-Arab newspaper *al-Hayat*. In 2001, he was appointed Deputy Minister of Defense and Aviation for Military Affairs with the rank of minister.

KHAMIS MUSHAYT. [khamīs mushayt; خميس مشيط; 42 44 - 18 18] A town, or group of villages, of the southern Saudi province of **'Asir**, about 20 miles from the provincial capital at **Abha**. The name derives from the Mushayt clan of the Shahran tribe, which dominates in the area, and its important Thursday market (Thursday in Arabic is *yawm al-khamis*). Khamis Mushayt's intermediate position between the sedentarized population of the mountains on the west and the nomadic tribes of the east, as well as its location on the main caravan route between **Yemen** and **al-Hijaz** virtually guaranteed its importance as a regional trade center. Recent prosperity has resulted from the establishment of a military base outside the city, significant because of Khamis Mushayt's proximity to the Yemen border.

KHARJ, AL-. [al-kharj; الخرج; 47 30 - 24 10] A major agricultural center and capital of a district of the same name in southern **Najd**, south of **Riyadh**. The first mention of al-Kharj was in the 18th century, as a result of its initial opposition to the **Wahhabi** movement. It fell to the **Al Sa'ud** in 1776 and was pillaged by an invading **Egyptian** army at the same time as the Saudi capital at **al-Dir'iyah** was destroyed. The oasis was incorporated into the present Saudi state not long after **Riyadh** was recaptured in 1902. The **Sa'ud al-Kabir**, the senior branch of the **Al Sa'ud** royal family, long have had close ties to the town. The oil company **ARAMCO** built a model farm at al-Kharj for King **'Abd al-'Aziz bin 'Abd al-Rahman** and Saudi army and air bases are located nearby. One of these, Prince Sultan Air Base, hosts a major US military command center which was utilized during the 2001-2002 war in **Afghanistan**.

KHASHAQJI, 'ADNAN BIN MUHAMMAD. (1935-) [khāshaqjī; عدنان بن محمد خاشقجي] Saudi businessman from a prominent **Makkah** family of Turkish origin. His father was the physician of King **'Abd al-'Aziz bin 'Abd al-Rahman**. 'Adnan attended Victoria College in Egypt along with King Husayn of **Jordan** and studied briefly in the United States before pursuing a commercial career. Although his business interests have covered many fronts, he is best known in the West for his role as an arms dealer. His business empire, concentrated in Triad Holdings, owned in partnership with two brothers, ran into financial difficulties in the 1980s. During the same decade, he acquired notoriety for his role in the Iran-Contra scandal and his involvement in the attempt to hide the wealth spirited out of the Philippines by its exiled President Ferdinand Marcos.

KHASHOGGI, 'ADNAN. *See* KHASHAQJI, 'ADNAN.

KHAWR. [khawr; pl. akhwār or khīrān; خور؛ اخوار؛ خيران] Arabic name for a bay or inlet, of which many are found along Saudi Arabia's coasts. Those along the **Gulf** tend to be very shallow and may be submerged only at high tide.

KHAWR AL-'UDAYD. [khawr al-'udayd; خور العديد; 51 25 - 24 20] A marshy inlet at the eastern base of the **Qatar** Peninsula. Sovereignty has been contested between the states of Qatar, Abu Dhabi, and Saudi Arabia. A 1974 boundary agreement between the **United Arab Emirates (UAE)** and Saudi Arabia appeared to award Saudi Arabia territory formerly held by the UAE, including a stretch of coastline on the **Gulf** between the Qatar Peninsula and the UAE. In the early 1990s, Saudi Arabia cut the highway between Abu Dhabi and Qatar and forced vehicles to travel along a newer road entirely in Saudi territory and to submit to Saudi customs.

KHAYBAR. [khaybar; خيبر; 39 13 - 25 44] An oasis in **al-Hijaz**, about 95 miles from **al-Madinah**. It is the site of a large walled town dating from the mid-to-late second millennium B.C., and Qasr Murhab [qaṣr murḥab; قصر مرحب], a large, pre-Islamic castle, sits atop a nearby rocky promontory. A large pre-Islamic dam, Sadd al-Hasid [sadd al-ḥaṣīd; سد الحصيد], exists some 20 miles to the south; of stepped stone construction, it is identical to **Sadd al-Samallaqi**. Khaybar was inhabited by Jewish tribes at the time of the Prophet **Muhammad**, who successfully besieged the oasis and later expelled its Jews. The town came under the control of the **Al Rashid** of **Ha'il** during the 19th century. It was taken over by the Sharif of **Makkah** in 1906 and then was captured by the **Al Sa'ud** in 1922.

KHUBAR, AL-. [al-khubar; الخبر; also spelled Khobar; 50 12 - 26 17] A town of the **Eastern Province** on the **Gulf** coast. It was founded as a fishing and pearling village in - 928 by members of the **Dawasir** tribe fleeing from Bahrain. In 1935, the oil company CALTEX (later **ARAMCO**) built a pier in order to land its equipment and in 1938, after the discovery of oil at nearby **Dhahran**, a storage and shipping terminal was added, thus enabling barges to take Saudi Arabia's first crude oil to nearby **Bahrain** for refining. Although al-Khubar declined as a port after the construction of a new deep-water port at nearby **al-Dammam**, it prospered as a residential and business center rivalling provincial capital al-Dammam. It also acquired notoriety in June 1996 when a truck bomb was set off outside a barracks at King 'Abd al-'Aziz Air Base in al-Khubar, killing 23 American servicemen and wounding nearly 400 others of various nationalities. The United States government has contended that the Saudi Hizbullah was responsible. *See also* OPPOSITION GROUPS.

KHURAYBAH. *See* 'ULA, AL-.

KHURMAH, AL-. [al-khurmah; الخرمة; 42 03 - 21 54] An oasis settlement astride the boundary between the regions of **al-Hijaz** and **Najd**. The forces of the **Al Sa'ud Imam 'Abd al-'Aziz bin Muhammad** were victorious over **al-Hashimi** Sharif Ghalib of **Makkah** in a nearby battle in 1798, and the population of the oasis, largely from the **Subay'** tribe, was converted soon after to the **Wahhabi** movement of **Islam** espoused by the Al Sa'ud. In the struggle after the First World War between the resurgent Al Sa'ud forces under Imam **'Abd al-'Aziz bin 'Abd al-Rahman** and King **Husayn bin 'Ali al-Hashimi** of Makkah, al-Khurmah was a long-standing bone of contention. As a result, it and the nearby village of Turabah saw repeated battles during 1918 and subsequent years. A British-imposed armistice left al-Khurmah in the hands of the Al Sa'ud, where it remained through the Saudi conquest of the entire Kingdom of al-Hijaz in 1924-1925. During the 1920s, al-Khurmah served as an important center of the **Ikhwan** movement

KHUWAH. [khūwah; خوة] A payment collected by **badu** tribes from weak tribes and settled merchants in return for providing protection or insurance against **ghazwah**, or desert raids.

KHUWAYTIR, 'ABD AL-'AZIZ BIN 'ABDULLAH AL-. (1927-) [al-khuwaytir; عبد العزيز بن عبد الله الخويطر] Saudi Arabia's Minister of Education from 1975 until 1995 when named Minister of State without Portfolio. Although born in **'Unayzah**, 'Abd al-'Aziz grew up in **Makkah** where his father was an official in the Ministry of Finance. He studied at Cairo University and did postgraduate work in London, becoming the first Saudi citizen to earn a Ph.D. He returned home to administrative positions at **King Sa'ud University** in **Riyadh** before being appointed first Minister of Health and then Minister of Education. Often used by King **Fahd bin 'Abd al-'Aziz** as an emissary to Arab governments, he was named Minister of State without

Portfolio in the new cabinet of 1995 and also served as Acting Minister of Finance and National Economy in the same year.

KING 'ABD AL-'AZIZ CITY FOR SCIENCE AND TECHNOLOGY (KACST). Established in 1977 and receiving its present name in 1985, KACST is an independent government institute serving as Saudi Arabia's principal research center in science and technology. Its activities include solar energy research projects, the Saudi Center for Remote Sensing, a national observatory, and the operation of the Institute for Petroleum and Petrochemicals Research, the Institute of Energy Research, the Institute of Natural Resources and Environmental Research, the Institute of Arid Lands Research, the Institute of Astronomy, and the Institute of Atomic Energy Research. It also operates the country's links to the Internet.

KING 'ABD AL-'AZIZ UNIVERSITY. Initially established as a private university in **Jiddah**, it was converted to a state university in 1971. Several faculties are located in nearby **Makkah**.

KING FAHD UNIVERSITY OF PETROLEUM AND MINERALS. Founded in **Dhahran** in the early 1960s as an independent college attached to the Ministry of Petroleum and Mineral Resources but managed by the Ministry of Higher Education. It was elevated to university status in 1975 but continues to emphasize technical disciplines.

KING FAYSAL FOUNDATION. A private foundation established in 1976 by the sons of King **Faysal bin 'Abd al-'Aziz** after his death. The foundation operates the King Faysal Center for Research and Islamic Studies on its premises in **Riyadh** and runs various charity programs. It is perhaps best known outside of the kingdom for the King Faysal International Prize which annually honors the top individuals in the fields of medicine, science, Arabic literature, Islamic studies, and service to **Islam**. In 2000, the Foundation opened al-Faysaliyah (al-Faisaliah) Center in 2000 as its showcase investment, one of the tallest buildings in Saudi Arabia and comprising a 30-story office tower, luxury hotel and apartments, and shopping mall.

KING FAYSAL UNIVERSITY. Created in 1975 in **al-Dammam**, with an agricultural and veterinary branch in **al-Hufuf**. King Faysal University serves a more general need in the **Eastern Province** than the **King Fahd University of Petroleum and Minerals** but is less highly regarded.

KING KHALID UNIVERSITY. Formed in 1998 from the **Abha** (capital of the southern province of **'Asir**) branches of **King Sa'ud University** and **Imam Muhammad bin Sa'ud University**. The university has four faculties: education, medicine, Islamic law and religion, and administrative studies.

KING SA'UD UNIVERSITY. Established by King **Sa'ud bin 'Abd al-'Aziz** in **Riyadh** in 1957, the university was renamed the University of Riyadh in 1964 when King Sa'ud was deposed. The original name was restored by

King **Khalid bin 'Abd al-'Aziz** during the university's silver jubilee. It remains the "flagship" university in the Saudi system and, with more than 30,000 students, the country's largest. Its huge new campus on the northern outskirts of Riyadh, costing $4 billion, was the biggest nonindustrial project in Saudi Arabia. The university has a branch at **al-Qasim** in central **Najd** and another branch at **Abha** in **'Asir** was absorbed into the new **King Khalid University**. The women's branch is located in the old campus in central Riyadh.

KUWAIT AND SAUDI ARABIA. The **amirate** of Kuwait, located in the northeastern corner of the **Arabian Peninsula**, sandwiched between Saudi Arabia and **Iraq**, was a **British**-protected state from 1899 until 1961 when it became fully independent. The Al Sabah, the ruling family, are from the **'Anazah** tribe of **Najd** and thus share a putative blood relationship with the **Al Sa'ud**. Along with other Najdi families (including the Al Khalifah who subsequently moved to **Bahrain** where they now form the ruling family), the Al Sabah settled in Kuwait in the early 18th century. Over the next several centuries, Kuwait served as a port and entrepôt for the tribal hinterland and trade was carried on with the merchants of **al-Qasim** and elsewhere in Najd. Kuwait provided asylum for the Al Sa'ud after their expulsion from Najd in 1891 and it was from Kuwait that **'Abd al-'Aziz bin 'Abd al-Rahman** launched his infiltration of **Riyadh** that marked the beginning of the Third Saudi State.

Ensuing relations between 'Abd al-'Aziz and succeeding amirs of Kuwait steadily deteriorated, however. Saudi grievances included Kuwait's giving sanctuary in 1916 to the **'Ajman** tribe during its rebellion against Riyadh and Kuwait's role in the resupplying of **Ottoman** garrisons during the First World War. Even more importantly, conflicting border claims led to several clashes between the two states in 1920, and 'Abd al-'Aziz initiated an economic blockade of Kuwait in 1921. The British High Commissioner of Iraq, Sir **Percy Cox**, awarded much of Kuwait's territory to Saudi Arabia at the 1922 **al-'Uqayr** conference, which resulted in a number of tribes switching their allegiance from the Al Sabah to the Al Sa'ud. Al-'Uqayr also established the Kuwaiti-Saudi **Neutral Zone**, as a result of the difficulty of assigning national sovereignty over tribal grazing lands. The Neutral Zone was divided between the two countries in 1966 but they continue to share equally the income from the former zone's **oil** concession. Additional problems arose in the late 1920s when the **Ikhwan** began raiding Kuwait without reference to 'Abd al-'Aziz. His efforts at breaking the power of the rebellious Ikhwan leaders drove them to seek refuge in Kuwait in 1930, and the British subsequently turned them over to 'Abd al-'Aziz.

Saudi-Kuwaiti relations gradually improved over the following decades, undoubtedly helped by the need to forge a common defense against the advancing tide of Arab radicalism in the 1950s. Saudi Arabia was one of the first countries to declare its support for Kuwait in 1961 when **Iraq** appeared to be on the verge of invasion and the kingdom sent troops to join the Arab peacekeeping force which replaced the initial British protecting troops. Further bonds were established through the two countries' similar positions in **OPEC**. After the outbreak of the Iran-Iraq War (1980-1988), Kuwait and Saudi Arabia were founding members of the **Gulf Cooperation Council (GCC)**: a Kuwaiti became the first Secretary-General of the organization and its headquarters were located in **Riyadh**. But lingering Kuwaiti suspicions of its larger neighbor were behind the amirate's reluctance to sign a bilateral security pact and Riyadh allegedly pressured the Al Sabah to suspend the elected National Assembly in 1986 and to resist its reinstatement.

All this paled in light of Iraq's invasion of Kuwait on 2 August 1990 and the possibility of a further Iraqi advance into Saudi Arabia. The kingdom permitted the establishment of a Kuwaiti government-in-exile at **al-Ta'if**, gave refuge to thousands of Kuwaitis, and marshaled the military contributions of a wide coalition of nations to force Iraq out of Kuwait in early 1991. *See* DESERT STORM, OPERATION.

Saudi-Kuwaiti relations remained close through the following decade. A minor irritant over remaining border questions was settled when the two countries agreed on the demarcation of their maritime borders in early 2001, some thirty years after land borders were settled.

KUWAIT WAR. *See* DESERT STORM, OPERATION.

- L -

LADIN, USAMAH BIN MUHAMMAD BIN. (c.1958-) [usāmah bin muhammad bin lādin; اسامه بن محمد بن لادن] One of many children of Muhammad bin Ladin, who had been born in the Hadramawt region of **Yemen** but emigrated to **Jiddah** where he gradually built up a construction business that eventually became Saudi Arabia's largest. Born about 1958 as the 17th of his father's reputed 50 or more children and of a Syrian mother, Usamah received an education in civil engineering at the university level inside the kingdom but does not seem to have played a major role in the family business. With the **Soviet** invasion of **Afghanistan**, he helped fund-raising activities in **Pakistan** and then joined the Afghani *mujahidin* (freedom fighters) to fight against the Soviet-backed government. On his return home, Usamah became known as one of the "Arab Afghans," a term for the young men who followed a radical religion-based ideology as a result of their experiences in Afghanistan.

Because of his extremist views, the Saudi government was suspicious of Usamah's intentions and withheld his passport in 1989. In 1991, Usamah left for Sudan, where he supported the Islamist government dominated by Hasan al-Turabi and established a number of businesses. His activities there led the Saudi government in 1994 to revoke his citizenship and freeze his assets in Saudi Arabia, and his family also disowned him. At the same time, he established the Committee for Advice and Reform in London and later created the radical Islamic movement **al-Qa'idah**, which advocated violence to achieve its goals. Prominent amongst them was driving the **United States** out of Saudi Arabia and the Islamic world.

In the following years, al-Qa'idah gained adherents in a number of Islamic countries and began to support terrorist activities around the world, notably in **Yemen** where it apparently was involved with the bombing of the US naval vessel, the USS *Cole*, in September 2000. The most spectacular attack was the hijacking of four American domestic airliners on 11 September 2001 and using them to destroy the World Trade Center in New York and severely damage the Pentagon in Washington. As a consequence, the United States attacked Afghanistan to destroy the Taliban régime there, which had allied itself with Usamah, and to kill or capture as many al-Qa'idah members as possible. Although Usamah bin Ladin was the chief target of this campaign, his whereabouts remained unknown through 2002. *See also* OPPOSITION GROUPS.

LAWRENCE, T. E. (THOMAS EDWARD). (1888-1935) Better known as Lawrence of Arabia, Lawrence was born in Wales. At Jesus College, Oxford, he became a protégé of archaeologist **D. G.** Hogarth, who provided him with his first field experience in the Middle East and utilized Lawrence's skills at cartography to help prepare maps for military use. After the outbreak of the First World War, Lawrence became an intelligence officer in the Middle East and accompanied Sir **Ronald Storrs** on a diplomatic mission to **al-Hijaz** in 1916, where Sharif **Husayn b. 'Ali** had just declared himself independent of the **Ottoman** Empire. Subsequently, he was detached to Sharif Husayn's army, under the command of Husayn's son **Faysal**, as a military adviser and helped to initiate a series of guerrilla raids against Ottoman forces and the Hijaz Railway. These culminated in the capture of al-'Aqabah (now in **Jordan**) in 1917. Shortly thereafter, Lawrence was captured by the Turks at Dir'ah in Syria and physically assaulted. With the failure to establish a Syrian kingdom at Damascus after the Armistice of 1918, Lawrence returned to England and resigned his commission. The next few years saw spells as a research fellow at Oxford and adviser on Arab affairs to Winston Churchill at the Colonial Office, as well as completion of the manuscript for *Seven Pillars of Wisdom* and the emergence of the Lawrence legend with the help of journalist Lowell Thomas. Partly in an attempt to escape the public eye, Lawrence joined the Royal Air Force (RAF) under an assumed name and, when exposed, joined the Royal Tank Corps. He was transferred back to the RAF in 1925 and, a few months after his discharge from the RAF in 1935, was killed in a motorcycle accident near his Clouds Hill cottage in Dorset. Other publications included *Revolt in the Desert* and *The Mint*.

LEBANON AND SAUDI ARABIA. An Arab state located on the eastern shore of the Mediterranean Sea and bordered on the south by Israel and on the east and north by Syria. Lebanon's delicate political balance between its Christian and Muslim sects was destroyed by the outbreak of a civil war in 1976 which lasted until 1990. The formal agreement ending the war, achieved with Saudi Arabia's assistance, was signed in **al-Ta'if**. Saudi Arabia's developing economy attracted many Lebanese over the years to the kingdom, with a reported 18,000 workers by 1974. Among them was **Rafiq Hariri**, who built up a massive conglomerate centered on construction and who returned to Lebanon in 1992 to serve as prime minister. The Trans-Arabian Pipeline carried Saudi crude from the **Eastern Province** to a refinery in

Lebanon's southern port of Sidon from 1950 until the route was closed as a result of the 1967 **Arab-Israeli** War. *See also* PIPELINES.

LIBERAL PRINCES. [al-umarā' al-ahrār; الامراء الاحرار; also known as Free Princes] A faction of the **Al Sa'ud** ruling family which advocated a liberalization of the Saudi political system in the late 1950s and early 1960s. Led by **Talal bin 'Abd al-'Aziz**, the informal grouping also included his full brother, **Nawwaf bin 'Abd al-'Aziz**, and half brothers **'Abd al-Muhsin bin 'Abd al-'Aziz**, **Badr bin 'Abd al-'Aziz**, **Fawwaz bin 'Abd al-'Aziz**, and **Majid bin 'Abd al-'Aziz**. The appointment of some of these princes to King **Sa'ud's** reform cabinet of 1960, along with associated commoners such as **'Abdullah al-Tariqi**, marked the apogee of the movement. It is probable, however, that King Sa'ud included them only to gain support in his rivalry with his full brother and Heir Apparent **Faysal bin 'Abd al-'Aziz**. A few months later in 1961, Talal was removed from his position as Minister of Finance after he attacked the Saudi government in a press conference in Beirut. He and some of the other princes spent several years in exile in Egypt before returning to the kingdom.

LIHYAN, LIHYANITES. [lihyān; لحيان] An Arab civilization of the seventh to third centuries B.C., conducting trade between **India**, **Yemen**, and the Mediterranean. Once sedentarized, the Lihyanite kingdom took ancient **Daydan** (now **al-'Ula**, north of **al-Madinah** and near **Mada'in Salih**) as their capital. The Lihyanites were likely a branch of **Thamud** and their civilization was influenced by first **Minaean** and then **Nabataean** culture. Although they adapted the Minaean script as their own, their language was North Arabian. Lihyanite inscriptions of the fifth century B.C. mention the god HLH, one of the first occurrences of the name of Allah.

- M -

MADA'IN SALIH. [madā'in ṣāliḥ; مدائن صالح; 37 58 - 26 51] Located in the northeastern corner of the country, not far from **al-'Ula**, Mada'in Salih was initially founded at the beginning of the first millennium B.C. as a northern outpost of the **Minaean** civilization of South Arabia. It was subsequently occupied by **Thamudic** and **Lihyanite** peoples. Along with Petra in **Jordan**, it became one of the two principal cities of the **Nabataean** kingdom, which flourished in northeastern Arabia from the end of the first millennium B.C. until engulfed by Roman expansion in the second century A.D. Mada'in Salih's most impressive monuments, the tombs carved from living rock and the imposing façades built into cliff faces, date from this period and are identical in construction to those of Petra. The city was well-known as the capital of the region of **Midian** to Greek, Roman, and Islamic geographers and historians under the name of Hagra, or al-Hijr in Arabic.

MADINAH, AL-. [al-madīnah or al-madīnah al-munawwarah; المدينة؛ المدينة المنورة; also spelled Medina; 39 00 - 24 00] The second holiest city in **Islam**, located in **al-Hijaz** province, 280 miles north of **Makkah** and 130 miles inland from the **Red Sea**. Under the name **Yathrib**, the settlement was an ancient trading and agricultural center. Its inhabitants gave sanctuary to the Prophet **Muhammad** and his Muslim followers, who had been forced to leave hostile **Makkah**. As a consequence, the name was changed to al-Madinah ("The City," short for Madinat al-Nabi, "The City of the Prophet") and it became the capital of the first Islamic state. The Jewish tribes of al-Madinah betrayed the Muslim forces during the battles with the armies of Makkah and they were, as a result, driven from al-Madinah and eventually all of al-Hijaz. Al-Madinah has been closed to non-Muslims ever since.

The city today is dominated by the Mosque of the Prophet, which is reputed to contain not only the grave of Muhammad, but of his immediate successors as heads (caliphs) of the Islamic community, Abu Bakr and 'Umar, and of his daughter Fatimah. Although a visit to al-Madinah is not required during the **hajj** (pilgrimage), many pilgrims, especially the **Shi'ah**, make the journey anyway. There are also Shi'ah among the population of al-Madinah, including the **Nakhawilah** community and some of the surrounding tribes. Because of its significance in Islam, al-Madinah displays a racially heterogenous population, representing many of the countries in which Islam is found. The pilgrimage remains the principal source of income for the city. The altitude (2,500 feet) and the intersection of **wadis** at al-Madinah account for extensive date cultivation, as well as grapes and other fruits.

MAGHAYIR SHU'AYB. *See* BIDA', AL-.

MAHD AL-DHAHAB. [mahd al-dhahab; مهد الذهب; 40 52 - 23 30] Town and region of **al-Hijaz** about 100 miles southeast of **al-Madinah**. Its name, "cradle of gold," indicates its economic role. Gold mining has been carried out there since the second millennium B.C. Mining was reintroduced in 1989, with nearly 500 pounds of gold produced in the first six months. A second gold mine was reopened at Sukhaybarat (185 miles east of al-Madinah) in 1991.

MAHFUZ, BIN. [bin mahfūz; بن مهفوظ] A prominent **banking** family of **Jiddah** headed by Khalid bin Mahfuz. Like many merchant families of **al-Hijaz**, the family originated in the Hadramawt region of **Yemen**. The family established the National Commercial Bank (NCB), the first bank in Saudi Arabia and the largest private bank in the Arab world. In the early 1990s, questions were raised about the NCB's stability and Khalid bin Mahfuz resigned as the bank's chief operating officer in 1992 after having been indicted in New York for contravening US banking laws. In the late 1990s, Khalid bin Mahfuz was suspected of ties to Islamic radical **Usamah bin Ladin** and reportedly placed under house arrest in **al-Ta'if**. The Mahfuz family also had interests in the Nimr Petroleum Company, a private Saudi company formed to exploit a Yemeni oil concession.

MAJID BIN 'ABD AL-'AZIZ AL SA'UD. (1936 or 1937-)
[ماجد بن عبد العزيز آل سعود] One of King 'Abd al-'Aziz's sons by an Armenian mother. At first, Majid was one of the **"Liberal Princes"** associated with half brother **Talal** but he broke with Talal in 1960 and became a businessman.

Appointed Minister of Municipal and Rural Affairs in 1975, he was transferred as **Amir** of **Makkah** after the Great Mosque was seized in 1979, a position he held until 1999.

MAJLIS. [majlis; pl. majālis; مجلس؛ مجالس] Most frequently used throughout the **Arabian Peninsula** to mean an informal gathering held on a regular basis at a private home, often in a purpose-built building or in a room separated from the rest of the house. An individual may hold a regular majlis on the same night each week (or perhaps two or even three majlises on different evenings). Some majlises may acquire reputations as evenings for gossip, light discussion, poetry, or other verbal entertainment; alternatively, a majlis may be a venue for serious discussion of culture or politics. Members of the royal family, government ministers, governors of provinces, and important merchants also hold regular majlises which any member of the public, citizen or expatriate, may attend. Through these majlises, personal contact is theoretically, and in many instances actually, maintained with all levels of society. Private citizens have the opportunity to present petitions requesting help with personal problems; at the same time, the majlis provides the political leadership with a barometer of public opinion. In a more formal sense, majlis means council or assembly, *e.g.* Majlis al-Wuzara' or Council of Ministers, and **Majlis al-Shura** or Consultative Council.

MAJLIS AL-SHURA. [majlis al-shūrá; مجلس الشورى] A consultative council with this name has functioned in Saudi Arabia since 1926. However, this original council, originally formed just for **al-Hijaz** and never formally disbanded, gradually became defunct as its aging members died. Announcements of the imminent establishment of a new Majlis al-Shura were made at various critical times since 1960, notably after the **Yemen** revolution of 1962, after the accession of King **Khalid** in 1975, following the seizure of the Great Mosque at **Makkah** in 1979, and after the **Iraqi** invasion of **Kuwait** in 1990. Impressive quarters were constructed for the council in the King's Office and Council of Ministers' Complex in the mid-1980s. King Fahd finally announced the creation of the Majlis al-Shura in 1992 and appointed Minister of Justice **Muhammad bin Ibrahim bin Jubayr** as Speaker. The council's 60 members were appointed in 1993 when the council met for the first time. The membership was increased to 90 appointed members during the second session (1997-2001) and increased again to 120 members for the third term (2001-2005). The members are principally businessmen, academics, retired military officers, and several Shi'ah appointees; there are no Al Sa'ud or government officials. The membership does not include **women** either, although women have been invited to take part in sessions that dealt with matters affecting women. As an advisory body, the council discusses and passes resolutions on matters put before it by the **government**, generally on financial, Islamic, and social-affairs matters. It is subdivided into 11 committees. Dr. Salih bin 'Abdullah bin Humayd was named Speaker in 2002, replacing Muhammad bin Jubayr on the latter's death.

MAKKAH. [makkah or makkah al-mukarramah; مكة؛ مكه المكرمة; also spelled Mecca; 39 49 - 21 27] The holiest city of **Islam**, located in **al-Hijaz** province about 50 miles inland from the **Red Sea**. Its origins are shrouded in mystery but Islamic tradition says it was established by the Prophet Ibrahim (Abraham), who built the **Ka'bah** in its precincts. Makkah was already well-known as a trading center and sacred enclosure by about A.D. 500 when the **Quraysh** tribe established themselves as the leaders of the city and the surrounding hinterland. **Muhammad**, the future Prophet of Islam, was born in Makkah, by tradition in the year A.D. 570. His message of a religion promising equality for all did not sit well with the patrician merchants of the city and he and his small band of followers were forced to leave Makkah for **Yathrib** (later **al-Madinah**) in A.D. 622. This event, known as the **hijrah**, marks the beginning of the Muslim calendar.

After the **Muslims** attacked Makkan caravans, Makkah retaliated by attacking al-Madinah and a number of fierce battles were fought in which the Muslims gained the upper hand. A conciliation was reached in 630 and Muhammad was able to reenter Makkah, which then became the paramount city in Islam. Before his death in 632, Muhammad performed the **hajj** (pilgrimage) and the details of his act have determined ever since the precise ritual of the hajj, which takes place annually in Makkah and its suburbs of **Mina** and **'Arafat**. At the heart of the city is the Great Mosque, containing the sacred Ka'bah, a small stone building of ancient origin, and the Well of **Zamzam**.

Because of its centrality to Islam, Makkah was the largest city in Arabia until the last few decades and its population was estimated at 70,000 in the early part of the 20th century. Makkah has no agriculture and is dependent on fresh supplies from **al-Ta'if**, 75 miles to the southeast, and imported goods from the port of **Jiddah**, about 50 miles to the west. The city is surrounded on three sides by harsh and barren hills, which capture the intense summer heat and reflect it at night. Makkah's present population, estimated at about 1½ million, is swelled by approximately two million pilgrims during the hajj.

MALIK, BANI. [banī mālik; sing. mālikī; الي، بني] A tribe of Saudi Arabia's southern highlands, in the Bajilah area north of **Abha** and between the **Bilharith** tribe on the north and the **Zahran** on the south.

MAMDUH BIN 'ABD AL-'AZIZ AL SA'UD. (1940-) [mamdūh; ممدوح بن عبدالعزيز آل سعود] One of King **'Abd al-'Aziz**'s sons by a mother from the **Ruwala** tribe. Educated in the **United States**, Saudi Arabia, and **Egypt**, he served as Amir of **Tabuk** before being named Head of the Office of Strategic Studies in the King's Office about 1987.

MANASIR, AL-. [al-manāṣīr; sing. manṣūrī; المناصير؛منصوري] A widespread tribe, mostly nomadic, of eastern Arabia, extending from al-Dhafrah desert of **Najd** into **Qatar** and the **United Arab Emirates**.

MANSUR BIN 'ABD AL-'AZIZ AL SA'UD. (1922-1951) [عبد العزيز آل سعود
منصور بن] A son of King **'Abd al-'Aziz** by an Armenian mother. A highly
regarded and rising figure, he served as Director of the Royal Household,
Chief of the Royal Cabinet, and Minister of Defense (1940-1951) until his
death in Paris from kidney disease.

MAQNA. See BIDA', AL-.

MARIA THERESA THALER. See RIYAL.

MAS'ARI, MUHAMMAD BIN 'ABDULLAH AL-. [mas'arī;
محمد بن عبد الله المسعري] A physics professor at **King Sa'ud University** who
had studied in Germany and the **United States**, Muhammad was a member
of the Committee for the Defense of Legitimate Rights (CDLR), established
in part by his father, Shaykh 'Abdullah bin Sulayman al-Mas'ari, and served
as the group's spokesman. Arrested after the CDLR announced itself in May
1993, he escaped to London six months later where he set up CDLR
headquarters. Acting under Saudi pressure, the British government denied
political asylum to al-Mas'ari in November 1994 and sought to exile him
to the Caribbean island of Dominica. The order subsequently was overturned
by an immigration appeals court and Muhammad was allowed to remain
in **Britain**. See also OPPOSITION GROUPS.

MASJID. See MOSQUE.

MECCA. See MAKKAH.

MEDIA. The state in Saudi Arabia exercises strong control over local media
through the Ministry of Information. Most media exercise careful self-
censorship to avoid **government** action and their news coverage tends to
concentrate on safe local issues, sports, and international news. There are
at least eight Arabic newspapers, including *'Ukaz, al-Bilad, al-Jazirah, al-
Madinah al-Munawwarah, al-Nadwah, al-Riyad,* and *al-Yawm.* These are
published in either **Jiddah** or **Riyadh**, apart from *al-Yawm* (al-Dammam).
One of the newest papers is *al-Watan,* published in the southern city of **Abha**,
which in 2001-2002 acquired a reputation for aggressive reporting. In addition,
there are two English-language dailies, the *Arab News* and the *Saudi Gazette,*
both published in Jiddah. There are also a number of weekly and monthly
publications.

Television broadcasting began in the kingdom in 1965 from stations
in Riyadh and Jiddah. Presently, the Ministry of Information provides three
television channels, two in Arabic and one in English (which began life as
ARAMCO television), as well as AM, FM, and shortwave radio services
(radio broadcasting began in 1948 in Jiddah and in 1964 in Riyadh).

In the 1990s, Saudi businessmen began to invest heavily in the
international Arabic media. Prince **Khalid bin Sultan**, an army general and
son of the Defense Minister, took control of the respected Lebanese daily
al-Hayat while the rival *al-Sharq al-Awsat,* also based in London and

established in 1978, belongs to Prince Ahmad bin Sultan, son of the Governor of Riyadh.

Saudi business interests also extended about the same time into satellite television. The Middle East Broadcasting Center (MBC) was started in London by **Walid al-Ibrahim**, a businessman with close ties to King **Fahd bin 'Abd al-'Aziz**, and prominent businessman **Salih Kamil**. A year later MBC purchased the United Press International (UPI) wire service. Salih Kamil subsequently sold out his interest in MBC and started Arab Radio and Television (ART), based in Cairo, with a strong minority stake belonging to Prince **al-Walid bin Talal**. Prince Khalid bin 'Abdullah bin 'Abd al-Rahman Al Sa'ud started Orbit, based in Rome, in 1994. Orbit initially carried the BBC's Arabic television service, but when the latter broadcast a critical program on the kingdom, it was dropped from Orbit and the BBC folded the service. Many of its personnel, however, were hired by the new Jazeera (al-Jazirah) channel in nearby **Qatar**. Satellite dishes are officially banned in the kingdom although they are widely used.

MEDINA. *See* MADINAH, AL-.

MIDIAN. [midyan; مدين] The pre-Islamic name of the region of northwestern Arabia, with its sometime capital at **Mada'in Salih**. Regarded by traditional Islamic historians as the homeland of the **Thamudic** civilization, it also served as the heart of the later but still pre-Islamic **Nabataean** kingdom.

MILITARY AND DEFENSE. In the early days of his rule, King **'Abd al-'Aziz bin 'Abd al-Rahman** relied on three types of armed forces: regulars, generally drawn from the towns and used to staff garrisons; **badu** (bedouin) levies, drawn from tribal allies of the **Al Sa'ud**; and the **Wahhabi** warriors of the **Ikhwan**, drawn from newly sedentarized badu tribes. Eventually, the Ikhwan turned against 'Abd al-'Aziz and he was forced to break their power using the new White Army, nucleus of the present National Guard.

The kingdom's first attempt at military rationalization, undertaken after the 1934 Saudi-Yemeni war, resulted in the creation of the Royal Saudi Army. While its mission was defense against external threats, the Army remained smaller and less important than the National Guard until well into the 1960s, when the Royal Guard was incorporated in the Army and oil income provided the means for major arms purchases and expansion costs. Further efforts at modernization included the establishment of the Office of the Minister of Defense in 1944, and creation of the present Ministry of Defense and Aviation (MODA) as part of the first Council of Ministers in 1953. Several **British** training teams worked in the country in the 1930s and assistance from the **United States** began as a consequence of the emergence of American strategic interest in the **Gulf** at the time of the Second World War, but these efforts bore little fruit until the removal of King **Sa'ud bin 'Abd al-'Aziz**.

The return of Sa'ud's brother **Faysal** as Prime Minister in October 1962 gave high priority to the reform and modernization of the Saudi armed forces. The lessening isolation of Saudi Arabia from the outside world, the eruption of multiple potential threats to the kingdom in the 1960s, and the British withdrawal from the Gulf in 1971 all played their part in provoking greatly increased concern about the defensive capabilities of the kingdom's armed forces. Saudi Arabia's oil provided the income with which to purchase an expensive arsenal and ensure the assistance of the United States. As a consequence, the last three decades have seen dramatic changes in the structure and capabilities of all components of the Saudi armed forces.

Formally, the High Defense Council determines policy, although in practice the King's decisions are final. The Council was established in 1961 with membership consisting of the King, the Ministers of Defense and Aviation, Finance and National Economy, Communications, and Foreign Affairs, and the Chief of Staff. The Minister of Defense and Aviation (**Sultan bin 'Abd al-'Aziz Al Sa'ud** since 1962) controls the Army, Air Force and Navy, while the National Guard (commanded by Heir Apparent **'Abdullah bin 'Abd al-'Aziz** since 1963) theoretically falls under the control of the Minister of the Interior, along with the Frontier Force, the Coast Guard, and internal security forces. In practice, however, the National Guard is answerable only to Prince 'Abdullah and, through him, to the King.

In the 1930s, a few British aircraft were purchased and some Saudi pilots were trained by Italy, but these putative efforts at an air force capability really had no impact until the massive expansion programs begun three decades later. To an even greater degree than the other Saudi services, US guidance and assistance has shaped the development of the Royal Saudi Air Force (RSAF). The **Yemen** civil war of the 1960s provoked fighter purchases and eventually the RSAF settled on American F-5 aircraft. This burgeoning relationship extended into the 1970s with the F-15 and later US-built AWACS radar planes. Efforts to acquire additional and more advanced equipment ran afoul of the **Arab-Israeli Conflict** and the pro-Israeli lobby in the US Congress. Subsequently, the kingdom went to Europe for the purchase of the Anglo-German Tornado aircraft. Air bases are located at **Riyadh, Dhahran, al-Ta'if, Khamis Mushayt, Tabuk, Hafar al-Batin**, and **al-Sharurah**, and total personnel is about 20,000.

Unlike American military organization, Air Defense forms a fourth Saudi service, independent of the Air Force, Army, and Navy, with a strength of about 16,000. In 1988, the kingdom secretly purchased a number of CSS-2 "East Wind" ballistic missiles with conventional warheads from the People's Republic of **China**; their discovery by the United States government caused a temporary diplomatic row.

Since the late 1970s, the US has also stepped up its assistance to the Royal Saudi Army (RSA). During the 1970s and 1980s, the US Army Corps of Engineers was heavily involved in army construction, particularly in the building of major facilities at Khamis Mushayt, Tabuk, and al-Sharurah, and the King Khalid and As'ad Military Cities (located at Hafar al-Batin and **al-Kharj** respectively). These bases have helped to expand RSA strength from its older bases at **Jiddah, al-Dammam**, and al-Ta'if to strategic points closer to potential threats. With some 75,000 uniformed personnel, the Army is the largest service. Plans announced after the war to liberate Kuwait in 1991 to double or even triple its size were never acted upon.

The Royal Saudi Navy (RSN) was the last of the Saudi armed forces to emerge. Formed as an adjunct of the Army in 1957, it received its first naval officer as commander in 1963 and only began functioning as a separate force in 1969. The Navy's headquarters are at Riyadh, with principal bases at Jiddah on the **Red Sea** and at **al-Jubayl** on the Gulf. There are about 16,000 Navy personnel. **France** has been instrumental in the Navy modernization program.

A lineal descendant of the tribal levies, the National Guard's personnel traditionally were recruited from the tribes of **Najd**. Consequently, it is not surprising that the National Guard's primary allegiance is to the Al Sa'ud dynasty even more than the state. Just as it served to protect the position of the Al Sa'ud at the time of the Ikhwan rebellion, the Guard continues to serve as a counterweight to the more recently created Army. Only in recent years has the attempt been made to modernize the Guard and expand its role from an essentially tribal levy into a well-equipped and trained fighting force on modern lines, using wheeled vehicles instead of the army's preference for tracked vehicles. For years, many guardsmen were either part-time or pensioners from the earlier days of 'Abd al-'Aziz's expansionary moves, and "phantom guardsmen" allegedly were enrolled by **shaykhs** to receive additional payments. This has become increasingly less true although it is difficult to estimate the total manpower, with figures of 75,000 to 100,000 common.

Saudi Arabia's armed forces, under the leadership of Prince **Khalid bin Sultan Al Sa'ud**, played an important role in **Operation Desert Storm** to liberate **Kuwait** from the Iraqi occupation in 1991. The Iraqi threat has spurred intentions to modernize and expand the country's armed forces, although continuing financial difficulties have limited expenditures, particularly in the latter half of the 1990s. The biggest arms sale was a $9 billion purchase of 72 F-15S aircraft from the United States in 1993. Defense spending has ranged between $17 billion and $22 billion annually during the late 1990s and early 2000s, one of the highest proportions in the world. *See also* FOREIGN AFFAIRS.

MINA. [mīnā; منى ; also spelled Muna] A small town about three miles from **Makkah**, traditionally associated with the site where Abraham (Ibrahim) was called upon to sacrifice his son Ishmael (Isma'il). Mina was also the site of a pre-Islamic fair, similar to that of **'Ukaz**. During the annual **Islamic** pilgrimage **(hajj)**, the pilgrims come to Mina after **'Arafat** and throw stones at three symbolic pillars. Mina should not be confused with the Arabic word for port, mīnā'.

MINAEAN. *See* SOUTH ARABIAN CIVILIZATIONS.

MISH'AL BIN 'ABD AL-'AZIZ AL SA'UD. (1926-) [mish'al; مشعل بن عبدالعزيز آل سعود] A son of King **'Abd al-'Aziz** by an Armenian mother, he replaced his full brother **Mansur** as Minister of Defense following the latter's death in 1951. Dropped from the defense portfolio by King **Sa'ud** in 1956, he later served as **Amir** of **Makkah** (1963-1971) before being removed by King **Faysal**. He subsequently has devoted himself to business interests.

MISHARI BIN SA'UD AL SA'UD. (r. 1820) [mishārī; مشاري بن سعود آل سعود]
Apparently succeeded his brother **'Abdullah bin Sa'ud** briefly as the fifth leader of the **Al Sa'ud** state, during the chaotic period following the invasion of **Egypt's** Ibrahim Pasha in 1818. But Mishari was soon captured by a rival and turned over to the **Ottomans**.

MIT'AB BIN 'ABD AL-'AZIZ AL SA'UD. (1928-) [mit'ab;
متعب بن عبد العزيز آل سعود] One of King **'Abd al-'Aziz**'s sons by an Armenian mother. His earlier positions included Deputy Minister of Defense (1951-1956) under his full brother **Mish'al** and **Amir** of **Makkah** (1959-1960). He later held the positions of Minister of Public Works and Housing (1975-1980) and Minister of Municipalities and Rural Affairs (1980-1983) before returning to Public Works and Housing.

MOSQUE. [masjid, pl. masājid; مسجد؛ مساجد] The **Islamic** place of worship. Because **Muslims** are required to pray at five set times during the day (although not necessarily at a mosque), nearly every neighborhood will have at least one mosque. A larger central mosque, the jami' [jāmi'; جامع], is also the site of the gatherings of Muslims for the Friday noon sermon [khuṭbah; خطبة]. The largest and most important mosque in Saudi Arabia is the Great Mosque of **Makkah**, which contains the **Ka'bah**, the holiest site in all Islam. The second-most important mosque is the one in **al-Madinah** containing the remains of the Prophet **Muhammad**.

MU'AMMAR, 'ABD AL-'AZIZ AL-. (c. 1905-c. 1990) [عبد العزيز المعمر] A Saudi bureaucrat who, although reared in Riyadh, apparently came from the old Al Mu'ammar family of al-'Uyaynah in **Najd** (which drove the 18th-century religious reformer **Muhammad bin 'Abd al-Wahhab** into exile at the **Al Sa'ud** settlement of **al-Dir'iyah**). 'Abd al-'Aziz served as **Amir** of **Yanbu'** until appointed Amir of **Jiddah** in 1932, then was transferred in 1935 to Amir of **al-Ta'if**.

MU'AMMAR, 'ABD AL-'AZIZ AL-. (1923-1980s?) [عبد العزيز المعمر] Regarded as part of the "liberal" group associated with **'Abdullah al-Tariqi** (later Oil Minister) and **Talal bin 'Abd al-'Aziz Al Sa'ud**, 'Abd al-'Aziz served as Director of Labor before being appointed as a royal adviser to King **Sa'ud** in 1961. However, his leftist reputation and pressure by the King's half brother Talal led to his dismissal soon after and posting abroad as Ambassador to Switzerland. Upon coming to the throne in 1964, King **Faysal** recalled him from Switzerland. Believing him to be a communist, the King had him jailed in **al-Hufuf** where he remained for 10 years. He died in Saudi Arabia.

MUBARRAZ. [mubarraz; مبرز; 49 34 - 2522] The second largest town of **al-Ahsa'** oasis in the **Eastern Province**, two miles north of **al-Hufuf**. Its population is mixed, with only a few tribesmen; about 20 percent of its population is **Shi'ah**.

MUFTI. [muftī; مفتي] An **Islamic** religious official qualified to issue a formal religious opinion (**fatwa**). In most Islamic countries, the Grand Mufti is the senior religious figure and is generally appointed by the government. The kingdom had a Grand Mufti until the last incumbent, Shaykh Muhammad bin Ibrahim Al al-Shaykh, died in 1969. Thereafter, the mufti's areas of responsibility were divided between the Ministry of Justice, the Supreme Council of the Judiciary [al-majlis al-a'lá lil-qaḍāh; المجلس الاعلى للقضاة], the Departments of Religious Research, Legal Opinions, Islamic Propagation and Guidance [idārat al-buḥūth al-'ilmīyah wal-iftā' wal-da'wah wal-irshād; ادارة البحوث العلمية والافتا، والدعوة والارشاد], all created in 1970, and the Council of the Assembly of Senior **'Ulama'** [majlis hay'at kibār al-'ulamā'; مجلس هيئة كبار العلما،], created in 1971 and which meets with the King every week. King **Fahd** restored the position of Grand Mufti in 1993 when he appointed the archconservative religious scholar Shaykh **'Abd al-'Aziz bin 'Abdullah bin Baz** to the position. Upon the latter's death in 1999, Shaykh 'Abd al-'Aziz bin 'Abdullah **Al al-Shaykh** was appointed Mufti in his place.

MUHAMMAD, THE PROPHET. The Prophet of **Islam**, born in **Makkah**, by tradition in A.D. 570, and died in 632. Born after the death of his father 'Abdullah, Muhammad was raised first by his grandfather 'Abd al-Muttalib and then after his grandfather's death, by his uncle Abu Talib, who headed the **Hashimi** clan of the **Quraysh** tribe. Following in the Qurayshi tradition, Muhammad became a merchant and accompanied several caravans abroad. Among the caravans he managed were those of a wealthy widow named **Khadijah**, whom Muhammad married when he was 25 and she was 40. Khadijah bore him two sons (both died in childhood) and four daughters. His prosperity gave him time for contemplation and preaching. About 610, Muhammad began to seclude himself in a cave outside Makkah, where he received the first in a series of revelations from the Angel Gabriel [Jabrā'īl; جبرائيل]. These revelations eventually constituted the **Qur'an** (Koran), the holy book of Islam.

　　His propagation of the new religion of Islam provoked the hostility of the Quraysh, who resented the message of egalitarianism and feared it would disrupt the prosperity of Makkah, which was built on income received from pilgrims to the pagan shrines in the city. After Muhammad's uncle Abu Talib died, leadership of the Hashimi clan passed to a hostile uncle, and persecution of Muhammad and the **Muslims** increased. In 622, Muhammad slipped out of Makkah and eventually made his way to **Yathrib**, where he had been invited by some of the inhabitants who had been converted to Islam earlier. He was soon joined there by 70 Muslims from Makkah and these emigrants [al-muhājirīn; المهاجرين] were soon joined by converted townspeople of Yathrib [al-anṣār; الانصار]. Thereafter, Yathrib became known as Madinat al-Nabi (City of the Prophet), or **al-Madinah** in short. This migration (the **hijrah**) resulted in the creation of the first Islamic state and thus marks the first year of the Islamic calendar.

A Muslim raid on a Makkan caravan prompted the Quraysh to gather an army to fight the Muslims and in 624 a battle took place at **Badr** (south of al-Madinah). Although outnumbered 1,000 to 300, the Muslims won the battle. The following year, however, a larger Makkan force of 3,000 defeated 700 Muslims at **Uhud** (outside al-Madinah), who were weakened because of desertions. Then in 627, an even larger Makkan force, accompanied by **badu** (bedouin) and Jewish tribesmen, attacked al-Madinah but were stymied by a defensive trench. After the Makkans gave up their unsuccessful siege of al-Madinah, hostilities between the two cities virtually ceased. An attempt by Muhammad and his followers to perform the **hajj** (pilgrimage) at Makkah in 628 was not allowed, but a treaty was signed permitting the hajj in the following year.

The expansion and growing power of al-Madinah led increasing numbers of tribes to convert to Islam, and by the time of Muhammad's death most of the **Arabian Peninsula** had been converted. In 632, Muhammad performed the "Farewell Pilgrimage," which provided the example by which all future pilgrimages were performed, and he died two months later. He was succeeded by Abu Bakr, his second convert to Islam (his wife Khadijah had been the first) and father of Muhammad's favorite wife 'A'ishah. Abu Bakr, who took the title caliph (*khalifah*), was succeeded by 'Umar, then 'Uthman, and then 'Ali, cousin and son-in-law of Muhammad. All descendants of Muhammad are through al-Hasan or al-Husayn, the sons of 'Ali and Fatimah bint Muhammad. 'Ali was tricked into giving up the office of caliph to a cousin, Mu'awiyah, who then became the first of the Umayyad dynasty, based in Damascus.

MUHAMMAD AL-FAYSAL (OR MUHAMMAD BIN FAYSAL) AL SA'UD. (1937-) [محمد الفيصل آل سعود] A son of King **Faysal bin 'Abd al-'Aziz**, Muhammad was educated in the **United States**, where in 1963 he became the first **Al Sa'ud** prince to receive a university degree. On his return to Saudi Arabia, Muhammad began working his way up the ranks of government and was named Deputy Minister of Agriculture and Water for Desalination Affairs in 1971. In that capacity, he gained international attention for advancing a scheme to tow icebergs from the Antarctic to Saudi Arabia to provide fresh water. Apparently because he did not receive a ministerial portfolio in the October 1975 cabinet following the death of his father, Muhammad left government service. He subsequently turned his attention to Islamic banking, becoming involved in Dar al-Mal al-Islami (Switzerland) and the Faysal Islamic Banks established in several Arab countries.

MUHAMMAD BIN 'ABD AL-'AZIZ AL SA'UD. (1910-1988) [محمد بن عبد العزيز آل سعود] A son of King **'Abd al-'Aziz** by a mother from the **Al Jiluwi** branch of the family. Prominent in the early fighting which established the Third Saudi State, he led the Saudi forces which conquered **al-Madinah** and served as its **Amir** (Governor) from 1926 to 1954. An implacable opponent of King **Sa'ud**, he was at the forefront of the forces within the royal family which deposed Sa'ud in 1965. When **Faysal** became King, Muhammad was passed over as Crown Prince in favor of **Khalid**, it is said because of his uncontrollable rages and personal conduct. He remained a respected elder of the **Al Sa'ud** until his death, although he gained brief notoriety in the West in 1977 for ordering the execution of his granddaughter and her lover, as dramatized in the film *Death of a Princess*.

MUHAMMAD BIN 'ABD AL-WAHHAB. (1703/1704-1792)

[محمد بن عبدالوهاب] An **Islamic** theologian and founder of the movement known by the outside world as **Wahhabism**. Muhammad was born in the small **Najdi** town of **al-'Uyaynah** to a religious family of the Bani Sinan tribe (a branch of the **Bani Tamim**). Muhammad was sent to various Islamic centers for theological training, including **al-Madinah**, Basra, Baghdad, Isfahan, and Qum. Upon his return to al-'Uyaynah, Muhammad began expounding his conservative views of **Sunni** Islam, based on the teachings of Ibn Hanbal and Ibn Taymiyah. His reception was cool and in 1744 he was forced to flee to the small village of **al-Dir'iyah**. There, **Muhammad bin Sa'ud**, the head of the **Al Sa'ud** family, took him in, was converted to his teachings, and married his daughter. The alliance between Muhammad bin 'Abd al-Wahhab and the Al Sa'ud spread the ascetic message of Wahhabism throughout Najd and beyond. His descendants are known as the **Al al-Shaykh**, or, "the family of the Shaykh" (*i.e.* of Muhammad 'Abd al-Wahhab).

MUHAMMAD BIN FAHD BIN 'ABD AL-'AZIZ AL SA'UD. (1950-)

[محمد بن فهد بن عبد العزيز آل سعود] Son of King **Fahd bin 'Abd al-'Aziz**, Muhammad was noted as a prominent and aggressive businessman prior to his appointment as **Amir** (Governor) of the **Eastern Province** in 1985, replacing the last of several **Al Jiluwi** amirs. He was also appointed a member of the new Royal Family Council established in 2000.

MUHAMMAD BIN SA'UD AL SA'UD. (r. 1742-1765) [محمد بن سعود آل سعود]

The head of a then-minor family of **al-Dir'iyah** in **Najd**, Muhammad gave sanctuary to Islamic reformer **Muhammad bin 'Abd al-Wahhab** in 1744. Converted to the latter's ascetic view of **Islam** (later popularly known as "**Wahhabism**"), Muhammad bin Sa'ud married his daughter and used *jihad* (holy war or struggle) to convert most of Najd to Wahhabism by his death in 1765. This was the beginning of the First Saudi State and the Al Sa'ud dynasty.

MUHAMMAD BIN SA'UD BIN 'ABD AL-'AZIZ AL SA'UD. (1934-)

[محمد بن سعود بن عبد العزيز آل سعود] A son of King **Sa'ud** who held numerous positions under his father, including Royal Chamberlain (1953-1959), Head of the Diwan (1959-1960), and Minister of Defense (1960-1962). After a long spell in business with his sons, he returned to public service as **Amir** of **al-Bahah** in the 1980s.

MURABBA' PALACE, AL-. [al-murabba'; المربع] The last of the traditional **Najdi** palaces occupied by the **Al Sa'ud** leaders, built in the 1930s to the north of old **Riyadh**. The word means square.

MURRAH, AL. [āl murrah; sing. murrī; مري؛ مرة، آل] A large and old nomadic tribe of "pure" lineage, with territory lying between the **Gulf** coast and **Najd**, and ranging from the hinterland of the port of **al-'Uqayr** in the north to **Jabrin** (Yabrin) oasis and the **Rub' al-Khali** desert in the south. Well-known in the past for harrying caravans between the Gulf and Najd, the Al Murrah strongly opposed the **Ottomans** and then Imam **'Abd al-'Aziz bin 'Abd al-Rahman Al Sa'ud**. They were the principal **badu** (bedouin) tribe involved in the sedentarization project at **Harad**.

MUSA'ID BIN 'ABD AL-RAHMAN AL SA'UD. (c. 1922-) [musā'id; مساعد بن عبد الرحمن آل سعود] A son of Imam **'Abd al-Rahman**, the father of King **'Abd al-'Aziz** and thus an uncle of Kings **Sa'ud**, **Faysal**, **Khalid**, and **Fahd**. Appointed Head of the Bureau of Grievances in 1954 and serving briefly as Minister of the Interior in 1960, his most important position was as Minister of Finance from 1962 to 1975. Musa'id is highly esteemed for his literary and scholarly interests, his religious conviction, and his honesty.

MUSLIM. [muslim, pl. muslimūn or muslimīn (m.); and muslimah (fem. sing.), muslimāt (fem. pl.); مسلم؛ مسلمون؛ مسلمين؛ مسلمة؛ مسلمات؛ س]; sometimes spelled Moslem] One who believes in **Islam**. Islam is divided into many different sects and movements, and a Muslim can be **Sunni**, a member of the main community or "orthodox" Islam; or **Shi'i**, a member of the largest breakaway sect which itself contains several subsects; or even a member of one of various smaller sects. Nearly all Saudis are Sunnis, apart from a significant Shi'i minority in the **Eastern Province**. Most Saudis generally adhere to the **Hanbali** school of jurisprudence within Sunni Islam and follow the movement established by **Muhammad 'Abd al-Wahhab**, known in the West as **Wahhabism**.

MUSMAK, AL-. [al-musmak; المسمك] A mud-brick fort in **Riyadh**. In January 1902, young **'Abd al-'Aziz bin 'Abd al-Rahman Al Sa'ud** brought a small band of 30 men from Kuwait and captured al-Musmak from its **Al Rashid** garrison, thus restoring Al Sa'ud control over Riyadh.

MUTAWWI'. [muṭawwi', pl. muṭawwi'īn; مطلوع؛ مطوعين] Literally meaning volunteer, mutawwi' is often translated as a member of the "religious" or "morality" police. Formed at the beginning of the 20th century, the mutawwi'in are organized into local committees and bear responsibility for enforcing the adherence of the public to **Islamic** behavior as interpreted within **Wahhabism**. These committees were historically important in consolidating **Al Sa'ud** authority in **Najd** by spreading Wahhabism to the **badu** (bedouin) and they were also a key instrument in converting **al-Hijaz** to Wahhabi views after its conquest in the 1920s. Subsequently the committees were incorporated into the civil service. At present, they come under the control of the **'ulama'** (religious scholars) through the Committee for Encouraging Virtue and Preventing Vice [hay'at al-amr bil-ma'rūf wal-nahī 'an al-munkar; هيئة الامر بالمعروف والنهي عن المنكر]. They are frequently criticized for high-handed behavior and lack of proper training. This was particularly true for their role in preventing girls in Makkah from leaving a school during a fire in early 2002, a number of whom died as a result.

MUTAYR, AL-. [al-muṭayr; sing. muṭayrī; المطير؛ مطيري] One of the principal nomadic tribes of Saudi Arabia, with territory extending across northern **Najd** and into **Kuwait** and **Iraq** via the Wadi al-Batin. The Mutayr are also closely tied to the **Harb** and **al-'Utaybah** tribes. In Najdi politics, the Mutayr traditionally were opposed to the **Al Rashid** rulers of **Ha'il** and were loyal to the **Al Sa'ud** of **Riyadh**. An exception occurred in the 1920s, when the Mutayri shaykh **Faysal al-Duwish** led the tribe into rebellion against Imam **'Abd al-'Aziz Al Sa'ud** as part of the **Ikhwan**.

MUZDALIFAH. [muzdalifah; مزدلفة] A locality about three miles from **Makkah**, associated with the **Islamic** pilgrimage (**hajj**). After leaving **'Arafat**, pilgrims spend the night at Muzdalifah before going on to **Mina**.

- N -

NABATAEAN. [al-nabaṭīyah, pl. al-anbāṭ; النبطية؛ الانباط] A pre-Islamic Arab civilization, of North Arabian origin as distinct from the **South Arabian civilizations** such as Sabaean and Minaean. Originally comprising a nomadic tribe in the area of modern **Jordan**, the Nabataeans gradually moved into Edomite territory and made Petra (near al-'Aqabah in southern Jordan) their capital. Surrounded by mountains and almost impregnable, Petra became a key city on the caravan routes from the Sabaean territories in **Yemen** to the Mediterranean. The Nabataeans were able to resist incursions by successors of Alexander the Great and later became allies of Rome. Reaching its apex just before Christ, the Nabataean kingdom stretched from Damascus in the north to **Mada'in Salih** in the south. But Petra was conquered by Rome and became a Roman province in A.D. 106. Lacking a script for their North Arabian language, the Nabataeans were forced to use Aramaic writing. This gradually evolved into the Arabic alphabet of the **Qur'an** (Koran) and Modern Standard Arabic.

NABK, AL-. *See* QURIYAT, AL-.

NABONIDUS. *See* TAYMA'.

NAFUD, AL-. [al-nafūd; النفود; also spelled Nefud] Generally meaning a sandy desert with dunes, al-Nafud is used more specifically to refer to the great desert which separates Syria from **Iraq** and occupies the eastern half of **Jordan** and much of northern Saudi Arabia. Although there are no settlements, it is crossed regularly by the great **badu** (bedouin) tribes, such as the **'Anazah**, **Shammar**, **al-Dhafir**, and al-Muntafiq.

NAJD. [najd; adjective, najdī; نجد؛ نجدي] The interior region of Central Arabia and one of the most important provinces of Saudi Arabia, as it is the home of the **Al Sa'ud** ruling family and the birthplace of the modern Saudi state.

The word means highland or plateau, and is used as a place-name for similar plateaux elsewhere in the Arab world. Ancient **al-Yamamah** was vaguely commensurate with modern Najd, particularly the southern half. Most of the province is quite arid, extremely hot in the summer and cold in the winter, with an occasional **oasis** settlement (most of which appear to date only from the 14th-16th centuries) interspersed among grazing lands utilized by **badu** (nomadic) tribes. Bounded on the east by **al-Dahna'** desert and on the west by **Jabal Tuwayq** and **al-Hijaz**, Najd contains three main divisions: northern Najd or **Jabal Shammar**, central Najd or **al-Qasim**, and southern Najd. The latter is often known simply as Najd, and includes the towns and districts of **Riyadh** (the capital of Saudi Arabia), **al-'Arid, al-Kharj**, al-Mahmal, **Sudayr, Washm**, and, to the south, al-Hawtah, al-Aflaj, and **Wadi al-Dawasir**. While Jabal Shammar traditionally looked north across **al-Nafud** desert and west to al-Hijaz, and while al-Qasim lay at the intersection of trade routes between al-Hijaz, Syria, **Iraq**, and **Kuwait**, southern Najd tended to be more isolated, with its trade restricted to **al-Ahsa'** in the east and the **Gulf** entrepôts of **Kuwait** and **Bahrain**.

For the last 250 years, Najd has frequently been under the control of the Al Sa'ud, beginning with the First Saudi State (1744-1818) and continuing with the Second Saudi State (1843-1891). Suzerainty over Najd was claimed in the latter part of the 19th century by the **Ottoman** Empire but was never exercised directly, although Ottoman backing helped the **Al Rashid** dynasty of **Ha'il** (in Jabal Shammar) to drive the Al Sa'ud from all of Najd by 1891. The creation of the Third Saudi State (1902-present) under King **'Abd al-'Aziz bin 'Abd al-Rahman** and his sons, began with the ouster of the Al Rashid from Riyadh and southern Najd in 1902. This was followed by the restoration of Saudi authority over al-Qasim and eventually the recapture of Ha'il in 1921, enabling 'Abd al-'Aziz to assume the title of Sultan of Najd (*see* INTRODUCTION for more detail). Najd remains the kingdom's most conservative region because of its traditional isolation and its role as the birthplace of **Muhammad 'Abd al-Wahhab** and his ascetic Wahhabi movement.

NAJRAN. [najrān; نجران; 44 10 - 17 30] An **oasis** settlement and provincial capital, located in the extreme south of Saudi Arabia along the **Yemen** border. Najran is one of the most ancient settlements in Saudi Arabia, the site first of a **Seleucid**-influenced settlement about the ninth century B.C. It flourished as a trading center along the cross-Arabian route to **Thaj** (near the Gulf in northeastern Saudi Arabia) under the Minaean and Sabaean civilizations of **South Arabia**. Najran was mentioned by the geographer Strabo in the first century B.C. as the "Town of the Seven Wells." The main archaeological site at al-Ukhdud in Wadi Najran, not far from the modern city, contains remains of an impressive masonry temple with Sabaean inscriptions and remnants of a large surrounding wall. Other pre-Islamic sites along Wadi Najran include al-Qaryah al-Qadimah, the Jabal 'Ajamah ruins, and al-Ukhdud South.

In the centuries preceding **Islam**, the population of Najran was Christian until a ruler was converted to Judaism and many Christians were subsequently massacred. This resulted in an Abyssinian expedition in A.D. 570 to Najran to protect its Christian inhabitants. Like the rest of Arabia, the people of Najran converted to Islam during the time of the Prophet **Muhammad**. Traditionally, Najran also has been home to an Isma'ili community (a subsect of **Shi'ah** Islam), headed by the Makrami family. Although autonomous in recent centuries, the city fell within the Yemeni sphere of influence until captured by the Al Sa'ud during the 1934 Saudi-Yemeni war. Because of its border location, a major military garrison is located outside the town. Najran was attacked by the Egyptian air force during the Yemen civil war of the 1960s.

NAKHAWILAH. [nakhawilah; نخولة] A **Shi'ah** community of **al-Madinah**, apparently of mixed race and lower social class, traditionally living in the village of al-'Awali. The name means "date palm cultivator," which was their profession until the transformation of al-Madinah into a modern city resulted in less need of their services. Since then they have tended to integrate into the larger community.

NATIONAL GUARD. *See* MILITARY AND DEFENSE.

NATURAL GAS. Although Saudi Arabia has extensive reserves of natural gas, expansion of its production was long delayed by reliance on its massive **oil** reserves, the largest in the world. Until the mid-1990s, most gas production was utilized inside Saudi Arabia to power electricity production, desalinate water, and to provide fuel for petrochemical industries, even though the kingdom had the fourth largest gas reserves in the world. But growing domestic demand and low crude oil prices caused Saudi **ARAMCO** to announce in 1997 that it would invest $5.4 billion over the following five years in the expansion of its gas supply network and to double its production from 3.5 billion cubic feet per day to 7 billion. As part of this effort, nine international oil companies were selected in 2001 to participate in a number of gas projects, including the development of three new fields and the creation of new power plants, transmission pipelines, and water desalination plants. This marked the first major foreign investment in the Saudi oil sector since ARAMCO was nationalized in 1975.

NAWWAF BIN 'ABD AL-'AZIZ AL SA'UD. (1933 or 1934-)
[نواف بن عبدالعزيز آل سعود] One of King **'Abd al-'Aziz**'s sons by an Armenian mother. He was educated privately in the United States and was Commander of the Royal Guard (1952-1956) until removed by King Sa'ud. When his full brother **Talal** resigned as minister of finance in 1961, Nawwaf succeeded him for six months. He was appointed as a Special Adviser on Gulf Affairs to King **Faysal** in 1968 but retired to private life in 1975. Considered to be close to Crown Prince **'Abdullah bin 'Abd al-'Aziz**, he was named Director of General Intelligence in early September 2001 in an unexpected appointment replacing **Turki al-Faysal Al Sa'ud**.

NAYIF BIN 'ABD AL-'AZIZ AL SA'UD. (1934-) [نايف بن عبد العزيز آل سعود]
A son of King **'Abd al-'Aziz** and full brother of King **Fahd bin 'Abd al-**
'Aziz, thus making him one of the influential **"Sudayri Seven"** or Al Fahd.
Nayif served first as Deputy **Amir** (Deputy Governor) and then as Amir
of **Riyadh** (appointed in 1953-1954 at the age of about 20), Amir of **al-**
Madinah, and, after a spell in business, Deputy Minister of the Interior (1970).
He succeeded his brother Fahd as Minister of the Interior in 1975, a position
he still holds. In this position, he oversees the internal security of the country
and often expresses the official viewpoint on when controversial issues occur,
such as high-profile crimes, hijackings, and terrorist acts. He went to Tehran
in 2001 in his official capacity to sign a mutual security agreement with Iran.

NAZIR, HISHAM BIN MUHYI AL-DIN AL-. (1934-) [al-nāzir;
هشام بن محي الدين الناظر] Born in **Jiddah** to a prominent **Makkah** family, he
attended Victoria College in Alexandria and received an M.A. from the
University of California, Los Angeles. Nazir joined the Saudi government
in the Department for Petroleum and Minerals, rising to Deputy Minister
when **Ahmad Zaki Yamani** was named Minister in 1962. In 1968, he was
appointed President of the Central Planning Organization (CPO) and then
Minister of Planning when that portfolio was created in 1975. He was
influential as the principal architect of Saudi Arabia's development plans
through the **oil** boom years and was a guiding force behind the enormous
al-Jubayl and **Yanbu'** industrialization project. He replaced Yamani as
Minister of Petroleum and Mineral Affairs in 1986 and became the first Saudi
Chairman of the Board of **ARAMCO** in 1988. He was dropped from the
cabinet in 1995. *See also* DEVELOPMENT PLANNING.

NEUTRAL ZONES. One of the most intractable problems in drawing definitive
borders between Arabian countries has been drawing lines across the
traditional migratory routes and grazing lands of nomadic tribes. When the
1922 boundary conference at **al-'Uqayr**, involving **Iraq**, **Kuwait**, and **Najd**
(later Saudi Arabia), became stalemated over this issue, Sir **Percy Cox**, the
High Commissioner of Iraq, drew two Neutral Zones. An inland zone was
shared between Iraq and Najd until divided equally in 1980. The other zone
lay along the Gulf coast between Kuwait and Saudi Arabia and was divided
equally in 1966, except for the adjacent islands, ownership of which was
subsequently disputed (*see* QARU AND UMM AL-MARADIM). An offshore
oil concession was jointly awarded to the Japanese-owned Arabian Oil
Company, which discovered oil in 1960 but lost the concession in 2000.
The income from this concession continues to be shared equally between
Kuwait and Saudi Arabia, except during the Iran-Iraq War when the proceeds
were given to Iraq. Onshore concessions belong to Kuwait Oil Company
(following the nationalization of the interests of the previous holder Aminoil)
and Getty Oil (now a subsidiary of TEXACO) on behalf of Saudi Arabia.

NEWSPAPERS. *See* MEDIA.

NIEBUHR, CARSTEN. (1733-1815) A German member of a Danish expedition to the Middle East and India during 1760-1767. The party visited **Jiddah** in Arabia, as well as Mocha and Sanaa in **Yemen.** After the expedition reached Bombay, Niebuhr soon became the sole surviving member. He eventually made his way back to Copenhagen via Muscat in **Oman**, Persia, and Mesopotamia. Niebuhr's accounts of his travels were published as *Description of Arabia* (1772) and *Travels Through Arabia* (1774).

NORTHERN FRONTIER PROVINCE. [al-ḥudūd al-shamālīyah; الحدود الشمالية] One of the 14 main provinces (or **amirates**) of Saudi Arabia, ranking next to the bottom in the number of inhabitants (less than 150,000). Its origins date back only to the late 1940s and the construction of **TAPLINE**, the oil **pipeline** crossing northern Saudi Arabia from the **Eastern Province** to a terminus on the Mediterranean. A province was established along the course of the pipeline, bordering **Iraq** and **Jordan**, and has been known by its present name since 1957. TAPLINE was also responsible for the creation of the settlement of **'Ar'ar**, which serves as the provincial headquarters.

NU'AYMI, 'ALI BIN IBRAHIM AL-. (1935-) [nu'aymī; علي بن ابراهيم النعيمي] Born in the **Eastern Province**, he received degrees in geology from Lehigh University and Stanford University in the **United States.** Joining **ARAMCO** in 1947, he rose through the ranks to become president and chief executive of ARAMCO and a close adviser to the Minister of Petroleum and Mineral Resources **Hisham Nazir**, who he replaced in 1995.

- O -

OASIS. [Arabic wāḥah, pl. wāḥāt; واحة؛واحات] Any place in a desert area where there is sufficient water for agricultural production. Larger oases are often composed of a number of settlements and have sustained cultivation for centuries (and in some cases for millennia). Oases such as **Tayma'** and al-**Jawf** in the northwest of Saudi Arabia have been inhabited for several thousand years. While many oases belong to a single tribe or may be divided between two or three tribes, the old and widespread oases such as **al Ahsa'** and **al-Qatif** (both in the **Eastern Province**) exhibit a mixed and often non-tribal population.

OIL. The first oil concession in Saudi Arabia was signed with the **Eastern and General Syndicate** in 1923 for exploration in **al-Ahsa'** region, but a lack of capital forced the company to let the concession lapse. In 1933, King **'Abd al-'Aziz bin 'Abd al-Rahman** agreed to a 60-year concession covering the **Eastern Province** with Standard Oil of California (SOCAL), which had broken the **British** monopoly in the region by discovering oil in **Bahrain** in 1932. SOCAL's success in gaining the Saudi concession over its British rivals was due principally to its willingness to pay $250,000 in gold upon King 'Abd al-'Aziz's signature, as well as royalties of four gold shillings per ton in the event oil was found. Oil was discovered in **Dhahran** in 1935 and, in 1938, production and exports to the parent company's refinery in

Bahrain began. The outbreak of the Second World War put a halt to activities but production began in earnest after the war.

By 1948, ownership of the concession, by then known as **ARAMCO** (Arabian American Oil Company), was divided between SOCAL (30%), TEXACO (30%), Standard Oil of New Jersey (later Exxon, 30%), and SOCONY Vacuum (later Mobil, 10%). The production levels in 1949 of ½ million barrels per day (mbd) doubled by 1955 and jumped to 3½ mbd by 1960. The growing scarcity of worldwide oil resources in the 1960s and 1970s meant that Saudi production continued to increase each year, eventually reaching an average in excess of 10 mbd. The worldwide recession and oversupply of oil in the 1980s forced adjustments within **OPEC** and Saudi Arabia became the organization's "swing producer." As the kingdom's production capacity exceeded its current requirements, it agreed to reduce its production levels in an attempt to keep the total amount of OPEC production in balance with demand.

By the end of the decade this role had pushed production down to less than 4 mbd and drained Saudi financial reserves at rates in excess of $1 billion per month, thus prompting the Saudi government to declare an end to this policy. Production levels remained depressed until after the **Iraqi** invasion of **Kuwait** in August 1990; the following year saw a return to daily production in excess of 8 mb. This level remained relatively constant through the decade and production at the end of 2001 was about 7.7 mbd. (*See* APPENDIX G, tables 11 through 13, for details of production, exports, and reserves.)

While Saudi ARAMCO (under 100% Saudi ownership since 1980) remains the largest producer in Saudi Arabia, it is not the only one. In 1960, oil was discovered in Japan's Arabian Oil Company offshore concession in the Saudi-Kuwaiti **Neutral Zone**. Saudi ARAMCO took over the concession when it expired in 2000. Saudi ARAMCO, the world's largest oil firm, continues to consolidate its position within the oil industry. In 1988, it became a major partner with TEXACO in retail marketing in the eastern and southern United States and in the 1990s expanded its downstream activities into Greece and Asia. At the same time, Riyadh solicited international investment in its upstream expansion within the kingdom. Initially this was aimed at participation by some of the major international oil companies in exploitation of Saudi **natural gas** reserves. Several private Saudi oil companies are engaged in exploration outside the kingdom.

There is also a political aspect to oil, most obviously in Saudi Arabia's adherence to the Arab oil embargo against the United States and several other countries in 1973-1974 in response to the October 1973 **Arab-Israeli** war. But the kingdom has not repeated this action and stated repeatedly during the second Palestinian *intifadah* (uprising) against Israeli occupation in the first few years of the 2000s that it would not institute a new embargo against the United States. Over the last several decades, the kingdom has increasingly seen its role as ensuring stability between production and pricing and has acted in concert with the oil-consuming nations, within OPEC, and with other global oil producers to maintain a stable price within $5 either direction of a targeted $25 a barrel. When rising oil prices in mid-2000 threatened this objective, King **Fahd bin 'Abd al-'Aziz** announced that

Saudi Arabia's oil policies were directed toward preventing a global economic recession. Riyadh was one of the prime architects of OPEC's system of production quotas and led negotiations with other non-OPEC exporters to curb production levels to maintain stable prices.

OJJEH, AKRAM SUBHI. (1918-c. 1991) [ijjah; اكرام صبحي إجة] A wealthy Saudi businessman of Syrian origin. His principal company was Techniques d'Avant Garde (TAG), which had close links to French business interests, but he was also active as a middleman in arms sales. He was married to the daughter of Syrian Defense Minister Mustafa Tlas and died in Paris.

OLAYAN, SULAYMAN. *See* 'ULAYAN, SULAYMAN.

OMAN AND SAUDI ARABIA. The ancient name of all of the eastern horn of the **Arabian Peninsula**, the name Oman today refers to the territory encompassed within the independent Sultanate of Oman. It took only a few decades after the founding of the First Saudi State before its expansionism took it into Oman: a Saudi expedition ventured onto Oman's Batinah Coast (on the Gulf of Oman) and the ancient city of Suhar was sacked in 1803. Four years later, a joint Saudi-Qasimi (the Qasimi family controlled the northern ports of the Trucial States, now the **United Arab Emirates**) army fought its way down the Batinah to the outskirts of the Omani capital at Muscat. The Omani Al Bu Sa'id rulers attempted to enlist Persian aid, as well as British, in an effort to forestall the Saudi advance but to no avail. By 1814, the Najdi invaders had plundered Muscat's twin city of Matrah and swept into the eastern reaches of Oman, converting the important Bani Bu'Ali tribe to **Wahhabism** in the process. But Saudi fortunes waned with the death of their general, Mutlaq al-Mutayri, the death of the Saudi imam **'Abdullah bin Sa'ud**, and the sacking of the Saudi capital by the **Egyptians** in 1818. Subsequent Saudi invasions of Oman occurred in 1830, 1845, 1854, and 1864. Their eviction from **al-Buraymi** oasis in 1869 introduced a respite of nearly a century, although the Saudis continued to press their claims to large amounts of Omani territory in border negotiations with Britain (acting on behalf of the smaller **Gulf** states).

In August 1952, a Saudi army contingent occupied one of the villages of al-Buraymi and used it as a conduit for the flow of arms and money to dissidents in the Omani interior. With the breakdown of an international arbitration tribunal, the British-officered Trucial Oman Scouts ousted the Saudi garrison from al-Buraymi in October 1955. The Saudis continued to provide moral and material assistance to the Omani dissidents, supporting their cause in the **Arab League** and **United Nations**, providing them with a haven in **al-Dammam**, and training their army.

It was not until Sultan Qabus bin Sa'id overthrew his father in 1970 and met King **Faysal bin 'Abd al-'Aziz** in **Riyadh** in 1971 that Saudi support for the Omani rebels was finally stopped and diplomatic relations established between the two countries for the first time. Saudi Arabia provided some assistance to the Omani government during the rebellion (1965-1975) in its southern province of Dhufar (after having provided arms to the first dissidents in the early 1960s well before the Marxists took charge). In the 1980s, under agreements reached within the **Gulf Cooperation Council** (of which both countries are members), Saudi Arabia provided financial assistance to Oman to strengthen its defenses. In 1991, King **Fahd bin 'Abd al-'Aziz** and Sultan Qabus announced the settlement of their common frontiers, thus ending a troubling factor in bilateral relations since the Buraymi crisis of the 1950s. The final documents regarding the demarcation were signed in **Riyadh** in July 1995.

OPPOSITION GROUPS. Although political parties always have been banned in Saudi Arabia, a small number of opposition groups has existed over the years, generally based outside the country and with miniscule followings. Technically, the first opposition to the Third Saudi State came from the **Ikhwan** in the 1920s. A key armed element in **Imam** (later King) **'Abd al-'Aziz**'s conquest of the various parts of what is now Saudi Arabia, disgruntled tribal leaders transformed the Ikhwan into an implacable foe on politico-religious grounds. The rebellion had to be put down by force at the end of the 1920s. Leaving aside tribal uprisings, the earliest formal opposition organizations appeared in **al-Hijaz** after its conquest by the **Al Sa'ud** during the 1920s. The first of these appears to have been the Hijaz National Party [al-hizb al-watanī al-hijāzī; الحزب الوطني الحجازي], founded in 1924 to uphold the independence of al-Hijaz. After the area fell to the Al Sa'ud, the party's leaders took refuge in **Egypt** for 10 years, but returned after an amnesty in 1935 and accepted ambassadorial and other official posts. There may have been links to the Free Hijazi Party [hizb al-ahrār al-hijāzī; الاحرار الحجازي حزب], in which the **Dabbagh** family was prominent and which was stymied in its preparation for a rebellion in **'Asir** in 1932.

   In the 1950s, a newer, more ideological assortment of opposition groups appeared. Some would argue that the small clique of liberal government officials of the 1950s, including then-Oil Minister **'Abdullah al-Tariqi** and **'Abd al-'Aziz al-Mu'ammar**, formed a group known as Young Najd [najd al-fatīy; نجد الفتي]. Some of these liberals, who allied themselves with the "**Liberal Princes**" faction of **Talal bin 'Abd al-'Aziz Al Sa'ud** and his brothers, were included in King **Sa'ud**'s short-lived "reformist" government of 1960-1961, but lost their positions and went into exile soon after.

   While the Young Najd was reform oriented, other groups and individuals sought to overthrow the Al Sa'ud régime, often through violence. Attempts had been made to assassinate King 'Abd al-'Aziz in 1945 and King **Sa'ud** in 1957-1958. Several military officers were arrested in 1962 and, in 1966, 17 Yemenis were executed after bombs were planted at various sites in **Riyadh**. In May 1969, large numbers of Hadramis (from South **Yemen**) and **Ghamidi** tribesmen were arrested. This was followed a month later by a purge of Air Force officers, along with policemen and civilians, with arrests continuing into 1970. The 1969 arrests apparently included the first arrests of Saudi **women**. Arrests of military personnel carried into 1970 and several hundred **Shi'ah** from **al-Ahsa'** were also arrested at the end of that year on suspicion of being members of the Ba'th Party. Another series of detentions of Army officers was carried out in 1977.

A number of ideologically leftist and revolution-oriented groups appeared about this time, although they remained small, largely ineffective, and, for the most part, operated outside the country. One of the earliest was the Union of Peoples of the Arabian Peninsula (UPAP) [ittiḥād shaʻb al-jazīrah al-ʻarabīyah; اتحاد شعب الجزيرة العربية], a Nasirist organization founded by **Nasir al-Saʻid** following his escape from Saudi Arabia after organizing a strike among **ARAMCO** workers in 1953. The UPAP claimed to have been responsible for the bombings inside the kingdom in 1966 and apparently was weakened severely by the wave of arrests in 1969-1971, as well as by the decline of Egyptian President Jamal ʻAbd al-Nasir's (Nasser) popularity in the Arab world. UPAP members were later instrumental in the formation of the People's Democratic Party and the Socialist Labor Party (see below). Nasir al-Saʻid returned briefly to public attention at the time of the takeover of the Great Mosque in **Makkah** in November 1979, when he implausibly claimed to have planned the incident. He disappeared in Beirut a few weeks later.

A contemporaneous group was the Saudi branch of the Arab Socialist Baʻth Party [ḥizb al-baʻth al-ʻarab al-ishtirākī; حزب البعث العرب الاشتراكي], founded in 1958, first with Syrian and then with **Iraqi** support. Its most effective activity seems to have been publication of the magazine, *Voice of the Vanguard* [sawt al-ṭalīʻah; صوت الطليعة], in Baghdad. The organization became moribund when Iraq improved relations with Saudi Arabia in the 1980s.

The left wing of the party seceded in the 1960s to form several splinter groups, eventually reorganizing under the name of the Popular Democratic Party [al-ḥizb al-dīmūqrāṭī al-shaʻbī; الحزب الديموقراطي الشعبي] in 1970. Most of its members were arrested by 1972 while the remainder used Aden as a base for producing the magazine, *New Peninsula* [al-jazīrah al-jadīdah; الجزيرة الجديدة], and beaming radio broadcasts to the kingdom. Links established with Nasir al-Saʻid's UPAP led to the formation of the League of the Sons of the Arabian Peninsula [rābiṭat abnā' al-jazīrah al-ʻarabīyah; الجزيرة العربية رابطة ابنا]. After a general amnesty following King **Faysal bin ʻAbd al-ʻAziz's** assassination and King **Khalid bin ʻAbd al-ʻAziz's** accession, most members returned to Saudi Arabia and gave up political activity. A 1971 splinter group was the Popular Struggle Front [jabhat al-niḍāl al-shaʻbī; جبهة النضال الشعبي]. A more substantial splinter group was the Socialist Labor Party, founded in 1972 with ties to the Popular Front for the Liberation of Palestine (although these ceased by the late 1970s). The organization was seriously weakened by a 1982 round-up of its members.

The Communist Party of Saudi Arabia (CPSA) [al-ḥizb al-shuyūʻī fī al-saʻūdīyah; الحزب الشيوعي في السعودية] grew out of the ARAMCO Workers' Committee, whose arrest precipitated the 1953 strike and which became the National Reform Front [jabhat al-iṣlāḥ al-waṭanī; جبهة الاصلاح الوطني] in 1954. As the objectives became more socialist and militant, the organization was renamed the National Liberation Front (NLF) [jabhat al-taḥrīr al-waṭanī; جبهة التحرير الوطني] in 1958 and links were established with the National Liberation Front of **Bahrain**. It also suffered a setback when a number of members and/or sympathizers were arrested in 1968-1969. In 1975, the name was changed to the Communist Party of Saudi Arabia, a rather grandiose title for a group thought to number only about 30 individuals. Faced with the growing appeal of **Islamic** movements and the disintegration of the **Soviet Union**, it renamed itself the Democratic Assembly of Saudi Arabia [al-tajammuʿ al-dīmūqrāṭī fī al-saʿūdīyah; التجمع الديموقراطي في السعودية] and began to espouse the cause of democratic reform.

With the rise of Islamic extremism in the 1970s and 1980s, a new breed of opposition appeared, operating at first with often considerable backing from the Islamic Republic of **Iran** after its establishment in 1979. However, the first strike against the régime by the Islamic right came from a neo-Ikhwan movement under **Juhayman bin Muhammad al-ʿUtaybi** which captured the Great Mosque in Makkah in November 1979. It took several weeks with considerable bloodshed to oust the invaders.

Not surprisingly, Iranian support went mainly to Shiʿah groups, most prominently the Organization of the Islamic Revolution in the Arabian Peninsula (OIRAP) [munaẓẓamat al-thawrah al-islāmīyah fī al-jazīrah al-ʿarabīyah; منظمة الثورة الاسلامية في الجزيرة العربية], following the guidance of Ayatollah Muhammad al-Shirazi of al-Qum (Iran) and led by Shaykh Hasan Musa al-Saffar, a Saudi national. It claims to have been formed in 1976 although its name clearly echoes the 1979 Islamic revolution in Iran. The OIRAP took claim for the unrest among the Shiʿah of the **Eastern Province** in 1979-1980. The 1987 riots during the **hajj** (pilgrimage) in Makkah (which left more than 400 dead) were initially thought to have been instigated solely by Iranian pilgrims but links to indigenous Saudi underground organizations were later alleged.

A like-minded party is the strongly pro-Khomeini Hizbullah of al-Hijaz [ḥizb allāh al-ḥijāz; حزب الله الحجاز], founded in 1987 among Shiʿah students who had studied in the Shiʿi centers of Najaf (Iraq) and Qum (Iran). (The reference to al-Hijaz is intended to include all of Saudi Arabia.) Its publications have included "The Victory" [al-fatḥ; الفتح] and "Letter from the Holy Places" [risālat al-ḥaramayn; رسالة الحرمين]. Many of the party's supporters in the Eastern Province were arrested in April 1988 for sabotage, including an explosion in an Eastern Province gas plant in 1987, an explosion at the **Raʾs Tanurah** refinery and a fire at a petrochemical plant in **al-Jubayl** in 1988. Four members were publicly executed in al-Dammam in September 1988. One of these groups and/or their sympathizers were probably also responsible for the bomb set off in Riyadh in 1985 (which killed one and injured three), and the planting of several bombs in Riyadh in 1989. The **United States** government has contended that it was responsible for the truck bombing of American military barracks at al-Khubar in 1996.

The 1990s witnessed the emergence of other Islamic opposition, including both anti-régime activists within the country and several organizations in exile. An early development was the submission of an "advisory memorandum" to King **Fahd** in August 1992, detailing grievances against the régime, including the repression of its citizens and its close ties to the United States. This memorandum appears to have been the genesis of the Committee for the Defense of Legitimate Rights (CDLR), more accurately translated as the Committee for the Defense of **Shariʿah** [Islamic law] Rights, founded in May 1993 by a group of well-known religious conservatives, including

Shaykh **'Abdullah bin Sulayman al-Mas'ari**, a former judge and head of the Saudi diwan of ombudsmen. 'Abdullah's son **Muhammad**, the spokesman of the group, was quickly arrested after the group's formation but escaped six months later to **Britain**, where he set up an office of the CDLR in exile. His organization received extensive media attention in the West and faxed its publications to many addressees in the kingdom. The British government denied his application for political asylum in November 1994 but its attempt to deport him was overturned by an appeals court. During the process of fighting the order, a rift developed between Mas'ari and his colleague, Dr. **Sa'd al-Faqih**, who left CDLR to found the Movement for Islamic Reform in Arabia. Thereafter the CDLR began to seek a wider Islamic audience, possibly because it had lost much of its Saudi funding to the rival group.

Other prominent religious figures such as Shaykh **Salman al-'Awdah** and Shaykh **Safar al-Hawali** were also calling for reform of the government and criticizing the basing of American and other Western forces in the holy land of Arabia during and after the **Kuwait** War. Tapes of their sermons circulated widely within the kingdom and they acquired a large following. In 1994, following public protests led by the two figures, the Saudi government arrested both along with more than a hundred of their sympathizers, especially in al-Qasim. More arrests followed over the next year or two, including that of Shaykh **Hamud bin 'Uqla' al-Shu'aybi**, who was held for two months in 1995. Most of those detained, including 'Awdah and Hawali, were released in 1999.

CDLR's establishment of a London office was preceded by another organization, the Committee for Advice and Reform, created by **Usamah bin Ladin**. Usamah had left the kingdom to fight in the war waged against the Soviets in **Afghanistan**. On his return home, Usamah became known as one of the "Arab Afghans," a term for the young men who followed a radical religion-based ideology as a result of their experiences in Afghanistan. His extremist views were anathema to the Saudi government, which withheld his passport during 1989-1991. In 1991 he found it expedient to move on to Sudan, where he supported the Islamist government dominated by Hasan al-Turabi and established a number of businesses. His activities there led the Saudi government in 1994 to revoke his citizenship and freeze his assets in Saudi Arabia. At the same time, he established the Committee for Advice and Reform in London, which seems to have cooperated with the more moderate CDLR in criticizing the Saudi régime.

American and Saudi pressure on the government of Sudan forced Usamah to relocate to Afghanistan in 1996. By this time, the tentacles of his **al-Qa'idah** movement appear to have stretched to a number of countries, notably Egypt and Yemen as well as Saudi Arabia. Although the specifics are hazy, Usamah seems to have had close ties with the Aden-Abyan Islamic Army in southern Yemen, which kidnapped a group of tourists in December 1998. A number of their captives were killed in a firefight with Yemeni soldiers and the head of the "army" was tried in Yemeni courts, convicted, and executed. But adherents, many of them "Arab Afghans," remained at large in remote areas of the country. It is widely thought that some of them, in conjunction with

Usamah bin Ladin, were responsible for the bomb attack on the American naval vessel, the USS *Cole*, in Aden harbor in September 2000. The four Saudis executed for the November 1995 bombing of a building in Riyadh used by an American training team for the Saudi Arabian National Guard, killing five Americans and two Indians, claimed to be influenced by Muhammad al-Mas'ari and Usamah bin Ladin.

On 11 September 2001, apparent members of al-Qa'idah hijacked four airliners on domestic flights in the United States and used them as flying bombs to destroy the World Trade Center in New York and to damage the Pentagon in Washington. As a consequence, American President George W. Bush declared a "war on terror" and carried out a military campaign in Afghanistan to destroy that country's Taliban régime and to kill or capture as many al-Qa'idah members as possible.

It is clear from the 11 September hijackings that Usamah had acquired a number of Saudi adherents, as 15 of the 19 hijackers were of Saudi nationality. A significant number of the Saudis involved came from the southern and western regions of the kingdom, areas that traditionally have nursed grievances against the central region of Najd, home of the ruling Al Sa'ud family, and have benefited relatively less from oil income. In addition, at least 45 Saudis were killed in the 2001 war in Afghanistan and at least 240 more Saudis were captured.

ORGANIZATION OF ARAB PETROLEUM EXPORTING COUNTRIES (OAPEC). Founded in 1968 to promote the interests of the Arab members of the more inclusive **Organization of Petroleum Exporting Countries** (OPEC). It was originally composed of the more traditional Arab oil producers (Saudi Arabia, **Kuwait**, and Libya) but, following the 1969 revolution in Libya, it expanded to include Algeria, **Bahrain**, **Egypt**, **Iraq**, **Qatar**, Syria, Abu Dhabi, and Dubai (which withdrew from OAPEC in the early 1970s). Tunisia's membership was suspended at its own request in 1986. Contrary to popular myth, the "Arab oil boycott" following the October 1973 **Arab-Israeli** War was not an OAPEC action. The organization has established a number of oil-related enterprises, including the Arab Maritime Petroleum Transport Corporation (1973), the Arab Shipbuilding and Repair Yard in Bahrain (1975), the Arab Petroleum Investments Corporation (1975), the Arab Petroleum Services Company (1977), and the Arab Petroleum Training Institute (1978). A Saudi, **'Abd al-'Aziz bin 'Abdullah al-Turki**, has been Secretary-General since 1990.

ORGANIZATION OF THE ISLAMIC CONFERENCE (OIC). A grouping of 56 Islamic states established at the first summit of the leaders of the Islamic world in 1969. Saudi Arabia was the principal force behind the creation of the OIC, originally as a counter to an Arab League dominated by radical Arab states. OIC summits to discuss and advance global Islamic interests have been held regularly at three-year intervals since then. More frequent meetings are held by member foreign and information ministers. In 1970, a permanent secretariat was created with its headquarters in **Jiddah** and the organization has created a number of subunits dealing with cultural heritage, trade, Islamic banking, and Islamic universities. The attendance of Heir Apparent **'Abdullah bin 'Abd al-'Aziz** at the 1997 OIC summit in Tehran marked the most senior visit by a Saudi to **Iran** since the 1979 revolution and spurred a rapprochement between the two countries.

ORGANIZATION OF PETROLEUM EXPORTING COUNTRIES (OPEC). An international organization composed of 12 oil-exporting Third World countries, including Saudi Arabia. OPEC was founded in 1960 to assure its members a stable price for their petroleum; headquarters were subsequently established in Vienna. The organization carried considerable clout following the October 1973 **Arab-Israeli** War and into the early 1980s because of a worldwide **oil** scarcity. However, the subsequent oil glut which stretched well into the 1990s and the emergence of a competing bloc of non-OPEC oil-exporting countries (NOPEC) severely taxed OPEC's ability to function as a cohesive group and its attempts to fix a minimum price for its crude oil and to establish country production quotas foundered on undercutting by member states. The late 1980s were characterized by increased bickering within the organization, the refusal of Saudi Arabia to continue its financially disastrous "swing producer" role, and finally the invasion in 1990 of one OPEC member (**Kuwait**) by another (**Iraq**), ostensibly because of Kuwait's blatant disregard of its OPEC quota amongst other reasons. In late 1992, Ecuador became the first member to secede from OPEC. By the beginning of the 21st century, OPEC's share of world oil production had fallen to about 36 percent, even though its members controlled 80 percent of global oil reserves.

OTTOMAN EMPIRE AND SAUDI ARABIA. The Ottoman dynasty was descended from a principality in Anatolia founded by a Turkish clan in the 13th century. The Ottoman state conquered Constantinople in 1453 (renaming it Istanbul) and began a gradual expansion that established Istanbul's authority across most of the Arab world, as well as what is now Turkey and the Balkans. The Ottomans first penetrated the **Arabian Peninsula** in the 16th century, moving down the **Red Sea** coast from Palestine to occupy **al-Hijaz**, including the holy cities of **Makkah** and **al-Madinah**, and continuing to **Yemen**. But Istanbul's power waned in the succeeding centuries. When the **Al Sa'ud** carried the **Wahhabi** banner out of **Najd** in the early 19th century, capturing al-Madinah in 1810, Istanbul was forced to ask its nominal viceroy of **Egypt**, Muhammad 'Ali, to send an expedition to punish the invaders of the Holy Places. Makkah and al-Madinah were soon retaken and, by 1818, Muhammad 'Ali's son, Ibrahim Pasha, had demolished the Wahhabi threat by razing the Al Sa'ud capital of **al-Dir'iyah** and carrying off the Saudi leader to be executed. A second Egyptian campaign was mounted in 1838 to deal with the reemergence of the Al Sa'ud threat and a second Saudi leader was captured.

A recrudescence of Ottoman expansionism in the Arabian Peninsula began with the appointment of Midhat Pasha as Governor-General of Baghdad in 1868 and reached full flower during the reign of Sultan Abdülhamid (r. 1876-1909). One jaw of the pincers enveloping the Peninsula covered the Red Sea coast, including much of Yemen, while the other was busy with extending influence along the Gulf. Ottoman garrisons were established in **al-Ahsa', al-Qatif, al-Qasim**, and **Qatar**, while the ruler of **Kuwait** rather vaguely acknowledged Istanbul's authority. Even though Istanbul was unable to establish direct mastery over the interior, the alliance with the **Al Rashid** dynasty of **Ha'il** allowed the latter to extend their control gradually over all **Najd**, driving the Al Sa'ud to seek refuge in Kuwait in 1891.

Subsequently, however, further Ottoman expansion was precluded by **British** protection of the small shaykhdoms of the **Gulf**. The Al Thani of Qatar drove the small Ottoman garrison out in 1893 and Istanbul renounced all claims to Qatar in the unratified Anglo-Turkish convention of 1913. Even Kuwait slipped from Istanbul's grasp by accepting protected status under the British in 1899. Elsewhere, the Ottoman position in Arabia was threatened by the recrudescence of Saudi power under **'Abd al-'Aziz bin 'Abd al-Rahman** following his retaking of **Riyadh** in 1902. Despite a brief period during which 'Abd al-'Aziz accepted recognition as the Ottoman *qa'im-maqam* (governor) of Najd, the Al Sa'ud aligned themselves with the British against Istanbul. 'Abd al-'Aziz succeeded first in driving the Ottomans out of al-Ahsa' and al-Qatif in 1913. Then, with British support, he began to recover central Najd from the Al Rashid while Sharif **Husayn al-Hashimi** in al-Hijaz declared himself independent of Istanbul in 1916. The last significant Ottoman stronghold, al-Madinah, was besieged by Hashimi troops in 1917 as the forces of the Al Sa'ud were advancing at the same time on the Al Rashid capital at Ha'il. The small garrison in al-Madinah, which held out throughout the war and surrendered only in 1919, was the last of the Ottoman presence in Arabia.

It is worth noting that the new Saudi Arabian kingdom absorbed two remnants of the Ottoman legacy. First, the administrative system of al-Hijaz had been fashioned by the Ottomans, was left unchanged by the brief Hashimi kingdom, and then was adopted nearly wholesale by the Saudis. Second, a number of officials of Turkish origin remained in al-Hijaz after the Ottoman retreat and their families have integrated into Saudi society. Perhaps the best known example is that of **'Adnan Khashaqji** (Khashoggi).

- P -

PAKISTAN AND SAUDI ARABIA. The kingdom has enjoyed close and friendly relations with fellow Muslim state Pakistan since the latter country became independent in 1947. In part, Saudi strategy has been based on the supportive role that the larger Pakistan can play in regional security. From 1983 until 1987, Pakistan loaned a tank brigade and more than 10,000 soldiers to help bolster the kingdom's defenses; several thousand other Pakistani pilots, technicians, and advisers continued to serve in Saudi Arabia on secondment or private contract. Many other Pakistanis are employed throughout the kingdom as professionals and as skilled and unskilled labor. It has been speculated that Saudi Arabia has also supported Pakistan's development of nuclear weaponry, although there is no real evidence for this.

Another underlying reason for the close relationship lies in personal ties between the elites in both countries. Many wealthy Saudis enjoy hunting in Pakistan and have built houses there. Saudi Heir Apparent Prince **'Abdullah bin 'Abd al-'Aziz** made Pakistan the last visit in his 1998 world tour and Pakistani military ruler General Pervez Musharraf made his first trip abroad to the kingdom a year later. In 2000, Saudi Arabia agreed to allow exiled former Pakistani Prime Minister Nawaz Sharif to reside in the kingdom. The **Saudi Fund for Development** provided Pakistan with $285 million in loans during the period 1975-2001.

PALGRAVE, WILLIAM GIFFORD. (1826-1888) An English ex-soldier and Jesuit priest, Palgrave journeyed through Arabia in 1862-1863 on an obscure mission for Napoleon III, travelling to **Jabal Shammar, Riyadh**, and **al-Qatif** before making his way down the **Gulf** littoral. His account of these travels was published as *Narrative of a Year's Journey Through Central and Eastern Arabia* (1865), but numerous inaccuracies and mistakes have cast doubt on his veracity.

PELLY, LEWIS. (1825-1895) An army and political officer of the Government of India. Pelly was named Political Agent in Zanzibar in 1860 and then officiating Political Resident in the Persian Gulf (PRPG) in 1861. His position was made permanent in 1862 and he held it until 1872. Strong willed and sometimes narrow-minded, Pelly understood his role in the **Gulf** as that of an agent of Western civilization and acted forcefully to thwart **Wahhabi** expansionism along the Gulf littoral. In 1861, he made an epic journey to **Riyadh** to meet the **Al Sa'ud** Imam **Faysal bin Turki** in an attempt to mend frayed relations and to forestall French ambitions in the region. While his mission had little political impact, as Faysal died shortly afterwards and the French challenge was short-lived, Pelly's account, published by the Government of India as *Report on a Journey to the Wahabee Capital of Riyadh in Central Arabia* (1865), added considerably to Europe's knowledge of the history, geography, and flora and fauna of central Arabia. He later held important posts in India and eventually became a Member of Parliament.

PERIPLUS OF THE ERYTHRAEAN SEA. A descriptive account of the **Red Sea** and surrounding lands, written by an anonymous Greek author about A.D. 50-60. The narrative provides some of the earliest written references about the inhabitants of Arabia and early Arabian civilizations.

PERSIAN GULF. *See* GULF, THE.

PETRA. *See* NABATAEANS.

PETROLINE. *See* PIPELINES.

PETROMIN. [General Organization for Petroleum and Minerals] PETROMIN was established in 1962 as a state **oil** company with the goal of diversifying the economy away from its sole dependence on crude oil production by the addition of such sources of income as minerals and petrochemicals. Other PETROMIN ventures have included upstream activities in oil and mineral exploration, and downstream activities in the establishment of refineries for the domestic and export markets and the creation of a supertanker fleet. A gold mine at **Mahd al-Dhahab** in **al-Hijaz** began production in 1989 under PETROMIN supervision.

PHARAON. *See* FARA'AWN.

PHILBY, H. ST. JOHN B. (1885-1960) A 20th-century British diplomat turned traveler and writer. Philby joined the Indian Political Service in 1907 and served in Iraq from 1915 to 1917. Sent to treat with Imam **'Abd al-'Aziz bin 'Abd al-Rahman Al Sa'ud** in 1917, he ended up crossing the **Arabian Peninsula** from **Kuwait** to **Jiddah** in the first of his many journeys of Arabian exploration. After subsequently serving in Iraq and Transjordan, Philby resigned from British government service and settled in Jiddah. He became a businessman and close adviser to King 'Abd al-'Aziz. He also converted to **Islam**, acquiring a Muslim wife and family (in addition to his English family). Philby was noted as an indefatigable explorer of Arabia, including becoming the second European to cross the great **Rub' al-Khali** sand desert, as well as a prolific author of books on Arabia. After King 'Abd al-'Aziz's death in 1953, Philby was temporarily banished from the kingdom and died in Beirut in 1960. His son Kim gained notoriety when he defected to Moscow in 1963 as he was about to be exposed as a Soviet spy in British intelligence.

PIPELINES. The Trans-Arabian Pipeline (TAPLINE) was built by **ARAMCO** in 1950 to carry crude oil from the Saudi oil fields in the **Eastern Province** across Syria, **Jordan**, and **Lebanon** to a terminal at Sidon, Lebanon. The line suffered endless problems with transit fees across the above countries and the Lebanese civil war put an end to its operations in Sidon. TAPLINE continued to operate fitfully through the mid-1980s but only to supply a small refinery in Jordan; it was closed down in 1990 in Saudi protest at Jordan's refusal to condemn the **Iraqi** invasion of **Kuwait**. PETROLINE was constructed in 1981 by **PETROMIN** to carry up to 1.9 mbd of crude oil from the Gulf oil fields to **Yanbu'** on the **Red Sea**. During the Iran-Iraq War, PETROLINE was expanded to provide **Iraq** with a safe terminal for its oil: known as IPSA-1 (the Iraq Pipeline Across Saudi Arabia) and completed in 1986, this pipeline boasted a capacity of 3 mbd shared by Saudi Arabia and Iraq. In 1989, all Iraqi oil was transferred to a new independent pipeline, IPSA-2, which terminated near Yanbu'. Iraqi use of this pipeline was suspended after Iraq's invasion of Kuwait in August 1990. Saudi Arabia confiscated the disused IPSA-2 in June 2001 following a series of Iraqi border incursions (and claiming the decision was taken because of Iraq's failure to repay the war loans provided during the Iran-Iraq War). Riyadh announced plans to convert the pipeline to carry natural gas.

POLITICAL PARTIES. *See* OPPOSITION GROUPS.

POLITICS. *See* GOVERNMENT.

POPULATION. There are no reliable early population figures for the kingdom. A sample census in 1974 put the total resident population at 7 million, of which nearly 47 percent were under the age of 16. The 1992 census recorded nearly 17 million people, including 4.6 million expatriates. By 1999, total population was estimated at 21.3 million, including 5.7 million expatriates. The kingdom's population is projected to reach nearly 34 million by 2015, in large part because of explosive population growth rates, estimated at 4.5 percent in 1990 and 2.6 percent in 1999. Some 50 percent of all Saudis are under the age of 18. Much of this population growth has been in the country's urban centers. The capital **Riyadh** has a population estimated at 3.5 million in 2001, while **Jiddah**, **Makkah**, and **al-Madinah** all have more than a million residents. **Al-Ta'if** and the **Dhahran-al-Dammam** conurbation in the **Eastern Province** are not much smaller.

PROVINCES. *See* GOVERNMENT.

- Q -

QADI. [qāḍī, pl. quḍāh; قضاة؛قضي] A judge or magistrate in **Islamic** jurisprudence.

QAHTAN. [qahtān; qahtānī; قحطان؛ قحطاني] Among the oldest tribes of Arabia and one of the few to have retained its ancient identity. There are two major divisions today: the settled elements of southern Qahtan, which live on the eastern slopes of **'Asir** province, and the northern Qahtan, which are generally nomadic and stretch from the **Rub' al-Khali** desert up into southern **Najd**.

QA'IDAH, AL-. [al-qā'idah; القاعدة] A radical Islamic organization founded by Saudi activist **Usamah bin Ladin** about 1994, drawing upon other "Arab Afghans" and disaffected young Muslims in Saudi Arabia, **Yemen**, **Egypt**, and other Islamic countries as members. From 1996, Usamah and the organization made their headquarters in **Afghanistan**, establishing close ties to the country's reactionary Taliban régime. Al-Qa'idah apparently had ties to the Aden-Abyan Islamic Army in Yemen, which kidnapped a number of foreign tourists in 1998, some of whom were killed in a firefight with government troops, and seems to have organized the September 2000 attack on a US naval vessel in Yemen's Aden harbor. On 11 September 2001, 19 al-Qa'idah members hijacked four American domestic airliners and used them to destroy the World Trade Center in New York and severely damage the Pentagon in Washington, killing more than 3,000 people. The **United States** and allies subsequently destroyed al-Qa'idah bases in Afghanistan, killed hundreds of its members, and captured hundreds more, many of whom were taken to an American base at Guantánamo Bay in Cuba. The whereabouts of al-Qa'idah's leader, Usamah bin Ladin, however, could not be established through 2002, and it was believed that al-Qa'idah members and units remained at large in a number of countries. An attack on a French oil tanker off the coast of **Yemen** and the bombing of several nightclubs on the island of Bali in Indonesia, both in October 2002, were attributed to a resurgence of al-Qa'idah activities. *See also* OPPOSITION GROUPS.

QARAMITAH, AL-. [al-qarāmiṭah; sing. qarmaṭī; قرامطة؛ قرمطي; also known as Carmathians] An early splinter from the Isma'ili subsect of **Shi'ah Islam**, which originated in **Iraq** in the late ninth century A.D. and consisted of a movement of peasants and the dispossessed taking their name from one of the founders, Hamdan Qarmat. Al-Qaramitah created a secret society, emphasizing the equality of all workers and a belief in communal property, as well as a readiness to kill other **Muslims** who did not accept their convictions. They were a factor in the uprising of the Zanj (African blacks) at Basra in A.D. 868-883 and they established a state in eastern Arabia, based on **al-Hufuf**, in 899, as well as a stronghold at Salamyah in northern Syria. From these bases, al-Qaramitah sought to overthrow orthodox Islam by subversion and outright attack. Under the leadership of Abu Sa'id al-Hasan al-Jannabi, the movement conquered **al-Yamamah** about A.D. 903 and invaded **Oman**. Al-Jannabi's son conducted raids across lower Iraq and attacked **Makkah** in 930, taking away the sacred Black Stone of the **Ka'bah**, which was recovered only in 951. Their heretical beliefs and violent aggressiveness meant that al-Qaramitah were not tolerated and the movement disappeared about a century later.

QARQANI, KHALID "ABU WALID" AL-. (c. 1890-?) [al-qarqānī; القرقاني [خالد (ابو وليد)] A native of Tripoli (now in Libya) who was said to have fought the Italians before retiring in exile to Egypt. Apparently brought to Saudi Arabia in 1930 by **Hafiz Wahbah**, he engaged in business in **Jiddah**, accompanied **Karl Twitchell** on his water and mineral surveys, and served as a trusted adviser to King **'Abd al-'Aziz** on border disputes, oil negotiations, and international treaties. A strong Arab nationalist, he was appointed a Minister of State in the first council of ministers established by King **Sa'ud** in 1954. He had retired to Libya in the 1960s where he is buried.

QARU AND UMM AL-MARADIM. [qārū; umm al-marādim; قارو؛ ام المرادم; 48 39 - 28 41] Two uninhabited islands lying offshore from the former Kuwait-Saudi Arabian **Neutral Zone**. When the two states agreed to divide the Neutral Zone in 1965, the question of sovereignty over these islands was left for later settlement. Saudi Arabia was reported to have occupied the islands in the late 1970s. **Iraq** occupied one or both as part of their invasion of **Kuwait** in 1990 but were subsequently ousted. They appear not to be physically occupied after that but the question of whether sovereignty belongs to Kuwait or Saudi Arabia still seems unsettled.

QASIM, AL-. [al-qaṣīm; qaṣīmī; القصيم؛ قصيمي] A province in central Arabia and traditionally the central district of historic **Najd**. Flat, almost featureless, and about 80 miles across, al-Qasim is dominated by the Wadi al-Rummah, along which are situated the two main settlements of **Buraydah** and **'Unayzah**. Frequently autonomous throughout modern history, the region was contested between the **Al Rashid** family of **Shammar** (northern Najd) and the **Al Sa'ud** family of **Riyadh** (southern Najd) in the late 19th and early 20th centuries. Endowed with relatively plentiful water supplies from the Wadi al-Rummah and its tributaries, al-Qasim has always supported a substantial sedentary population based on agriculture. In recent years, the region has been the center of an explosion of commercial wheat farming. Many of its people are from the **Bani Tamim**, but other tribes, such as **'Anazah, 'Utaybah, Harb, al-Mutayr**, and **Bani Khalid**, are represented. Its location in the center of Arabia also meant that the towns of al-Qasim were the focal points of long-distance caravan trade linking Basra (in **Iraq**), **Kuwait**, Damascus (in Syria), **Ha'il**, Riyadh, and **al-Hijaz**. As a consequence of the resultant broad worldview, the emphasis on education (many Qasimis traditionally were sent abroad for studies), and reputation as hard workers (many Qasimis were among the workers building the Suez Canal), the Saudi state in this century has often relied on Qasimis to fill top positions.

QATAR AND SAUDI ARABIA. The state of Qatar, independent since 1971, is located entirely on a peninsula of the same name jutting into the **Gulf** from the Arab littoral. Qatar's land boundary across the base of the peninsula is shared with Saudi Arabia. Ties have traditionally been close between the two countries, and between the **Al Sa'ud** and Qatar's ruling family, the Al Thani. In part, this is because many of Qatar's tribes, from which the majority of the population is derived, straddle the border with Saudi Arabia. In addition, most Qataris are not only **Sunni Muslims** but follow the **Wahhabi** path, as is the case in Saudi Arabia.

In October 1992, the close ties between Qatar and the kingdom were jeopardized by a Saudi attack on a Qatari border post, which left several Qatari soldiers dead and caused Qatar to suspend the two countries' 1965 border accord. When Riyadh refused to back down, Qatar began to suspend its participation in meetings of the **Gulf Cooperation Council** (GCC). A settlement was reached on the eve of the December 1992 GCC summit, which apparently confirmed Qatar's jurisdiction over the border post while recognizing Saudi sovereignty in the land corridor separating Qatar from the **United Arab Emirates**. However, the agreed demarcation of the border was not carried out and several more incidents involving fishing boats occurred during 1994, leading to more Qatari boycotts of some GCC meetings. Relations were further complicated the following year when Saudi Arabia appeared to support ex-**Amir** Khalifah bin Hamad Al Thani in his attempts to regain his control of Qatar after being ousted by his son Hamad. Matters were patched up in 1996 when the two countries agreed to proceed with demarcation of their common border; the final demarcation maps were signed in March 2001.

QATIF, AL-. [al-qaṭīf; القطيف; 49 58 - 26 36] The second largest **oasis** in the **Eastern Province**, adjoining the **Gulf** coast north of **al-Dammam**; also the name of the largest town of the oasis. Other towns include al-Sayhat and Safwah, and there are nearly three dozen villages. The oasis was an important trading center and Christian center from early times and had a long connection with Darin on nearby **Tarut Island**. The present town of al-Qatif dates from approximately the same period of the eighth-ninth centuries, and it was held by the Portuguese in the 16th century. Al-Qatif is unique in Saudi Arabia in that the great majority of its population consists of indigenous but non-tribal Arabs of the **Shi'ah** sect. It was the site of Shi'ah demonstrations after the **Iranian** revolution in 1979, protesting Saudi government neglect.

QIRSH. [qirsh, pl. qurūsh; قرش؛ قروش] A subunit of the national currency, the Saudi **riyal**. One riyal contains 100 qurush.

QUNFUDHAH, AL-. [al-qunfudhah; القنفذة; 41 15 - 19 08] A traditional port and fishing town on the **Red Sea**, administratively at the southern tip of the province of **Makkah**. Formerly under **Ottoman** control, al-Qunfudhah was recognized by the British as belonging to the **Idrisi amir** of '**Asir** in 1915, incorporated into the Kingdom of **al-Hijaz** in 1916, and finally fell to the Saudis in 1924. The name in Arabic means hedgehog.

QUR'AN, AL-. [al-qur'ān; القرآن] Frequently spelled Koran, it is the holy book of **Islam**, revealed by God (Allah) to **Muhammad the Prophet** through the Angel Gabriel [Jabrā'īl; جبرائيل]. It serves as the primary source of authority and doctrine in Islam, before the **Sunnah** (the example by word and deed of Muhammad the Prophet).

QURAYSH. [quraysh; sing. qurayshī; قريش؛ قريشي] The tribe of the Prophet **Muhammad**. Originating in North Arabia, the Quraysh settled in **Makkah** and by the time of the Prophet's birth had become the leading merchants of Makkah and its hinterland.

QURAYSHI, 'ABD AL-'AZIZ AL-. (1930-) [عبدالعزيز القريشي] A Saudi bureaucrat, born in Ha'il and educated in the **United States**. After heading the State Railways (1961-1968) and the General Personnel Bureau (1968-1974), he became a Minister of State (1971-1974). From 1974, he spent many years as Governor of the **Saudi Arabian Monetary Agency**. Among his business interests, he is Chairman of the Saudi International Bank.

QURIYAT, AL-. [al-qurīyāt; القريات; 57 55 - 23 20] A province (**imarah**) in extreme northwestern Saudi Arabia, bordering **Jordan** and taking its name from a system of oasis settlements in the Wadi Sirhan, collectively known as Quriyat al-Milh, "the villages of salt," because of the considerable salt deposits located in the area. These include al-Nabk [النبك], Kaf [kāf; كاف], Manwah [منوة], al-Qarqar [القرقر], al-Hadithah [al-hadīthah; الحديثة], and Ithra [ithrā; اثرا]. Along with al-Jawf, at the southern end of **Wadi Sirhan**, al-Quriyat contains some of Arabia's oldest settlement sites, dating from the middle of the second millennium B.C. Ithra contains ruins of a **Nabataean** palace, remnants of an Iron Age settlement are perched on top of Jabal al-Sa'idi [jabal al-sa'īdī; جبل السعيدي] outside Kaf, and what is possibly Arabia's oldest irrigation network was built near al-Hadithah at the end of the first millennium B.C. Al-Quriyat has the smallest population of any province, with a total of perhaps only 40,000. The original provincial capital of Kaf was regarded as unsuitable because of the prevalence of **sabkhah**s (salt marshes) and malaria, and it was moved to al-Nabk.

QUSAYBI, AL-. [al-quṣaybī; القصيبي; also spelled Gosaibi] An important merchant family of the **Eastern Province**, with commercial interests in **Najd** and elsewhere in the kingdom. Although settled in **al-Ahsa'**, the family has strong ties to **Bahrain**, where a member of the family, 'Abd al-'Aziz, served as King **'Abd al-'Aziz'**s agent and de facto ambassador for many years. Another family member, 'Abd al-Rahman, was made a Minister of State in 1955. But the best known politician in the family is Ghazi bin 'Abd al-Rahman, who received his Ph.D. from the University of London and taught at Riyadh University (now **King Sa'ud University**) before entering government service. He was appointed Minister of Industry and Electricity in King **Khalid'**s 1975 cabinet of technocrats and later shifted to Minister of Health. In 1984, Ghazi published a poem in a Saudi newspaper embodying a veiled attack on corrupt members of the royal family and was abruptly dismissed from his position. He subsequently served as the Saudi ambassador to Bahrain until appointed ambassador to the United Kingdom in July 1992. He was named Minister of Water in September 2002. He is well known as a poet and author, and some of his books have been translated into English.

- R -

RABADAH, AL-. *See* DARB ZUBAYDAH.

RADIO. *See* MEDIA.

RAHMAH BIN JABIR. *See* DAMMAM, AL-.

RAHMAH, JABAL. [jabal rahmah; جبل رحمة] The "Mount of Mercy." A small hill in the plain of **'Arafat**, near **Makkah**. On the second day of the Islamic pilgrimage (**hajj**), the pilgrims gather at Jabal Rahmah for the "Standing" [al-wuquf; الوقف], which is an essential part of the pilgrimage.

RAILROADS. Saudi Arabia possesses only one working railroad, built in 1951 and running for 350 miles between **al-Dammam** on the **Gulf** coast and the capital at **Riyadh**, via the oasis of **al-Ahsa'**. A second parallel line linking Riyadh with **al-Hufuf** in al-Ahsa' oasis was completed in 1985. There has been some discussion of rail links between al-Dammam and **al-Jubayl** in the **Eastern Province** and even between Riyadh and **Jiddah** on the **Red Sea**. The Hijaz Railway was built between 1900 and 1908 by the **Ottomans** to move supplies and troops across Syria and **Jordan** to **al-Madinah** in **al-Hijaz**. It was destroyed in 1917 as part of the Arab Rebellion against the Ottomans under Sharif **Husayn bin 'Ali al-Hashimi**.

RAJIHI, AL-. [al-rājihi; الراجحي] One of the wealthiest Saudi merchant families, with estimates of the total family fortune ranging up to $3 billion. The heart of the family business was long al-Rajhi Company for Currency Exchange and Commerce, established by four brothers (Sulayman, Muhammad, Salih, and 'Abdullah) from al-Buqayrah in **al-Qasim**. The company was converted in 1988 into al-Rajhi Banking Investment Corporation, the kingdom's first Islamic bank.

RAMADAN. [ramaḍān; رمضان] The ninth month of the **Islamic** calendar, during which all **Muslims** are expected to abstain from eating, drinking, smoking, and sexual activity between sunrise and sunset. The breaking of the fast is followed by the holiday of **'Id** al-Fitr.

RA'S TANŪRAH. [ra's tanūrah; رأس تنورة; 50 10 - 26 39] A port in the **Eastern Province**, created in 1939 when an oil **pipeline** from **Dhahran** was extended to a terminal built several miles out into the shallow waters of the **Gulf** for the transshipment of Saudi crude **oil** by sea to a refinery in **Bahrain**. The site of Jawan [jāwān; جاوان] a few miles to the northeast contains a **Seleucid** tomb complex.

RASHID, AL. [āl rashīd; rashīdī; آل رشيد؛رشيدي] A 19th-century central Arabian dynasty, based on the town of **Ha'il** in northern **Najd** and derived from a shaykhly clan of the **Shammar** tribe. The progenitor, 'Abdullah bin Rashid, had been made governor of Ha'il by the **Al Saud** Imam **Faysal bin Turki** in 1835 but, during the latter's five-year exile in Cairo, 'Abdullah was able to make himself virtually independent of the Al Sa'ud by the time of his death in 1848. When civil war broke out amongst the Al Sa'ud on Faysal's death in 1865, 'Abdullah's son and successor Talal (r. 1848-1868) declared his independence. But it was another son Muhammad (r. 1869-1897) who proved to be the strongest personality in Najd and who worked gradually to consolidate a network of tribal alliances and thus expand Rashidi domination over all Najd and westwards into **al-Jawf**.

The Saudi capital at **Riyadh** fell to Muhammad in 1884 and he forced Saudi Imam **'Abd al-Rahman bin Faysal** into exile in Kuwait in 1891. But Muhammad's successor, 'Abd al-'Aziz bin Mit'ab, was unable to hold the new state together. **'Abd al-'Aziz bin 'Abd al-Rahman Al Sa'ud** recaptured Rashidi-occupied Riyadh in 1902 and restored southern Najd to Saudi rule. Shortly afterwards al-Jawf fell to Shaykh Nuri al-Sha'lan of the **Ruwala** tribe, leaving the Rashidi dynasty in direct control of only Jabal Shammar, **al-Qasim**, and the oasis of **Tayma'**. The death of 'Abd al-'Aziz bin Mit'ab in 1906 in battle against the combined forces of the Al Sa'ud and the **Mutayr** tribe ushered in a disastrous sequence of murders of Rashidi leaders by family members. By 1914, al-Qasim had switched allegiance to the Al Sa'ud.

A principal enabling factor in the rise of the Al Rashid was an alliance with the **Ottomans**, but, with the outbreak of the First World War, this association was also to hasten the Rashidi downfall. **Britain** paid 'Abd al-'Aziz a small subsidy to keep the Al Rashid occupied, and when Sharif **Husayn bin 'Ali al-Hashimi** of **Makkah** declared the Arab Revolt against the Ottomans in 1916, the Al Rashid faced opposition from the southwest as well. A brief resurgence of Rashidi authority over al-Jawf following the end of the war was terminated by the assassination of Rashidi ruler Sa'ud bin 'Abd al-'Aziz by a cousin. An agreement concluded soon afterwards with the Saudi Imam reduced the Rashidi state to a Saudi protectorate. However, fighting continued between the **Ikhwan** forces of the Al Sa'ud and some sections of the Shammar, leading Saudi Imam 'Abd al-'Aziz to occupy Ha'il on 4 November 1921 without bloodshed. He incorporated Jabal Shammar into his Najdi state, removed the remaining members of the Al Rashid family to Riyadh, married the widow of Sa'ud bin 'Abd al-'Aziz, and adopted her children.

RAUNKIAIER, BARCLAY. (1888-1915) A Danish geographer and explorer whose 1912 journey into central Arabia was sponsored by the Royal Danish Geographical Society. Travelling from **Kuwait**, Raunkiaier visited **Buraydah**, **Riyadh**, and **al-Hufuf**, reaching the **Gulf** again at **al-'Uqayr**. His account of his travels, first published in Denmark, was translated into English and published as *Through Wahhabiland on Camel-Back* (1916).

RAWWAFAH. [rawwāfah; رواقة; 37 15 - 27 00 approx.] Archaeological site of a way station on the ancient trade route via the Wadi Rum between northwestern Arabia and the Levant, located some 45 miles southeast of modern **Tabuk**. It contains the impressive ruins of a Nabataean-Roman temple built and dated A.D. 166-169, nearly a half century after the collapse of the **Nabataean** kingdom.

"RED" LINE. Saudi Arabia had expanded rapidly since the **"Blue" Line** of 1913 established the de facto eastern boundary of **Najd** (then technically part of the **Ottoman** Empire and later the territorial basis of the Third Saudi State). Consequently, on 3 April 1935, King **'Abd al-'Aziz bin 'Abd al-Rahman Al Sa'ud** presented the **British** with a border claim (the "Red" Line) that ran considerably to the east of the former boundary. The "Red" Line would have placed the base of the Qatar Peninsula, the **Khawr al-'Udayd** region, the edges of al-Dhafrah desert, and nearly all of the **Rub' al-Khali** desert in Saudi territory. Negotiations concerning this boundary were held in London and Riyadh throughout 1935; in the same year the British proposed a modification of the Saudi claim that became known as the **Riyadh Line**.

RED SEA. The body of water separating the western coast of Saudi Arabia from Africa. Stretching from the Suez Canal and the Gulf of al-'Aqabah in the north to the Straits of Bab al-Mandab in the south, the Red Sea is approximately 1,400 miles long and 240 miles across at its widest point. Besides Saudi Arabia, other states bordering on the Red Sea are **Egypt**, Israel, **Jordan**, Sudan, Ethiopia, and **Yemen**. **Jiddah** is the principal Saudi point on the sea, but other ports include **Yanbu'** to the north and **Jizan** to the south. Long an important highway for trade, the Red Sea was also the key route by which **Muslim** pilgrims on the **hajj** (pilgrimage) entered Arabia before the advent of the airplane.

RIJAL AL-MA'. [rijāl al-mā'; رجال الماع] A tribe of 'Asir, located in the mountains southwest of Abha. The tribe was a principal supporter of the Idrisi family in its attempts to assert its independence in the early 20th century.

RIYADH. [al-riyād; الرياض; 39 43 - 24 38] Saudi Arabia's capital and largest city. Located in the southern Najd, it became the seat of the Al Sa'ud ruling family after the destruction by an Egyptian army of their ancestral home at nearby al-Dir'iyah in 1818. It was lost to the rival Al Rashid dynasty of Ha'il in 1891. But in 1902, 'Abd al-'Aziz bin 'Abd al-Rahman infiltrated the town with a small band of followers, launched a surprise attack on al-Musmak fortress, and succeeded in capturing the Al Rashid governor. Over the next two decades, the Al Sa'ud used Riyadh as their base to extend their authority once again over all of Najd. From the late 1920s, Saudi Arabia had two capitals, with the King resident in Riyadh, the capital of Najd, but most of the ministries and embassies located in al-Hijaz. By 1955, most government ministries and head offices had moved to Riyadh; the Foreign Ministry and foreign embassies remained in Jiddah until 1985 when they were required to move to the capital.

Riyadh's population was estimated at only 30,000 in 1930 and 169,000 in 1962, but the oil boom (beginning in 1974) dramatically transformed the city and caused its population to increase to 1.2 million in the 1974 census and to an estimated 3.5 million by the beginning of the 21st century. Very little of the old city remains intact. Riyadh is the inland terminus of a railroad from al-Dammam on the Gulf coast, and the previous international airport has become a major air force base. Both King Sa'ud University and Imam Muhammad bin Sa'ud University are located here. The present airport, King Khalid International Airport, was opened in 1983. The skyline has been enhanced in recent years by two skyscrapers, the 30-story al-Faysaliyah Center [see KING FAYSAL FOUNDATION] and the Kingdom Tower, owned by Prince al-Walid bin Talal Al Sa'ud.

RIYADH LINE. A proposed boundary line between Saudi Arabia and the British-protected states of the Gulf, presented by the British to Saudi Arabia on 25 November 193-5 The Riyadh Line was essentially a modification of the Saudi "Red" Line presented earlier in 1935, which advanced the Saudi border a considerable distance eastward of the earlier de facto frontier established by the 1913 "Blue" Line. Although the Riyadh Line represented British willingness to concede much of the additional territory the Saudis claimed, it would have prevented Saudi ownership of the base of the Qatar Peninsula and the strategic Khawr al-'Udayd area. This British "presentation" was academic as Saudi Arabia immediately rejected it. A boundary conference held in al-Dammam early in 1952 was equally unsuccessful and the problem continued to fester until Saudi Arabia announced even more expansive boundaries in August 1952 and backed them up with an armed occupation of al-Buraymi oasis. After the Trucial Oman Scouts removed the Saudi force from al-Buraymi in 1955, the British Government made a unilateral declaration defining the Modified Riyadh Line (MRL) as the de facto border.

It was amended by the 1974 Saudi-UAE border agreement but the 1990 Saudi-Oman border agreement very largely followed the MRL.

RIYAL. [riyāl; pl. riyālāt; ريالات؛ريال; also spelled rial] Saudi Arabia's unit of currency, abbreviated SR (ISO designation SAR), and consisting of 100 **qirsh** (pl. qurush). The name derives from the Spanish "real de plata" and is also used for the currency units of **Oman**, **Qatar**, and **Iran**. The "riyal faransi," in use throughout much of Arabia and Eastern Africa until recently, was the Maria Theresa thaler or dollar. This was a large silver coin originally minted by the Austro-Hungarian Empire but later copied in a number of countries; regardless of the actual date of minting, all Maria Theresa thalers bear the date of 1780.

ROYAL FAMILY COUNCIL. *See* SAʿUD, AL.

RUBʿ AL-KHALI, AL-. [al-rubʿ al-khālī; ربع الخالي] An Arabic phrase meaning the Empty Quarter, it is the largest desert of Arabia and one of the largest sand deserts in the world. It lies astride much of the southern and southeastern borders of Saudi Arabia, and the undemarcated frontiers over its sands long provided vexing border disputes with the Trucial States (later **United Arab Emirates**), the Sultanate of **Oman**, South Yemen (the People's Democratic Republic of Yemen), and North Yemen (the Yemen Arab Republic); the two Yemens later merged to form the Republic of **Yemen**. Habitation is extremely sparse, consisting of only a few small **badu** (bedouin) tribes such as al-ʿAwamir, Rawashid, **al-Manasir**, Saʿar, **al-Dawasir**, **Al Murrah**, and al-Duruʿ, who generally refer to it simply as al-Rimal (the Sands). The first European to cross it was Bertram Thomas in 1929-1930 (from Salalah in southern Oman to **Qatar**). Thomas was closely followed by **H. St. John B. Philby** (from the Saudi or northern side). The Western explorer best acquainted with it, however, remains Wilfred Thesiger.

RUSSIA. *See* SOVIET UNION.

RUWALA, AL-. [al-ruwalā; sing. ruwaylī; الروالا؛ رويلي; also spelled Rwala] A tribe of the Al Musallim branch of the **ʿAnazah**. Although the ʿAnazah are spread across Saudi Arabia, the Ruwala are principally in Syria, where they have long been an important force in Syrian politics, and in **Jordan**.

RYAN, ANDREW. [Sir] (1867-1949) British diplomat appointed as first British Minister at Jiddah in May 1929. His memoirs were published posthumously as the *Last of the Dragomans* (1951).

- S -

SABAEAN. *See* SOUTH ARABIAN CIVILIZATIONS.

SABBAN, MUHAMMAD SURUR AL-. (1898-1970s?) [al-sabbān; محمد سرور السبان] The son of a slave of the Sabban family of **Jiddah**, Muhammad became the dynamic force behind the family's hide and skin business. He later became a clerk in the Jiddah municipality under King **Husayn bin 'Ali al-Hashimi** and was alleged to have made an attempt on the life of **Imam** (later King) **'Abd al-'Aziz**, for which he was jailed in **Riyadh**. Upon his return to **al-Hijaz** in 1929, he became a protégé of **'Abdullah Sulayman**, the head of finances for al-Hijaz, and began to build a business empire for himself. Under King **Sa'ud**, he replaced 'Abdullah Sulayman as Minister of Finance in 1954. At first close to Crown Prince **Faysal**, he later became an enemy and was forced to leave the country when King Sa'ud turned over his executive powers to his brother in 1960. He returned in 1962 when Sa'ud attempted to regain power. He was not forgiven by Faysal for his support of Sa'ud until 1966, when he was named Secretary-General of the newly formed Constituent Assembly of the Muslim World League.

SABKHAH. [sabkhah; pl. sibākh; سبخة؛ سباخ] A salt flat or depression in the ground in which water gathers, either on or under the sandy surface. Often appearing deceptively as hard ground, sabkhahs can prove treacherous to both animals and vehicles. They are common along the shores of the **Gulf** and also occur inland, even deep in the **Rub' al-Khali** desert.

SADD AL-HASID. *See* KHAYBAR.

SADD AL-SAMALLAQI. [sadd al-samallaqī; سد السملقي] An impressive pre-Islamic dam located in Wadi Liyyah, about 19 miles south of **al-Ta'if** in western Saudi Arabia. The dam is built of unmortared stones, measures more than 650 feet in length and is over 30 feet wide with a plastered top. It was in use until the Islamic Middle Ages when it collapsed.

SADLEIR, GEORGE FORSTER. (1789-1859) A British official sent by the Government of India in 1819 as the first emissary to the **Al Sa'ud**. In his pursuit of the nomadic Saudi leader, Sadleir ventured from the **Gulf** deeper into **Najd** and eventually emerged on the **Red Sea** coast, thus becoming the first European to cross the Arabian Peninsula. His account of his travels was published as *Diary of a Journey Across Arabia* (1819).

SA'ID, NASIR AL-. [ناضر السعيد] A political activist who organized a strike in the **ARAMCO** oil company in 1953 and subsequently fled the country. In exile, he formed the Union of the Peoples of the Arabian Peninsula (UPAP), which claimed responsibility for a wave of bombings in the kingdom in late 1966. Although the organization declined thereafter, al-Sa'id remained active principally by writing virulently anti-**Al Sa'ud** tracts. He disappeared in Beirut in December 1979 and it is widely believed that he was abducted by Group 17 of the PLO, acting for Saudi Arabia, and killed. *See also* OPPOSITION GROUPS.

SAKAKA. [sakākā; سكاكا; 40 12 - 29 59] An oasis town to the northwest of **al-Jawf** town and now the capital of al-Jawf province. A number of archaeological sites are in and around Sakaka. At al-Rajajil [al-rajājīl; الرجاجيل], some eight miles south of Sakaka, are impressive standing stone pillars 10 feet tall, bearing inscriptions and early graffiti; they are thought to have been erected as early as 2000 B.C. **Thamudic** inscriptions and graffiti of the third-second centuries B.C. have been found on hills outside the village of Qarah (قرة; between Sakaka and al-Rajajil). A few centuries later, a semi-rectangular well was cut into solid rock, together with stairs along its sides, at Bi'r Sisar [bi'r sīsar; بئر سيسر] in Sakaka oasis. About 150 years ago, Qasr Za'bil [قصر زعبل], an impressive large fort with four towers, was built on a promontory overlooking the oasis.

SALAFIYIN, AL-. [al-salafīyīn; sing. salafī; السلفيين؛ سلفي] A term of recent introduction for the **Sunni** religious opposition in Saudi Arabia, although their detractors refer to them as *usuliyin* [uṣulīyīn; اصوليين] (fundamentalists). The term *salafiyah* is derived from *al-salaf* (also *al-aslaf*, the "ancestors" or the first generations of **Muslims**) and was used as the name of the Islamic reform movement founded by Egyptian scholar Muhammad 'Abduh (1849-1905). His movement was a reaction to the modern, Western-dominated world, and he and his followers argued that the answers to many modern dilemmas could be found within the traditions of **Islam**. In recent years, the use of the word *al-salafiyin* has been appropriated by Muslims in various countries who advocate a more literal return to the purity of the early Islamic community; they are often described in the West as "fundamentalists." The *salafiyin* in Saudi Arabia do not appear to have any connection with Muhammad 'Abduh's movement.

SALMAN BIN 'ABD AL-'AZIZ AL SA'UD. (1926-) [سلمان بن عبد العزيز آل سعود] Son of King **'Abd al-'Aziz** and full brother of King **Fahd**, thus making him one of the influential **"Sudayri Seven"** or Al Fahd. The highly regarded Governor of Riyadh for 40 years, Salman is considered a close confidant of the King and is often given tasks far beyond his official position. His sons include 'Abd al-'Aziz (deputy minister in the Ministry of Oil and Minerals), Ahmad (owner of al-Sharq al-Awsat newspaper), Fahd (a former Deputy **Amir** of the **Eastern Province** and businessman, died 2001), and Sultan (the first and only Arab astronaut and Secretary-General of the Higher Council for **Tourism** since 2000).

SARAWAT, AL-. [al-sarawāt; or sing. al-sarāh; السروات؛ السراة] A relatively narrow strip of escarpment (the word in Arabic means hills or tops) stretching from the high mountains of **Yemen** in the south to the vicinity of **al-Ta'if**, where the mountainous terrain levels out into less prominent hills. On the west, the often sheer escarpment falls dramatically to the **Tihamah** coastal plain; on the east, there is a more gradual shading into the sloping plains of al-Mashriq (sometimes called **Najd**), eventually turning to desert. In modern usage, the area of al-Sarawat is also considered to be southern **al-Hijaz** and **'Asir**. Al-Sarawat boasts some of the most fertile territory in Saudi Arabia, because of its higher rainfall, and it also contains the country's only forests (best seen outside of **Abha** and at **al-Shafa** near al-Ta'if). Consequently, it is heavily cultivated and supports a relatively dense population. Typically, the tribes of the region occupy bands from the Tihamah across al-Sarawat into al-Mashriq. Historically, the region tended to fall under the control of al-Hijaz to the north or Yemen to the south, or otherwise was torn by local rivalries. Although briefly dominated by the **Wahhabis** of Najd in the early 18th century, it came permanently under Saudi control only in the 1920s. Since the beginning of the **oil** era, there has been substantial migration to other, more prosperous, parts of the kingdom, as well as from the countryside to the towns, such as Abha and **Khamis Mushayt**.

SA'UD, AL. [āl sa'ūd; آل سعود] The dynasty ruling the Kingdom of Saudi Arabia for more than two centuries. The family generally is believed to have originated from the **'Anazah** tribe of central **Najd**, although some opinion holds that it comes from the Bani Hanifah. The family's ancestor, Mani' bin Rabi'ah al-Muraydi, was said to have come from **al-Qatif** and founded the settlement of **al-Dir'iyah**, a few miles north of the present-day capital of **Riyadh**, in 1446-1447. The family was not particularly important until its head, **Muhammad bin Sa'ud**, welcomed **Islamic** reformer **Muhammad bin 'Abd al-Wahhab** to al-Dir'iyah in 1744. Converted to the latter's ascetic vision of Islam, since then popularly known as **Wahhabism**, Muhammad bin Sa'ud began a campaign to spread it throughout Najd and the rest of Arabia. This was the beginning of the First Saudi State.

However, the success of the Al Sa'ud aroused the antagonism of the **Ottoman** Empire and its viceroy in **Egypt**, Muhammad 'Ali, was sent to Arabia to extinguish the Wahhabi/Saudi flame. Success was achieved with the sacking of al-Dir'iyah in 1818, and the family's seat was subsequently moved to Riyadh where it has remained ever since. The family's fortunes revived under **Turki bin 'Abdullah**, who founded the Second Saudi State, but the apex of the Al Sa'ud empire was reached under his son **Faysal bin Turki**, who regained many of the territories won by his predecessors and added new ones. However, this was followed by another disastrous period in the late 19th century, in which the Al Sa'ud were forced to give up their homeland of Najd to a rival family, the **Al Rashid** of Ha'il, and flee to **Kuwait**.

It was not until **'Abd al-'Aziz bin 'Abd al-Rahman** recaptured Riyadh in 1902 that the foundations were laid for the Third Saudi State. By the early 1930s, 'Abd al-'Aziz (commonly known in the West as Bin Sa'ud) had extended his authority over all the territory now comprising Saudi Arabia, including Najd in the center, **al-Hijaz** in the West, **al-Ahsa'** and the **Eastern Province**, and **'Asir** and neighboring territories in the south. In 1932, the country's present name of the Kingdom of Saudi Arabia was adopted. On 4 June 2000, King **Fahd** announced formation of an 18-member Royal Family Council, with Heir Apparent **'Abdullah bin 'Abd al-'Aziz** as its head; it was intended to deal with family matters, much like similar councils in other **Gulf Cooperation Council** states.

DYNASTIC LIST OF THE AL SA'UD (given in order of their rule and with dates of rule in parentheses; some individuals ruled more than once; most dates are approximate). A separate entry has been made for each name.
1. Muhammad bin Sa'ud (r. 1742-1765)
2. 'Abd al-'Aziz bin Muhammad (r. 1765-1803)
3. Sa'ud bin 'Abd al-'Aziz (r. 1803-1814)
4. 'Abdullah bin Sa'ud (r. 1814-1818)
5. Mishari bin Sa'ud (r. 1820)
6. Turki bin 'Abdullah (r. 1824-1834)
7 & 10. Faysal bin Turki (r. 1834-1838 and 1843-1865)
8. Khalid bin Sa'ud (r. 1839-1841)
9. 'Abdullah bin Thunayan Al Thunayan (r. 1841-1843)
11 & 14. 'Abdullah bin Faysal (r. 1865-1871 and 1875-1889)
12. Sa'ud bin Faysal (r. 1871-1875)
13 & 15. 'Abd al-Rahman bin Faysal (r. 1875 and 1889-1891)
16. 'Abd al-'Aziz bin 'Abd al-Rahman (r. 1902-1953)
17. Sa'ud bin 'Abd al-'Aziz (r. 1953-1964)
18. Faysal bin 'Abd al-'Aziz (r. 1964-1975)
19. Khalid bin 'Abd al-'Aziz (r. 1975-1982)
20. Fahd bin 'Abd al-'Aziz (r. 1982-)
   'Abdullah bin 'Abd al-'Aziz (Heir Apparent and First Deputy Prime Minister)
   Sultan bin 'Abd al-'Aziz (likely to succeed 'Abdullah; Second Deputy Prime Minister)

CADET BRANCHES. The term Al Sa'ud applies to the descendants of Sa'ud bin Muhammad bin Muqrin, father of the first Saudi **Imam** Muhammad. Two recognized cadet branches derive from Muhammad's brothers, *i.e.* the Al Farhan and the Al Thunayan. Two more cadet branches derive from the brothers of **Faysal bin Turki**, the creater of the mid-19th-century Second Saudi State: the Al Turki and the **Al Jiluwi**. Members of the latter have been prominent in service to the Saudi imams as governors of various localities and provinces; the only governors the Eastern Province knew from 1913 until 1985 were Al Jiluwi.

The final division results from the two sons of Faysal bin Turki, Sa'ud and 'Abd al-Rahman. The descendants of King **'Abd al-'Aziz bin 'Abd al-Rahman** comprise the main line of the royal family and are entitled to be called "royal highness." But the descendants of 'Abd al-Rahman's elder brother Sa'ud settled in **al-Kharj** and became estranged from the family. Known as **al-'Ara'if**, they claimed the imamate for themselves in 1910. With the failure of their rebellion, they were forced to flee to al-Ahsa', and following the absorption of that area into the Saudi State, the branch then dispersed to **al-Hijaz** and **Bahrain**. Subsequently, Imam 'Abd al-'Aziz allowed the descendants of Sa'ud to return. The Imam gave their head, Sa'ud bin 'Abd al-'Aziz, the appellation of Sa'ud al-Kabir (Sa'ud the Elder)—to distinguish him from his own son, also named Sa'ud bin 'Abd al-'Aziz—and married Sa'ud to his sister Nura. Thus this cadet branch is known as the Al Sa'ud al-Kabir. While the descendants of 'Abd al-Rahman bin Faysal, apart from the progeny of King 'Abd al-'Aziz, are called "highness" or "prince," members of the other cadet branches do not carry the title and are usually addressed as "excellency." *See* Appendix B for the genealogical relationship of cadet branches.

SA'UD AL-FAYSAL (OR SA'UD BIN FAYSAL) AL SA'UD. (1940-) [سعود آل سعود الفيصل] One of a number of prominent and capable sons of King **Faysal bin 'Abd al-'Aziz**. After education in the United States, Sa'ud served as Deputy Minister for Petroleum Affairs before being promoted to Foreign Minister following his father's death in 1975. A full brother is **Turki al-Faysal**, the former head of Saudi intelligence.

SA'UD AL-KABIR, AL. [آل سعود الكبير] One of the cadet branches of the royal family. *See* SA'UD, AL; 'ARA'IF, AL-.

SA'UD BIN 'ABD AL-'AZIZ AL SA'UD. (r. 1803-1814) [سعود بن عبد العزيز آل سعود] Succeeded his father **'Abd al-'Aziz bin Sa'ud** as the third leader of the **Wahhabi Al Sa'ud** state. Sa'ud appears to have been the most capable of his brothers, as well as the eldest, and had led his father's army in many of its conquests. One of his first accomplishments as leader was the capture of **Makkah** and **al-Madinah** in 1805, and in subsequent years he extended the domain of the Al Sa'ud farther than it had ever been: including all of **al-Hijaz**, northwest into the Syrian desert to the outskirts of Damascus, and northeast into the **Iraqi** desert, as well as southeast to Ra's al-Khaymah (in the present-day **United Arab Emirates**) and southwest to Zabid in **Yemen**. His exploits at expanding the realm of the Al Sa'ud and his banning of the *mahmal* (the covering for the holy **Ka'bah** in Makkah) during the **hajj** (pilgrimage) caused the **Ottoman** Empire to order its viceroy in **Egypt**, Muhammad 'Ali, to take action against the Sa'udi state. By 1813, Muhammad 'Ali had gained control of Makkah, al-Madinah, and **al-Ta'if**. During his rule, Sa'ud also attempted to improve the system of administration and deepen the state's control over the tribes. At the same time, his reluctance to delegate any authority to his sons or other family members and his strict observance of Wahhabi tenets did not endear him to his people. Sa'ud died of fever in his capital at **al-Dir'iyah** in 1814 and was succeeded by his eldest son **'Abdullah**.

SA'UD BIN 'ABD AL-'AZIZ AL SA'UD. (r. 1953-1964) [سعود بن عبد العزيز آل سعود] The 17th leader of the Saudi state and the first of the sons of King **'Abd al-'Aziz bin 'Abd al-Rahman** (r. 1902-1953) to succeed him. Sa'ud was born in 1926 of a mother from the **Bani Khalid** tribe; his older full brother was 'Abd al-'Aziz's eldest son Turki, who died of influenza in 1919. From 1926 to 1953, Sa'ud served as Viceroy of **Najd** while his younger half brother (later King) **Faysal** acted as Viceroy of **al-Hijaz**. It can be argued that, by this arrangement, 'Abd al-'Aziz was placing greater trust in Faysal, who was nearly autonomous in al-Hijaz. Nevertheless, as the elder brother, Sa'ud was proclaimed Heir Apparent in 1933, in itself a radical departure from the traditional policy of allowing the strongest family member to emerge as leader after the incumbent's death. This division of responsibilities between the two brothers set the stage for a fierce rivalry lasting for more than a third of a century.

Despite the misgivings caused by the profligacy of Sa'ud and his followers during the final years of 'Abd al-'Aziz's weakening reign, Sa'ud was duly recognized as successor on his father's death in 1953. The bitterness between the new King and Faysal erupted soon after the latter, with the backing of many senior princes, made efforts to put a brake on uncontrolled royal spending. By 1958, the economy had reached the point of catastrophe and in March Sa'ud was forced to relinquish much of his decision-making power to Faysal, who immediately instituted reforms. King Sa'ud struck back by touring his country and dispensing gifts to the tribes in an effort to portray his brother as parsimonious. He also curried support within the Al Sa'ud by striking an incongruous alliance with half brothers **Talal** and **Nawwaf** and their fellow **"liberal princes."** In December 1960, King Sa'ud refused to sign the new budget prepared by Faysal and forced him to withdraw from the political scene. Although portfolios in Sa'ud's new government went to Talal and others of the "liberal princes," it soon became clear that no reforms were intended.

The financial situation after King Sa'ud's return to power was not so perilous as before, since some of Faysal's budgetary improvements were carried over and **oil** revenues were mounting. But Sa'ud's wooing of **Egyptian** revolutionary president Jamal 'Abd al-Nasir (Nasser) did not stop Nasir's intrigues and propaganda against the **Al Sa'ud**. The final break came in 1962 with Egypt's intervention in the **Yemen** civil war against the Saudi-backed royalists and the bombing of several Saudi towns along the Yemen border by the Egyptian air force. The Al Sa'ud took action once again and Sa'ud was forced to appoint Faysal as Prime Minister in October 1962. He spent much of the next year in travel and hospitals throughout Europe. On his return to **Riyadh** in late 1963, he discovered that he retained only minimal authority and his bitter attacks on Faysal backfired.

In March 1964, the leading **'ulama'** (religious scholars) issued a **fatwa** (ruling) that Sa'ud was unfit to rule and a few days later the senior princes of the Al Sa'ud stripped him of all but his title. That came in November when Faysal was named King upon Sa'ud's enforced abdication. Sa'ud's subsequent voluntary exile in Greece, accompanied by a huge retinue and most of his reputed 53 sons and 54 daughters, was marred by a period spent in Cairo in 1966 where the ex-King played into the hands of Egyptian propaganda by denouncing his abdication and claiming that the **United States** government had helped to overthrow him. Sa'ud died in Greece on 23 February 1969. Most of his sons were prominent in public offices only during their father's reign, among them **Fahd** (Minister of Defense, 1956-1960), **Muhammad** (Minister of Defense, 1960-1962), 'Abdullah (Amir of Makkah, 1960-1962), and Badr (Amir of Riyadh, 1962-1963).

SA'UD BIN FAYSAL AL SA'UD. (r. 1871-1875) [سعود بن فيصل آل سعود] The 12th leader of the **Wahhabi** Al Sa'ud state. While his father **Faysal** still ruled, Sa'ud was embroiled in serious rivalry with his elder brother **'Abdullah**, who had been named as heir: 'Abdullah was regarded as the leader of the fanatically religious party while Sa'ud was seen as the champion of the moderate or liberal faction. Seven months after his father's death, Sa'ud left **Riyadh** and began to gather supporters among the tribes and shaykhs of **al-Ahsa'** in the east; the east soon fell to Sa'ud's forces and 'Abdullah's army was routed when it tried to recapture al-Ahsa'. Sa'ud captured Riyadh in 1870, causing 'Abdullah to flee to the tribes of the north, where he established an alliance with the **Ottomans** which allowed them to take over al-Ahsa'. Sa'ud sent his younger brother **'Abd al-Rahman bin Faysal** to negotiate in Baghdad with the Ottomans for return of al-Ahsa'. Unsuccessful after two years, 'Abd al-Rahman set off for Riyadh, stopping on the way to launch a fruitless attack on al-Ahsa'. Estranging the population of **Najd** by his reliance on tribal allies from eastern Arabia, Sa'ud was expelled from Riyadh in 1871. Although he managed to recover the capital in the following year, he was wounded in a battle against other tribes and died in Riyadh in 1875.

SAUDI ARABIAN AIRLINES. Formed as a division of the Ministry of Defense and Aviation in 1946 with three DC-3 airplanes, the airline began international service in 1947 with a route to 'Amman, **Jordan**. By 1963, it had received the status of a commercial corporation with its own board of directors and flights began to Europe in 1967. By the late 1980s, Saudi Arabian Airlines served 46 international destinations and carried more than ten million passengers. It also serves many domestic destinations scattered throughout the kingdom, as well as the main civil airports in **Jiddah**, **Riyadh**, and **al-Dammam**. The airline gained headlines in the financial world when it agreed in 1996 to purchase 61 aircraft from Boeing and McDonnell Douglas for some $7.5 billion. Its working name was changed from Saudi Arabian Airlines to Saudia in 1972 but reverted to Saudi Arabian Airlines in 1996. Plans to privatize the airline were announced as early as 1996 but were hampered by the airline's continued unprofitability, caused largely by underpriced domestic fares and free travel by members of the royal family.

SAUDI ARABIAN BASIC INDUSTRIES CORPORATION (SABIC). A public corporation established in 1976 to run hydrocarbon and mineral-based industries throughout the kingdom, particularly in the new industrial cities of **al-Jubayl** and **Yanbu'**, and to reduce the country's dependence on **oil** exports. SABIC began operations in 1979 and in the following year, three petrochemical companies were created, followed by a steel rolling mill and an iron and steel plant. One of SABIC's purposes is to establish public industrial companies which can then be transferred to the private sector. By the late 1980s, 17 projects were in operation, producing petrochemicals, plastics, fertilizer, iron and steel products, and aluminum. By 1995, SABIC was producing 5 percent of the world's petrochemicals. Expansion of petrochemicals, however, has been hampered by difficult negotiations with the European Union on the amount of duties on exports to Europe. *See also* INDUSTRY.

SAUDI ARABIAN MONETARY AGENCY (SAMA). The kingdom's central bank, founded in 1951 as the first Saudi public corporation and headed for many years by **Anwar 'Ali**, a **Pakistani** expert seconded from the International Monetary Fund (IMF). SAMA was responsible for introducing the Saudi **riyal** (SR) in the mid-1950s, as well as the first paper currency, and of course it supervises the Saudi **banking** sector. In additional roles, the Governor of SAMA was chairman of the first formal development committee in 1958 and SAMA continues to serve as the country's investment authority, managing some $80 billion (in 2002) of foreign reserves, down from a high of $145 billion in 1982. SAMA also supervises Saudi Arabia's stock market, which lists some 70 companies and is the largest in the Arab world with a capitalization of $58 billion.

SAUDI FUND FOR DEVELOPMENT (SFD). Beginning operations in 1975 with a capital of SR 10 billion ($2.74 billion), the SFD is one of the principal channels for the disbursement of Saudi Arabia's foreign aid. The fund is controlled by a board whose director is the Minister of Finance and National Economy. Funds are provided only to governments on a soft-loan basis. Between its inception and 1988, the SFD had funded $5.38 billion in 266 loans to 59 countries, especially in Africa and Asia. The Arab Bank for Economic Development in Africa has been a major recipient of Saudi funding and Riyadh put up 20 percent of the initial capital of the Islamic Development Bank. By 2001, the SFD had loaned a total of nearly $6 billion to 63 countries on four continents.

SAYYID. [sayyid, pl. sādāt; fem. sayyidah; سيد؛ سيدة؛ سادات] Honorific for a descendant of the Prophet **Muhammad**, similar to **sharif**.

SELEUCID KINGDOM. (312-64 B.C.) Founded by Seleucus I Nicator, one of Alexander the Great's leading generals, in Babylonia two years after Alexander's death. In the following years, Seleucus extended his control to the Indus Valley in the east and to Anatolia and Thrace in the west. The kingdom, reduced to a much shrunken state in Syria, was finally conquered by the Romans in 64 B.C. Seleucid sites located in modern Saudi Arabia include **al-Hina**, Jawan (near **Ra's Tanurah**), and **Tarut Island**, while Seleucid influence was to be seen in such prominent centers as **Najran** and **Thaj**.

SHAFA, AL-. [al-shafā; الشفا; 42 35 - 23 25] A highland area a few miles outside of the city of **al-Ta'if** in **al-Hijaz** region. With its cool air and juniper forests, al-Shafa is a popular summer resort and resembles the highland areas of **'Asir** and **Yemen**.

SHAKESPEAR, W. H. I. (WILLIAM). As the (British) Political Agent in Kuwait in 1910, Captain Shakespear became the first **British** official to meet and deal personally with **Imam** (later King) **'Abd al-'Aziz bin 'Abd al-Rahman**. After the outbreak of the First World War, Shakespear was sent to **Najd** to enlist 'Abd al-'Aziz's support against the **Ottomans**. He finally caught up with the Saudi leader in January 1915, on the eve of a battle with the **Al Rashid** at Jarrab, near **al-Zilfi**. During the course of the battle, a wing composed of 'Abd al-'Aziz's tribal allies collapsed and Shakespear, who had accompanied the Saudi forces in British uniform, was killed.

SHAMMAR. [shammar; sing. shammarī; شمر؛ شمرى] An important tribe, or confederation of tribes, centered on the Jabal Shammar region of northern **Najd**. After spreading into the Syrian desert several centuries ago, they were split in two by the **'Anazah** tribe. The southern sections have been the predominant power in Jabal Shammar, even over other tribes and the settlements, as was evidenced during the late 19th century when the Shammari family of **Al Rashid**, based at **Ha'il**, ruled much of Najd with the support of the **Ottomans** and even occupied **Riyadh**, the seat of the **Al Sa'ud**, before declining. In tribal relationships, the Shammar traditionally have gotten on well with al-Muntafiq but have had hostile relations with **al-Dhafir**, **al-Huwaytat**, and frequently with **al-Mutayr**.

SHAMS, 'UMAR. (1923-) [عمر شمس] A Saudi bureaucrat born in **Jiddah** to a family of Indian origin. After approximately 15 years in the Ministry of Finance, he was transferred to the Ministry of the Interior about 1953. Three years later, he became Deputy Director-General of Security and took over as Chief of the General Intelligence Directorate in 1963, a job he held until retirement in 1975. He made himself valuable to the government in 1968 when he rolled up an alleged Communist underground.

SHARI'AH. [shar'īah; شريعة] The body of law which governs many aspects of life in **Islam**. Although based on the **Qur'an** (Koran) and the **Sunnah** (the example set by the Prophet **Muhammad** in his deeds and sayings), various interpretations of the shari'ah rely upon the individual judgment [ra'y; رعي] of the judge [**qādī**; قاضي], analogy [qiyās; قياس], and/or consensus [**ijmā'**; اجماع] of the theological community. These differing interpretations have been consolidated into four schools of Islamic jurisprudence: the Hanafi, **Hanbali**, Maliki, and Shafi'i. A Muslim may belong to whichever school he chooses and have legal action concerning him conducted by a *qadi* of that school. Among the **Sunnis** of Saudi Arabia (Sunnism being the main body of Islam; other sects do not follow the above four schools of interpretation), the great majority belong to the Hanbali school, from which the Muwahhidun or **Wahhabi** movement emerged.

SHARIF. [sharīf, pl. ashrāf; fem. sharīfah; شريف؛ اشراف؛ شريفة] Honorific for a descendant of the Prophet **Muhammad**, similar to **sayyid**. Sharif was used in **al-Hijaz** by the **al-Hashimi** family as a religious/political title. Following the **Iraqi** invasion of **Kuwait** in 1990, King Husayn of **Jordan** revived the title, presumably to emphasize his membership in the Hashimi family and descent from the Prophet.

SHARURAH, AL-. [al-sharūrah; الشرورة; 47 08 - 17 15] A point deep in the **Rub' al-Khali** desert, close to the **Yemen** border. Its strategic location and the perceived threat from former South Yemen led the Saudi government in the 1980s to build an elaborate military infrastructure there, including the King Khalid Air Base and the 11th Imam Sa'ud al-Kabir Army Brigade.

SHAYKH. [shaykh; pl. shuyūkh or mashāyikh; شيخ؛ شيوخ؛ مشايخ; sometimes spelled shaikh or sheik] A title ordinarily given to the chief of a tribe. The term is also used as an honorific title for respected male elders and religious figures, as well as the title of members of ruling families in the smaller states of the **Gulf** (which are frequently referred to as "shaykhdoms").

SHAYKH, AL AL-. [آل الشيخ] Literally, the family of the **Shaykh**, *i.e.* the descendants of the 18th-century religious reformer **Muhammad 'Abd al-Wahhab.** Today, the Al al-Shaykh constitute perhaps the second-most important family in Saudi Arabia, next to the ruling **Al Sa'ud** with whom they have extensively intermarried. In the past, the Al al-Shaykh predominated in the **'ulama'** (religious scholars), among the **qadis** (religious judges) and **imams** (prayer leaders), and in the faculty and administration of the Islamic **universities**. In recent times, however, many family members have taken up other nonreligious government positions, including ministerial portfolios.

SHAYKH, HASAN BIN 'ABDULLAH AL AL-. (1933 or 1934-1987) [حسن بن عبد الله آل الشيخ] Born in **al-Madinah** in 1933 or 1934 and educated in religious studies in **Makkah**, he held a number of judicial positions before being appointed Minister of Education by King **Sa'ud** in 1962 and then Minister of Higher Education by King **Faysal** in 1975. He also served as Acting Minister of Health (1967-1970) and later headed the Supreme Council of King 'Abd al-'Aziz Research Center. He died in Riyadh in 1987.

SHI'AH, SHI'I. [shī'ah; sing. shī'ī; شيعة؛ شيعي; sometimes spelled Shi'ite] A Shi'i is a member of the Shi'ah sect of **Islam**, the largest surviving sect to break away from the **Sunni** (or orthodox) main body of Muslims. The Shi'ah believe that leadership of the Islamic community should have continued through the descendants of the Prophet **Muhammad**'s grandsons. The Zaydi or Fiver subsect of Shi'ah holds that there were only five such leaders or imams; the Zaydis are today confined to **Yemen**. The Isma'ili or Sevener subsect believes that seven imams existed while the Ja'fari or Ithna'ashari or Twelver Shi'ah believe there were 12 imams. Ja'fari Shi'ism is the state religion of **Iran**, and adherents form the largest single sect in **Iraq** and **Bahrain**, as well as substantial minorities in **Kuwait** and other parts of the Middle East. There are up to 500,000 Ja'fari Shi'ah in Saudi Arabia, concentrated in the **Eastern Province** oases of **al-Qatif**, which is well over 90 percent Shi'ah, and **al-Ahsa'**, about half Shi'ah. The majority of these are Hasawi while others are **al-Baharinah** (related to similar communities in Bahrain and elsewhere in the Gulf), while a few are 'Ajam (*i.e.* of Persian descent). Because Saudi oil lies in the Eastern Province, a considerable proportion of the employees of the oil company **ARAMCO** have been Shi'ah. The Shi'ah of Saudi Arabia have not been highly active politically since the demonstrations in al-Qatif in 1979-1980, but they maintain grievances against the Saudi government because of drastic actions taken against Shi'i communities and mosques then and before at the time of the Saudi conquest. Another small Shi'ah community, known as the **Nakhawilah**, exists in **al-Madinah** in **al-Hijaz**, and a small Isma'ili community resides in **Najran** in the south. Several sections of **badu** (bedouin) tribes in al-Hijaz are also Shi'ah.

SHU'AYBI, HAMUD BIN 'UQLA' AL-. (c. 1925-2002) [ḥamūd bin 'uqlā' al-shu'aybī; حمود بن عقلا.الشعيبي] Prominent religious figure and critic of the Saudi government. Although blind, he became a leading Islamic scholar and counted a **mufti** (the country's senior religious authority), a minister of justice, and a minister of Islamic affairs among his students. In 1995, he was dismissed from his teaching position at the **Buraydah** branch of **Imam Muhammad bin Sa'ud University** and subsequently arrested and held for two months. In October 2001, he issued a **fatwa** (religious opinion) opposing American intervention in **Afghanistan** against the Taliban and **al-Qa'idah**. He died in his hometown of Buraydah in January 2002.

SIBILAH. [sibilah; سبلة; 45 00 - 26 30 approx.] A plain between **al-Zilfi** and **al-Artawiyah** in central **Najd**, site of a battle on 30 March 1929 between the forces of Imam **'Abd al-'Aziz bin 'Abd al-Rahman** Al Sa'ud and the rebellious **Ikhwan**, led by **Sultan bin Bijad bin Humayd** and **Faysal al-Duwish**. The overwhelming victory by 'Abd al-'Aziz broke the back of the Ikhwan rebellion.

SIRHAN, WADI. [wādī sirḥān; وادي سرحان; 38 15 - 30 30] A large valley in extreme northeastern Saudi Arabia, near the city of **al-Jawf** and the border with **Jordan**, serving for several millennia as a principal caravan route between the **Arabian Peninsula** and the Mediterranean. It is the site of some of Arabia's oldest archaeological sites, particularly around al-Jawf and, to the north, Quriyat al-Milh, in **al-Quriyat** province. In modern times, the wadi was held by the **Al Rashid amirate** until the First World War. The British, negotiating on behalf of Transjordan (later Jordan), recognized Al Sa'ud sovereignty over most of the wadi in 1925. More recently, the wadi was the site of a government settlement scheme implemented in large part to augment the government's authority among the **badu** (bedouin) roaming across the Saudi-Jordanian border. The plight of the badu during the long drought beginning in 1957 led to government-assisted relief efforts in 1961. But involvement of the badu in agricultural projects (also begun in 1961) failed when they left the farms to return to pasture as soon as the rains returned. The settlement was finally abandoned in 1972.

SOUTH ARABIAN CIVILIZATIONS. Traditionally, the Arab race was divided into northern and southern branches. Although the Arabic language and alphabet of today is North Arabian, the earliest flowering of Arab civilization occurred in southern Arabia. The first of the three preeminent kingdoms to flourish in the area of present-day **Yemen** during the pre-Islamic period was that of the Sabaeans. The Sabaeans are the earliest known Arabian polity, with references in late cuneiform inscriptions and Greek literature, as well as Assyrian and Hebrew records (the Biblical Sheba). Their kingdom, which existed roughly during the period 750-115 B.C., was based first on Saba' and later on Ma'rib and prospered due to a monopoly of the spice trade. Caravan routes were established from present-day Dhufar (in southern **Oman**) and the Hadramawt (in eastern Yemen) north to Syria and the Mediterranean, and a number of Sabaean colonies were established along the way, including **Makkah** and Petra. The Minaean state rose to the north of the Sabaeans in al-Jawf region of modern Yemen, with centers at Qarnaw [qarnāw; قرناو], modern Ma'in [ma'īn; معين], and Yathil [yathīl; يثيل], modern Baraqish [barāqish; براقش]. Their colonies in northern Arabia included **al-'Ula, al-Jawf, Tayma'**, and **Mada'in Salih** in modern Saudi Arabia, and Ma'in in modern **Jordan**. The Minaeans were able to fend off the challenges from the rival kingdoms of Qataban and Hadramawt but were subsumed by the Himyaritic kingdom (115 B.C. until ca. A.D. 300). The Minaean and Himyaritic languages essentially were dialects of Sabaean, known today only through numerous inscriptions in both South and North Arabia. The decline of the South Arabian civilizations and the rise of northern trade rivals such as Makkah, as well as the predominance of the North Arabian language at literary fairs such as **'Ukaz**, are given as reasons why South Arabian was replaced by North Arabian as the Arabic language of the **Qur'an** (Koran) and present-day usage. South Arabian languages survive only in the mountains of southern Oman and southeastern Yemen, and the island of Socotra.

SOVIET UNION (RUSSIA) AND SAUDI ARABIA. The Soviet Union was the first country to recognize **'Abd al-'Aziz bin 'Abd al-Rahman** as King of **al-Hijaz** and **Najd** in 1927 and had sent a minister to **Jiddah**. But Soviet attempts at commercial success in Jiddah were stymied by a Saudi trade embargo in 1928. When Prince (later King) **Faysal bin 'Abd al-'Aziz** visited the Soviet Union at the end of his European tour in 1932, the Soviets proposed a commercial treaty and treaty of friendship in return for a £1 million loan. The King declined. In 1938, the Soviet ambassador left Jiddah and diplomatic relations, although never formally suspended, lapsed.

Apart from an August 1956 meeting in Tehran between King **Sa'ud** and the Soviet ambassador to Iran, Saudi Arabia staunchly steered clear of any ties with Moscow, declaring the Marxist state to be incompatible with **Islam** and suspicious of Soviet ties to the radical Arab states. Not only did Soviet support to Syria, **Iraq**, **Egypt** (before 1972), and various Palestinian groups worry **Riyadh**, but the Soviets had also established a military presence in Marxist South **Yemen**, supported the Dhufar rebellion in **Oman**, and financed subversive groups in various Arab **Gulf** countries. Farther afield, the Saudis shared American concerns over Soviet activities in Asia (especially Muslim **Afghanistan**) and Africa, and they were ready to provide financial support to anti-Soviet governments and movements.

It was not until the mid-1980s that the first signs of a rapprochement appeared. Foreign Minister **Sa'ud al-Faysal**, son of the late King Faysal, journeyed to Moscow in 1983. Then Faysal bin Fahd, the eldest son of King **Fahd** and President of the Youth Welfare Authority, visited the Soviet Union in 1985 at the head of a football delegation and held talks in Moscow with

Soviet Foreign Ministry officials as well. Two years later, the new Saudi Minister of Petroleum and Mineral Affairs **Hisham al-Nazir** included Moscow in his itinerary of countries to coordinate oil strategies and shortly afterwards Soviet diplomats showed up at an official function of the Saudi embassy in London. Sa'ud al-Faysal returned to Moscow, accompanied by the Saudi ambassador to the US, Prince **Bandar bin Sultan**, at the beginning of 1988 to hold discussions on the Iran-Iraq War. This was followed by the first visit by a Soviet official to Saudi Arabia since 1938.

Although the reestablishment of diplomatic relations seemed inevitable, Riyadh continued to hold back, citing the Soviet presence in Afghanistan as an obstacle. Even the establishment of Soviet relations with Oman (1985), the **United Arab Emirates** (UAE) (1985), and **Qatar** (1988) was not enough to convince Riyadh. A flurry of activity in early 1990 resulted in a formal announcement of resumption of relations on 17 September 1990 following discussions in Moscow between Sa'ud al-Faysal and President Mikhail Gorbachev. (The announcement was followed a few months later by the establishment of relations between the Soviet Union and **Bahrain**, the last of the **Gulf Cooperation Council** [GCC] states to do so.) An immediate benefit to the Soviet Union was the announcement that Riyadh would provide a substantial loan of about $1.5 billion. In early 1992, following the demise of the Soviet Union, it was confirmed that the remainder of the loan would be paid to the Commonwealth of Independent States. Subsequently, ties were established with the various Muslim ex-Soviet republics of Central Asia.

Subsequent Saudi-Russian ties were normal but uneventful. Russian Prime Minister Viktor Chernomyrdin included Riyadh on his 1994 Gulf tour. Shots were fired at the Russian consulate in Jiddah in 2000 but the Saudi government concluded that it resulted from personal motives and was not related to the Russian campaign in Muslim Chechnya.

SR. Abbreviation for the Saudi **riyal**, the currency of Saudi Arabia.

STOCK MARKET. *See* SAUDI ARABIAN MONETARY AGENCY.

STORRS, RONALD. [Sir] (1881-1955) British official in the Middle East in first quarter of the 20th century. After education at Charterhouse and Pembroke College, Cambridge, Storrs entered the Egyptian Civil Service and was appointed Oriental Secretary at the British Agency in Cairo in 1909. During 1914, he was involved in negotiations with Sharif **Husayn bin 'Ali al-Hashimi** and in 1917 he was appointed Assistant Political Officer to the Anglo-French political mission of the Egyptian Expeditionary Force. In that capacity, he worked with Sir **Percy Cox** in Mesopotamia on means of persuading Saudi Imam **'Abd al-'Aziz bin 'Abd al-Rahman** from allying himself with the Ottomans. Storrs was sent to Riyadh to negotiate with 'Abd al-'Aziz but never arrived. Similarly, he was to accompany Cox to meet Sharif Husayn at **al-Ta'if** but the mission never took place as the Sharif refused to guarantee Cox's security as he crossed the desert. Later in 1917, Storrs was appointed military governor of Jerusalem and then civilian governor of Jerusalem and

Judea in 1920 at the beginning of the Palestine mandate. He became governor of Cyprus in 1926 and published his memoirs in 1937.

SUBAY'. [subay'; sing. subay'ī; سبيع؛سبيعي] A widespread tribe of **Najd** whose territory extends from northeastern **'Asir** up into Najd, especially around Ranyah (the tribal seat), **al-'Arid, Washm, Riyadh,** and **al-Qasim.** A Subay'i family provides the governors of the important Qasimi town of **'Unayzah.** In the early 20th century, the presence of a section of the Subay' in Wadi **al-Khurmah** created a border dispute between Imam **'Abd al-'Aziz bin 'Abd al-Rahman Al Sa'ud,** who claimed sovereignty over the Najdi and **Wahhabi** tribe, and Sharif **Husayn bin 'Ali al-Hashimi of al-Hijaz,** who appointed the wadi's governor.

SUDAYR, AND AL-SUDAYRI. [sudayr; al-sudayrī; pl. al-sadārah; سدير؛السديري؛السدارة] A district of southern **Najd,** about 145 miles long, abutting **al-Qasim** province of central Najd on the north and **al-'Arid** district on the south. The most important towns are al-Majma' (the capital) and **al-Zilfi.** The **Bani Tamim** tribe, along with another inferior tribe of Bani Khadir, form the predominant population, although elements of **al-Dawasir,** Fadul, **'Anazah,** and **'Utaybah** also live there. Apart from a brief period at the end of the 19th century, Sudayr has belonged to the **Al Sa'ud** since 1862. The region has given its name to its most prominent family, al-Sadarah (sing. Sudayri), an offshoot of al-Dawasir. A Sudayri became a key 19th-century general for the Al Sa'ud and the connection between the two families has been particularly close ever since.

"SUDAYRI SEVEN." Informal term applied to the seven sons of King **'Abd al-'Aziz bin 'Abd al-Rahman** by the same mother, Hussah bint Ahmad **al-Sudayri.** Together, they form the most powerful bloc within the royal family and therefore in Saudi Arabia. The seven, also known as the Al Fahd, are (with their positions as of early 2002): **Fahd** (King), **Sultan** (Minister of Defense and Aviation), 'Abd al-Rahman (Deputy Minister of Defense and Aviation), Turki (Deputy Minister of Defense and Aviation until 1978 and now in private business), **Nayif** (Minister of the Interior), **Salman** (Governor of Riyadh), and **Ahmad** (Deputy Minister of the Interior).

SULAYMAN (AL-HAMDAN), 'ABDULLAH BIN. (c. 1887-1954) [al-hamdān; عبد الله بن سليمان الحمدان] A self-made government official originally from **'Unayzah** in **Najd.** 'Abdullah served in the employ of the **al-Qusaybi** merchant family of the **Eastern Province** for some years before replacing his brother as a clerk for King **'Abd al-'Aziz bin 'Abd al-Rahman.** By 1928, he had acquired firm control of the finances of **al-Hijaz** province and was promoted to Finance Minister in 1932. Perhaps the principal figure behind the emergence of the country's rudimentary bureaucracy, 'Abdullah also had a say in many other government matters, including agriculture, **hajj** (pilgrimage) affairs, defense, and the King's household. Retained in the first cabinet announced after King 'Abd al-'Aziz's death in 1953, despite the antipathy of King **Sa'ud** and Crown Prince **Faysal,** he was forced to resign from the government in 1954. 'Abdullah had employed his son 'Abd al-'Aziz as his deputy, but after 'Abdullah's ouster in 1954, 'Abd al-'Aziz turned to private business and made an immense fortune through construction projects undertaken by his ROLACO organization.

SULTAN. [sulṭān; سلطان] A common personal name as well as a traditional title. The head of the **Ottoman** Empire was known as the sultan, **Imam 'Abd al-'Aziz bin 'Abd al-Rahman Al Sa'ud** adopted the title of Sultan of **Najd** before proclaiming himself King of Saudi Arabia, and the ruler of **Oman** is still a sultan. The entity ruled by a sultan is a sultanate [Arabic, sulṭanah; سلطنة]

SULTAN BIN 'ABD AL-'AZIZ AL SA'UD. (1924-) [سلطان بن عبد العزيز آل سعود] Son of King **'Abd al-'Aziz** and full brother of King **Fahd bin 'Abd al-'Aziz**, thus making him one of the influential **"Sudayri Seven"** or Al Fahd. He first served as **Amir** of **Riyadh**. After King 'Abd al-'Aziz's death, Sultan became a key supporter of Heir Apparent (later King) **Faysal**, serving as Minister of Agriculture, Minister of Communications, and then, in 1962, Minister of Defense and Aviation—the position he continues to hold (purportedly making him the longest-serving cabinet minister in the world). He received his other principal appointment of Second Deputy Prime Minister upon the accession of his full brother Fahd in 1982; this title indicates his position as second in line for the throne behind Crown Prince **'Abdullah bin 'Abd al-'Aziz**. Like many in the **Al Sa'ud**, Sultan has extensive business interests, which make him a wealthy man. However, continuing questions about his health make it less than certain that he, like 'Abdullah, will eventually take his place as King. The most prominent among his sons are **Khalid**, Deputy Minister of Defense and Aviation for Military Affairs, and **Bandar**, Ambassador to the United States.

SULTAN BIN BIJAD BIN HUMAYD. [bijād; سلطان بن بجاد بن حميد] Often called Bin Bijad, Sultan was paramount **shaykh** of the **'Utaybah** tribe and one of the principal leaders of the **Ikhwan** movement, having settled in the Ikhwan settlement of **al-Ghatghat** in 1914. A prominent commander of Ikhwan forces during the conquest of **al-Hijaz** in the mid-1920s, Sultan appeared to have expected an appointment as either governor of al-Hijaz or commander of all Saudi forces as a reward. However, Imam **'Abd al-'Aziz bin 'Abd al-Rahman** Al Sa'ud failed to give him any position (possibly out of fear of Sultan's reputation as a devout **Wahhabi** and high standing amongst the Ikhwan). The refusal apparently led the shaykh to join with **Faysal al-Duwish**, paramount shaykh of the **Mutayr** tribe, in a meeting of Ikhwan in 1926 where they listed their complaints against the Saudi leader. A year later, Shaykh Sultan and Shaykh Faysal led the Ikhwan in revolt against 'Abd al-'Aziz. The fighting dragged on until the Battle of **Sibilah** in 1929, when the Ikhwan forces were severely beaten and Shaykh Sultan was captured and imprisoned in Riyadh. His settlement at al-Ghatghat was razed.

SULUBAH, AL-. [al-ṣulubah; ṣulubī; الصلبة؛ صلبي] A collection of small groups, not necessarily a tribe, without known "origin" ranging across northern **Najd**, particularly north of the **Shammar** tribes and eastwards toward **Kuwait** and **Iraq**. Regarded as inferior by the "pure" tribes in whose territories they roam, traditionally they have been menders and metalworkers and have used donkeys rather than camels.

SUNNAH, AL-. [al-sunnah; السنة] From the word meaning "practice" or "custom," the Sunnah is the collection of sayings and doings of the Prophet **Muhammad**. In **Islam**, only the **Qur'an** (Koran) carries more importance and legal standing. Many aspects of Islamic ritual, *e.g.* the number of daily prayers and the procedure to be followed, are derived from the Sunnah, rather than the Qur'an. The sayings of the Prophet are known as the **hadith**.

SUNNI. [sunnī; سني] The main body or the orthodox sect of **Islam**. All other Islamic sects, such as the **Shi'ah**, have broken away from the Sunnis. Within Sunnism, there are four schools of interpretation of the **shari'ah** (Islamic law). Most Saudi Arabians are Sunni. The name derives from **al-Sunnah**, the collected traditions of the sayings and deeds of the Prophet **Muhammad**.

SURUR, MUHAMMAD. *See* SABBAN, MUHAMMAD SURUR AL-.

- T -

TABUK. [tabūk; تبوك; 36 35 - 28 23] Town and province (**imarah**) of the same name in extreme northwestern Saudi Arabia, bordering on the Red Sea and the Gulf of al-'Aqabah. The province includes the oasis of **Tayma'** and port of al-Wajh. The total population is small, perhaps 200,000. A Royal Saudi Air Force base is located at Tabuk town.

TAFRAH. [tafrah; طفرة] The Arabic word for leap or upswing, used in Saudi Arabia and the **Gulf** to refer to the heady period of the **oil** boom (1974 to the early 1980s).

TAHIR, 'ABD AL-HADI HASAN. (1931-) ['abd al-hādī ḥasan ṭāhir; عبد الهادي حسن طاهر] Saudi bureaucrat born in **al-Madinah**. A protégé of former Oil Minister **Ahmad Zaki Yamani**, Tahir was a Director-General of the Ministry of Petroleum from 1961, Governor-General of **PETROMIN** from 1962, and a Minister of State from 1978. He was fired in 1986 shortly after Yamani and then dropped from the board of directors of **ARAMCO** in the following year.

TA'IF, AL-. [al-ṭā'if; الطائف; 40 25 - 21 16] A highland city of **al-Hijaz** region, about 75 miles southeast of the holy city of **Makkah** and about 5,000 feet above sea level. Al-Ta'if is located in a sandy plain but, blessed with plentiful water, it is surrounded by fruit and vegetable gardens, the produce of which is sent to Makkah and **Jiddah**. The city has long been the summer residence of Makkah's wealthier citizens and, in recent decades, of the Saudi kings as well. Al-Ta'if was the first major settlement of al-Hijaz to fall to the **Al Sa'ud** in 1924, and the **Ikhwan** armies who first entered the city, plundered it and massacred many of its residents. The nearby district of **al-Shafa** is a popular summer resort.

TALAL BIN 'ABD AL-'AZIZ AL SA'UD. (1931-) [talāl; طلال بن عبد العزيز آل سعود] Son of King **'Abd al-'Aziz.** After appointment as Comptroller of the Royal Household at the age of 19, Talal was appointed Minister of Communications on his father's death. But he was transferred as ambassador to **France** and Spain following an intra-family dispute. Upon his return in 1957, he became the leader of the so-called **"Liberal Princes"** (along with full brother **Nawwaf** and half brothers **Badr, Fawwaz, 'Abd al-Muhsin,** and **Majid**), advocating a constitutional and more representative government. King **Sa'ud bin 'Abd al-'Aziz,** locked in a bitter struggle for power with his brother **Faysal** (Heir Apparent at the time), made an alliance with Talal's group. As a result, Talal was named Minister of Finance in King Sa'ud's new cabinet of 1960, while two of his cohorts also received portfolios. However, it soon became clear that King Sa'ud had no intention of introducing political reforms and Talal left for Lebanon (his mother was a Lebanese of Armenian origin and his first wife was the daughter of Lebanese politician Riad Solh). He earned the hostility of both the King and Prince Faysal for attacking the government at a press conference in Beirut, and the "liberal princes" spent several years in exile cooperating with **Egypt.** Talal returned to the kingdom in 1963 and made his peace with Faysal but devoted himself to business interests. In the mid-1980s, he became president of the Arab Gulf Program for UN Development (AGFUND) and was appointed a member of the new Royal Family Council in 2000. His son **al-Walid** has become a prominent global businessman.

TAMIM, BANI. [banī tamīm; sing. tamīmī; بني تميم؛ تميمي] A famous tribe in the pre-Islamic history of Arabia, the Bani Tamim have become almost completely sedentarized and occupy a number of oasis settlements in **Najd, al-Qasim,** and **Jabal Shammar.**

TAPLINE. *See* PIPELINES.

TARIQI, 'ABDULLAH BIN HAMUD AL-. [al-ṭāriqī; عبد الله بن حمود الطارقي؛ also spelled Tariki] (1919-1997) Former Minister of Petroleum and Mineral Affairs. Born in **al-Zilfi** in **Najd,** he studied at Cairo University and then received his M.A. from the University of Texas. After a period of employment with TEXACO, he returned to Saudi Arabia and joined the government, rising to Director-General of Petroleum and Mineral Affairs in the Ministry of Finance and National Economy at the end of 1954. He was one of the first Saudis to sit on the board of the oil company **ARAMCO** and was instrumental in the establishment of the **Organization of Petroleum Exporting Countries (OPEC).** Although a protégé of Crown Prince **Faysal,** he was included in King **Sa'ud's** "liberal" cabinet of 1960 as the first Minister of Petroleum and Mineral Affairs. When Faysal was made Prime Minister in 1962, Tariqi was replaced by **Ahmad Zaki Yamani**. He subsequently left the kingdom and became an independent oil consultant, founding the *Arab Oil and Gas Journal* and acquiring an increasing reputation as an Arab radical and proponent of the nationalization of the oil industry. After residence in **Egypt** and **Kuwait**, he eventually returned to Riyadh to establish a consultancy, although he spent most of his last decade in Cairo where he died in 1997.

TARUQ AL-AFRIQI, MUHAMMAD. (b. ?-1961) [tārūq al-afrīqī; محمد طاروق الافريقي] A soldier born in Nigeria and commissioned into the **Ottoman** army after graduation from the Istanbul Military Academy. He apparently fought against the Italians in Tripolitania and against the Bulgarians in the Balkan War before resigning and retiring to Syria. After service as aide-de-camp to Amir **'Abdullah** of Transjordan, he came to Saudi Arabia in 1939 to command the kingdom's small armed forces. He left sometime in the 1940s and died in Damascus.

TARUT ISLAND. [tārūt; تاروت; 50 05 - 26 35] An island in the **Gulf**, just offshore from **al-Qatif** oasis. Two harbors were active on the island during the third millennium B.C.: the **Seleucid** settlement at Sanabis [sanābis; سنابس] on the northeastern corner and Darin [dārīn; دارين] in the south. Remains of steatite, alabaster, lapis lazuli, and copper implements have been found on the island and it is thought that Tarut was connected to the famous civilization of Dilmun. Darin was the site of a Nestorian bishopric in the early Christian era. Tarut town contains a Portuguese fort of the 16th-17th centuries and another fort dated to A.H. 1302 (c. A.D. 1875) exists in Darin.

TAYMA'. [taymā'; تيما; 38 29 - 27 37] An **oasis** of northwestern Saudi Arabia, about halfway between **Ha'il** and **Tabuk**. The district of Tayma' was attached to Tabuk province in 1950, reassigned to Ha'il two years later, and returned to Tabuk more than a decade ago. In ancient times, Tayma' occupied a central position astride the trade routes between the interior of Arabia, the Holy Places of **al-Hijaz**, **Egypt**, the Levant, and southern Mesopotamia (present-day **Iraq**). Although a large walled town was situated there during the mid-to-late second millennium B.C., Tayma' reached its peak in the first millennium B.C. under the influence of the Minaean and Sabaean civilizations of **South Arabia**. Tayma' was famed as the sixth century B.C. refuge of **Nabonidus**, the last king of the Neo-Babylonian Empire which had collapsed because of the Achaemenid invasion. There are thousands of pre-Islamic inscriptions in the vicinity, especially atop Jabal Ghunaym [جبل غنيم], a few miles southeast of the oasis. The **Thamudic** inscriptions from Tayma' are the earliest known. The present-day settlement is still surrounded by the ancient walls of the first millennium B.C., nearly two miles in length with some sections standing to a height of nearly 13 feet. The well of Bi'r al-Haddaj [bi'r al-haddāj; الهداج بئر] inside modern Tayma' is thought to date from the same period and is the place where the Tayma' Stone, which bears an important religious inscription written in ancient Aramaic and is now in the Louvre, was discovered in 1884. The walls enclose a great mass of mounds of archaeological interest which have yet to be explored.

TELEVISION. *See* MEDIA.

THAJ. [thāj; ثاج; 48 43 - 26 53] A large and massively walled, **Seleucid**-influenced settlement of the ninth-second centuries B.C. Approximately 65 miles from the **Gulf** coast, south of **al-Jubayl** and west of **al-Qatif,** Thaj stood at the northern end of the important trans-Arabian trading routes which crossed **al-Yamamah** (modern **Najd**) and connected Mesopotamia and the Gulf with **Najran** and the **South Arabian** civilizations located in present-day **Yemen**.

THAMUD, THAMUDIC. [thamūd; ثمود] An ancient Arab tribe mentioned in the **Qur'an** (Koran) and now extinct. Speculation gives their origin as **Yemen** from where they emigrated to the environs of **Makkah**. In the eighth century B.C., they were subjugated by the Assyrian King Sargon II and forced to relocate in the mountains of northern **al-Hijaz,** where Thamudic settlements have been found at **Mada'in Salih, Tayma'**, and **al-'Ula**. Their language was North Arabian (akin to classical Arabic), although they used a South Arabian script, similar to the Safaitic and **Lihyanite** peoples, to whom they were related.

THUNAYAN, AL. [āl thunayān; آل ثنيان] One of the cadet branches of the royal family. *See* SA'UD, AL.

TIHAMAH. [tihāmah; تهامة] The coastal plain along the **Red Sea** in southwestern Saudi Arabia and **Yemen**. Although the term Tihamah was formerly used for the plain along the entire length of **al-Hijaz,** in modern usage it is considered to end at **Jiddah** and **Makkah**. Thus, the provinces containing the Saudi Tihamah are the southern part of **Makkah** province, the western tips of **al-Bahah** and **'Asir**, and nearly all of **Jizan**. The plain is not very fertile and is noted for its high temperatures and humidity during the summer. Lightly populated, the principal towns and ports include al-Lith, **al-Qunfudhah**, and Jizan. Many tribes located primarily in the neighboring **al-Sarawat** highlands also have subunits in the Tihamah. Political control generally was fragmented until portions of the Tihamah gradually came under Saudi suzerainty through the 1920s.

TIRAN ISLAND. [tīrān; تيران; 34 34 - 27 56] A small and uninhabited island at the mouth of the Gulf of al-'Aqabah at the northern end of the **Red Sea**. Although Tiran and neighboring Sanafir [sanāfir; سنافير] Island legally belong to Saudi Arabia, they were occupied by **Egypt** in 1950 because of their strategic location. Israel captured Tiran in the 1956 **Arab-Israeli** War but subsequently withdrew. Israeli forces reoccupied the island as a result of the 1967 war and reopened the strait to its shipping. They held Tiran until leaving in 1982 in line with their withdrawal from Sinai.

TOURISM. Saudi Arabia has sought to exploit tourism, beginning with domestic tourism and tourists from other GCC states and by pilgrims staying on after the annual **hajj** (pilgrimage). The country's many historical sites and the cool highlands of the south are the primary draws. A Higher Council for Tourism was set up in 2000 with Prince **Sultan bin Salman** (the first and only Arab astronaut) as its Secretary-General. Tours by selected groups of Westerners began soon after, although the kingdom had not permitted individual tourist visas by 2002.

TRADE. Saudi Arabia's principal export for half a century has been crude **oil**. Minerals (including **natural gas** and gold as well as oil) account for more than 80% of all exports, with the next largest export being petrochemicals. Total exports in 2000 were worth SR 290 billion or about $77 billion and the most important destinations were the **United States**, Japan, South Korea, Singapore, **India**, Holland, and **France** (*see* APPENDIX G, tables 7 and 9). The biggest items of imports were machinery and electrical equipment (22%) and transportation equipment (18%). Total imports in 2000 were worth SR 113 billion or about $30 billion. The United States was the biggest source of imports, followed by Japan, Germany, and the United Kingdom (*see* APPENDIX G, tables 8 and 10). The decline in oil prices during the 1990s led to a long period of negative balance of payments (*see* APPENDIX G, table 6), which were covered by running down reserves, delays in government payments, and borrowing, mostly domestically but also internationally.

TURKI, 'ABD AL-'AZIZ BIN 'ABDULLAH AL-. (1936-) [al-turkī; عبد العزيز بن عبد الله التركي] A Saudi bureaucrat born in **Jiddah** and educated in Cairo. He worked at the Banque de l'Indochine, the United States Embassy, and for **ARAMCO** before joining the Ministry of Petroleum and Minerals in 1966. Named Deputy Minister of Petroleum and Minerals in 1975, he retained his position even after his mentor, **Ahmad Zaki Yamani**, was removed as minister in 1986. Al-Turki has been the Secretary-General of **Organization of Arab Petroleum Exporting Countries** (OAPEC) since 1990.

TURKI, AL. [āl turkī; آل تركي] One of the cadet branches of the royal family. *See* SA'UD, AL.

TURKI AL-FAYSAL (OR TURKI BIN FAYSAL) AL SA'UD. (1945-) [turkī al-fayṣal; تركي الفيصل آل سعود] One of the prominent and capable sons of King **Faysal bin 'Abd al-'Aziz**. Turki returned from postgraduate studies in London to join Saudi intelligence, becoming its head in 1978. His full brother **Sa'ud al-Faysal** is Foreign Minister. Turki was replaced as Director of the General Intelligence Directorate in early September 2001 by his uncle **Nawwaf bin 'Abd al-'Aziz** Al Sa'ud. He was named ambassador to the United Kingdom in late 2002.

TURKI BIN 'ABD AL-'AZIZ AL SA'UD. (1900-1919) [turkī;
تركي بن عبد العزيز آل سعود] King 'Abd al-'Aziz's eldest son and considered his likely successor until he died in the 1919 influenza epidemic. He was a full brother of King **Sa'ud.** Turki is also the name of another son (born 1934) of King 'Abd al-'Aziz by Hussah bint Ahmad al-Sudayri, thus making him one of the so-called **"Sudayri Seven"** and a full brother of King **Fahd.** He was appointed Deputy Minister of Defense in 1969 but was forced to resign in 1978 as a result of his marriage to the daughter of Saudi eccentric Muhammad al-Fassi. He has not held a public position since then.

TURKI BIN 'ABDULLAH AL SA'UD. (r. 1824-1834) [turkī;
تركي بن عبد الله آل سعود] The sixth leader of the **Wahhabi Al Sa'ud** state and a grandson of its founder **Muhammad bin Sa'ud.** Turki is generally considered the founder of the Second Saudi State. He was responsible for moving the Al Sa'ud capital from destroyed **al-Dir'iyah** to **Riyadh,** where it remains today, and he organized the forces of the Al Sa'ud and allies in **Najd** to oust the **Egyptian** occupiers. A rival family member was responsible for assassinating Turki in 1834, but his son **Faysal bin Turki** returned from eastern Arabia and successfully besieged Riyadh, killing the pretender and succeeding his father.

TUWAYJIRI, 'ABD AL-'AZIZ BIN 'ABD AL-MUHSIN AL-. (1915-) [al-tuwayjirī; عبد العزيز بن عبد المحسن التويجري] Born in a prominent family of **Najd,** he has been the Assistant Deputy Commander of the National Guard since 1975 and a top assistant to Crown Prince **'Abdullah bin 'Abd al-'Aziz.**

TUWAYQ, JABAL. [jabal ṭuwayq; جبل طويق] A dominant geological feature of central Arabia, consisting of a range of hills running north-south from **Sudayr** district of southern **Najd** into **al-'Arid** district, where the range splits into two.

TWITCHELL, KARL S. (1885-1968) An American engineer who had carried out water surveys for **Charles R. Crane** in Abyssinia and **Yemen** before being chosen to undertake the first geological survey of Saudi Arabia in 1931. His report that there were strong indications of **oil** in the **Eastern Province** led to his temporary employment by the American oil company SOCAL (which held the oil concession for **Bahrain**) as it tried, successfully in the end, to outbid a British rival for the Saudi oil concession.

- U -

'UBAYD, AL-. *See* JUBAYL, AL-.

'UBAYD, THURAYA BINT AHMAD. (ca. 1945-) [thurayā bint aḥmad 'ubayd; ثريا بنت احمد عبيد] International bureaucrat appointed head of the **United Nations Population Fund** in 2000. After an education in Cairo, she became the first Saudi woman to receive a government scholarship to study in the **United States.** She eventually received her doctorate in English literature from Wayne

State University and pursued a career in the United Nations, particularly in the Arab world.

UHUD. [uhud; احد] A hill just outside **al-Madinah** and the site of a major battle in A.D. 625 between a **Qurayshi** army from **Makkah** and the nascent **Muslim** forces of al-Madinah. Already vastly outnumbered, the Muslims were weakened by the defection of some of the Madinans and suffered a crushing defeat. Even the Prophet **Muhammad** was wounded and 72 of the 700 Muslim fighters were killed and buried at the scene of the battle.

'UKAZ. ['ukāz; عكاظ] The site of a pre-Islamic fair, about 25 miles north of **al-Ta'if** in **al-Hijaz**, renowned as the place where famous poets recited their latest verses. Because it was one of the principal occasions on which people from around the **Arabian Peninsula** gathered, it also served as a location for preachers and religious figures to proselytize. The fair was subsequently banned by the Prophet **Muhammad**, although a market continued to be held on the spot into the 'Abbasid period (eighth ninth centuries A.D.). 'Ukaz was pillaged in A.D. 760 by the extremist **al-Qaramitah** (Carmathian) movement. Ruins of a number of buildings are still visible, including some associated with 'Ukaz's utilization as a way station on the Pilgrims' Road. *'Ukaz* (also spelled Okaz) is also the name of a contemporary Saudi newspaper.

UKHDUD, AL-. *See* NAJRAN.

'ULA, AL-. [al-'ulā; العلا; 37 55 - 26 38] The modern name of an ancient **oasis** located along Wadi al-'Ula north of **al-Madinah** and only 13 miles south of **Mada'in Salih**. The site of Khuraybah, north of the modern town, was the ancient capital of the kingdom of Daydan [daydān, ديدان; also spelled Dedan] which existed about 3,000 years ago, and the site may have been occupied before that. Following the Daydanite period, **Lihyanite**, **Thamudic**, and probably also **Nabataean** settlements were established at the site. In addition to Khuraybah, significant sites in the oasis include rock cut tombs north of the modern town, inscriptions and graffiti (**Minaean**, Lihyanite, Thamudic and Nabataean) scattered throughout the wadi, and Mahlab al-Naqah [mahlab al-nāqah; محلب الناقة], a rock-cut water tank associated with the Prophet Salih of the **Qur'an** (Koran).

'ULAMA'. ['ulamā', sing. 'ālim; عالم؛ علما; also spelled ulema] Arabic term for theologians or religious scholars. They are responsible for interpreting the **shari'ah** (Islamic law) and their interpretation varies according to which school of jurisprudence they follow. Those *'ulama'* who judge cases according to Islamic law are the **qadis** [qāḍī; pl. quḍā'; قاضي؛ قضا], while those who give opinions on matters not covered in the **Qur'an** (Koran) or **Sunnah** are known as *faqih*s [faqīh; pl. fuqahā'; فقيه؛ فقها].

In modern times, the influence of the 'ulama' in various Islamic states has depended on the degree of secularization experienced. They probably exert more influence in Saudi Arabia than in any other country and new government policies are undertaken only after receiving a favorable ruling [**fatwá**; فتوى] from the 'ulama'. This responsibility falls to an inner circle of several dozen 'ulama', dominated in the past by the **Al al-Shaykh** family (*i.e.* the descendants of **Muhammad 'Abd al-Wahhab**). Key issues requiring the approval of the *'ulama'* before action was taken have included approval of the deposition of King **Sa'ud** in 1964, the recapture of the Great Mosque of **Makkah** in 1979, and the hosting of American and other Western troops during the campaign to liberate **Kuwait** from **Iraq** in 1990-1991. They also constitute the Committee for Encouraging Virtue and Preventing Vice [hay'at al-amr bil-ma'rūf wal-nahī 'an al-munkar; هيئة الامر بلمعروف والنهي عن المنكر], which uses the "morality" police (**mutawwi'in**) to control public behavior and make sure that prayer times are observed in offices and shops. In addition, the *'ulama'* also are in charge of Islamic education and operated the General Presidency for Girls' Education until 2002. The long time head of the Saudi *'ulama'* was Shaykh **'Abd al-'Aziz bin Baz** until his death in 1999. In the **Shi'ah** sect, the term *mullah* is generally substituted for *'alim.*

'ULAYAN, SULAYMAN BIN SALIH AL-. (1918-2002) ['ulayān; سليمان بن صالح العليان] also spelled Olayan] Extremely successful Saudi businessman from **Najd**. He was born in **'Unayzah** in 1918 and, after attending the American missionary school in **Bahrain**, began his career as an employee of and then a contractor for **ARAMCO**. From there he branched out into import activities and began to make investments in the **United States** from the 1940s. The fortune he established was estimated at nearly $8 billion in 2002. His son Khalid succeeded him as chairman of the Olayan Group, assisted by Sulayman's three daughters who have long held important positions within the business.

UMM. [umm; ام] Mother or source; sometimes used as part of a place-name.

UMM AL-MARADIM. *See* QARU AND UMM AL-MARADIM.

UMM AL-QURA. [umm al-qurá; ام القرى] Another name for **Makkah**, it translates as the "mother of cities." The name was also used for the official gazette during the short-lived Kingdom of **al-Hijaz** and then later during the Third Saudi State. It is also the name of a university, established in the course of the Third Development Plan as a subordinate offshoot of **King 'Abd al-'Aziz University**. Umm al-Qura became an independent university in 1981, specializing in Islamic disciplines, as well as education and engineering.

UMM AL-ZAMUL. [umm al-zamūl; ام الزمول; 55 47 - 22 40] A small well in the **Rub' al-Khali** desert at the point where the territorial boundaries of Saudi Arabia, the **United Arab Emirates** (more precisely, the **amirate** of Abu Dhabi), and the Sultanate of **Oman** meet, and whose sovereignty was long a matter of dispute among the governments of these states. (The above coordinates are necessarily approximate as the Saudi border agreement with the United Arab Emirates specifies different coordinates than the border agreement with Oman.)

'UMRAH. ['umrah; عمرة] The "lesser" pilgrimage to **Makkah**, which can be performed at any time, as opposed to the **hajj**, or "greater" pilgrimage, which must be performed during the Islamic month of Dhu al-Hijjah. The *'umrah*, involving circumambulation of the **Ka'bah** in the Great Mosque of Makkah as well as several other rituals, in fact constitutes one part of the hajj.

'UNAYZAH. ['unayzah; عنيزة; 43 59 - 26 06] Key city of **al-Qasim** province of **Najd**, located on the south bank of Wadi al-Rummah, about 15 miles from its traditional rival of **Buraydah**. Its population is estimated at 70,000. Long known as a center of long-distance trade (caravans operated to the **Gulf** coast, **al-Hijaz**, and north to Syria and Basra [in present day **Iraq**]), 'Unayzah is considered to date from the 13th century, although earlier settlements occupied the site. Caught up in the 19th-century struggle between the **Al Sa'ud** and the **Al Rashid**, 'Unayzah backed young **'Abd al-'Aziz bin 'Abd al-Rahman Al Sa'ud** in his attempt to revive the Al Sa'ud state. Thus, it has been part of Saudi Arabia since 1904. Because it has long been a center of education, 'Unayzah provided the first educated Saudi officials for the new kingdom, as well as many current Saudi politicians and educational figures, including the kingdom's first Ph.D. recipient.

UNITED ARAB EMIRATES (UAE) AND SAUDI ARABIA. Formerly known as the Trucial States (or the Trucial Coast or Trucial Oman), the UAE is a union of seven small states (Abu Dhabi, Dubai, Sharjah, Ra's al-Khaymah, 'Ajman, Umm al-Qaywayn, and al-Fujayrah) formed in 1971 when **Britain** withdrew its responsibility for foreign affairs and defense. The expansion of the First Saudi State reached the shores of the **Gulf** by the early 19th century and a longstanding alliance was forged with the al-Qasimi (pl. al-Qawasim) rulers of Ra's al-Khaymah, who converted to the **Wahhabi** creed. The dissipation of al-Qasimi power in the Gulf by the British sacking of Ra's al-Khaymah in 1819, coincidental with the decline of the First Saudi State after its capital at **al-Dir'iyah** was destroyed by an Egyptian army in 1818, led to the eventual emergence of the Bani Yas tribe, based on the settlements of Abu Dhabi and Dubai, as the predominant power along the Trucial Coast.
     The Bani Yas and allied tribes resisted Saudi claims of sovereignty and territory. In particular, the **amirate** of Abu Dhabi opposed the Saudi incursions into **al-Buraymi** oasis (some villages of which belonged to Abu Dhabi and the others to **Oman**), the last time being in 1952. With the breakdown of an international arbitration tribunal, the British-officered Trucial Oman Scouts ousted the Saudi garrison in October 1955. Conflicting border claims continued to bedevil Saudi-Abu Dhabi relations until the boundary agreement of 1974. While the terms were never published, the Saudis apparently gave up their claims to al-Buraymi and surrounding territory in exchange for a land corridor to the Gulf east of **Khawr al-'Udayd** (at the base of the **Qatar** Peninsula).
     Although the UAE and the kingdom subsequently became allies in the **Gulf Cooperation Council**, minor blowups occurred in the mid- and late 1990s over territorial questions, Saudi disagreement with the UAE's desire to normalize relations with **Iraq**, and the UAE's opposition to Saudi Arabia's

rapprochement with **Iran** at a time when the latter occupied three Gulf islands claimed by the UAE.

UNITED NATIONS AND SAUDI ARABIA. Saudi Foreign Minister (and later King) Prince **Faysal bin 'Abd al-'Aziz** participated in the San Francisco conference organizing the United Nations (UN) and the kingdom was a founding member of the UN when it was created in 1945. Saudi Arabia has been a staunch supporter of the UN ever since, although it has preferred to make its concerns known regarding international matters of interest through private and bilateral methods. The kingdom is also a member of various UN specialized entities, including the United Nations Conference on Trade and Development (UNCTAD), the United Nations Development Program (UNDP), the United Nations Educational, Scientific, and Cultural Organization (UNESCO), the United Nations Children's Fund (UNICEF), the United Nations Industrial Development Organization (UNIDO), the Office of the High Commission for Refugees (UNHCR), and the UN Relief and Works Agency (UNRWA). Saudi Arabia has also been seeking membership in the World Trade Organization (WTO) for some years, although the WTO does not fall within the UN framework.

UNITED STATES AND SAUDI ARABIA. Since its inception, the Saudi-American relationship has been fundamentally based on **oil**, although it has also encompassed strategic and political aspects. Oil provided the basis for the first direct contact when an American oil company, Standard Oil of California (SOCAL), which had discovered oil in nearby **Bahrain** in 1932, gained the concession for Saudi Arabia. SOCAL was soon joined by TEXACO and the new California Arabian Oil Company began producing oil in the late 1930s from its base at **Dhahran**. Production grew after the Second World War and Standard of New Jersey (later Exxon) and Standard Vacuum Oil (later Mobil) joined the earlier partners in the newly named Arabian American Oil Company (**ARAMCO**). Besides being a producing company, ARAMCO served as a channel between the Saudi and American governments and a principal agent in the development of Saudi Arabia. The company provided the government with advice and expertise on a wide variety of subjects. It instituted the first formal educational system for its Saudi employees, both at its headquarters in Dhahran and abroad, and its local purchases paved the way for the emergence of present-day indigenous commercial concerns in the **Eastern Province**.

US-Saudi diplomatic ties began with the establishment of a US legation in **Jiddah** in 1943. In February 1945, King **'Abd al-'Aziz bin 'Abd al-Rahman** met with President Franklin Roosevelt on a yacht in the Great Bitter Lake of the Suez Canal; one month later, Saudi Arabia abandoned its neutrality and declared war on Germany. A full embassy was subsequently established in Jiddah in 1948. Military ties between the two countries date from the same period. By 1943, the Pentagon deemed it desirable to establish its own air facilities in the **Gulf** (rather than rely on British ones) to link the Middle Eastern/North African theatre to South Asia and the Pacific. Negotiations over a base at Dhahran were started and the facility was completed shortly after the end of the war. The Dhahran airfield was used by the US until the agreement was terminated by mutual choice in 1962.

US teams were sent to survey Saudi military needs in 1944 and 1949, and the US Military Training Mission (USMTM) was established in 1953, replacing earlier British teams. The first arms transfers from the US to Saudi Arabia took place at this time as well, including M-41 light tanks and B-26 bombers. At first, the level of military assistance was extremely modest. Between 1950 and 1964, the grand total of sales agreements was only $87 million and deliveries totaled $75 million. But the level of sales agreements jumped to $342 million in 1965, and zoomed to over $2 billion in 1974. By 1980, nearly $35 billion in arms agreements had been negotiated, with over $11 billion of deliveries made. The pace of arms sales accelerated after the **Kuwait** War and, by early 1997, the total value of US-Saudi arms agreements totalled $93.8 billion.

The expansion of US-Saudi ties in the 1950s and 1960s, especially in military matters, was prompted by a number of factors. A principal one involved the growing importance of Saudi oil fields (and increasing levels of production) at a time when the world's oil supplies were growing short. Just as important was the emergence of the Arab "cold war" between the new, radical Arab republics and the older, traditional régimes, mostly monarchies. Not only did these new republics target Saudi Arabia and other monarchies friendly to the West, but the new régimes were increasingly aligned with the Communist bloc, thus doubly worrying Washington.

Saudi interest in an American partnership stemmed from its being subject to active aggression by such "progressive" Arab leaders as **Egypt**'s Nasir (Nasser) and **Iraq**'s Qasim. For its part, Washington sought allies against the **Soviet Union**'s encroachment in the Middle East. The complexities of the situation were clearly illustrated by the civil war in neighboring **Yemen** (1962-1967). Saudi Arabia provided as much aid as possible to the royalists fighting the Egyptian-backed republicans, and the US briefly posted a squadron of F-100 aircraft and paratroops in southwestern Saudi Arabia in case Egypt should use its troops in Yemen to attack Saudi Arabia directly.

The oil boom of the period after 1974 served to strengthen relations in the economic field. Initially, these ties favored Saudi Arabia as, until the early 1980s, the US imported over 20 percent of its oil from Saudi Arabia, more than any other country. Much of the kingdom's income was "recycled" back to the United States in the form of the purchase of American goods and services, as well as in extensive investment in the United States both by the Saudi government and by private Saudi investors. In addition, Saudi Arabia generally has worked for policies of moderation within the **Organization of Petroleum Exporting Countries** (OPEC), believing that both its own interests and the interests of the international oil market (producers as well as consumers) are best served by a reliable supply of oil at steady prices.

Increased American involvement in the kingdom's development was encouraged by the US government due to its favorable impact on recycling petrodollars. Other continuing aspects of the close cooperation between the two countries include the US/Saudi Joint Economic Commission (JECOR), which was created in 1974 and soon established several dozen projects involving technical expertise from the US Departments of Labor, Treasury, Interior, Agriculture, State, Transportation, Energy, and Health and Human Services. By the late 1980s, approximately 800 US specialists had assisted in one or more of JECOR's many training programs over the years, and the Saudi government had funded $1.8 billion in JECOR projects. At its peak, the number of Americans resident in the kingdom totalled over 60,000, with probably half or more connected to military projects.

Saudi-American ties have been strengthened by a mutual concern for the continued stability of the kingdom. Saudi displeasure over Egyptian President Anwar al-Sadat's separate peace with Israel had limited impact on the US-Saudi relationship, probably only because of increasingly volatile developments in the Gulf, alarming both Riyadh and Washington. The security threat posed by the militantly anti-US and anti-Saudi **Iranian** Revolution of 1979 seemed to tie in with a resurgence of populist **Islam**. Saudi fears seemed justified, at least briefly, by the November 1979 takeover of the Great Mosque at **Makkah** by Islamic extremists. Suspicions of Soviet designs on the Gulf were intensified by the brief border war between Saudi-backed North Yemen and Moscow-influenced South Yemen in early 1979 and then by the Soviet occupation of Afghanistan at the end of that year.

One consequence of the highly charged atmosphere over perceptions of a Soviet threat to Saudi Arabia and the Gulf region was an emerging US emphasis on direct and indirect military options in the Gulf. The Carter Doctrine was promulgated in January 1980 to provide a warning to Moscow that any move to the Gulf would be met by US force if necessary. Efforts were made to give teeth to that declaration through the Rapid Deployment Force, officially made the US Central Command in 1983. Pressure was put on Riyadh to permit access to Saudi military facilities by the Central Command on an emergency basis, and to allow the stockpiling of equipment there. Riyadh has continued to resist this kind of overt cooperation, as have some of the other states of the **Gulf Cooperation Council (GCC)**.

The priority given to a possible Soviet attack in American planning for Gulf contingencies was forced to undergo reevaluation with the outbreak of the Iran-Iraq War in September 1980. It finally became apparent in official Washington circles that threats to Gulf security from regional sources were as great as, if not greater than, Soviet incursions. With the fall of Pahlavi **Iran**, Saudi Arabia had become the only remaining "pillar" of US interests in the Gulf. Washington was determined to protect its influence in Saudi Arabia, even to the point of intervention if necessary (as expressed in the Reagan codicil to the Carter Doctrine). In addition, efforts were intensified to build up the Saudi military to the point of self-defense, if not some regional defense capability. In the latter stages of the Iran-Iraq War, with Iranian advances on land threatening Kuwait and Iranian attacks on seaborne shipping bound for Kuwaiti and Saudi ports becoming more aggressive, the US was drawn into the Gulf more directly. In 1987, Kuwaiti oil tankers were reflagged as US vessels and US military forces in the Gulf became involved in skirmishes with Iranian forces, including several attacks on Iranian offshore oil platforms that had been converted to military use.

The cessation of hostilities between Iran and Iraq in 1988 provided a respite from American military entanglement in the Gulf, but this interlude lasted only two years. Riyadh waited only a few days after the 2 August 1990 Iraqi invasion of Kuwait before requesting American and other Western assistance to defend the kingdom. Saudi Arabia not only allowed "coalition" forces full use of its territory and facilities to build up for the war, but also paid the United States some $14 billion in reimbursement for its war-related costs. (*See* DESERT STORM, OPERATION, for more detail on the invasion and war.) Once victory in Desert Storm had been achieved, Riyadh and its fellow GCC members seemed reconciled to a permanent dependence on an American defense umbrella. At the same time, however, the Saudis soon reiterated their opposition to the stationing of any foreign military presence on Saudi soil.

Washington has looked to Riyadh as the key to Arab moderation regarding Israel, as a "tool" to bring other Arab actors into the "moderate" camp. Riyadh sees itself more as a force behind Arab consensus on many matters, including Israel. Its insistence on consensus derives from the experience of the Arab cold war and reluctance to return to the extreme polarization of Arab politics during those years. The Arab summit at Khartoum in 1967, which put an end to that cold war, also created pan-Arab obligations for Riyadh, particularly in regard to **Arab-Israeli** matters. Saudi Arabia was also bound by the decision of the Arab summit at Rabat in 1975 to recognize the Palestine Liberation Organization (PLO) as the sole representative of the Palestinians.

Differing views on Arab-Israeli matters have long provided one of the few irritants in the relationship. During the June 1967 Arab-Israeli War, an impromptu labor strike at ARAMCO stopped oil production and a street demonstration in Dhahran got out of hand and a mob sacked facilities and housing at both the US air base and ARAMCO, although no Americans were injured. Another demonstration took place in Riyadh. The October 1973 Arab-IsraeliWar and resultant oil boycott marked a troubling undercurrent in the two countries' ties. As the fighting continued, Saudi Arabia and most other Arab oil producers reluctantly instituted production cutbacks and a boycott of the United States and the Netherlands for their pro-Israeli attitudes; the boycott was later extended to include Portugal, Rhodesia, and South Africa for their antiblack policies in Africa.

Indeed, Arab-Israeli differences have persisted as the major thorn in an otherwise increasingly intimate relationship. Saudi encouragement and midwifery produced the rise of the short-lived US/Saudi/Egyptian triangle of the 1970s. Saudi Arabia encouraged Sadat to turn from the Soviet Union to the United States. But Sadat's surprise decision to go to Jerusalem mocked Saudi concerns for a consensus approach and led to suspicions that Sadat's goal was a separate peace in which the other Arab states and the Palestinians would be sold out.

The "special relationship" prospered during the 1980s and even grew more intimate, despite the frustrations of the Arab-Israeli impasse. But there have been further irritations. The United States has sold an immense amount of weapons and other military equipment to Saudi Arabia over the years. At the same time, Saudi arms procurement has not followed an easy path.

US apprehensions over the apparent deterioration of "stability" in the Gulf led to an acrimonious debate over the sale of five Airborne Warning and Control System (AWACS) radar aircraft to the kingdom in 1982, over the objections of Israel and its supporters in the US, and those congressmen who feared that the Al Sa'ud state would collapse just as the Pahlavi régime had. The Saudi government, while anxious to maintain its close relations with Washington, including in the military realm, was notably and understandably reluctant to give carte blanche to a direct US military presence in the kingdom. The tug-of-war between the Pentagon's desire for facilities in Saudi Arabia and the Saudis' wish to keep out American military units (as opposed to American military advisers to the Saudi Armed Forces) continued through the tanker war of 1984.

As a consequence, Riyadh was forced to turn elsewhere for arms. In the al-Yamamah-I agreement (1985), Saudi Arabia placed orders for 72 British Aerospace Tornado combat aircraft and 60 other aircraft. Three years later, the Saudis turned to **Britain** again for the al-Yamamah-II agreement, which included another 50 Tornados as well as trainer aircraft, helicopters, minesweepers, and the construction of several air bases. The kingdom has also received arms and military assistance from **France**, as well as purchasing other arms from a variety of sources.

Another temporary flap in bilateral relations occurred in 1987 when the United States discovered that Saudi Arabia had secretly purchased a number of ballistic missiles from the People's Republic of **China**. Shortly afterwards, in what appeared to be a Saudi reaction to a strongly worded US protest, the American ambassador Hume Horan was declared persona non grata. Although Riyadh would not let the US inspect the missiles to see whether they had been modified to carry nuclear warheads, the kingdom subsequently signed the Nuclear Non-Proliferation Treaty. In large part, this episode was symptomatic of Saudi Arabia's difficulty in getting its arms requests approved by the US Congress.

Another potential point of friction is internal Saudi opposition to the closeness and even dependence of the Al Sa'ud on the United States. In part, this disquiet may be due to the traditionally conservative and insular nature of the country, but it also finds expression in pan-Arab sentiments (given US support for Israel) and Islamic political objections to partnership with the Christian West. Some activist religious leaders decried the continued American military presence in the country and their participation in demonstrations in 1994 and 1995 led to arrests. *See also* OPPOSITION GROUPS.

Saudi-American relations in the first years of the 21st century were troubled on two fronts. First, the campaign by Saudi-born **Usamah bin Ladin** against the American presence in Saudi Arabia and the Islamic world acquired a number of Saudi adherents. This was vividly demonstrated on 11 September 2001 when 19 members of his al-Qa'idah organization hijacked four domestic American aircraft and used them to destroy the World Trade Center in New York and damage the Pentagon in Washington. Fifteen of the hijackers were Saudis. For months afterwards, American media and popular opinion attacked the kingdom as being hostile to the United States and accused the Saudi government of nurturing terrorists and Saudi citizens of contributing funds to al-Qa'idah and other organizations. Several hundred Saudis living in the United States were detained, some for a number of months. Official relations between Riyadh and Washington, however, remained firm, particularly after the kingdom arrested some Saudis suspected of involvement and acted on Washington's request to close suspect financial institutions. There was some agitation in the US to move US troops—and the state-of-the-art military command center at **al-Kharj** out of the kingdom, partly in response to perceived Saudi disquiet over their presence.

At about the same time, bilateral relations were also impacted by the deterioration in Arab-Palestinian relations as a result of the second Palestinian *intifadah* (uprising) which began in September 2000. The election of Ariel Sharon as Israeli prime minister and his institution of hard-line policies vis-à-vis the Palestinian Authority led to a wave of suicide bombings against Israeli military and civilian targets in 2002. When Sharon ordered the army into Palestinian towns and villages in response and sought to oust President Yasir Arafat, public opinion in Saudi Arabia was as aroused as elsewhere in the Arab world, and demonstrations in the kingdom attacked both Israel and the United States for supporting Israel.

UNIVERSITIES. The first Saudi university graduates returned from **Egypt** in 1945 and shortly afterwards **shari'ah** (Islamic law) institutes were opened in **Makkah** and **Riyadh**. The first proper university, **King Sa'ud University**, was established in Riyadh in 1957, at the insistence of the Minister of Education (later King), **Fahd bin 'Abd al-'Aziz**. Today, total enrollment in higher education in the kingdom is about 350,000. Of the eight universities (all are listed under separate entries), five offer more secular curricula: King Sa'ud University, Riyadh; **King 'Abd al-'Aziz University, Jiddah**; **King Fahd University of Petroleum and Minerals, Dhahran**; **King Faysal University, al-Dammam** and **al-Hufuf**; and **King Khalid University, Abha**. The remaining three concentrate on Islamic religious and legal disciplines: **Imam Muhammad bin Sa'ud University**, Riyadh; **Islamic University, al-Madinah**; and **Umm al-Qura University**, Makkah. All the universities, administered by the Ministry of Higher Education, are segregated by sex, and five have women's branches. In addition, the General Presidency for Girls' Education, under the supervision of the **'ulama'** (religious scholars), operates a dozen Colleges of Education throughout the country, which produce mostly schoolteachers.

'UQAYLAT. ['uqaylāt; sing. 'uqaylī; عقيلى؛عقيلات] The guild-like corporations of livestock merchants of **al-Qasim** of central Arabia who in times past travelled around the **Arabian Peninsula** and to Syria and **Iraq** to sell their animals. The term was also used more generally to refer to Qasimis who worked abroad in the days before oil.

'UQAYR, AL-. [al-'uqayr; العقير; also spelled Oqair; 50 13 - 25 39] A traditional port on Saudi Arabia's **Gulf** coast, and the site of border negotiations in 1922 between **'Abd al-'Aziz bin 'Abd al-Rahman Al Sa'ud**, the **Imam** of **Najd**, and Sir **Percy Cox**, the High Commissioner of **Iraq** and representing the interests of **Kuwait** and **Bahrain**. To cut through the stalemated negotiations, Cox allegedly gave Iraq much of the territory claimed by Najd and balanced it by giving Najd much of Kuwait's territory. To resolve the intractable problem of **badu** (bedouin) tribes moving across grazing grounds, Cox also proposed the creation of two **Neutral Zones**, one between Iraq and Saudi Arabia and the other between Kuwait and Saudi Arabia.

'UTAYBAH, AL-. [al-'utaybah; sing. 'utaybī; العتيبة؛عتيبي] An important nomadic tribe of **Najd**, with some settled sections in **al-Hijaz**. The tribe's territory is concentrated in the central Arabian plateaux and ranges from **al-Qasim** in the east to the highlands east of **al-Ta'if**. Traditionally ferocious, the 'Utaybah were on poor terms with Imam **'Abd al-'Aziz bin 'Abd al-Rahman Al Sa'ud** and often raided Saudi territories in Najd earlier in the 20th century. Conversely, they acknowledged the authority of the King of al-Hijaz until the Saudi conquest. Their traditional enemies are the **Harb**.

'UTAYBI, JUHAYMAN BIN MUHAMMAD BIN SAYF AL-. [juhaymān; جهيمان بن محمد بن سيف العتيبي] Leader of the **Ikhwan** group which seized the Great Mosque of **Makkah** in 1979. His father was among the Ikhwan members who rebelled against **Imam 'Abd al-'Aziz bin 'Abd al-Rahman** in the late 1920s and allegedly was killed at the Battle of **Sibilah** (1929), which broke the back of the Ikhwan. Juhayman served in the National Guard for a number of years and then quit to attend the **Islamic University** in **al-Madinah**. On 20 November 1979, Juhayman led several hundred followers, mostly fellow religious students drawn from traditionalist Saudi tribes and from neighboring countries, into the Great Mosque of Makkah. There he proclaimed Muhammad bin 'Abdullah al-Qahtani, his brother-in-law, as the "*mahdi*" (the Islamic equivalent of a Messiah). The government, after soliciting a **fatwa** (religious opinion) sanctioning the use of force, moved into the mosque on 5 December and killed a number of the dissidents, including al-Qahtani, and capturing the rest. Juhayman and most of his followers were executed shortly afterwards. *See also* OPPOSITION GROUPS.

'UYAYNAH, AL-. [al-'uyaynah; العيينة] The most important town of central **Najd** in the mid-18th century, not far from **Riyadh**. The ruling Al Mu'ammar family of **Bani Tamim** forced the Islamic reformer **Muhammad bin 'Abd al-Wahhab** to leave the town, and he settled in **al-Dir'iyah** and struck a compact with the **Al Sa'ud** family which resulted in the spread of the **Wahhabi** version of **Islam**, as well as Saudi political power, across Najd and beyond.

- W -

WADI. [wādī, pl. wudyān; وادي؛وديان] Watercourse or valley, often used as part of a geographical name, *e.g.* Wadi al-Batin.

WAHBAH, HAFIZ. [ḥāfiẓ wahbah; حافظ وهبة] (1889-1965) A Saudi government official of Egyptian origin, Hafiz Wahbah was a long-time fixture in the Saudi government and an especially important figure in dealings with Europeans. Born in Cairo and educated at al-Azhar University, he became an ardent Arab nationalist as a student and was forced to leave **Egypt** to avoid arrest. Until 1918, he spent time in Istanbul, **India**, and Basra (**Iraq**), and was imprisoned several times for political agitation. After the 1918 armistice, he opened a school in **Bahrain** but was soon deported on political grounds; a similar episode followed in **Kuwait**. His first Saudi connection came in 1919 when he accompanied Prince (later King) **Faysal bin 'Abd al-'Aziz** to Europe and he became an adviser to King **'Abd al-'Aziz bin 'Abd al-Rahman** after being expelled from Kuwait. Appointed **Amir** of **Makkah** following the Saudi conquest of **al-Hijaz** in 1926, he soon rose to Deputy Viceroy of al-Hijaz (under Prince Faysal) but was then transferred to Acting Minister of Education, as well as Minister of the Interior. By the late 1920s, Wahbah was engaged in various diplomatic missions in Europe and the **Gulf**. He continued to carry out these tasks in his capacity as Adviser to the King through the 1960s. He was also accredited to the United Kingdom as Saudi Arabian minister (later ambassador) from 1930. He died in Rome in 1965.

WAHHABISM. [al-wahhābīyah; الوهابية] The movement within **Sunni Islam** founded by **Muhammad 'Abd al-Wahhab** (1703-1792). Influenced by the teachings of Ibn Hanbal (the founder of the **Hanbali** school of jurisprudence, generally considered the most conservative of the four schools within Sunni Islam) and Ibn Taymiyah, the Wahhabi movement is known for its austerity and literal interpretation of Islamic teachings. Generally speaking, the Wahhabi movement opposes innovations [bida'; بدع] within Islam and confines its recognition of sources of religious authority to the **Qur'an** (Koran), the **Sunnah** (the Traditions of the Prophet Muhammad), and the teachings of the four schools of Islamic law, principally the Hanbali. Wahhabism has been the creed of the **Al Sa'ud** since the mid-18th century when **Muhammad bin Sa'ud** employed its message and appeal to create the First Saudi State. Today, the majority of the indigenous population of Saudi Arabia, as well as that of neighboring **Qatar**, is Wahhabi. Wahhabism is a primary factor in the extreme conservatism of Saudi society today compared to its neighbors, displayed for example in forbidding the veneration of saints, the abhorrence of tombs and elaborate mosques, the absolute prohibition of alcohol, the segregation of the sexes, the rigid enforcement of prayer times by the so-called "religious police" (**mutawwi'in**), and the state's declared adherence to the **shari'ah** (Islamic law). Adherents prefer to be known as Muwahhidin [muwahhidīn; موحدين], or "unitarians," but this term is not much used outside Saudi Arabia and Qatar.

WALID, AL-, BIN TALAL BIN 'ABD AL-'AZIZ AL SA'UD. (1957-) [al-walīd; الوليد بن طلال بن عبد العزيز آل سعود; also spelled Alwaleed] Saudi businessman and son of former minister and noted royal family liberal **Talal bin 'Abd al-'Aziz**. Al-Walid's mother was the daughter of former Lebanese

Prime Minister Riad Solh and al-Walid was raised in Beirut and **Riyadh**, before receiving a business administration degree in California in 1979 and a master's degree from Syracuse University in 1985. His business interests are concentrated in the Kingdom Establishment for Trading and Contracting, which he founded in 1979, which has become the second largest company in Saudi Arabia with a 1998 turnover of about $4.5 billion. Starting in construction, travel agencies, and real estate, he eventually moved into banking and portfolio investment, with stakes in Citicorp, Saks Fifth Avenue, Eurodisney, TWA, Apple computers, Moevenpick, Planet Hollywood, Netscape, Daewoo, Canary Wharf, Teledesic, and America On-Line. He has invested in Lebanese and Palestinian redevelopment and has provided donations for charitable causes within and without the kingdom. He has also built the tallest building in Riyadh, the Kingdom Tower, at 990 feet tall. He was estimated in 2002 to be the 11th richest person in the world, with a fortune of $20 billion.

WALLIN, GEORG AUGUSTUS. (1811-1852) A Finnish scholar of Arabic and the Middle East, long associated with the university at Helsingfors (Sweden). In the first (1845) of Wallin's two epic journeys in Arabia, he travelled from Cairo across **al-Jawf** and **al-Nafud** desert to **Ha'il** in **Najd**, disguised as a Syrian Christian doctor. He was unable to go on to **al-Qasim** as intended and instead covertly joined the **hajj** (Islamic pilgrimage) to Makkah before returning to Cairo. In 1848, he made his way from Baghdad back to **Ha'il**, intending to travel on to **Riyadh**. But he was exposed as a Christian and was forced to return to Baghdad and thence to Helsingfors. He died in the midst of preparations for a third Arabian trip.

WAQF. [waqf; pl. awqāf; وقف؛اوقاف] An endowment, usually religious in nature, whereby income from property, frequently agricultural land or a shop, is dedicated in perpetuity to a specific purpose. A *waqf* may be used to fund the upkeep of a **mosque** or Qur'anic school, for example. In Saudi Arabia, administration and supervision of these endowments is handled by the Ministry of Hajj Affairs and Awqaf.

WASHM. [washm; وشم] A district at the northwestern edge of southern **Najd**, bordered by **Sudayr** to the north and **al-'Arid** to the south. Its capital is Shaqrah and its principal sedentary population is drawn from the Bani Zayd and **Bani Tamim**; the largest **badu** (bedouin) tribe is **al-'Utaybah**.

WHITE ARMY. *See* MILITARY AND DEFENSE.

WOMEN. Saudi Arabia's prevailing **Wahhabi** interpretation of **Islam** has meant that the country strictly enforces the segregation of men and women. Apart from a brief period of liberalization in the 1970s, segregation in the 2000s is as strict as it was traditionally. Women are required to be fully veiled in black *abayas* (encompassing robes) when in public, and the only men with whom they are allowed to mix are close relatives. While this policy does not prevent women from pursuing **education** (there were nearly 21,000 female university graduates in 1999) and working (an estimated 250,000 women work in Saudi Arabia), it does make any activity outside the home difficult. **Banks** have separate branches for women, both as customers and employees. Areas in buses and restaurants are set aside for sole use by women or families. Travel, employment, and most dealings with the government require the permission or intervention of a *mahram*, a male relative who is responsible for the woman. Not surprisingly, women became heavy users of the Internet after its introduction to the kingdom in the late 1990s.

Still, a few women have achieved prominence as newscasters, educators, scholars, and businesswomen. The country produces enough female schoolteachers to meet its needs, although there is great difficulty in assigning female teachers to remote parts of the country. Nursing and, increasingly, medical doctors provide career opportunities, as do banking and some employment in ministries. While foreign women are not subject to many of the restrictions applying to Saudi women, they must still be cloaked in public.

In 1990, a group of some 50 Saudi women staged a demonstration in **Riyadh** by driving their own cars. Although no law existed specifically prohibiting women from driving, the demonstrators were arrested by police. Most were fired from their jobs and prevented from traveling abroad for a year. A new law to prohibit women from driving was soon enacted. Despite occasional rumors about the law being revoked, no changes had been made by 2002.

The government began issuing identity cards to women on a voluntary basis in late 2001; previously, women were included on the cards of their father or brother. Saudi Arabia joined the United Nations Convention on Elimination of All Forms of Discrimination Against Women but simultaneously announced it would not be bound by any clauses that contradicted the **shari'ah** (Islamic law). A Saudi woman, **Thuraya bint Ahmad 'Ubayd**, was named head of the **United Nations** Population Fund in 2000.

- Y -

YAM. [yām; sing. yāmī; يامي ،يام] A principal tribe of southern Saudi Arabia, particularly around **Najran** on the **Yemen** border and (Yemeni) **al-Jawf**. It is **Shi'ah**, possibly Isma'ili.

YAMAMAH, AL-. [al-yamāmah; اليمامة] A small district and minor settlement of southern **Najd** in the vicinity of **al-Kharj**. However, the name al-Yamamah is of great antiquity and originally seems to have referred to a much larger region between **al-Rub' al-Khali** desert in the south and **al-Ahsa' oasis** in the north and east, thus comprising the inland counterpart to the coastal area of al-Bahrayn (in the older, larger sense of that name). Al-Yamamah seems to have corresponded roughly to what is today the southern division of **Najd** and, in this sense, the term remained in use through the 'Abbasid or medieval period. The name al-Yamamah has also been used to designate the Saudi purchase of British Tornado aircraft and associated work. *See* BRITAIN AND SAUDI ARABIA.

YAMANI, AHMAD ZAKI. (1930-) [zakī yamanī; احمد زكي يماني] Son and grandson of **Jiddah** merchants, Ahmad was one of the early generation of Saudis to receive education abroad (LL.B. Cairo University and LL.M. Harvard), and he returned to become the first Saudi to join the Bureau of Experts in the King's Office in 1958. His aptitude and intelligence commended him to King **Faysal bin 'Abd al-'Aziz**, who named him to the key post of Minister of Petroleum and Mineral Resources in 1962. But his flamboyance and prominence on the international stage helped to turn King Faysal's successors against him, and reports of disagreements over the handling of Saudi Arabia's **oil** policy were rife until Ahmad was abruptly dismissed in 1986. Unlike another prominent commoner politician dismissed from cabinet office, **Ghazi al-Qusaybi**, Ahmad was not forced into exile and has continued to practice law in **Riyadh**, as well as establishing a Centre for Global Energy Studies in London. Of no relation to former Information Minister Muhammad 'Abduh al-Yamani.

YANBU'. [yanbu'; ينبع; also spelled Yanbo; 37 55 - 24 10] A coastal settlement of **al-Hijaz** on the **Red Sea**, traditionally serving as a port for the city of **al-Madinah**. Formerly, Yanbu' was divided into the port itself, Yanbu' al-Bahr, and an inland agricultural settlement of Yanbu' al-Nakhl. Yanbu' apparently acquired its name from the proliferation of springs in the vicinity. In the 1970s, it became the center, along with **al-Jubayl** on the **Gulf**, of a massive **industrial** development scheme, including **oil** refining, petrochemical industries, and heavy manufacturing complexes based on hydrocarbon fuels. Yanbu' was planned as the smaller of the two sites, with two petroleum refineries, a natural gas processing plant, a petrochemical complex, other light industries, an industrial port and a new city of 100,000 inhabitants. Energy for these projects was to be supplied via oil and gas **pipelines** from the **Eastern Province**.

YASIN, YUSUF. [yāsīn; يوسف ياسين] (1890-1962) Saudi official of Syrian origin, born in Latakia. A pupil of the prominent Islamic reformer Rashid al-Rida, Yusuf became a schoolmaster in Jerusalem and later was attached to the **al-Hashimi** entourage in **al-Hijaz**, joining King **Faysal al-Hashimi** in Damascus after its liberation from the **Ottomans**. By 1925, he had transferred his allegiance to the **Al Sa'ud** and was entrusted with launching the official gazette, **Umm al-Qura**. Later, he was promoted to Deputy Foreign Minister, in which capacity he negotiated foreign treaties and accompanied King **'Abd al-'Aziz bin 'Abd al-Rahman** to **Egypt** in 1945 for his meeting with President Franklin Roosevelt. Contemporary diplomats regarded him as a strong Arab nationalist and ardent **Muslim**. He was appointed a Minister of State in the first council of ministers established by King **Sa'ud** in 1954. As a member of the Saudi delegation in the **al-Buraymi** arbitration tribunal in The Hague (1955), accusations that he had attempted to influence the witnesses led to British withdrawal from the tribunal.

YATHRIB. [yathrib; يثرب] The original name of **al-Madinah** in **al-Hijaz**. Its inhabitants invited the Prophet **Muhammad** and his small band of **Muslims**

to settle in Yathrib when they were being persecuted in **Makkah**. Thus, Yathrib, or al-Madinah, became the first capital of the Islamic state.

YEMEN AND SAUDI ARABIA. In April 1990, the Republic of Yemen (ROY) was formed from a merger of the Yemen Arab Republic (YAR; 1962-1990), also known as North Yemen, and the People's Democratic Republic of Yemen (PDRY; 1967-1990), also known as South Yemen. Saudi Arabia's attitude toward the new state was reflective of its traditional ambivalence about Yemen throughout the 20th century. The Imamate of Yemen (an imamate was a religious monarchy headed by an **imam**), which preceded the YAR in North Yemen, and the kingdom had been long-standing rivals. Following the departure of the **Ottomans** after the First World War, both Saudi Arabia and Yemen laid claim to the province of '**Asir** but it fell to King '**Abd al-'Aziz bin 'Abd al-Rahman** in the mid-1920s. In 1934, the two monarchies fought a short but sharp border war, during which Saudi forces penetrated far down Yemen's **Red Sea** coast. The resultant Treaty of al-Ta'if (1934) gave the provinces of **Jizan** and **Najran** to Saudi Arabia, a decision which still rankles many Yemenis, and defined the Yemeni-Saudi border inland from the Red Sea to a point south of Najran. The rest of the frontier was still being demarcated in early 2002.

In September 1962, an Egyptian-inspired coup d'état resulted in the declaration of the Yemen Arab Republic and the flight of the Yemeni imam, Muhammad al-Badr of the Hamid al-Din dynasty, to the northern mountains of his country. A long and bloody civil war ensued, with **Egypt** supporting the republican forces with troops and money while Saudi Arabia provided the royalist forces with a haven, arms, and more money. Yemen came to serve as a battlefield-by-proxy of the two competing forces in Arab politics of the era: the progressive republics, exemplified by Jamal 'Abd al-Nasir's (Nasser) Egypt, and the conservative monarchies, most prominently Saudi Arabia. The fighting raged on until the June 1967 Arab-Israeli War forced Egypt to withdraw its more than 70,000 troops. It soon became clear that neither of the Yemeni sides could prevail outright and negotiations finally resulted in a national reconciliation in 1970.

For the first time, Saudi Arabia began to play a direct role in Yemeni politics. The Saudi view of North Yemen has been dichotomous. On the one hand, **Riyadh** desired a North Yemeni régime strong enough to act as a bulwark against radical South Yemen. On the other hand, Saudi Arabia feared the emergence of a strong North Yemen, given its larger indigenous population, the hundreds of thousands of Yemeni workers in Saudi Arabia, and long-standing Yemeni popular hostility toward the kingdom. Consequently, to protect itself against the perceived South Yemeni threat, Riyadh propped up North Yemen by extending diplomatic backing, providing budgetary support and development aid, and transferring arms. At the same time, however, the Al Sa'ud indulged in intrigues in North Yemeni politics, playing off politicians in the capital against each other and bolstering the northern tribes against the YAR government. It is widely believed in Yemen that Riyadh was behind the assassination of the popular YAR President Ibrahim al-Hamdi in 1977, and also that the Saudis played a key behind-the-scenes role in the election of 'Ali 'Abdullah Salih as Hamdi's eventual successor.

While the Saudis had been opposed to the British presence in Aden, they were not prepared for **British** withdrawal in 1967 to produce a South Yemeni government led by the radical National Liberation Front. The old aristocracy in Aden's hinterland fled to exile in Saudi Arabia and elsewhere, and the Saudis supported a variety of dissident armies along South Yemen's borders. For their part, the South Yemeni leaders verbally attacked the **Al Sa'ud** and the other ruling families in the **Gulf**. The enmity reached a nadir with a South Yemeni attack on the Saudi border post at al-Wadiyah in 1969, which was followed by a retaliatory air strike on the PDRY. During the same period, the Aden government also threw its backing behind the Marxist rebellion in **Oman**'s southern province of Dhufar.

It was not until the mid-1970s that Riyadh perceived that a rapprochement might be possible, through the medium of South Yemeni President Salim Rubayyi' 'Ali. The latter's visit to Riyadh in 1976 resulted in the establishment of diplomatic relations and agreement on a modest aid program. However, the outbreak of fighting in Aden in June 1978 resulted in the capture and execution of Salim Rubayyi' 'Ali by his hard-line rivals. The animosity between Riyadh and Aden was renewed, tempered slightly by the ouster of pro-Moscow leader 'Abd al-Fattah Isma'il in 1982 and then by the emergence of a relatively moderate government out of the ashes of the January 1986 civil war in South Yemen.

The Saudi attitude toward the merger of North and South Yemen in 1990 seemed predictably ambivalent. The submergence of South Yemen's radical ruling party by the North's more moderate military leadership was welcomed but the prospect of an even larger, unified, anti-monarchical and anti-Saudi Yemen was equally worrying. The new Republic of Yemen's vacillation over the **Iraqi** invasion of **Kuwait** in August 1990 provoked a furious Saudi response: all aid to Yemen was cut off and most of the hundreds of thousands of Yemenis resident in the kingdom were forced to leave. In 1992, the Saudi government issued warnings to a number of international oil companies operating concessions granted by the Yemeni government, contending that they were operating in Saudi territory and should desist.

The decision in 1994 of the former leaders of South Yemen to secede from the northern-dominated Republic of Yemen resulted in a disastrous civil war ending in the southerners' defeat. Saudi Arabia tacitly supported the southerners in the conflict, in part because of Yemen's perceived support of Iraq. It took several years for relations to improve slightly, with Yemeni President 'Ali 'Abdullah Salih's visit to Saudi Arabia, the kingdom's lifting of the ban on Yemeni employment, and the establishment of joint committees to discuss mutual problems. Still, the dispute over the two countries' mutual border continued to bedevil ties and there were reports of occasional Saudi-Yemeni skirmishes. Although an agreement to respect the 1934 al-Ta'if arrangement was signed by both parties in early 1995, long and tortuous negotiations were required before the final border treaty of 12 June 2000. The resultant lessening of tensions led to the awarding of a contract for border demarcation, the removal of many of the troops stationed along the border, and reinstitution of Saudi financial assistance to Yemen.

- Z -

ZAHRAN. [zahrān; sing. zahrānī; زهران؛ زهراني] One of the largest tribes of **al-Bahah** Province, with both nomadic and settled sections ranging from the **Tihamah** plain along the **Red Sea** to the mountains of **al-Sarawat**. The Zahran have a reputation as a warrior tribe and their traditional enemies were the **Bani Ghamid**. The tribe fought for the **Idrisi** family in the early part of the 20th century.

ZAHRAN, AL-. *See* DHAHRAN.

ZAKAT. [zakāt; زكاة; also spelled zakah] The Islamic alms tax, which is one of the five fundamental obligations of every **Muslim** and is variably levied on production. As state and religion were inseparable in early **Islam**, zakat has continued to be collected, at least periodically, in Saudi Arabia. It is now levied on Saudi companies but not on individuals whose payment is voluntary. Zakat has also had political significance, as Saudi claims to **al-Buraymi** and other parts of eastern Arabia relied on the record of previous collections of zakat from inhabitants of the area. Originally used as a principal source for aiding the poor, the widowed, the orphaned, and the disabled, the importance of zakat has diminished in recent years owing to the much greater largesse available for social welfare programs in general through the accumulation of revenues from petroleum products.

ZAMIL, AL-. [al-zāmil; الزامل] A prominent Saudi merchant family, originating in the town of **'Unayzah** in **al-Qasim** but important in the **Eastern Province**. Al-Zamil Group activities range from consumer imports to construction and manufacturing. One member of the family, 'Abd al-'Aziz bin 'Abdullah, served as Minister of Industry and Electricity while his brother 'Abd al-Rahman served as Deputy Minister of Commerce.

ZAMZAM. [zamzam; زمزم] A well near the **Ka'bah** in the Great Mosque at **Makkah**. According to **Islamic** beliefs, the well derived from a spring which appeared when Hagar and her son Ishmael [Ismā'īl; اسماعيل] were wandering in the desert after being expelled by Abraham [Ibrāhīm; ابراهيم]. The water of Zamzam is drunk by the pilgrims during the **hajj** (pilgrimage) and bottles of its water are taken back to homes throughout the Islamic World.

ZILFI, AL-. [al-zilfī; الزلفي; 44 00 -26 00] A town of central **Najd** at the border between **Sudayr** district and **al-Qasim** province, about 60 miles east of **Buraydah**. It marks the northern end of the **Jabal Tuwayq**. Al-Zilfi's inhabitants are drawn from the Bani Khadir, **al-Dawasir**, **al-'Utaybah**, **Shammar**, and Fadul.

ZUBAYDAH. *See* DARB ZUBAYDAH.

APPENDIX A: RULERS IN THE AL SA'UD DYNASTY
(with order and dates of rule)

Sa'ud bin Muhammad bin Muqrin

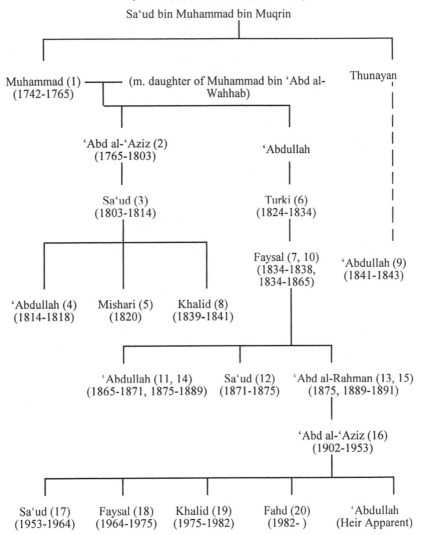

APPENDIX B: THE AL SA'UD:
RELATIONSHIP OF CADET BRANCHES

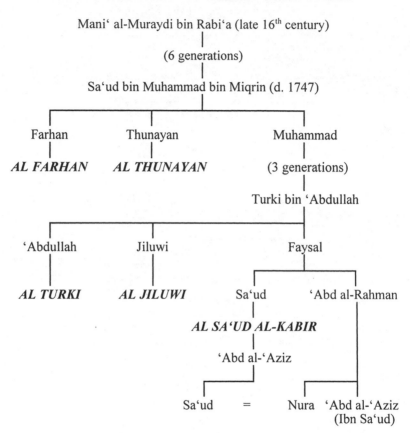

Mani' al-Muraydi bin Rabi'a (late 16th century)

(6 generations)

Sa'ud bin Muhammad bin Miqrin (d. 1747)

Farhan

AL FARHAN

Thunayan

AL THUNAYAN

Muhammad

(3 generations)

Turki bin 'Abdullah

'Abdullah

AL TURKI

Jiluwi

AL JILUWI

Faysal

Sa'ud

AL SA'UD AL-KABIR

'Abd al-'Aziz

'Abd al-Rahman

Sa'ud   =   Nura 'Abd al-'Aziz
(Ibn Sa'ud)

APPENDIX C: PROMINENT DESCENDANTS OF IMAM 'ABD AL-RAHMAN BIN FAYSAL

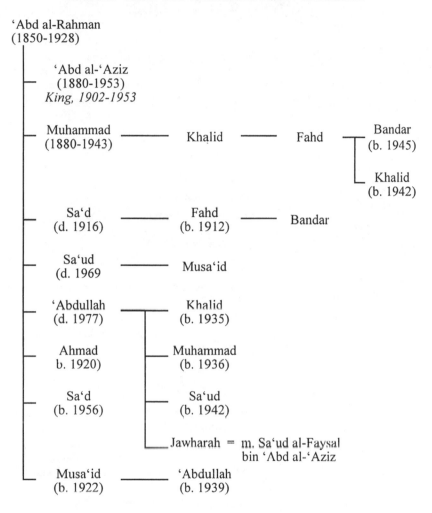

'Abd al-Rahman
(1850-1928)

'Abd al-'Aziz
(1880-1953)
King, 1902-1953

Muhammad ——— Khalid ——— Fahd ——— Bandar
(1880-1943)   (b. 1945)
                                               Khalid
                                               (b. 1942)

Sa'd ——— Fahd ——— Bandar
(d. 1916)   (b. 1912)

Sa'ud ——— Musa'id
(d. 1969

'Abdullah ——— Khalid
(d. 1977)   (b. 1935)

Ahmad   Muhammad
b. 1920)   (b. 1936)

Sa'd   Sa'ud
(b. 1956)   (b. 1942)

              Jawharah = m. Sa'ud al-Faysal
                          bin 'Abd al-'Aziz

Musa'id ——— 'Abdullah
(b. 1922)   (b. 1939)

167

APPENDIX D: PROMINENT DESCENDANTS OF KING 'ABD AL-'AZIZ BIN 'ABD AL-RAHMAN

N.B. This chart lists all the sons of King 'Abd al-'Aziz but only a few of his grandsons and none of his great-grandsons, principally those who have held senior government positions or have been prominent for other reasons. Some dates of birth are approximate and not all positions held may be current.

'Abd al-'Aziz bin 'Abd al-Rahman (1880-1953)

Turki (1900-1919)	Died in influenza epidemic
Faysal	Minister of Labor and Social Affairs (1961-1962); Minister of the Interior (1962)
Sa'ud (1902-1969)	King (1953-1964)
Fahd	Minister of Defense (1956-1960)
Muhammad	Minister of Defense (1960-1962); Amir of al-Bahah (?-)
Khalid	Commander of National Guard (1956-1961)
Sa'd	Commander of National Guard (1961-1963)
'Abd al-Rahman	Deputy Minister of Defense (1982-)
Mish'al	Amir of Najran (early 1990s-)
Faysal (1904-1975)	King (1964-1975)
'Abdullah	Minister of Health (1951-1954); Minister of the Interior (1951-1959)
Muhammad	Deputy Minister of Agriculture and Water for Desalination Affairs (1970s); principal in Dar al-Mal al-Islami and Faysal Islamic Banks
Khalid	Amir of 'Asir (1971-)
Sa'ud	Minister of Foreign Affairs (1975-); Chairman, Supreme Council for Petroleum Affairs
Turki	Director-General of Intelligence (1978-2001)

'Abd al-'Aziz bin 'Abd al-Rahman (1880-1953)

Muhammad (1910-1988)	Passed over as Heir Apparent in favor of his brother Khalid in 1982
Khalid (1912-1982)	King (1975-1982)
Nasir (1920-)	
Sa'd (1920-)	
Fahd (1921-)	King (1982-)
Faysal (1946-1999)	President of General Presidency of Youth Welfare (1972-1999)
Sa'ud	Deputy Director-General of Intelligence (1992-); Vice-President of General Intelligence (1985-)
Sultan	Vice-President of General Presidency of Youth Welfare (1982-)
Muhammad (1950-)	Amir of the Eastern Province (1985-)
'Abd al-'Aziz (c. 1974-)	Minister of State without Portfolio (1998-); Head of Council of Ministers Affairs (2000-)
Mansur (1922-1951)	Minister of Defense (1944-1951); died of kidney disease
'Abdullah (1923-)	Commander of National Guard (1963-); Heir Apparent and First Deputy Prime Minister (1982-)
Mut'ib	Assistant Deputy Commander of National Guard for Military Affairs
'Abd al-'Aziz	Adviser in Heir Apparent's Court (1990s-)
Bandar (1923-)	
Faysal	Amir of al-Qasim (1992-)
Musa'id (1923-)	
Faysal	Executed in 1975 for assassination of King Faysal
Sultan (1924-)	Minister of Defense and Aviation and Inspector General (1962-); Second Deputy Prime Minister (1982-)

169

'Abd al-'Aziz bin 'Abd al-Rahman (1880-1953)

─Khalid — Commander of Air Defense Forces (1984-1991); commanded Arab and Islamic coalition forces during Kuwait War (1990-1991); Assistant Minister of Defense and Aviation and Inspector-General for Military Affairs (2001-)

─Bandar (1949-) — Ambassador to the United States (1983-)

└Turki — Deputy Minister of Information (1980s-)

'Abd al-Muhsin (1925-) — Minister of the Interior (1960-1961); one of "Liberal Princes" of 1960s

└Sa'ud — Amir of Ha'il (1999-)

─Mish'al (1926-) — Minister of Defense (1951-1956); Amir of Makkah (1963-1971)

'Abd al-Rahman (1931-) — Vice Minister of Defense and Aviation and Inspector-General (1983-)

─Talal (1931-) — Leader of "Liberal Princes" of 1960s; President of Arab Gulf Program for UN Development (AGFUND)

└al-Walid (1957-) — Prominent businessman and investor

─Mishari (1932-2000)

─Badr (1933-) — One of "Liberal Princes" of 1960s; Deputy Commander of National Guard (1968-)

─Nayif (1933-) — Minister of the Interior (1975-)

└Muhammad — Assistant to the Minister of the Interior (2000-)

─Nawwaf (1934-) — One of "Liberal Princes" of 1960s; Adviser to King Faysal on Gulf Affairs (1968-1975); Director-General of Intelligence (2001-)

─Turki (1934-) — Vice Minister of Defense (1969-1982)

─Fawwaz (1934-) — Amir of Makkah (1971-1980)

─'Abd al-Ilah (1935-) — Amir of al-Qasim (1980-1992)

─Salman (1936-) — Amir of Riyadh (1962-)

─Sultan (1956-) — First Arab astronaut; Secretary-General of the Higher Council for Tourism (2000-)

─'Abd al-'Aziz — Deputy Minister of Oil and Minerals (1995-)

─Ahmad — Owner of *al-Sharq al-Awsat* newspaper

└Fahd (d. 2001) — Deputy Amir of the Eastern Province (1986-1991); businessman

'Abd al-'Aziz bin 'Abd al-Rahman (1880-1953)

Majid (1936-) Amir of Makkah (1980-1999)

Mish'al Governor (muhafiz) of Jiddah (1990s-)

Thamir (1937-1958) Committed suicide in the United States

Ahmad (1941-) Vice Minister of the Interior (1975-)

Mamduh (1941?-) President of Strategic Studies Bureau in the King's Office (1970s-)

'Abd al-Majid (1941-) Amir of al-Madinah (1986-1999); Amir of Makkah (1999-)

Hidhlul (1941-)

Mashhur (1942-)

Sattam (1943-) Deputy Amir of Riyadh (1968-)

Miqrin (1943-) Amir of Ha'il (1980-1999); Amir of al-Madinah (1999-)

Hamud (1947-)

Sources: Compiled from a variety of published sources and interviews in Saudi Arabia and elsewhere. Important sources of biographical information include:
① Brian Lees. *Handbook of the Al Saud Ruling Family of Saudi Arabia.* London: Royal Genealogies, 1980.
② David Holden and Richard Johns. *The House of Saud.* New York: Holt, Rinehart and Winston, 1982.
③ Gary Samuel Samore. "Royal Family Politics in Saudi Arabia (1953-1982)." Ph.D. dissertation, Harvard University, 1983.

APPENDIX E: AL-HASHIMI SHARIFS OF MAKKAH AND THEIR DESCENDANTS

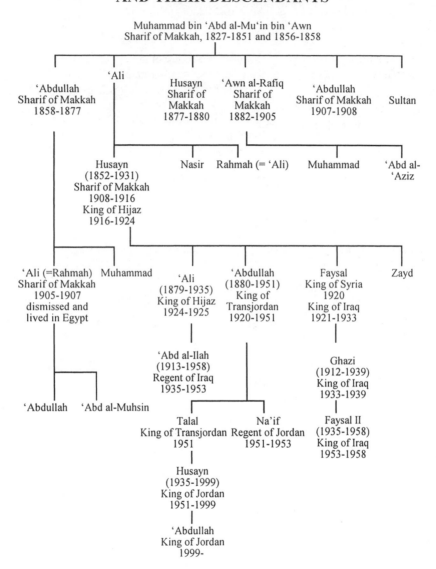

Note: A member of the rival Dhawi Zayd clan (which held the title of Sharif before 1827) was appointed Sharif during 1851-1856 and again in extreme old age during 1880-1882, after the murder of Sharif Husayn bin Muhammad.

Sources:

① C.E. Dawn. "Hashimids." *Encyclopædia of Islam*, 2nd ed., Vol. 3, p. 264.
② David George Hogarth. *Hejaz Before World War I: A Handbook*. Reprint of 1917 2nd ed.; Cambridge: Oleander Press, 1978.
③ Randall Baker. *King Husain and the Kingdom of Hejaz*. Cambridge: Oleander Press, 1979.

APPENDIX F: THE BASIC LAW
OF SAUDI ARABIA

Promulgated by royal decree on 1 March 1992. Adapted from text provided by the Saudi Arabia Ministry of Information, online at <www.saudinf.com>.

General Principles

Article 1. The Kingdom of Saudi Arabia is a sovereign Arab Islamic State. The religion is Islam. The constitution is the Holy Qur'an and the Prophet's Sunnah [traditions]. The language is Arabic. The capital is Riyadh.

Article 2. Its national holidays are 'Id al-Fitr (a religious feast celebrated on the 1st of Shawal, the 10th month of the Islamic calendar) and 'Id al-Adha (a religious feast celebrated on the 10th of Dhu al-Hijjah, the 12th month of the Islamic calendar). The calendar is Hijri (lunar).

Article 3. Its national flag is green in color, the width equal to two thirds of length, with the article of faith (translated as "There is no God but Allah, Muhammad is Allah's Messenger") inscribed in the center with a drawn sword underneath.

Article 4. The State's emblem consists of two intersecting swords with a datepalm in the upper space between them. Both the national anthem and the decorations awarded by the State shall be determined by the law.

System of Government

Article 5.
    (a) The system of government in Saudi Arabia shall be monarchical.
    (b) The dynasty right shall be confined to the sons of the Founder, King 'Abd al-'Aziz bin 'Abd al-Rahman Al Sa'ud, and the sons of sons. The most eligible among them shall be invited, through the process of "bay'ah" [allegiance], to rule in accordance with the Book of God and the Prophet's Sunnah.
    (c) The King names the Crown Prince and may relieve him of his duties by Royal Order.
    (d) The Crown Prince shall devote full time to his office and to any other duties which may be assigned to him by the King.
    (e) The Crown Prince shall assume the powers of the king on the latter's death pending the outcome of the "bay'ah".

Article 6. Citizens shall pledge allegiance to the King on the basis of the Book of God and the Prophet's Sunnah, as well as on the principle of "hearing is obeying" both in prosperity and adversity, in situations pleasant and unpleasant.

Article 7. The regime derives its power from the Holy Qur'an and the Prophet's Sunnah which rule over this and all other State Laws.

Article 8. The system of government in the Kingdom of Saudi Arabia is established on the foundation of justice, "Shura" [consultation], and equality in compliance with the shari'ah [the revealed law of Islam].

Constituents of Saudi Society

Article 9. The family is the nucleus of Saudi society. Its members shall be brought up imbued with the Islamic Creed which calls for obedience to God, His Messenger and those of the nation who are charged with authority; for the respect and enforcement of law and order; and for love of the motherland and taking pride in its glorious history.

Article 10. The State shall take great pains to strengthen the bonds which hold the family together and to preserve its Arab and Islamic values. Likewise it is keen on taking good care of all family members and creating proper conditions to help them cultivate their skill and capabilities.

Article 11. The Saudi society shall hold fast to the Divine Rope. Its citizens shall work together to foster benevolence, piety and mutual assistance; and it avoids dissension.

Article 12. The State shall foster national unity and preclude all that may lead to disunity, mischief and division.

Article 13. Education aims at the inculcation of the Islamic creed in the young generation and the development of their knowledge and skills so that they may become useful members of society who love their homeland and take pride in its history.

Economic Principles

Article 14. All God-given resources of the country, both under and above ground, or in territorial waters, or within terrestrial and maritime limits to which the State jurisdiction extends, as well as the revenues accruing therefrom shall be owned by the State as specified by the law. Likewise the law shall specify the means to be employed for the utilization, protection and development of these resources in a manner conducive to the promotion of the State's interest, security and economy.

Article 15. No concessions shall be awarded or permission given for the utilization of the country's natural resources, except as permitted by the law.

Article 16. Public property is sacrosanct. It shall be protected by the State and preserved by both citizens and foreign residents.

Article 17. Ownership, capital and labor are the fundamentals of the Kingdom's economic and social life. They are private rights that serve a social function in conformity with shari'ah.

Article 18. The State shall guarantee the freedom and inviolability of private property. Private property shall be not be expropriated unless in the public interest and the confiscatee is fairly compensated.

Article 19. Collective confiscation of properties shall be prohibited. Confiscation of private properties shall only be effected in accordance with a judicial verdict.

Article 20. Taxes and fees shall be imposed only on the basis of fairness and when the need arises. They shall only be imposed, amended, abolished or remitted in accordance with the law.

Article 21. Zakat [alms tax] shall be levied and dispensed to its legitimate beneficiaries.

Article 22. Economic and social development shall be achieved in accordance with a methodical and equitable plan.

Rights and Duties

Article 23. The State shall protect the Islamic Creed and shall cater to the application of shari'ah. The State shall enjoin good and forbid evil, and shall undertake the duties of the call to Islam.

Article 24. The State shall maintain and serve the Two Holy Mosques. It shall ensure the security and safety of all those who call at the Two Holy Mosques so that they may be able to visit or perform the pilgrimage and "umrah" [minor pilgrimage] in comfort and ease.

Article 25. The State shall be keen to realize the aspirations of the Arab Muslim nations with regard to solidarity and unity while enhancing its relations with friendly states.

Article 26. The State shall protect human rights in accordance with shari'ah.

Article 27. The State shall guarantee the right of its citizens and their families in an emergency of in case of disease, disability and old age. Likewise it shall support the social security system and encourage individuals and institutions to contribute to charitable pursuits.

Article 28. The State shall provide job opportunities to all able-bodied people and shall enact laws to protect both the employee and the employer.

Article 29. The State shall foster sciences, arts and culture. It shall encourage scientific research, shall preserve Arab and Islamic heritage and shall contribute to Arab, Islamic and human civilization.

Article 30. The State shall provide public education and shall commit itself to the eradication of illiteracy.

Article 31. The State shall be solicitous for promoting public health and shall provide medical care to every citizen.

Article 32. The State shall seek to conserve, protect and develop the environment and prevent pollution.

Article 33. The State shall build and equip the armed forces to defend the Islamic faith, the Two Holy Mosques, the society and the homeland.

Article 34. Defending the Islamic faith, the society and the homeland shall be the duty of each and every citizen. Rules of military service shall be spelled out by the law.

Article 35. The rules which govern the Saudi Arabian nationality shall be defined by the law.

Article 36. The State shall ensure the security of all its citizens and expatriates living within its domains. No individual shall be detained, imprisoned or have his actions restricted except under the provisions of the law.

Article 37. Houses are inviolable. They shall not be entered without the permission of their owners, nor shall they be searched except in cases specified by the law.

Article 38. Punishment shall be restricted to the actual offender. No crime shall be established as such and no punishment shall be imposed except under a judicial or law provision. No punishment shall be imposed except for acts that take place after enaction of the law provision governing them.

Article 39. Mass media, publication facilities and other means of expression shall function in a manner that is courteous and fair and shall abide by State laws. They shall play their part in educating the masses and boosting national unity. All that may give rise to mischief and discord, or may compromise the security of the State and its public image, or may offend against man's dignity and rights shall be banned. Relevant regulations shall explain how this is to be done.

Article 40. All forms of correspondence, whether conveyed by telegraph, post or any other means of communication shall be considered sacrosanct. They may not be confiscated, delayed or read, and telephones may not be tapped except as laid down in the law.

Article 41. Foreign residents in the Kingdom of Saudi Arabia shall abide by its regulations and shall show respect for Saudi social traditions, values and feelings.

Article 42. The State shall grant political asylum, if so required by the public interest. The law and international agreements shall define the procedures and rules for the extradition of common criminals.

Article 43. The "majlis" of the King and the "majlis" of the Crown Prince shall be open to all citizens and to anyone who may have a complaint or a grievance. Every individual shall have the right to communicate with public authorities regarding any topic he may wish to discuss.

Powers of the State

Article 44. The powers of the State shall comprise:
— The Judicial Power
— The Executive Power
— The Organizational Power
All these powers shall cooperate in performing their duties according to this Law and other regulations. The King is the ultimate source of all these authorities.

Article 45. The source of ifta' [religious ruling] in the Kingdom of Saudi Arabia is the Holy Qur'an and the Prophet's Sunnah. The law shall specify the composition of the Senior 'Ulama' Board and of the Administration of Religious Research and Ifta' and its jurisdictions.

Article 46. The judicial authority is an independent power. In discharging their duties, the judges bow to no authority other than that of shari'ah.

Article 47. Both citizens and foreign residents have an equal right to litigation. The necessary procedures are set forth by the law.

Article 48. Courts shall apply the provisions of shari'ah to cases brought before them, according to the teachings of the Holy Qur'an and the Prophet's Sunnah as well as other regulations issued by the Head of State in strict conformity with the Holy Qur'an and the Prophet's Sunnah.

Article 49. Subject to the provisions of article 53 of this law, the courts shall have jurisdiction to deal with all kinds of disputes and crimes.

Article 50. The King, or whomsoever he may deputize, shall be concerned with the implementation of the judicial verdicts.

Article 51. The law specifies the formation of the supreme judicial council and its functions as well as the organization and jurisdiction of the courts.

Article 52. Judges are appointed and their service is terminated by a Royal Order upon a proposal by the supreme judicial council as specified by the law.

Article 53. The law defines the structure and jurisdiction of the Court of Grievances.

Article 54. The law shall specify the reference, organization and jurisdictions of the Board of Investigation and Public Prosecution.

Article 55. The King shall undertake to rule according to the rulings of Islam and shall supervise the application of shari'ah, the regulations, and the State's general policy as well as the protection and defense of the country.

Article 56. The King shall be the Prime Minister and shall be assisted in the performance of his duties by members of the Council of Ministers according to the rulings of this law and other laws. The Council of Ministers Law shall specify the Council's Powers with regard to internal and external affairs, organizing government bodies and co-ordinating their activities. Likewise the Law shall specify the conditions which the Ministers must satisfy, their eligibility, the method of their accountability along with all other matters related to them. The Council of Ministers' law and jurisdiction shall be modified with this Law.

Article 57.
(a) The King shall appoint the Deputy Prime Minister and Cabinet Ministers and may relieve them of their duties by a Royal order.
(b) The Deputy Prime Minister and Cabinet Ministers shall be jointly responsible before the King for the applications of shari'ah, the laws and the State's general policy.
(c) The King shall have the right to dissolve and re-form the Council of Ministers.

Article 58. The King shall appoint ministers, deputy ministers and officials of the "excellent grade" category and he may dismiss them by a Royal order in accordance with the rules of the law. Ministers and heads of independent authorities shall be responsible before the Prime Minister for their ministries and authorities.

Article 59. The law shall prescribe the provisions pertaining to civil service, including salaries, bonuses, compensation, privileges and retirement pensions.

Article 60. The King shall be the Supreme Commander of the armed forces and shall appoint military officers and terminate their service in accordance with the law.

Article 61. The King shall have the right to declare a state of emergency and general mobilization as well as war.

Article 62. If danger threatens the safety of the Kingdom, the integrity of its territory, the security of its people and their interests, or impedes the performance of State institutions, the King shall take necessary and speedy measures to confront this danger. If the King feels that these measures may better be permanent, he then shall take whatever legal action he deems necessary in this regard.

Article 63. The King receives Kings and heads of state, appoints his representatives to other countries and accepts accreditation of the representatives of other countries to the Kingdom.

Article 64. The King awards medals in the same manner as specified by the law.

Article 65. The King may delegate parts of his authority to the Crown Prince by a Royal order.

Article 66. In the event of his traveling abroad, the King shall issue a Royal Order deputizing the Crown Prince to run the affairs of the State and look after the interests of the people as stated in the Royal Order.

Article 67. Acting within its term of reference, the Organizational Power shall draw up regulations and by-laws to safeguard public interests or eliminate corruption in the affairs of the State in accordance with the rulings of the shari'ah. It shall exercise its powers in compliance with this law and the two other laws of the Council of Ministers and the Majlis al-Shura [Consultative Council].

Article 68. The Majlis al-Shura shall be constituted. Its law shall determine the structure of its formation, the method by which it exercises its special powers and the selection of its members. The King shall have the right to dissolve the Majlis al-Shura and re-form it.

Article 69. The King may call the Council of Ministers and Majlis al-Shura to hold a joint meeting to which he may invite whomsoever he wishes for a discussion of whatsoever issues he may like to raise.

Article 70. Laws, treaties, international agreements and concessions shall be issued and modified by Royal Decrees.

Article 71. Laws shall be published in the official gazette and they shall take effect as from the date of their publication unless another date is stipulated.

Financial Affairs

Article 72.
(a) The law shall determine the management of State revenues, and the procedures of their delivery to the State Treasury.
(b) Revenues shall be accounted for and expended in accordance with the procedures stated on the law.

Article 73. No obligation shall be made to pay funds from the State Treasury except in accordance with the provisions of the budget. Should the provisions of the budget not suffice for paying such funds, a Royal Decree shall be issued for their payment.

Article 74. State property may not be sold, leased or otherwise disposed of except in accordance with the law.

Article 75. The regulations shall define the provisions governing legal tender and banks, as well as standards, measures and weights.

Article 76. The law shall determine the State's fiscal year. The budget shall be issued by a Royal Decree which shall spell out revenue and expenditure estimates for the year. The budget shall be issued at least one month before the beginning of the fiscal year. If, owing to overpowering reasons, the budget is not issued on time and the new fiscal year has not yet started, the validity of the old budget shall be extended until a new budget has been issued.

Article 77. The concerned authority shall prepare the State's final accounts for the expired fiscal year and shall submit it to the Prime Minister.

Article 78. The budgets and final accounts of corporate authorities shall be subject to the same provisions applied to the State budget and its final accounts.

Control and Auditing Authorities

Article 79. All State revenues and expenditures shall be kept under control, so shall its fixed and liquid (mobile) assets which will be checked to ascertain that they are properly utilized and maintained. An annual report thereon shall be submitted to the Council of Ministers. The law shall name the control and auditing authority concerned, and shall define its terms of reference and accountability.

Article 80. Government bodies shall be monitored closely to ensure that they are performing well and applying the law properly. Financial and administrative violations shall be investigated and an annual report thereon shall be submitted to the Council of Ministers. The law shall name the authority to be charged with this task and shall define its accountability and terms of reference.

General Provisions

Article 81. The implementation of this law shall not violate the treaties and agreements the Kingdom has signed with other countries or with international organizations and institutions.

Article 82. Without prejudice to the provisions of article 7 of this law, none of the provisions of this law shall, in any way, be obstructed unless it is a temporary measure taken during the time of war or in a state of emergency as specified by the law.

Article 83. No amendments to this law shall be made except in the same manner in which it has been issued.

APPENDIX G: STATISTICAL TABLES

Table 1. Saudi Arabia: Basic Facts

Area	Total: 1,960,582 sq km (slightly more than one-fifth the size of the US) Land 1,960,582 sq km; water 0 sq km
Land boundaries	Total: 4,415 km. Border countries: Iraq 814 km, Jordan 728 km, Kuwait 222 km, Oman 676 km, Qatar 60 km, UAE 457 km, Yemen 1,458 km
Coastline	2,640 km
Elevation extremes	Lowest point: Gulf 0 m Highest point: Jabal Sawda' 3,133 m
Land use	Arable land 2%, permanent crops 0%, permanent pastures 56%, forests and woodland 1%, other 41%; irrigated land 4,350 sq km (1993 est.)
Population	22,757,092; includes 5,360,526 nonnationals (July 2001 est.) Growth rate: 3.27% (2001 est.)
Age structure	0-14 years 42.52% (male 4,932,465; female 4,743,908); 15-64 years 54.8% (male 7,290,840; female 5,179,393); 65 years and over 2.68% (male 334,981; female 275,505) (2001 est.)
Currency	Saudi riyal (SAR). Currency code: SAR. Common abbreviation: SR.
Exchange rate	SR 1 = US$ 3.745 (fixed vis-à-vis US dollar since June 1986)
Radio	Radios 6.25 million (1997); broadcast stations AM 43, FM 31, shortwave 2 (1998)
Television	Televisions 5.1 million (1997), broadcast stations 117 (1997)
Internet country code	.sa
Communications	Railways 1,390 km (1992); highways 146,524 km (paved 44,104 km, unpaved 102,420) (1997 est.); waterways none.

Table 1 (continued). Saudi Arabia: Basic Facts

Pipelines	crude oil 6,400 km, petroleum products 150 km, natural gas 2,200 km (includes natural gas liquids 1,600 km)
Ports and harbors	al-Dammam, al-Jubayl, Duba, Jiddah, Jizan, Rabigh, Ra's al-Khafji, Mishab, Ra's Tanurah, Yanbu' al-Bahr, Madinat Yanbu' al-Sina'iyah
Airports	206 (2000 est.)
Military expenditures	$18.3 billion (fiscal year 2000) 13% of GDP (fiscal year 2000)

Source: Adapted from US Central Intelligence Agency, *World Factbook 2001*; online at <www.odci.gov>.

Table 2. Saudi Arabia: Social and Economic Indicators

	1996	1999	2000
Population, total (in millions)	18.7	20.2	20.7
Population growth (annual %)	2.6	2.6	2.6
Life expectancy at birth (years)	..	..	72.5
Fertility rate, total (births per woman)	..	..	5.5
Mortality rate, infant (per 1,000 live births)	..	..	18.2
Mortality rate, under-5 (per 1,000 live births)	..	..	22.7
Urban population (% of total)	83.4	85.1	85.7
Illiteracy rate, adult male (% of males 15+)	19.8	17.7	16.9
Illiteracy rate, adult female (% of females 15+)	39.1	34.6	33.1
Surface area (million sq km)	2.1	2.1	2.1
Forest area (sq km)	..	..	15,040
GNI, Atlas method (current billion US$)	137.5	139.3	149.9
GNI per capita, Atlas method (current US$)	7,360	6,900	7,230
GDP (current $)	141.3	142.9	173.3
GDP growth (annual %)	1.4	-0.8	4.5
Inflation, GDP deflator (annual %)	9.1	12.1	16.1
Agriculture, value added (% of GDP)	6.1	..	..
Industry, value added (% of GDP)	55.7	..	..
Services, etc., value added (% of GDP)	38.2	..	..
Exports of goods and services (% of GDP)	46.5	40.6	49.6
Imports of goods and services (% of GDP)	30.0	27.2	25.7

Table 2 (continued). Saudi Arabia: Social and Economic Indicators

Gross capital formation (% of GDP)	18.0	18.9	16.3
Fixed line & mobile telephones (per 1,000 people)	105.4	169.4	200.9
Personal computers (per 1,000 people)	39.8	57.4	60.2
Internet users (thousands)	5	100	200
Paved roads (% of total)	29.8	..	..
Aircraft departures (thousands)	100.7	106.9	109.0
Trade in goods as a share of GDP (%)	62.6	55.1	66.0
Net barter terms of trade (1995=100)	132.0	132.0	..
Aid per capita (current US$)	1.2	1.4	1.5

Source: Adapted from World Bank Group, *World Development Indicators* (April 2002); online at <http://worldbank.org>.

Table 3. Annual Saudi Arabian Government Revenues and Expenditures
(actual)   (in million Saudi riyals)

Year	Total Revenues			Total Expenditures	Deficit/ Surplus
	Oil	Non-Oil	Total		
1389/90 (1969)	5,119	549	5,668	—	—
1390/91 (1970)	7,122	818	7,940	6,418	1,522
1391/92 (1971)	9,585	1,435	11,120	8,303	2,817
1392/93 (1972)	13,480	1,888	15,368	10,148	5,220
1393/94 (1973)	39,285	2,420	41,705	18,595	23,110
1394/95 (1974)	94,190	5,913	100,103	32,038	68,065
1395/96 (1975)	93,481	9,903	103,384	81,784	21,600
1396/97 (1976)	121,191	14,766	135,957	128,273	7,684
1397/98 (1977)	114,042	16,617	130,659	138,048	-7,389
1398/99 (1978)	115,078	16,427	131,505	147,971	-16,466
1399/00 (1979)	189,295	21,901	211,196	188,363	22,833
1400/01 (1980)	319,305	28,795	348,100	236,570	111,530
1401/02 (1981)	328,594	39,412	368,006	284,650	83,356
1402/03 (1982)	185,006	60,176	246,182	244,912	1,270
1403/04 (1983)	145,123	61,296	206,419	230,185	-23,766
1404/05 (1984)	121,348	50,161	171,509	216,363	-44,854
1405/06 (1985)	88,425	45,140	133,565	184,004	-50,439
1406/07 (1986)	42,464	34,034	76,498	137,422	-60,924
1407/08 (1987)	67,405	36,406	103,811	173,526	-69,715
1408/09 (1988)	48,400	36,200	84,600	134,850	-50,250

Table 3 (continued). Annual Saudi Arabian Government Revenues and Expenditures
(actual)   (in million Saudi riyals)

Year	Total Revenues			Total Expenditures	Deficit/ Surplus
	Oil	Non-Oil	Total		
1409/10 (1989)	75,900	38,700	114,600	149,500	-34,900
1410/11 & 1411/12 (1990 & 1991) ①	246,297	70,342	316,639	457,477	-140,838
1412/13 (1992)	128,790	40,857	169,647	211,340	-41,693
1413/14 (1993)	105,976	35,469	141,445	187,890	-46,445
1414/15 (1994)	95,505	33,486	128,991	163,776	-34,785
1415/16 (1995)	105,728	40,772	146,500	173,945	-27,445
1416/17 (1996)	135,982	43,103	179,085	198,117	-19,032
1417/18 (1997)	159,985	45,515	205,500	221,272	-15,772
1418/19 (1998)	79,998	61,610	141,608	190,060	-48,452
1419/20 (1999)	104,447	43,007	147,454	183,841	-36,387
1420/21 (2000) ②	214,424	43,641	258,065	235,322	22,743

Notes:
① Budget allocation for the fiscal year 1411/12 was amalgamated with the budget for 1410/11.
② In fiscal year 1420/1421 salaries of 13 months were paid.
Source: Saudi Arabia, Ministry of Finance and National Economy; online at <www.mof.gov.sa>.

Table 4. Saudi Arabia Government Budget by Sector

(in million Saudi riyals)

Sector	1997	1998	1999	2000	2001
Human Resource Development	41,595	45,498	42,792	49,284	53,010
Transport & Communications	6,890	8,517	5,197	5,534	5,732
Economic Resource Development	4,733	5,820	4,418	5,955	5,629
Health & Social Development	14,366	16,390	15,152	16,381	18,088
Infrastructure Development	1,588	2,160	1,707	2,067	2,532
Municipal Services	5,445	6,546	5,400	5,710	7,224
Defense & Security	67,975	78,231	68,700	74,866	77,111
Public Administration and Other	30,836	25,067	16,458	19,277	39,111
Government Lending Institutions ①	439	500	420	436	411
Local Subsidies	7,133	7,271	4,756	5,490	6,151
Total Expenditures	181,000	196,000	165,000	185,000	215,000
Total Revenues	164,000	178,000	121,000	157,000	215,000

Note: ① Includes transfer to Saudi Development Fund.
Source: Ministry of Finance and National Economy; online at <www.mof.gov.sa>.

Table 5. Current Price GDP at Current Prices by Economic Activity and Sector
(in million Saudi riyals)

Economic Activity	1992	1993	1994	1995	1996	1997	1998	1999	2000 ①
Agriculture, Fishing & Forestry	28,785	30,224	31,131	31,598	32,162	33,400	33,901	34,443	34,973
Mining & Quarrying - Oil & Nat Gas	174,942	147,703	146,984	163,777	200,321	200,941	129,480	173,102	269,379
Mining & Quarrying - Other Than Oil	1,936	2,013	2,104	2,114	2,172	2,315	2,385	2,464	2,552
Manufacturing - Oil	18,673	15,765	15,689	17,014	18,867	19,852	15,554	18,021	21,597
Manufacturing - Non Oil	20,580	22,021	23,783	25,805	28,117	30,732	32,422	34,465	37,170
Elec. Gas & Water	701	727	754	786	817	860	890	924	961
Construction	39,039	41,186	42,730	43,499	44,447	46,580	47,465	48,462	51,273
Wholesale Trade, Restaurants	31,239	32,332	32,978	34,421	35,577	37,000	37,222	37,557	39,116
Transport Storage & Communication	28,432	29,569	30,456	30,913	31,507	32,736	33,390	34,191	35,675
Financial Services-Dwellings	6,983	7,227	7,516	7,591	7,804	8,194	8,374	8,567	8,818
Financial Services-Non Dwellings	18,973	19,542	20,089	19,888	20,198	21,107	21,592	22,132	23,161
Community Social Services	12,595	12,973	13,362	13,562	13,800	14,352	14,682	15,034	15,597

Table 5 (continued). Current Price GDP at Current Prices by Economic Activity and Sector

(in million Saudi riyals)

Economic Activity	1992	1993	1994	1995	1996	1997	1998	1999	2000 ①
Less Imputed Bank Charges	-5,046	-5,500	-5,940	-6,059	-5,816	-5,961	-6,450	-7,065	-7,758
Producers of Government Services	74,466	78,783	80,100	86,243	90,402	97,232	100,284	103,094	106,795
GDP Excluding Import Duties	452,298	434,565	441,736	471,152	520,375	539,340	471,191	525,390	639,308
Import Duties	9,100	9,277	8,289	7,500	8,875	9,100	10,013	9,634	9,650
GDP Including Import Duties	461,398	443,842	450,025	478,652	529,250	548,440	481,204	535,024	648,958

Note: ① Preliminary.
Source: Central Department of Statistics, Ministry of Planning, Central Department of Statistics; online at <www.mof.gov.sa>.

Table 6. Saudi Arabia Balance of Payments Estimates
(in millions of Saudi riyals)

	1992	1993	1994	1995	1996	1997	1998	1999	2000
Current Account Balance	-66,437	-64,668	-39,273	-19,943	2,548	1,144	-49,245	1,542	53,689
Merchandise Trade FOB									
Imports	-113,278	-96,895	-79,862	-96,061	-94,967	-98,756	-103,117	-96,312	-103,890
Oil Exports (Excl Bunker Oil)	173,752	144,202	142,401	162,593	202,638	199,172	121,607	167,793	264,887
Other Exports	14,082	14,135	16,761	24,320	24,181	27,672	23,416	21,786	24,805
Re-Exports	1,527	1,312	1,762	2,321	2,471	1,795	1,868	1,886	1,545
Trade balance (FOB)	74,556	61,441	79,300	90,852	131,852	128,088	41,906	93,267	185,802
Services & Transfer Receipts									
Investment Income	27,629	23,250	15,101	18,678	19,200	21,555	21,757	21,764	12,543
Oil Sector (Bunker Oil)	491	434	428	490	610	599	365	505	860
Other	12,982	12,295	12,533	13,033	10,382	15,941	17,712	20,147	17,921
Total Receipts	41,102	35,979	28,062	32,201	30,192	38,095	39,834	42,415	31,325
Services & Transfer Payments									
Freight & Insurance	-11,328	-8,721	-7,587	-9,126	-9,012	-8,888	-9,280	-8,668	-9,350
Oil Sector Investments Income	-7,281	-8,613	-9,587	-8,179	-10,039	-11,127	-11,389	-10,811	-10,745

Table 6 (continued). Saudi Arabia Balance of Payments Estimates

(in millions of Saudi riyals)

	1992	1993	1994	1995	1996	1997	1998	1999	2000
Services & Transfer Payments (continued)									
Other Govt. Services	-67,803	-42,457	-35,821	-40,079	-44,202	-43,635	-31,164	-35,640	-54,002
Other Private Services	-45,511	-43,437	-25,848	-23,385	-38,146	-45,085	-23,149	-26,678	-31,628
Private Transfers	-50,172	-58,860	-67,792	-62,227	-58,097	-56,304	-56,003	-52,343	-57,713
Total Payments	-182,095	-162,089	-146,635	-142,996	-159,496	-165,039	-130,985	-134,141	-163,827
Net Services & Transfers									
Receipts-Payments	-140,993	-126,109	-118,573	-110,795	-129,304	-126,944	-91,151	-91,726	-132,113
Capital Movements & Reserves									
Net Capital Movements & Reserves	66,437	54,668	39,273	19,943	-2,548	-1,144	49,245	-1,542	-53,689
Oil Sector & Other Capital Transactions	-297	5,127	1,310	-7,030	-4,228	11,398	16,063	-2,921	-7,054
Other①	66,733	59,541	37,963	26,973	1,680	-12,542	33,182	1,379	—

Note: ① Including private capital, valuation adjustments, net errors and omissions.
Source: Saudi Arabian Monetary Agency; online at <www.mof.gov.sa>.

Table 7. Saudi Arabia's Exports to Major Trading Partners
(in million Saudi riyals)

Rank	Country	1996	1997	1998	1999	2000
1	USA	39,891	34,600	23,695	37,185	58,832
2	Japan	34,221	39,360	21,668	28,496	46,074
3	South Korea	23,931	23,150	13,886	20,429	31,273
4	Singapore	13,656	15,640	8,697	11,107	14,632
5	India	7,804	9,250	6,083	8,175	12,823
6	Holland	9,725	10,610	6,043	7,845	11,592
7	France	9,030	8,950	5,456	7,469	10,910
8	Taiwan	5,830	5,696	3,470	4,185	7,742
9	Bahrain	6,581	6,270	4,387	5,560	7,158
10	Italy	6,640	8,003	4,908	4,428	6,971
11	South Africa	530	1,029	1,608	3,880	6,621
12	UAE	6,779	7,375	4,912	4,710	5,886
13	China	858	1,582	1,231	2,352	5,630
14	Spain	4,980	4,230	3,050	3,388	5,013
15	Pakistan	2,026	1,948	1,520	2,562	4,766
16	Indonesia	1,380	1,650	2,280	3,318	4,071
17	Philippines	4,530	3,606	2,020	2,828	4,023
18	Greece	2,540	2,640	2,127	2,321	3,964
19	Thailand	2,990	2,980	1,607	2,100	3,578
20	Brazil	4,900	3,910	2,210	2,216	3,505

Source: Saudi Arabia Ministry of Planning, Central Department of Statistics; online at <www.mof.gov.sa>.

Table 8. Saudi Arabia's Imports from Major Trading Partners

(in million Saudi riyals)

Rank	Country	1996	1997	1998	1999	2000
1	USA	22,771	23,933	23,984	19,882	21,802
2	Japan	7,314	7,124	9,666	9,650	11,837
3	Germany	7,798	5,830	7,052	7,648	9,164
4	England	9,334	11,281	9,535	8,456	7,308
5	Italy	4,901	4,962	4,667	4,424	4,698
6	France	4,313	4,837	5,862	4,421	4,675
7	China	3,201	3,369	3,593	3,677	4,485
8	South Korea	2,940	2,619	3,884	3,801	3,846
9	Switzerland	4,856	6,221	4,828	3,523	3,693
10	India	2,241	2,584	3,058	2,770	3,132
11	Australia	1,263	1,751	1,978	2,273	2,907
12	Holland	1,770	2,067	1,829	1,971	2,387
13	Brazil	1,780	2,132	1,658	1,650	2,314
14	UAE	1,510	1,610	1,842	2,213	2,206
15	Sweden	1,288	189	1,373	1,441	1,813
16	Belgium	1,812	1,635	1,386	1,558	1,707
17	Indonesia	1,543	1,608	1,696	1,508	1,699
18	Spain	1,414	1,415	1,813	1,962	1,607
19	Taiwan	1,547	1,626	1,454	1,258	1,158
20	Malaysia	902	749	813	890	1,151

Source: Saudi Arabia Ministry of Planning, Central Department of Statistics; online at <www.mof.gov.sa>.

Table 9. Saudi Arabia's Exports by Major Items
(in million Saudi riyals)

Section	Title	1996	1997	1998	1999	2000
1	Animals & Animal Products	531	644	739	761	697
2	Vegetables & Vegetable Products	446	483	413	488	438
3	Fats & Oils	63	122	65	61	75
4	Prepared Foods, Tobacco Products	441	529	537	576	574
5	Mineral Products	203,746	200,264	122,466	168,735	266,226
6	Chemical Products	10,501	11,123	10,017	9,293	12,194
7	Plastics & Rubber	4,352	5,723	4,192	3,572	3,854
8	Leather Products	207	174	78	56	81
9	Wood Products	40	39	39	39	29
10	Paper Products	561	687	564	593	579
11	Textiles & Textile Products	633	768	748	645	567
12	Clothing Accessories	14	17	20	14	13
13	Stone & Glass Products	456	606	542	487	531
14	Precious Metals, Jewelry	1	8	127	83	36
15	Base Metals	2,523	3,157	2,342	2,358	2,145
16	Machinery & Electrical Equipment	1,418	1,505	1,489	1,343	1,454
17	Transportation Equipment	1,257	1,267	617	687	810
18	Miscellaneous Instruments	25	31	62	96	79
19	Arms & Ammunition	0	0	0	6	19
20	Miscellaneous Manufactured Items	214	295	328	193	151
21	Art Items & Others	1	1	2	1	1
	Total	227,430	227,440	145,390	190,087	290,552

Source: Saudi Arabia Ministry of Planning, Central Department of Statistics; online at <www.mof.gov.sa>.

Table 10. Saudi Arabia's Imports by Major Items
(in million Saudi riyals)

Section	Title	1996	1997	1998	1999	2000
1	Animals & Animal Products	5,071	4,891	5,107	5,312	5,675
2	Vegetables & Vegetable Products	7,674	7,905	6,868	7,637	8,278
3	Fats & Oils	800	654	880	927	784
4	Prepared Foods, Tobacco Products	4,411	5,298	4,761	4,191	5,531
5	Mineral Products	1,159	1,092	1,055	1,274	1,062
6	Chemical Products	3,382	8,712	9,249	9,496	9,512
7	Plastics & Rubber	3,777	3,453	3,753	3,488	4,130
8	Leather Products	355	371	381	381	394
9	Wood Products	1,463	1,332	1,434	1,259	1,444
10	Paper Products	2,295	1,915	2,305	2,087	2,356
11	Textiles & Textile Products	7,589	7,093	7,464	6,494	6,674
12	Clothing Accessories	1,120	1,025	1,082	935	899
13	Stone & Glass Products	1,749	1,472	1,460	1,392	1,931
14	Precious Metals, Jewelry	4,399	8,237	6,263	5,113	4,575
15	Base Metals	10,396	9,717	10,743	8,808	8,895
16	Machinery & Electrical Equipment	21,848	21,267	22,486	25,187	24,982
17	Transportation Equipment	15,903	16,737	20,705	15,201	19,996
18	Miscellaneous Instruments	2,897	3,039	2,950	3,102	3,048
19	Arms & Ammunition	411	1,001	987	636	788
20	Miscellaneous Manufactured Items	1,935	2,038	2,133	1,929	2,260
21	Art Items and Others	345	393	330	127	23
	Total	103,980	107,643	112,397	104,980	113,240

Source: Saudi Arabia Ministry of Planning, Central Department of Statistics; online at <www.mof.gov.sa>.

Table 11. Saudi Arabian Crude Oil Production
(in million barrels)

Year	Total	Percentage change	Daily Average
1962	599.76	10.96	1.64
1963	651.71	8.66	1.79
1964	694.13	6.51	1.90
1965	804.94	15.96	2.21
1966	948.57	17.84	2.60
1967	1,023.84	7.94	2.81
1968	1,113.71	8.78	3.04
1969	1,173.89	5.40	3.22
1970	1,386.67	18.13	3.80
1971	1,740.68	25.53	4.77
1972	2,201.96	26.50	6.02
1973	2,772.61	25.92	7.60
1974	3,095.09	11.63	8.48
1975	2,582.53	-16.56	7.08
1976	3,139.28	21.56	8.58
1977	3,357.96	6.97	9.20
1978	3,029.90	-9.77	8.30
1979	3,479.15	14.83	9.53
1980	3,623.80	4.16	9.90
1981	3,579.89	-1.21	9.81
1982	2,366.41	-33.90	6.48
1983	1,656.88	-29.98	4.54

Table 11 (continued). Saudi Arabian Crude Oil Production

(in million barrels)

Year	Total	Percentage change	Daily Average
1984	1,492.90	-9.90	4.08
1985	1,158.80	-22.38	3.17
1986	1,746.20	50.69	4.78
1987	1,505.40	-13.79	4.12
1988	1,890.10	25.55	5.16
1989	1,848.50	-2.20	5.06
1990	2,340.50	26.62	6.41
1991	2,963.00	26.60	8.12
1992	3,049.40	2.92	8.33
1993	2,937.40	-3.67	8.05
1994	2,937.90	0.02	8.05
1995	2,928.54	-0.32	8.02
1996	2,965.45	1.26	8.10
1997	2,924.28	-1.39	8.01
1998	3,022.27	3.35	8.28
1999	2,761.10	-8.64	7.56
2000	2,962.60	7.30	8.09

Source: Saudi Arabia, Ministry of Petroleum & Mineral Resources; online at: <www.mopm.gov.sa>.

Table 12. Saudi Exports of Crude Oil by Destination
(in million barrels)

Year	North America	Latin America	Western Europe	Middle East	Asia & E. Africa	Far East	Oceania	Total
1962	—	—	180.92	—	—	—	—	501.30
1963	—	—	199.74	—	—	—	—	544.83
1964	—	—	247.71	—	—	—	—	587.21
1965	—	—	301.09	—	—	—	—	678.83
1966	—	—	404.54	—	—	—	—	829.31
1967	—	—	425.15	—	—	—	—	888.57
1968	46.19	36.33	472.25	64.75	28.91	289.01	28.34	968.30 ①
1969	41.62	34.44	496.04	67.66	45.43	306.59	28.27	1,020.05
1970	20.82	50.59	608.09	69.84	50.64	347.45	26.74	1,174.17
1971	70.30	91.29	814.52	75.07	67.43	389.01	20.57	1,528.19
1972	90.31	115.15	1,130.36	71.31	57.30	518.69	9.41	1,992.53
1973	137.14	247.29	1,332.90	77.10	80.77	670.94	14.20	2,560.34
1974	139.80	342.02	1,526.68	79.40	36.85	743.95	22.98	2,891.68
1975	117.00	344.88	1,113.12	66.97	40.20	699.69	27.53	2,409.39
1976	171.15	490.96	1,268.86	83.18	31.74	860.60	33.15	2,939.64
1977	359.68	369.21	1,296.05	114.34	21.19	938.37	43.21	3,142.05
1978	509.20	139.04	1,092.28	94.87	13.83	928.60	34.88	2,812.70
1979	641.74	116.38	1,337.21	104.27	31.44	947.43	40.00	3,218.47
1980	619.11	127.41	1,432.30	98.66	43.43	1,008.06	46.72	3,375.69
1981	508.28	142.81	1,396.69	114.48	55.82	1,024.16	49.30	3,291.54
1982	171.05	93.93	727.72	76.95	37.59	913.46	37.70	2,058.40
1983	128.06	67.64	364.53	67.83	25.96	753.49	23.57	1,431.08

Table 12 (continued). Saudi Exports of Crude Oil by Destination

(in million barrels)

Year	North America	Latin America	Western Europe	Middle East	Asia & E. Africa	Far East	Oceania	Total
1984	83.32	37.13	247.87	52.07	20.36	705.74	21.40	1,167.89
1985	47.11	44.33	218.50	36.52	14.31	410.84	9.11	780.72
1986	243.15	78.90	458.72	81.93	1.93	321.47	3.92	1,190.02
1987	—	—	—	—	—	—	—	973.12
1988	359.42	67.95	356.70	78.99	13.51	346.72	22.19	1,245.49
1989	380.48	35.59	320.92	69.86	4.61	388.96	17.08	1,217.50
1990	481.04	59.71	380.19	77.35	32.71	593.10	18.32	1,642.42
1991	663.89	72.35	623.10	78.80	61.44	861.78	20.75	2,382.11
1992	614.84	67.67	636.24	78.20	35.48	958.19	18.36	2,408.98
1993	487.75	61.51	628.37	74.69	33.96	986.40	24.24	2,296.92
1994	521.41	60.35	601.77	81.52	35.15	957.36	17.70	2,275.27
1995	504.02	53.30	598.37	80.54	34.96	1,006.31	18.63	2,296.13
1996	490.66	47.15	530.62	83.61	35.24	1,031.49	17.24	2,236.01
1997	488.73	33.16	591.13	77.69	38.57	1,010.81	17.24	2,257.33
1998	544.24	31.42	645.73	76.49	49.61	971.35	13.64	2,332.48
1999	534.20	26.95	454.33	68.97	73.66	921.77	7.80	2,087.68
2000	577.17	22.47	483.80	60.44	79.45	1,044.67	14.38	2,282.38

Note: ① Including Petromin Exports.

Source: Ministry of Petroleum & Mineral Resources; online at <www.mopm.gov.sa>.

Table 13. Saudi ARAMCO Proved Natural Gas Liquid Reserves (Gross)

(in billion cubic feet)

Year	At Beginning of Year	Increase During Year	Annual Production	Annual Net Increase	Reserves at End of Year
1976	—	—	0.38	—	—
1977	—	—	0.45	—	—
1978	—	—	0.52	—	—
1979	—	—	0.63	—	65,861
1980	65,861	2,940	0.76	2,939	68,800
1981	68,800	2,001	0.92	2,000	70,800
1982	70,800	43,201	0.88	43,200	114,000
1983	114,000	5,001	0.68	5,000	119,000
1984	119,000	3,701	0.73	3,700	122,700
1985	122,700	3,401	0.65	3,400	126,100
1986	126,100	9,701	0.62	9,700	135,800
1987	135,800	6,001	0.71	6,000	141,800
1988	141,800	35,495	0.84	35,494	177,294
1989	177,294	3,062	0.86	3,061	180,355
1990	180,355	172	1.09	171	180,526
1991	180,526	-65	1.20	-66	180,460
1992	180,460	—	—	1,018	181,478
1993	181,478	—	—	453	181,931
1994	181,931	—	—	4,154	186,085
1995	186,085	—	—	5,843	191,928
1996	191,928	—	—	5,514	197,442

Table 13 (continued). Saudi ARAMCO Proved Natural Gas Liquid Reserves (Gross)
(in billion cubic feet)

Year	At Beginning of Year	Increase During Year	Annual Production	Annual Net Increase	Reserves at End of Year
1997	197,442	—	—	6,596	204,038
1998	204,038	—	—	6,794	210,832
1999	210,832	—	—	2,406	213,238
2000	213,238	—	—	5,452	218,690

Sources: Saudi Arabia, Ministry of Petroleum & Mineral Resources, and Saudi ARAMCO annual reports; online at <www.mopm.gov.sa>.

SELECTED BIBLIOGRAPHY

The numbers of entries in the following bibliography, to a certain extent, seem to indicate that a rich body of literature exists on Saudi Arabia. I have made the point elsewhere that the volume of published material on the Arabian Peninsula, including Saudi Arabia, is misleading:

> While the factual outlines of the development of the seven states are fairly well known, little work has been done to fill in the contours. All too often, new writing consists of a rehash of stories already told, frequently relying on the same secondary sources, or of superficial country surveys prompted by the region's high profile over the last decade or two.[1]

In many respects, that unevenness of scholarship is reflected in this bibliography: one of the largest of the sections which follow is on the economy. Meanwhile, the literature on anthropology and social issues is embarrassingly slight. Perhaps because of the country's traditional isolation, historical writing on the period between the early centuries of Islam and the modern era is scarce.

As a selective bibliography, certain classes of materials either have been excluded or only a small sample included. Arabic language sources are not comprehensive. General rules of inclusion have been to limit the selection to seminal books or those published recently or on topics of recent history. The preponderance of the English language among works in European languages reflects the kingdom's close ties to Britain and the United States. Items in other European languages, particularly French and German, have been included but not as systematically. For reasons of space, most publications which cover the Gulf as whole, or the six Gulf Cooperation Council states, and are only partly on Saudi Arabia, have been excluded.

Although information for this dictionary has been collected from a wide variety of sources, including interviews and personal observations in addition to published sources, particular use has been made of a number of more specialized reference works. Information on tribes and geographical places has been culled from a large variety of specialized compendia, including Hamad al-Jasir's *Mu'jam qabā'il al-mamlakah al-'arabīyah al-sa'ūdīyah*, Mahmud Taha Abu al-'Ala's *Jugrāfīyat shibh jazīrat al-'arab*, 'Umar Rida Kuhhalah's *Mu'jam qabā'il al-'arab*, J. G. Lorimer's *Gazetteer of the Persian Gulf, 'Oman, and Central Arabia*, the United Kingdom Admiralty's *A Handbook of Arabia* and *Western Arabia and the Red Sea*, and Sheila Scoville's *Gazetteer of Arabia*. The principal sources used for archaeology and pre-Islamic history are the Saudi Arabian Department of Antiquities and Museums' *Muqaddimah 'an: āthār al-mamlakah al-'arabīyah al-sa'ūdīyah*, and Abdullah Masry's "The History and Development of Human

---

[1] J. E. Peterson, "The Arabian Peninsula in Modern Times: A Historiographical Survey," *American Historical Review*, Vol. 96, No. 5 (December 1991), p. 1436.

Settlement in Saudi Arabia," as well as Philip K. Hitti's *History of the Arabs* and R. Dussaud's *La pénétration des Arabes en Syrie avant l'Islam.*

Much information on Islamic terms and history has been drawn from the *Encyclopaedia of Islam* (1st and 2nd editions) and Cyril Glassé's *The Concise Encylopaedia of Islam.* Background on individuals is contained in biographical dictionaries such as the *Who's Who of Saudi Arabia,* the *Who's Who of the Arab World, Burke's Royal Families of the World,* Khayr al-Din al-Zirkali's *Al-I 'lām: qāmūs tarājim,* Brian Lees's *Handbook of the Al Saud Ruling Family of Saudi Arabia,* and J. R. L. Carter's *Merchant Families of Saudi Arabia.* Considerable information is to be found as well in Holden and Johns (below), Lacey (below), and Gary Samuel Samore's "Royal Family Politics in Saudi Arabia (1953-1982)."

A good, if difficult to find, bibliographic source is the Saudi Arabian Institute of Public Administration's compilation of *Information Sources on Saudi Arabia.* The Saudi Arabia volume in the ABC-Clio series of country bibliographies, by Frank A. Clements, can also be recommended. A valuable, if dated, bibliographic review is provided by George Rentz in his "Literature on the Kingdom of Saudi Arabia."

A useful general introduction to the country is by Helen Chapin Metz and associates, *Saudi Arabia: A Country Study,* while sweeping popular histories are David Holden and Richard Johns, *The House of Saud,* and Robert Lacey, *The Kingdom: Arabia and the House of Saud.* The book edited by Ismail I. Nawwab, Peter C. Speers, and Paul F. Hoye, *Aramco and Its World: Arabia and the Middle East,* does an admirable job of placing the kingdom in the broader Arab context. *Modernity and Tradition: The Saudi Equation* by the present Minister of Information, Fouad al-Farsy, provides a wealth of basic, factual information. Noteworthy volumes of collected essays include Willard A. Beling, ed., *King Faisal and the Modernisation of Saudi Arabia,* Paul Bonnenfant, ed., *La Péninsule Arabique d'aujourd'hui,* and Tim Niblock, ed., *State, Society and Economy in Saudi Arabia.*

Publications on the history of the three Saudi states steadily grows in volume and quality. Alexei Vassiliev's *The History of Saudi Arabia* provides a broad overview of the country's history and is more readable than H. St. John B. Philby's *Saudi Arabia.* J. G. Lorimer's *Gazetteer of the Persian Gulf, 'Oman, and Central Arabia,* although only partially covering the kingdom, remains an unsurpassed compendium on historical outline, people, and places. Madawi al-Rasheed outlines the period of the Al Sa'ud in her *A History of Saudi Arabia.*

` In *Religion, Society and the State in Arabia: The Hijaz Under Ottoman Control, 1840-1908,* William Ochsenwald gives a portrait of western Saudi Arabia while Frederick Anscombe's *The Ottoman Gulf* provides insight into an aspect of Saudi history that heretofore received short shrift. In *The Cohesion of Saudi Arabia,* Christine Moss Helms dissects the state-building process of King 'Abd al-'Aziz, while Joseph Kostiner covers similar ground in his *The Making of Saudi Arabia, 1916-1936.* Other noteworthy historical works include John Habib's *Ibn Sa'ud's Warriors of Islam,* Madawi al-Rasheed's *Politics in an Arabian Oasis: The Rashidi Tribal Dynasty,* and Bayly Winder's *Saudi Arabia in the Nineteenth Century.*

The availability of archival material outside Saudi Arabia has made studies of the country's earlier foreign policy possible, among them Irvine Anderson's

Aramco, the United States and Saudi Arabia, Jacob Goldberg's *The Foreign Policy of Saudi Arabia,* Clive Leatherdale's *Britain and Saudi Arabia, 1925-1939,* and Gary Troeller's *The Birth of Saudi Arabia: Britain and the Rise of the House of Sa'ud.* The most important external sources of material on Saudi Arabia remain the Public Record Office in London and the National Archives in Washington, DC.

Most book-length studies of the economy appeared in the decade after the oil price revolution, when Saudi Arabia finally had the money to put its process of development in high gear, and have been overtaken by events, although Robert Looney's *Economic Development in Saudi Arabia* is more recent. Much detailed information lies in unpublished doctoral theses (as cited below) and government publications and websites. The Ministry of Planning's *Achievements of the Development Plans, 1390-1420 (1970-2000)* provides extensive statistical information on the economy as well as development. Although not specifically on Saudi Arabia, Daniel Yergin's *The Prize* provides a highly readable history of the international oil industry and Ian Skeet's *OPEC: 25 Years of Prices and Politics* ably outlines that organization and Saudi Arabia's role in it.

The political scene has been dissected by Mordechai Abir in *Saudi Arabia: Government, Society, and the Gulf Crises,* Alexander Bligh in *From Prince to King,* Fandy Mamoun in *Saudi Arabia and the Politics of Dissent,* Summer Scott Huyette in *Political Adaptation in Sa'udi Arabia: A Study of the Council of Ministers,* and Joseph Kechichian in *Succession in Saudi Arabia.*

Not surprisingly, Saudi Arabia's security matters and American concerns have produced a voluminous literature. The topic has been covered by Anthony Cordesman in a number of works, Thomas McNaugher in *Arms and Oil,* William Quandt in *Saudi Arabia in the 1980s,* and the present author's *Saudi Arabia and the Illusion of Security.* Regional relations have been the subject of Shahram Chubin and Charles Tripp in *Iran-Saudi Arabia Relations and Regional Order* and Gregory Gause in *Saudi-Yemeni Relations.*

Only a few anthropological or sociological studies have been published. A number of these have focused on women, such as Soraya Altorki's *Women in Saudi Arabia* and Eleanor Doumato's *Getting God's Ear.* Ethnographic studies include Donald Cole's *Nomads of the Nomads,* Motoko Katakura's *Bedouin Village,* and Frederico Vidal's *The Oasis of Al-Hasa.* A unique view of the town of 'Unayzah's development is provided by Altorki and Cole in *Arabian Oasis City.* Mai Yamani provides insight into the views of the kingdom's burgeoning youth in *Changed Identities: The Challenges of the New Generation in Saudi Arabia.* Saudi Arabia's nearly disappeared traditional architecture is discussed by Geoffrey King in his *The Traditional Architecture of Saudi Arabia* and William Facey surveys the capital in word and picture in his *Riyadh: The Old City From Its Origins Until the 1950s.*

A number of websites relevant to the study of Saudi Arabia complete the bibliography. These include both official Saudi Arabian government sites and a number of other sites that deal with the country. A representative selection of sites devoted to the Middle East are also included. All the sites listed were current as of early 2003.

Needless to say, the works mentioned in this brief survey represent only the tip of the iceberg and many more worthwhile references could be included.

GENERAL, BIBLIOGRAPHY, AND COLLECTIONS

Abu al-'Ala, Mahmud Taha. *Jugrāfīyat shibh jazīrat al-'arab, Vol. 1: Jugrāfīyat al-mamlakah al-'arabīyah al-sa'ūdiyah.* ("The Geography of the Arabian Peninsula; Vol. I: The Geography of the Kingdom of Saudi Arabia.") Cairo: Maktabat al-anjilū al-masrīyah, 1986.

Beling, Willard A., ed. *King Faisal and the Modernisation of Saudi Arabia.* London: Croom Helm; Boulder, CO: Westview Press, 1980.

Bonnenfant, Paul, ed. *La Péninsule Arabique d'aujourd'hui.* Paris: Centre National de la Recherche Scientifique, 1982.

Clements, Frank A. *Saudi Arabia: An Annotated Bibliography.* Oxford: Clio Press, 1979.

Dahlan, Ahmed Hassan, ed. *Politics, Administration and Development in Saudi Arabia.* Brentwood, MD: Amana Corporation; Jiddah: Dar al-Shorouq, 1990.

Farsy, Fouad al-. *Modernity and Tradition: The Saudi Equation.* London: Kegan Paul International, 1991. Distributed by Routledge, Chapman & Hall.

Graham, Douglas. *Saudi Arabia Unveiled.* Dubuque, IA: Kendall/Hunt, 1991.

Hariri-Rifai, Wahbi al-, and Mokhless al-Hariri-Rifai. *The Heritage of the Kingdom of Saudi Arabia.* Washington, DC: GDG Publications, 1990.

Harmon, Robert B. *Politics and Government in Saudi Arabia: A Selected Bibliography.* Monticello, IL: Vance Bibliographies, 1981. Public Administration Series, Bibliography P-739.

Hobday, Peter. *Saudi Arabia Today: An Introduction to the Richest Oil Power.* London: Macmillan, 1978.

Hoge, Badr El-. *Saudi Arabia: Caught in Time.* Reading: Garnet, 1996.

Hopwood, Derek, ed. *The Arabian Peninsula: Society and Politics.* London: George Allen and Unwin, 1972. Studies on Modern Asia and Africa, No. 8.

Lacey, Robert. "Saudi Arabia: A More Visible Role in the Middle East." *The World Today*, Vol. 38, No. 1 (January 1982), pp. 4-12.

Long, David E. *The Kingdom of Saudi Arabia.* Gainesville: University Press of Florida, 1997.

————. *Saudi Arabia.* Beverly Hills, CA: Sage Publications, for the Georgetown University Center for Strategic and International Studies, 1976. Washington Papers, No. 39.

Mackey, Sandra. *The Saudis: Inside the Desert Kingdom.* Boston: Houghton Mifflin, 1987.

McHale, T. R. "A Prospect of Saudi Arabia." *International Affairs* (London), Vol. 56, No. 4 (1980), pp. 622-647.

McLachlan, Keith. "Saudi Arabia: Political and Social Evolution." In Ian Richard Netton, ed., *Arabia and the Gulf: From Traditional Society to Modern States* (London: Croom Helm; New York: Barnes & Noble, 1986), pp. 91-106.

Manger, Thierry. *The Ark of the Desert.* Paris: Souffles, 1991.

Metz, Helen Chapin, ed. *Saudi Arabia: A Country Study.* Washington, DC: Library of Congress, Federal Research Division, 1993. Available online at <http://lcweb2.loc.gov/frd/cs/satoc.html>.

Minosa, Tchekof, photographs. Patricia Massari and Cherbel Dagher, text. *Najran: Desert Garden of Arabia.* Paris: Scorpio Editeur, n.d.

Nawwab, Ismail I., Peter C. Speers, and Paul F. Hoye, eds. *Aramco and Its World: Arabia and the Middle East.* Dhahran: Aramco, 1980.

Niblock, Tim, ed. *State, Society and Economy in Saudi Arabia.* London: Croom Helm, for the University of Exeter Centre for Arab Gulf Studies, 1982.

Peterson, J. E. *Security in the Arabian Peninsula and Gulf States, 1973-1984.* Washington, DC: National Council on US-Arab Relations, 1985. Occasional Paper No. 7.

Philby, H. St. John B. *Arabia of the Wahhabis.* London: Constable, 1928. Reprinted London: Frank Cass, 1977.

————. *Saudi Arabia.* London: Ernest Benn, 1955.

Rashid, Nasser Ibrahim, and Esber Ibrahim Shaheen. *King Fahd and Saudi Arabia's Great Evolution.* Joplin, MO: International Institute of Technology, 1988.

Refaei, Sheikh Abdul Aziz Al-. "Saudi Arabia." In *Not Oil Alone: A Cultural History of OPEC Member Countries* (Vienna: Organization of Petroleum Exporting Countries, n.d.), pp. 141-147.

Rentz, George. "Literature on the Kingdom of Saudi Arabia." *Middle East Journal,* Vol. 4, No. 2 (1950), pp. 244-249.

Ricks, Stephen D. *Western Language Literature on Pre-Islamic Central Arabia: An Annotated Bibliography.* Denver, CO: American Institute of Islamic Studies, 1991. Bibliographic Series, No. 10.

Sanger, Richard H. *The Arabian Peninsula.* Ithaca, NY: Cornell University Press, 1954.

Saudi Arabia. Institute of Public Administration. Library and Documents Center. Reference Service. *Information Sources on Saudi Arabia.* 2nd ed.; Riyadh, 1403/1983.

Saudi Arabia: One Hundred Years Later; Revised and Updated Proceedings of a Conference at the Center for Contemporary Arab Studies, 28 April 1999. Washington, DC: Georgetown University Center for Contemporary Arab Studies, 1999.

Scoville, Sheila A. *Gazetteer of Arabia: A Geographical and Tribal History of the Arabian Peninsula.* Graz: Akademische Druck Verlagsanstalt, 1979. Vol. I (A-E).

Stevens, J. H. *A Bibliography of Saudi Arabia.* Durham, England: Durham University Centre for Middle Eastern and Islamic Studies, 1971.

Stookey, Robert W., ed. *The Arabian Peninsula: Zone of Ferment.* Stanford, CA: Hoover Institution Press, 1984.

Sweel, Abdulaziz I. al-, and J. W. Wright, Jr. *Saudi Arabia: Tradition and Transition.* Westland, MI: Hayden-McNeil for the Saudi Arabian Cultural Mission to the US, 1993.

Twitchell, Karl S. *Saudi Arabia.* 3rd ed.; Princeton, NJ: Princeton University Press, 1958.

Wahba, Haliz. *Arabian Days.* London: Arthur Barker, 1964.

OIL

Ahrari, Mohammed. "OPEC, Saudi Arabia and Iran: The Dilemmas of Shared Power." *Strategic Studies*, Vol. 9, No. 1 (1985), pp. 80-95.

Arom, Eli. "Saudi Arabia's Oil Policy." *Jerusalem Quarterly*, No. 28 (Summer 1983), pp. 125-144.

Axelrod, Lawrence. "Saudi Oil Policy: Economic and Political Determinants." Ph.D. dissertation, Columbia University, 1989.

Bahgat, Gawdat. "Managing Dependence: American-Saudi Oil Relations." *Arab Studies Quarterly*, Vol. 23, No. 1 (Winter 2001), pp. 1-14.

Barger, Thomas. *Out in the Blue: Letters from Arabia, 1937-1940.* N.p., 2000.

Caroe, Olaf. *The Wells of Power: The Oil-Fields of South-Western Asia.* London: Macmillan, 1951.

Dowling, Greg. "ARAMCO and the Saudis." *Middle East Insight*, Vol. 14, No. 3 (May-June 1999), pp. 75-77, 88-89.

Gause, F. Gregory, III. "Saudi Arabia Over a Barrel." *Foreign Affairs*, Vol. 79, No. 3 (May-June 2000), pp. 80-94.

Gaynor, William Marshall. "Optimal Pricing and Production of an Exhaustible Resource: The Case of Saudi Arabian Crude Oil." Ph.D. dissertation, University of Maryland, 1983.

Golub, David B. *When Oil and Politics Mix: Saudi Oil Policy, 1973-1985.* Cambridge, MA: Harvard University, Center for Middle Eastern Studies, 1985. Harvard Middle East Papers, Modern Series, No. 4.

Hammoudeh, Shawkat M. "Optimal Oil Pricing Policy for Saudi Arabia." Ph.D. dissertation, University of Kansas, 1980.

Johany, Ali D. *The Myth of the OPEC Cartel: The Role of Saudi Arabia.* Chichester, MA: John Wiley and Sons, 1980.

Kaud, Nassar Ibrahim. "Optimal Oil Extraction, Exploration and Investment in an Underdeveloped Oil-Exporting Country: The Saudi Case." Ph.D. dissertation, University of Washington, 1985.

Kaufold, Howard S. "OPEC Portfolio Investment, Oil Supply and Worldwide Inflation." Ph.D. dissertation, Princeton University, 1981.

Kern, Nathaniel. "Oil: Fifty Years of Cooperation." *Middle East Insight*, Special Edition (1995), pp. 60-61.

Khattab, Mukhtar 'Abd al-Mun'im. "Al-siyāsah al-bitrūlīyah lil-mamlakah al-'arabiyah al-sa'udiyah mundhu awā'il al-saba'īn." ("Saudi Oil Policy Since the Beginning of the 1970s.") *Majallat dirāsat al-khalīj wal -jazīrah al-'arabīyah*, Vol. 14, No. 53 (January 1988), pp. 105-149.

Knauerhase, Ramon. "Saudi Arabian Oil Policies." *Current History*, Vol. 83, No. 489 (January 1984), pp. 29-32, 36-37.

Long, David E. "Saudi Oil Policy." *Wilson Quarterly* (Winter 1979), pp. 83-91.

Longrigg, Stephen. *Oil in the Middle East: Its Discovery and Development.* 3rd ed.; London: Oxford University Press, for the Royal Institute of International Affairs, 1968.

Mohamedi, Fareed. "Oil Prices and Saudi Choices." *Middle East Insight*, Vol. 14, No. 3 (May-June 1999), pp. 78-80.

Morano, Louis. "Multinationals and Nation-States: The Case of ARAMCO." *Orbis*, Vol. 23, No. 2 (1979), pp. 447-468.

Obaid, Nawaf E. *The Oil Kingdom at 100: Petroleum Policymaking in Saudi Arabia*. Washington, DC: Washington Institute for Near East Policy, 2000.

Philby, H. St. J. B. *Arabian Oil Ventures*. Washington, DC: Middle East Institute, 1964.

Placke, James. "Saudi Oil Industry Preparing for the New Millennium." In *Saudi Arabia: One Hundred Years Later; Revised and Updated Proceedings of a Conference at the Center for Contemporary Arab Studies, 28 April 1999* (Washington, DC: Georgetown University Center for Contemporary Arab Studies, 1999), pp. 11-13.

Quandt, William B. *Saudi Arabia's Oil Policy*. Washington, DC: Brookings Institution, 1982. A Staff Paper.

Rabie, Mohamed. "The Role of Saudi Arabia in the 1980s Oil Market." *American-Arab Affairs*, No. 3 (Winter 1982-1983), pp. 94-102.

Sahlawi, Mohammed A. Al-. "Saudi and Gulf Cooperation Council Oil Supply: An Econometric Analysis." *Journal of Energy and Development*, Vol. 11, No. 2 (Spring 1986), pp. 263-272.

Schneider, Steven A. *The Oil Price Revolution*. Baltimore: Johns Hopkins University Press, 1983.

Skeet, Ian. *OPEC: 25 Years of Prices and Politics*. Cambridge: Cambridge University Press, 1988.

Stevens, George P. "Saudi Arabia's Petroleum Resources." *Economic Geography*, Vol. 25, No. 3 (1949), pp. 216-225.

Taher, Abdulaziz Adeeb H. "World Oil Price Shocks and the Saudi Arabian Economy: A Macro Econometric Simulation." Ph.D. dissertation, University of Colorado, 1987.

Tuwaijri, Abdulrahman al-. "Exploration of Optimal Strategies for the Development of an Oil-Based Economy: The Case of Saudi Arabia." Ph.D. dissertation, Iowa State University, 1985.

U. S. General Accounting Office. *Critical Factors Affecting Saudi Arabia's Oil Decisions*; Report by the Comptroller General of the US. Washington, DC: GAO, 12 May 1978.

U. S. Senate. Committee on Foreign Relations. *The Future of Saudi Arabian Oil Production*; A Staff Report. Washington, DC: USGPO, 1979.

Wells, Donald A. "ARAMCO: The Evolution of an Oil Concession." In Raymond F. Mikesell, ed., *Foreign Investment in the Petroleum and Mineral Industries* (Baltimore: Johns Hopkins University Press, 1971), pp. 216-236.

Yergin, Daniel. *The Prize: The Epic Quest for Oil, Money, and Power*. New York: Simon & Schuster, 1991.

ECONOMY AND FINANCE

Aarts, Paul. "Saudi Arabia: From Fiscal Crisis to Political Crisis?" *JIME Review*, No. 29 (1995), pp. 23-34.

Abal-Khail, Mohammad Ali. "Economic Development in Saudi Arabia and Western Technology." *American-Arab Affairs*, No. 3 (Winter 1982-1983), pp. 1-4.

Abd al-Mawla, S. S. "Economic Policies and the Performance of the Private Sector in the Kingdom of Saudi Arabia." (in Arabic) *Majallat dirāsāt al-khalīj waljazīrah al-'arabīyah*, Vol. 21, No. 80 (1996), pp. 101-156.

Abdeen, Adnan, and Dale Shook. *The Saudi Financial System*. New York: John Wiley and Sons, 1984.

Abed, George, and Said H. Hitti. "The Economy and Finances of Saudi Arabia." *International Monetary Fund Staff Papers*, Vol. 21, No. 2 (1974), pp. 247-306.

Aburdene, Bassam. "Investment and Joint-Venture Experiences in Saudi Arabia." *American-Arab Affairs*, No. 11 (Winter 1984-1985), pp. 101-103.

Aburdene, Odeh. "U. S. Economic and Financial Relations with Saudi Arabia, Kuwait, and the United Arab Emirates." *American-Arab Affairs*, No. 7 (Winter 1983-1984), pp. 76-84.

Ahmed, Osama Saad. "Diversification Through Industrialization: The Saudi Experience." In Abbas Abdelkarim, ed., *Change and Development in the Gulf* (London: Macmillan, 1999), pp. 104-130.

Akhdar, Farouk M. H. "Multinational Firms and Developing Countries: A Case Study of the Impact of the Arabian American Oil Co. 'ARAMCO' on the Development of the Saudi Arabian Economy." Ph.D. dissertation, University of California, Riverside, 1974.

Alajaji, Adel Abdullah. "Obstacles to the Employment of Male Saudi University Graduates by the Private Sector in Saudi Arabia." Ed.D. dissertation, George Washington University, 1995.

Albraikan, Saud Mehmas. "OPEC Foreign Investment: The Case of Saudi Arabia." Ph.D. dissertation, University of Colorado, 1980.

ARAMCO Services Company. *Saudi ARAMCO and Its People: A History of Training*. Washington, DC, 1998.

Asfour, Edmund. "Saudi Arabia." In Charles Cooper and Sidney S. Alexander, eds., *Economic Development and Population Growth in the Middle East* (New York: American Elsevier, 1972), pp. 369-380.

Badr, Fayez Ibrahim. "Developmental Planning in Saudi Arabia: A Multidimensional Study." Ph.D. dissertation, University of Southern California, 1968.

Bakr, Mohammed A. *A Model in Privatization: Successful Change Management in the Ports of Saudi Arabia*. London: London Center of Arab Studies, 2001.

Barker, Paul. *Saudi Arabia: The Development Dilemma*. London: Economist Intelligence Unit, 1982.

Bashir, Faisal Saffooq Al-. "An Econometric Model of the Saudi Arabian Economy, 1960-1970." Ph.D. dissertation, University of Arizona, 1973.

Bowen-Jones, H. "Agriculture and the Use of Water Resources in the Eastern Province of Saudi Arabia." In May Ziwar-Daftari, ed., *Issues in the Development of Arab Gulf States* (London: MD Research Service, 1980), pp. 118-137.

Brown, A. *Oil, God and Gold: The Story of ARAMCO and the Saudi Kings*. N.p., 1999.

Carter, J. R. L. *Investors in Saudi Arabia: A Reference to Private Investment*. London: Scorpion, 1981.

Chaudhry, Kiren Aziz. *The Price of Wealth: Economics and Institutions in the Middle East*. Ithaca, NY: Cornell University Press, 1997.

————. "Economic Liberalization in Oil-Exporting Countries: Iraq and Saudi Arabia." In Iliya Harik and Denis J. Sullivan, eds., *Privatization and Liberalization in the Middle East* (Bloomington: Indiana University Press, 1992), pp. 145-166.

————. "The Price of Wealth: Business and State in Labor Remittance and Oil Economies." *International Organization*, Vol. 43 (Winter 1989), pp. 101-145.

Choudhry, Masudul Alam. *Manpower Planning and Policies of Saudi Arabia.* Jiddah: King Abdulaziz University, 1982.

Cleron, Jean Paul. *Saudi Arabia 2000: Strategy for Growth.* London: Croom Helm, 1978.

Crane, Robert D. *Planning the Future of Saudi Arabia: A Model for Achieving National Priorities.* New York: Praeger, 1978.

Daghistani, Abdulaziz Ismail. "Economic Development in Saudi Arabia: Problems and Prospects." Ph.D. dissertation, University of Houston, 1979.

Edens, David G., and William P. Snavely. "Planning for Economic Development in Saudi Arabia." *Middle East Journal*, Vol. 24, No. 1 (1970), pp. 17-30.

Elgari, Mohamed Ali. "The Pattern of Economic Development in Saudi Arabia as a Product of Its Social Structure." Ph.D. dissertation, University of California, Riverside, 1983.

Elzir, A. "Pétrole: pourquoi Ryad pousse à la baisse?" *Cahiers de l'Orient*, No. 3 (1986), pp. 215-227.

Endo, M. "Saudiization: Developments in the Early 1990s and Prospects for the Rest of the Decade." *JIME Review*, No. 35 (1996), pp. 75-92.

Farhan, Tareq Abdullah al-. "A Descriptive Analysis of Kuwait, Abu Dhabi, and Saudi Funds and Their Role in International Development." M.I.B.A. thesis, United States International University, 1985.

Fayez, Khaled Mohammed Ali Al-. "Economic Development of Saudi Arabia: A Case Study of the Government Propelled Economy." Ph.D. dissertation, Tufts University, Fletcher School of Law and Diplomacy, 1974.

Fozan, Mohammed Nasser. "Interest-free Loans Used by the Saudi Government as a Transfer Mechanism of Oil Revenue to the Private Sector." Ph.D. dissertation, University of Arizona, 1986.

Ghamdi, Abdullah al-. "Political Economy of Privatization: The Case of Saudi Arabia." Ph.D. dissertation, Florida State University, 1992.

Gottheil, Fred M. "The Manufacture of Saudi Arabian Economic Power." *Middle East Review*, Vol. 11, No. 1 (1978), pp. 18-23.

Griffith-Jones, Stephen. "The Saudi Loan to the IMF: A New Route to Recycling." *Third World Quarterly*, Vol. 4, No. 2 (1982), pp. 304-311.

Hajjar, B. al-, and J. Presley. "Constraints on Development: Small Businesses in Saudi Arabia." *Middle Eastern Studies*, Vol. 28, No. 2 (1992), pp. 333-351.

Hajrah, H. H. "Water Resources Development in Saudi Arabia." In *Alternative Strategies for Desert Development and Management* (New York: Pergamon Press, 1982, for UNITAR), pp. 840-849.

Hamed, Abdulwahed Khaled. "Capital Absorptive Capacity of Non-Oil Sectors in Saudi Arabia." Ph.D. dissertation, University of Wisconsin at Milwaukee, 1984.

Hamed, Faisal Hassan. "Privatization of State-Owned Enterprises." Ph.D. dissertation, Florida State University, 1986.

Hashim, Waheed Hamza. "Economic Decision Making: Oil and Development." In *Saudi Arabia: One Hundred Years Later; Revised and Updated Proceedings of a Conference at the Center for Contemporary Arab Studies, 28 April 1999* (Washington, DC: Georgetown University Center for Contemporary Arab Studies, 1999), pp. 15-16.

Hassanain, Mahjoob Ahmed. "An Economic Review of the Saudi Arabian Planning Framework (The Petroleum Economy of Saudi Arabia)." Ph.D. dissertation, University of Pittsburgh, 1971.

Hill, Enid. "Saudi Labor and Industrialization Policy in Saudi Arabia." *International Review of Modern Sociology*, Vol. 12, No. 1 (1982), pp. 147-174.

Hoftyzer, J., and J. Mixon. "National Origins of Saudi Arabia's Imports." *Journal of Energy and Development*, Vol. 14, No. 1 (1988), pp. 45-54.

Jamjoom, Mohamed Abdulwahid. "International Trade and Balance of Payments in a Mono-product Economy: A Case Study of the Saudi Arabian Kingdom." Ph.D. dissertation, University of Southern California, 1970.

Jarrah, M. al-. "Money, Income, and Prices in Saudi Arabia: A Cointegration and Causality Analysis." *Pakistan Economic and Social Review*, Vol. 34, No. 1 (1996), pp. 41-53.

Kalicki, Jan H. "A Vision for the U. S.-Saudi and U. S.-Gulf Commercial Relationship." *Middle East Policy*, Vol. 5, No. 2 (May 1997), pp. 73-78.

Kanovsky, Eliyahu. "The Woeful State of Saudi Finances." In Patrick Clawson, *Energy and National Security* (Washington, DC: National Defense University, Institute for National Strategic Studies, 1995; Strategic Forum, No. 26), pp. 63-75.

Kaslow, Amy. "US-Saudi Commercial Relations Since the Gulf War." *Middle East Insight*, Special Edition (1995), pp. 84-85.

Katani, Ahmad Kamal. "Policies and Models for Planning the Economic Development of the Non-Oil Sector of Saudi Arabia." Ph.D. dissertation, Iowa State University, 1971.

Khatrawi, Mohamed Ibn Faraj. "The Diversification Strategy for the Saudi Arabian Economy." Ph.D. dissertation, Georgetown University, 1976.

Khuthaila, Khalid Majid. "Saudi Arabia's Development: A Dependency Theory Perspective." Ph.D. dissertation, Syracuse University, 1984.

Knauerhase, Ramon. *The Saudi Arabian Economy*. New York: Praeger, 1975.

———. "Saudi Arabia's Economy at the Beginning of the 1970s." *Middle East Journal*, Vol. 28, No. 2 (1974), pp. 126-140.

Krimly, Rayed. "The Political Economy of Adjusted Priorities: Declining Oil Revenues and Saudi Fiscal Policies." *Middle East Journal*, Vol. 53, No. 2 (Spring 1999), pp. 254-267.

Kuwaiz, Abdullah Ibrahim, El-. "Comparison of the Actual and Optimal Pricing Policy for a Public Utility Operating in a Developing Country: A Case Study of Electricity in the City of Riyadh, Saudi Arabia." Ph.D. dissertation, St. Louis University, 1976.

Looney, Robert E. *Economic Development in Saudi Arabia*. Greenwich, CT: JAI Press, 1990.

———. *Saudi Arabia's Development Potential: Application of an Islamic Growth Model*. Lexington, MA: Lexington Books, 1982.

———. *Saudi Arabia's Economic Development Strategy.* Oslo: Norwegian Institute of International Affairs, 1980.

———. "Depressed Oil Revenues and Austerity: The Economics of Reduced Saudi Arabian Defense Expenditures." *Arab Studies Quarterly,* Vol. 10, No. 3 (1988), pp. 345-361.

———. "Future Viability of the Saudi Arabian Private Sector in an Era of Fiscal Austerity." *Journal of South Asian and Middle Eastern Studies,* Vol. 11 (Spring 1988), pp. 3-27.

———. "Growth Prospects of the Saudi Arabian Private Sector." *American-Arab Affairs,* No. 23 (Winter 1987-1988), pp. 65-74.

———. "The Impact of Defense Expenditures on the Saudi Arabian Private Sector." *Journal of Arab Affairs,* Vol. 6, No. 2 (Fall 1987), pp. 198-229.

———. "The Impact of Petroleum Exports on the Saudi Arabian Economy." In Robert W. Stookey, ed., *The Arabian Peninsula: Zone of Ferment* (Stanford, CA: Hoover Institution Press, 1984), pp. 37-64.

———. "Infrastructure Investment and Inflation in Saudi Arabia." *Journal of Energy and Development,* Vol. 14, No. 1 (1988), pp. 103-113.

———. "Patterns of Human Resource Development in Saudi Arabia." *Middle Eastern Studies,* Vol. 27, No. 4 (1991), pp. 668-678.

———. "The Relative Strength of Fiscal and Monetary Policy in Saudi Arabia." *Finance and Industry,* No. 9 (1988), pp. 21-29.

———. "Saudi Arabia: Measures of Transition from a Rentier State." In Joseph A. Kechichian, ed., *Iran, Iraq, and the Arab Gulf States* (New York: Palgrave, 2001), pp. 131-159.

———. "Saudi Arabian Budgetary Dilemmas." *Middle Eastern Studies,* Vol. 26, No. 1 (1990), pp. 76-87.

———. "Saudi Arabia's Development Strategy: Comparative Advantage vs. Sustainable Growth." *Orient,* Vol. 30, No. 1 (1989), pp. 75-96.

———. "Saudi Arabia's Fiscal Dilemma: Sustained Growth Versus Increased Vulnerability." *Journal of Arab Affairs,* Vol. 7, No. 2 (1988), pp. 155-173.

Luciani, Giacomo. "Arabie saoudite: l'industrialisation d'un état allocataire." *Maghreb-Machrek,* No. 129 (1990), pp. 76-93.

Malik, Ibrahim Mohammed al-. "Development Planning in Saudi Arabia: The Impact of the Oil Recession on Structure, Values, and Policy Outcomes." Ph.D. dissertation, St. Louis University, 1987.

Mallakh, Ragaei El. *An Overview of the Third Development Plan of Saudi Arabia* (1400-1405/1980-1985). Boulder, CO: International Research Center for Energy and Economic Development, 1981.

———. *Saudi Arabia: Rush to Development; Profile of as Energy Economy and Investment.* London: Croom Helm, 1982.

Mansoor, M. "Saudi Arabia: Economic Structural Adjustment and Outlook." *JIME Review,* No. 17 (1992), pp. 55-62.

Mansour, Hussein Omar. "The Discovery of Oil and Its Impact on the Industrialization of Saudi Arabia." Ph.D. dissertation, University of Arizona, 1973.

Masri, Zeinab Ismael El-. "The Demand for Money in Developing Economies: The Case of Libya, Saudi Arabia and Irak." Ph.D. dissertation, University of Missouri, Columbia, 1982.

Meyer-Reumann, Rolf. "The Banking System in Saudi Arabia." *Arab Law Quarterly*, Vol. 10, No. 3 (1995), pp. 207-237.

Mobarak, Nasser Abdulaziz al-. "From Order Taker to Policy Maker: The Expanding Role of Planning in the Socio-Economic Development of Saudi Arabia From 1932 to Present." Ph.D. dissertation, University of Pennsylvania, 1993.

Mohamedi, Fareed. "The Saudi Economy: A Few Years Yet to Doomsday." *MERIP Middle East Report*, Vol. 23, No. 6 (1993), pp. 14-17.

Moliver, Donald Matthew. *The Economy of Saudi Arabia.* New York: Praeger, 1980.

––––––. "Oil and Money in Saudi Arabia." Ph.D. dissertation, Virginia Polytechnic Institute and State University, 1978.

Moneef, Ibrahim A. Al-. *Transfer of Management Technology to Developing Countries: The Role of Multinational Oil Firms in Saudi Arabia.* New York: Arno Press, 1980.

Najjar, Mitri J. "Doing Business in Saudi Arabia." *Middle East Insight*, Special Edition (1995), pp. 86-89.

Nariya, H. "The Saudi Economy After the Gulf War." *JIME Review*, No. 14 (1991), pp. 27-37.

Nehme, Michael G. "Saudi Development Plans Between Capitalist and Islamic Values." *Middle Eastern Studies*, Vol. 30, No. 3 (1994), pp. 632-645.

Okruhlik, Gwen. "Image, Imagination, and Place: The Political Economy of Tourism in Saudi Arabia." In Joseph A. Kechichian, ed., *Iran, Iraq, and the Arab Gulf States* (New York: Palgrave, 2001), pp. 111-129.

Okruhlik, Mary Gwen. "Debating Profits and Political Power: Private Business and Government in Saudi Arabia." Ph.D. dissertation, University of Texas at Austin, 1992.

Otaibi, Sunhat Bader al-. "Linking Strategy, Information Technology and Performance in Financial Service Organizations: An Empirical Investigation in the Gulf Cooperation Council Countries (Saudi Arabia, Kuwait, Bahrain, Qatar, Oman, United Arab Emirates)." D.B.A. thesis, Southern Illinois University at Carbondale, 1992.

Pampanini, Andrea H. *Cities from the Arabian Desert: The Building of Jubail and Yanbu in Saudi Arabia.* Westport, CT: Praeger, 1997.

Peagam, Norman. "Saudi Arabia: Development Without Parallel." *Euromoney*, No. 314 (June 1995), suppl. pp. 229-246.

Presley, John R. *A Guide to the Saudi Arabian Economy.* London: Macmillan; New York: St. Martin's Press, 1984.

––––––. "Trade and Foreign Aid: The Saudi Arabian Experience." *Arab Gulf Journal*, Vol. 3, No. 1 (April 1983), pp. 41-59.

Pritzkat, Thomas. "The Hadrami Community in Saudi Arabia and the Rationale of Investing in the Homeland." In Rémy Leveau, Franck Mermier, and Udo Steinbach, eds., *Le Yémen Contemporain* (Paris: Éditions Karthala, 1999), pp. 399-418.

Roberts, John. "Saudi Ambitions." *Petroleum Review*, Vol. 46 (July 1992), pp. 314-316.

Ronall, J. O. "Banking Regulations in Saudi Arabia." *Middle East Journal*, Vol. 21, No. 3 (1967), pp. 399-402.

Saati, Abdul-Rahim Abdul-Hamid al-. "The Islamic Reform to the Saudi Arabian Financial System." Ph.D. dissertation, University of Colorado, 1987.

Sabab, Ahmed abdulla AI-Ali Al-. "An Inquiry into the Development of the Current Planning Institutions for Economic and Social Development in Saudi Arabia." Ph.D. dissertation, New York University, 1973.

Sabri, Sharaf. *The House of Saud in Commerce: A Study of Royal Entrepreneurship in Saudi Arabia.* New Delhi: I. S. Publications, 2001.

Saigh, Nassir Mohammed Al-. "A Method for Financing the Private Sector's Development Projects by Development Banks: The Saudi Arabian Experience." Ph.D. dissertation, University of Kentucky, 1979.

Salem, Ahmed Mohammed Al-. "Economic Viability of the Saudi Arabian Petrochemical Industry: Methanol as a Case Study." Ph.D. dissertation, University of California, Riverside, March 1987.

Salloom, Yousif ibn Ibrahim al-. *Strategic Planning and Development in the Kingdom of Saudi Arabia, 1932-1995 A.D.: A Historical Study.* Riyadh: n.p., 1997.

Saudi Arabia. Ministry of Planning. *Achievements of the Development Plans, 1390-1405 (1970-1985): Facts and Figures.* Riyadh, 1406/1986.

————. *Achievements of the Development Plans, 1390-1420 (1970-2000).* Riyadh, 2001? 18th Issue.

Shams, Mohamed Mahmod. "Oil Conservatism and Economic Development in Saudi Arabia." Ph.D. dissertation, University of Texas at Austin, 1984.

Shaw, Paul F. "Saudi Arabian Manpower Requirements." In George S. Roukis and Patrick J. Montana, eds., *Workforce Management in the Arabian Peninsula: Factors Affecting Development* (Westport, CT: Greenwood Press, 1986), pp. 95-112.

Shea, Thomas W. "Measuring the Changing Family Consumption Patterns of ARAMCO's Saudi Arab Employees, 1962 and 1968." In Derek Hopwood, ed., *The Arabian Peninsula: Society and Politics* (London: George Allen and Unwin, 1972), pp. 231-254.

Sheikh, A. A. A. H. al-. "Agriculture and Economic Development, With Special Emphasis on a Strategy for Saudi Arabian Economic Development." Ph.D. thesis, University of Edinburgh, 1971.

Shreeve, Gavin, and Stephen Timewell. "Summer Wishes, Winter Dreams." *Banker*, Vol. 140 (November 1990), pp. 74-76, 78-89.

Shuaibi, Saleh M. Al-. "Human Resources Development in Saudi Arabia." Ph.D. dissertation, University of Pittsburgh, 1984.

Soufi, Adnan Abdulfattah. "A Conceptual Model for Managing the Portfolio of Saudi Arabia's Reserve Funds." D.B.A. dissertation, George Washington University, 1984.

Sowfi, Wahib A., and Richard T. Mayer. "Saudi Arabia or the West: Alternative Relationships Between the Public and Private Sectors." *Journal of South Asian and Middle Eastern Studies*, Vol. 10 (Fall 1986), pp. 78-87.

Suraisy, Jobarah Eid. "Development of a Dualistic Economy: A Case Study of Saudi Arabia." Ph.D. dissertation, University of Colorado, 1978.

Szyliowicz, Joseph. "The Prospects for Scientific and Technological Development in Saudi Arabia." *International Journal of Middle East Studies*, Vol. 11, No. 3 (August 1979), pp. 355-372.

Takroni, Mohamed Habib. "Evaluating Loan Repayment in the Saudi Arabian Agriculture Sector by Means of Farm Credit Interdependent System." Ph.D. dissertation, Oklahoma State University, 1980.

Tarabzune, Muhiadin Rashad. "An Analysis of the Effect of Capitalizing Exploration and Development Costs in the Petroleum Industry—With Emphasis on Possible Economic Consequences in Saudi Arabia." Ph.D. dissertation, University of Arkansas, 1975.

Tbeileh, Faisal. "The Political Economy of Legitimacy in Rentier States: A Comparative Study of Saudi Arabia and Libya." Ph.D. thesis, University of California, Los Angeles, 1991.

Thiemann, E. "Beziehungen von Staat and Auslandskapital im Industrialisie-rungsprozess Saudi-Arabiens." *Asia Africa-Lateinamerica*, Vol. 15, No. 5 (1987), pp. 833-846.

Tuncalp, S., and A. al-Ibrahim. "Saudi Arabia's Petrochemical Industry: Growth and Performance." *Journal of Energy and Development*, Vol. 16, No. 2 (1991), pp. 287-306.

Turner, Louis. *The Political and Economic Impact of Saudi Arabia's Industrialization Policies*. Oslo: Norwegian Institute of International Affairs, 1980.

Virchow, F. "Bildungssystem and Wertewandel in Saudi-Arabien." *Orient*, Vol. 28, No. 4 (1987), pp. 557-589.

Weintraub, Sidney. "Saudi Arabia's Role in the International Financial System." *Middle East Review*, Vol. 10, No. 4 (1978), pp. 16-20.

Wells, Donald A. *Saudi Arabian Development Strategy*. Washington, DC: American Enterprise Institute for Public Policy Research, 1976.

———. "The Effects of Saudi Industrialization on Employment." *Journal of Energy and Development*, Vol. 11, No. 2 (Spring 1986), pp. 273-284.

Wilson, Peter W. *A Question of Interest: The Paralysis of Saudi Banking*. Boulder, CO: Westview Press, 1991.

Woodward, Peter N. *Oil and Labor in the Middle East: Saudi Arabia and the Oil Boom*. New York: Praeger, 1988.

Young, Arthur N. *Saudi Arabia: The Making of a Financial Giant*. New York: New York University Press, 1983.

———. "Financial Reform in Saudi Arabia." *Middle East Journal*, Vol. 14, No. 4 (1960), pp. 466-469.

Yousuf, Ala'a al-. *Kuwait and Saudi Arabia: From Prosperity to Retrenchment*. Oxford: Oxford Institute for Energy Studies, 1990.

EXPLORATION

Blunt, Lady Anne. *A Pilgrimage to Najd*. 2 vols. London: John Murray, 1881.

Burckhardt, John Lewis. *Travels in Arabia*. London: n.p., 1829.

Burton, Sir Richard F. *Personal Narrative of a Pilgrimage to Al Medinah and Meccah*. 2 vols.; London: George Bell and Sons, 1907.

de Gaury, Gerald. *Arabian Journey and Other Desert Travels*. London: 1950.

Doughty, Charles M. *Travels in Arabia Deserta*. London: Jonathan Cape and The Medici Society, 1926.

McLoughlin, Leslie. "Abdullah Philby's Crossing of the Empty Quarter." *Asian Affairs* (London), Vol. 22, No. 2 (1991), pp. 142-151.

Meulen, Daniel van der. *The Wells of Ibn Saud.* London: John Murray, 1957.

Palgrave, William Gifford. *Narrative of a Year's Journey Through Central and Eastern Arabia (1865).* Reprinted in 2 vols. Farnborough, Hants.: Gregg International, 1969.

Pelly, Lewis. *Report on a Journey to the Wahabee Capital of Riyadh in Central Arabia (1865).* Bombay: Printed for Government at the Education Society's Press, Byculla, 1866. Repr. Cambridge: Oleander Press, 1978; Naples: Falcon Press, 1978.

Philby, H. St. John B. *Arabian Days.* London: Robert Hale, 1948.

————. *Arabian Highlands.* Ithaca, NY: Cornell University Press, 1952.

————. *Arabian Jubilee.* New York: John Day, 1953.

————. *The Empty Quarter.* London: Constable, 1933; New York: Henry Holt, 1933.

————. *Land of Midian.* London: Ernest Berm, 1957.

————. "Riyadh: Ancient and Modern." *Middle East Journal,* Vol. 13, No. 2 (1959), pp. 129-142.

Sadleir, George Forster. *Diary of a Journey Across Arabia (1819).* Reprinted Cambridge: Oleander Press, 1977.

Wallin, Georg August. *Travels in Arabia (1845 and 1848).* Repr. Cambridge: Oleander Press, 1979; Naples: Falcon Press, 1979. Intro. material by W. R. Mead and M. Trautz.

Wellsted, J. R. *Travels in Arabia.* 2 vols. London: John Murray, 1838. Reprinted Graz: Akademische Druke, 1978.

Wolfe, Michael, ed. *One Thousand Roads to Mecca: Ten Centuries of Travelers Writing About the Muslim Pilgrimage.* New York: Grove, 1997.

GEOGRAPHY

Abu-Dawood, Abdul-Razzak S., and P. P. Karan. *International Boundaries of Saudi Arabia.* New Delhi: Galaxy, 1990.

Abu-Ela, M. T. "A Geographical Study of Man and His Environment in al-Ahsa Province (Saudi Arabia)." Ph.D. thesis, Trinity College, Dublin, 1960.

Blehed, Abdel Rahman Saud al-. "Aspects of Emergence and Change in Asir, Saudi Arabia." Ph.D. thesis, Dept. of Geography, University of Southampton, June 1982.

Chaline, C. "Ryad ou un urbanisme de l'abondance." *Information Géographique,* Vol. 51 (1987), pp. 45-51.

Daghistani, Abdal-Majeed Ismail. *Riyad: Developpement et planning urbains.* Riyadh: Ministry of Information, Interior Information, 1985.

Duncan, G. O. "The Planning and Development of the City of Jeddah, 1970-1984." Ph.D. thesis, Oxford University, 1988.

Elawy, Ibrahim S. Al-Abdullah Al-. "The Influence of Oil Upon Settlement in Al-Hasa Oasis, Saudi Arabia." Ph.D. thesis, University of Durham, 1976.

Facey, William. *Riyadh: The Old City From Its Origins Until the 1950s.* London: Immel, 1992.

Fadaak, Tarek Ali. "Urban Housing Policy Evaluation in the Kingdom of Saudi
    Arabia." Ph.D. dissertation, Portland State University, 1984.
Felemban, Abdulaziz H. "Regional Physical Planning in Saudi Arabia: An
    Evaluation of the Western Region Plan and a Proposal for a Methodology
    for the Kingdom." Ph.D. thesis, University of East Anglia, 1976.
Gil-Har, Y. "Delimitation Boundaries: Trans-Jordan and Saudi Arabia." *Middle
    Eastern Studies*, Vol. 28, No. 2 (1992), pp. 374-384.
Hajrah, H. H. "Public Land Distribution in Saudi Arabia." Ph.D. thesis, University
    of Durham, 1974.
Kelly, J. B. "Arabian Frontiers and Anglo-American Relations." *Government
    and Opposition*, Vol. 27, No. 3 (Summer 1992), pp. 369-384.
Mojtahed-Zadeh, Pirouz. "A Geopolitical Triangle in the Persian Gulf: Actions
    and Reactions Among Iran, Bahrain, and Saudi Arabia." *Iranian Journal
    of International Affairs*, Vol. 6, No. 1-2 (Spring-Summer 1994), pp. 47-59.
Roberts, John. "The Saudi-Yemeni Boundary Treaty." *Boundary and Security
    Bulletin*, Vol. 8, No. 2 (Summer 2000), pp. 70-73.
Saleh, Nassir A. "Provincial and District Delimitation in the Kingdom of Saudi
    Arabia." In John I. Clarke and Howard Bowen-Jones, eds., *Change and
    Development in the Middle East: Essays in Honour of W. B. Fisher* (London:
    Methuen, 1981), pp. 305-317.
Schofield, Richard. "Negotiating the Saudi-Yemeni International Boundary."
    British-Yemeni Society Journal, Vol. 8 (July 2000), pp. 7-20.
Shurafa', Muhammad al-. *Al-mintaqah al-sharqīyah min al-mamlakah al-'arabīyah
    al-sa'ūdīyah.* ("The Eastern Region of the Kingdom of Saudi Arabia.")
    Dammam: Tihāmah, 1992.
Stivers, William. "A Note on The Red Line Agreement." *Diplomatic History*,
    Vol. 7 (1979), pp. 23-34.
Ward, Philip. *Ha'il: Oasis City of Saudi Arabia.* Cambridge: Oleander Press,
    1983.
Wilkinson, John. *Arabia's Frontiers: The Story of Britain's Blue and Violet Lines.*
    London: I. B. Tauris; New York: St. Martin's Press, 1991.

HISTORY AND ARCHAEOLOGY

General, Early, and Archaeology

Aladieh, Salamah Salih Sulayman. "Mecca Trade Prior to the Rise of Islam."
    Ph.D. thesis, School of Oriental Studies, University of Durham, 1991.
Azmeh, Aziz al-. "Wahhabite Polity." In Ian Richard Netton, ed., *Arabia and
    the Gulf: From Traditional Society to Modern States* (London: Croom Helm;
    New York: Barnes & Noble, 1986), pp. 75-90.
Dostal, Walter. "Mecca Before the Time of the Prophet: Attempt of an
    Anthropological Interpretation." *Der Islam*, Vol. 68, No. 2 (1991), pp. 193-
    231.
Dussaud, R. *La pénétration des Arabes en Syrie avant l'Islam.* Paris: P. Geuthner,
    1955.

Edens, Chris. "In Ancient Times: The Archeology of Saudi Arabia." *Middle East Insight*, Vol. 14, No. 3 (1995), pp. 96-104.

Erris, Tarik Sultan El-. "Saudi Arabia: A Study in Nation Building." Ph.D. dissertation, American University, 1965.

Faraj, Nasir al-. *Qiyam al-'arash al-sa'ūdi: dirāsah tārīkhīyah lil-'alāqāt al-sa'ūdīyah al-brītānīyah.* ("The Rise of the Saudi Throne: A Historical Study of British-Saudi Relations.") London: al-Safā lil-Nashr wal-Tawzī', 1988.

Ghanem, Isam. "The Legal History of Asir (al-Mikhlaf al-Sulaymai)." *Arab Law Quarterly*, Vol. 5, No. 3 (1990), pp. 211-214.

Healey, John F. "Report on Epigraphic Work at Mada'in Salih." In R. B. Serjeant, R. L. Bidwell, and G. Rex Smith, eds., *New Arabian Studies*, Vol. 1 (Exeter: University of Exeter Press, 1993), pp. 228-230.

Hitti, Philip K. *History of the Arabs.* 10th ed. London: Macmillan, 1970.

Jrais, Ghithan Ali. "The Social, Industrial, and Commercial History of the Hejaz Under the Early 'Abbasids, 132-232/749-847." Ph.D. thesis, Victoria University of Manchester, 1989.

Lacey, Robert. *The Kingdom: Arabia and the House of Saud.* New York: Harcourt Brace Jovanovich, 1982.

Lorimer, J. G., comp. *Gazetteer of the Persian Gulf, 'Oman, and Central Arabia.* Calcutta: Superintendent, Government Printing, Vol. 1: 1915; Vol. 2: 1908. Reprinted Farnborough, Hants.: Gregg International, 1970; Shannon: Irish Universities Press, 1970; in six volumes. Reprinted London: Archive Editions, 1989.

Masry, Abdullah Hassan. "The History and Development of Human Settlement in Saudi Arabia." In Ahmed Hassan Dahlan, ed., *Politics, Administration and Development in Saudi Arabia* (Brentwood, MD: Amana Corporation; Jidda: Dar al-Shorouq, 1990), pp. 7-28.

Mazrou, Hamid I. al-. "The Canon and Proportion of Pre-Islamic Arabian Sculptures." *New Arabian Studies*, Vol. 5 (2000), pp. 183-187.

Mortel, R. T. "Aspects of Mamluk Relations with Jedda During the Fifteenth Century: The Case of Timraz al-Mu'ayyadi." *Journal of Islamic Studies*, Vol. 6, No. 1 (1995), pp. 1-13.

———. "Taxation in the Amirate of Mecca During the Medieval Period." *Bulletin of the School of Oriental and African Studies*, Vol. 58, No. 1 (1995), pp. 1-16.

Rasheed, Madawi al-. *A History of Saudi Arabia.* Cambridge: Cambridge University Press, 2002.

Rashid, 'Abd al-'Aziz al-. *Al-Rabadah: A Portrait of Early Civilisation in Saudi Arabia.* London: Longman, 1986.

Rashid, Dari b. Fuhayd al-, relater, and Wadi' al-Bustani, writer. *Nubdah tārīkhīyah 'an najd.* ("Historical Fragment [Pamphlet] on Najd.") Riyadh: Manshūrāt dār al-yamāmah lil-bahth wa-tarjimah wal-nashr, 1966?

Rashid, Saad A. al-. *Darb Zubaydah: The Pilgrim Road from Kufa to Mecca.* Riyadh: Riyad University Libraries, 1980.

Robin, Christian, ed. "L'Arabie antique de Karib'îl à Mahomet," *Revue du Monde Musulman et de la Méditerranée* (Editions Edisud), No. 61 (1991-1993).

Said, Abdulrahman H. "Saudi Arabia: The Transition from a Tribal Society to a Nation-State." Ph.D. dissertation, University of Missouri, Columbia, 1979.

Saudi Arabia. Department of Antiquities and Museums. *Muqaddimah 'an: āthār al-mamlakah al-'arabīyah al-sa'ūdīyah.* ("Introduction to the Monuments of the Kingdom of Saudi Arabia.") Riyadh, 1975.
Vassiliev, Alexei. *The History of Saudi Arabia.* London: Al Saqi Books, 2000. Originally published in 1998 as *The History of Saudi Arabia, 1745-1994.*
Zedan, Faysal Muhammad. "Political Development of the Kingdom of Saudi Arabia." PhD. dissertation, Claremont Graduate School, 1981.
Zayla'i, Ahmad 'Umar al-. "A Kufic Inscription from Ḥamdānah in Southern Hijaz Referring to Amir Ibrahim bin Ziyad." In G. Rex Smith, J. R. Smart, and B. R. Pridham, eds., *New Arabian Studies*, Vol. 3 (Exeter: University of Exeter Press, 1996), pp. 258-266.

18th and 19th Centuries: The First and Second Saudi States

Alorabi, Abdulrahman S. M. "The Ottoman Policy in the Hejaz in the Eighteenth Century: A Study of Political and Administrative Developments: 1143-1202 A.H./1731-1788 A.D." Ph.D. dissertation, University of Utah, 1988.
Anscombe, Frederick F. *The Ottoman Gulf: The Creation of Kuwait, Saudi Arabia, and Qatar.* New York: Columbia University Press, 1997.
Baran, Michael. "The Rashidi Amirate of Hayl: The Rise, Development and Decline of a Premodern Arabian Principality, 1835-1921." Ph.D. dissertation, University of Michigan, 1992.
Cook, Michael. "The Expansion of the First Saudi State: The Case of Washm." In C. E. Bosworth et al., eds., *The Islamic World: From Classical to Modern Times; Essays in Honor of Bernard Lewis* (Princeton, NJ: Darwin Press, 1989), pp. 661-699.
Dahlan, Ahmad b. Zini; compiled and edited by Ahmad Amin Tawfiq. *Tārīkh ashrāf al-hijāz 1840-1883: khilāsat al-kalām fī bayān umarā' al-balad al-harām.* ("History of the Sharifs of al-Hijaz 1840-1883: Summary of the Word in the Statement of the Amirs of the Holy Land.") London: Dār al-Sāqī, 1993.
Faroqhi, Suraiya. *Pilgrims and Sultans: The Hajj Under the Ottomans.* London: I. B. Tauris, 1994.
Frankl, P. J. L. "Lieutenant Jopp's Report on a Visit to Hufuf, 1257/1841." In R. B. Serjeant, R. L. Bidwell, and G. Rex Smith, eds., *New Arabian Studies*, Vol. 1 (Exeter: University of Exeter Press, 1993), pp. 215-227.
Hithlayn, Sultan b. Khalid b., and Zakariya Kurshun. *Tārīkh qabīlat al-'Ajmān: dirāsah withā'iqīyah.* ("History of al-'Ajman Tribe: A Documentary Study.") Kuwait: Dhāt al-Silāsil, 1998.
Hurgronje, C. Snouck. *Mekka in the Latter Part of the Nineteenth Century (1931).* Reprinted Leiden: E. J. Brill, 1970.
Ibrahim, 'Abd al-'Aziz 'Abd al-Ghani. *Sirā' al-umarā': 'alāqat najd bil-quwá al-siyāsīyah fī al-khalīj al-'arabī 1800-1870; dirāsah withā'iqīyah.* ("Struggle of the Amirs: Najd's Relations with the Political Powers in the Arabian Gulf 1800-1870; A Documentary Study.") London: Dār al-Sāqī, 2nd ed., 1992.
Linabury George. "The Creation of Saudi Arabia and the Erosion of Wahhabi Conservatism." *Middle East Review*, Vol. 11, No. 1 (1978), pp. 5-12.
Nakhlah, Muhammad 'Arabi. *Tārīkh al-ahsā' al-siyāsī (1818-1914).* ("Political History of al-Ahsa' [1818-1914].") Kuwait: Dhāt al-Silāsil, n.d.

Ochsenwald, William. *Religion, Society and the State in Arabia: The Hijaz Under Ottoman Control, 1840-1908*. Columbus: Ohio State University Press, 1984.
————. "The Jidda Massacre, 1858." *Middle Eastern Studies*, Vol. 13, No. 3 (1977), pp. 314-326.
————. "Ottoman Subsidies to the Hijaz, 1877-1886." *International Journal of Middle East Studies*, Vol. 6, No. 3 (1975), pp. 300-307.
Philby, H. St. John B. *Arabia of the Wahhabis*. London: Constable, 1928. Reprinted London: Frank Cass, 1977.
Rasheed, Madawi al-. *Politics in an Arabian Oasis: The Rashidi Tribal Dynasty*. London: I. B. Tauris, 1991.
————. "Durable and Non-Durable Dynasties: The Rashidis and Sa'udis in Central Arabia." *British Journal of Middle Eastern Studies*, Vol. 19, No. 2 (1992), pp. 144-158. Reprinted as "Dynasties durable et non durables: le Al Rachīd et les Sa'ūd en Arabie centrale." *Maghreb-Machrek*, No. 147 (1995), pp. 13-25.
————. "The Rashidi Dynasty: Political Centralization Among the Shammar of North Arabia." In R. L. Bidwell, G. Rex Smith, and J. R. Smart, eds., *New Arabian Studies*, Vol. 2 (Exeter: University of Exeter Press, 1994), pp. 140-152.
Winder, R. Bayly. *Saudi Arabia in the Nineteenth Century*. London: Macmillan, 1965.
Zdanowski, Jerzy. "Military Organization of the Wahhabi Amirates (1750-1932)." In R. L. Bidwell, G. Rex Smith, and J. R. Smart, eds., *New Arabian Studies*, Vol. 2 (Exeter: University of Exeter Press, 1994), pp. 130-139.

20th Century: The Third Saudi State

Abadha, Faruq 'Uthman. *Siyāsat brītānīyā fī 'asīr ithnā' al-harb al-'alimīyah al-ulá 1914-1918*. ("British Policy in 'Asir During the First World War, 1914-1918.") Kuwait: Manshūrat majallat al-dirāsat al-khalīj wal-jazīrah al-'arabīyah, 1983. No. 9.
Abdul-Aziz, Moudi M. Tr. from Arabic by Basil Hatim with Ron Buckley. *King Abdul Aziz and the Kuwait Conference 1923 1924*. London: Echoes, 1993.
Alangari, Haifa. *The Struggle for Power in Arabia: Ibn Saud, Hussein, and Great Britain, 1914-1924*. Reading: Ithaca Press, 1997.
Armitage, St. John. "The Keystone of the Partnership, Saudi-American Relations: An Englishman's View." *Middle East Insight*, Special Edition (1995), pp. 57-59.
————. "Saudi Arabia: The Diamond Jubilee." *Asian Affairs* (London), Vol. 24, Pt. 1 (February 1993), pp. 17-29.
Ayalon, Ami. "The Hashemites, T. E. Lawrence and the Postage Stamps of the Hijaz." In Asher Susser and Aryeh Shmuelevitz, eds., *The Hashemites in the Modern Arab World: A Festschrift in Honour of the Late Professor Uriel Dann* (London: Frank Cass, 1994), pp. 15-30.
Baba, N. "Nasser's Pan-Arab Radicalism and the Saudi Drive for Islamic Solidarity: A Response for Security." *India Quarterly*, Vol. 48, Nos. 1-2 (1992), pp. 1-22.

Bang, Anne Katrine. *The Idrisi State in 'Asir, 1906-1934: Politics, Religion, and Personal Prestige.* Bergen, Norway: Bergen Studies on the Middle East and Africa, 1996.

———. "'This Is an Announcement to the People ...'—The Bayan of 1912 by Muhammad b. 'Ali al-Idrisi in 'Asir." In G. Rex Smith, J. R. Smart, and B. R. Pridham, eds., *New Arabian Studies,* Vol. 4 (Exeter: University of Exeter Press, 1997), pp. 1-38.

Benoist-Mechin, Jacques. *Arabian Destiny.* London: Elek Books, 1957.

de Gaury, Gerald. *Arabia Phoenix.* London: George G. Harrap, 1946.

Eddy, William A. "FDR Meets Ibn Saud." *Middle East Insight,* Special Edition (1995), pp. 38-46.

Eilts, Hermann Frederick. "The United States and Saudi Arabia: A Half-Century Overview." *Middle East Insight,* Special Edition (1995), pp. 14-31.

Fadil, Sdaka Y. "The Impact of the Unification of Saudi Arabia on Regional Stability." In *Saudi Arabia: One Hundred Years Later; Revised and Updated Proceedings of a Conference at the Center for Contemporary Arab Studies, 28 April 1999* (Washington, DC: Georgetown University Center for Contemporary Arab Studies, 1999), pp. 7-9.

Faqih, Muhammad. *Takawwun al-taba'īyah al-sa'ūdīyah: qarā'ah tārīkhīyah sūsūlūjīyah fī takawwun al-taba'īyah fī al-jazīrah al-'arabīyah.* ("Formation of the Saudi Nationality: Socio-Historical Reading of the Formation of Nationality in the Arabian Peninsula.") Beirut: Maktabat al-faqīh, 1991.

Glubb, John Bagot. *War in the Desert: An R.A.F. Frontier Campaign.* London: Hodder and Stoughton, 1960.

Gold, Isador Jay. "The United States and Saudi Arabia, 1933-1953: Post-Imperial Diplomacy and the Legacy of British Power." Ph.D. dissertation, Columbia University, 1984.

Goldberg, Jacob. *The Foreign Policy of Saudi Arabia: The Formative Years, 1902-1918.* Cambridge, MA: Harvard University Press, 1986.

Goldrup, Lawrence Paul. "Saudi Arabia 1902-1932: The Development of a Wahhabi Society." Ph.D. dissertation, University of California, 1971.

Habib, John S. *Ibn Sa'ud's Warriors of Islam: The Ikhwan of Najd and Their Role in the Creation of the Sa'udi Kingdom, 1910-1930.* Leiden: E. J. Brill, 1978. Social, Economic and Political Studies of the Middle East, Vol. 27.

Hamad, Turki Hamad Turki Al-. "Political Order in Changing Societies; Saudi Arabia: Modernization in a Traditional Context." Ph.D. dissertation, University of Southern California, 1985.

Hart, Parker T. *Saudi Arabia and the United States: Birth of a Security Partnership.* Indianapolis: Indiana University Press, 1998. Published in association with the Association for Diplomatic Studies and Training.

Helms, Christine Moss. *The Cohesion of Saudi Arabia: Evolution of Political Identity.* London: Croom Helm; Baltimore: Johns Hopkins University Press, 1981.

Holden, David, and Richard Johns, with James Buchan. *The House of Saud: The Rise and Rule of the Most Powerful Dynasty in the Arab World.* New York: Holt, Rinehart and Winston, 1982.

Jazairi, Mohamed Zayyan Al-. "Saudi Arabia: A Diplomatic History, 1924-1964." Ph.D. dissertation. University of Utah, 1971.

Jubeir, Adel A. al-. "The Resilience of the Saudi State." *Middle East Insight*, Special Edition (1995), pp. 62-75.

Juma, Rabih Lutfi. *Ḥālat al-amn fī 'ahd al-mālik 'abd al-'azīz.* ("The Security Situation in the Time of King 'Abd al-'Aziz.") Riyadh: dārat al-mālik 'abd al-'azīz, 1982. Matbū'āt dārat al-mālik 'abd al-'azīz, No. 23.

Kedourie, Elie. "The Surrender of Medina, January 1919." *Middle Eastern Studies*, Vol. 13, No. 1 (1977), pp. 124-143.

Kelly, John B. *Eastern Arabian Frontiers.* London: Faber, 1964.

————. "Eastern Arabian Frontiers." *Middle Eastern Studies*, Vol. 1, No. 3 (1965), pp. 307-312.

————. "Sovereignty and Jurisdiction in Eastern Arabia." *International Affairs* (London), Vol. 34, No. 1 (1958), pp. 16-24.

Khatrash, Futuh 'Abd al-Muhsin al-. *Tārīkh al-'alāqāt al-sa'ūdīyah al-yamanīyah, 1927-1934.* ("History of Saudi-Yemeni Relations, 1927-1934.") Kuwait: Dhāt al-Silāsil, 1983.

Knauerhase, Ramon. "Saudi Arabia: Fifty-Five Years of Economic Change." *Current History* (January 1983), pp. 23, 35-36.

Kostiner, Joseph. *The Making of Saudi Arabia, 1916-1936: From Chieftaincy to Monarchical State.* New York: Oxford University Press, 1993.

————. "Britain and the Challenge of the Axis Powers in Arabia: The Decline of British-Saudi Cooperation in the 1930s." In Michael J. Cohen and Martin Kolinsky, eds., *Britain and the Middle East in the 1930s: Security Problems, 1935-39* (Houndmills, UK: Macmillan, 1992), pp. 128-143.

————. "The Hashimite 'Tribal Confederacy' of the Arab Revolt, 1916-1917." In Edward Ingram, ed., *National and International Politics in the Middle East: Essays in Honor of Elie Kedourie* (London: Frank Cass, 1986), pp. 126-143.

————. "Prologue of Hashemite Downfall and Saudi Ascendancy: A New Look at the Khurma Dispute, 1917-1919." In Asher Susser and Aryeh Shmuelevitz, eds., *The Hashemites in the Modern Arab World: A Festschrift in Honour of the Late Professor Uriel Dann* (London: Frank Cass, 1994), pp. 47-64.

————. "Tracing the Curves of Modern Saudi History." *Asian and African Studies*, Vol. 19, No. 2 (July 1985), pp. 219-244.

Krimly, Rayed Khalid. "The Political Economy of Rentier States: A Case Study of Saudi Arabia in the Oil Era, 1950-1990." Ph.D. dissertation, George Washington University, 1993.

Leatherdale, Clive. *Britain and Saudi Arabia, 1925-1939: The Imperial Oasis.* London: Frank Cass, 1983.

Lesch, D. "The Saudi Role in the American-Syrian Crisis of 1957." *Middle East Policy*, Vol. 1, No. 3 (1992), pp. 33-48.

Linabury, George Ogden. "British-Saudi Arab Relations, 1902-1927: A Revisionist Interpretation." Ph.D. dissertation, Columbia University, 1970.

Melamid, Alexander. "The Buraimi Oasis Dispute." *Middle East Affairs,* Vol. 7, No. 2 (1956), pp. 56-62.

Mousa, Suleiman. "Sharif Husayn and Developments Leading to the Arab Revolt." In R. B. Serjeant, R. L. Bidwell, and G. Rex Smith, eds., *New Arabian Studies*, Vol. 1 (Exeter: University of Exeter Press, 1993), pp. 36-53.

Nakamura, S. "The Ikhwan Movement and Tribal Politics (1912-1920)." *Annals of the Japan Association for Middle East Studies*, No. 15 (2000), pp. 127-152.

Nehme, Michel G. "Saudi Arabia 1950-80: Between Nationalism and Religion." *Middle Eastern Studies*, Vol. 30, No. 4 (October 1994), pp. 931-943.

Nuaim, Mishary Abdalrahman Al-. "State Building in a Non-Capitalist Social Formation: The Dialectics of Two Modes of Production and the Role of the Merchant Class, Saudi Arabia 1902-1932." Ph.D. dissertation, University of California, Los Angeles, 1986.

Pfullmann, U. "Thronfolge in Saudi-Arabien: Vom Anfang der wahhabitischen Bewegung bis 1953; Der matrilinearer Background im 'Abd al-'Aziz-Zweig der Al Sa'ud-Dynastie." *Archiv Oriental*, Vol. 63, No. 3 (1995), pp. 162-179.

Podeh, Elie. "Ending an Age-Old Rivalry: The Rapprochement Between the Hashemites and the Saudis, 1956-1958." In Asher Susser and Aryeh Shmuelevitz, eds., *The Hashemites in the Modern Arab World: A Festschrift in Honour of the Late Professor Uriel Dann* (London: Frank Cass, 1994), pp. 85-108.

Rasheed, Madawi al-, and Loulouwa al-Rasheed. "The Politics of Encapsulation: Saudi Policy Towards Tribal and Religious Opposition." *Middle Eastern Studies*, Vol. 32, No. 1 (1996), pp. 96-119.

Rashid, Ibrahim al-, ed. *Documents on the History of Saudi Arabia*. Salisbury, NC: Documentary Publications, 1976. 3 vols.

———, ed. *Saudi Arabia Enters the Modern World: Secret U. S. Documents on the Emergence of the Kingdom of Saudi Arabia as a World Power, 1936-1949*. Salisbury, NC: Documentary Publications, 1980. Documents on the History of Saudi Arabia, Vols. 4-5.

———, ed. *The Struggle Between the Two Princes: The Kingdom of Saudi Arabia in the Final Days of Ibn Saud*. Salisbury, NC: Documentary Publications, 1985. Documents on the History of Arabia, Vol. 8.

Rawaf, Othman Yasin al-. "The Concept of the Five Crises in Political Development—Relevance to the Kingdom of Saudi Arabia." Ph.D. dissertation, Duke University, 1980.

———. "Islam, Modernity, and Moderation: Saudi Arabia's Unifying Force." *Middle East Insight*, Special Edition (1995), pp. 90-95.

Ruwaithy, Abdulmuhsin Rajallah al-. "American and British Aid to Saudi Arabia, 1928-1945." Ph.D. dissertation, University of Texas at Austin, 1990.

Sanger, Richard H. "Ibn Saud's Program for Arabia." *Middle East Journal*, Vol. 1, No. 1 (1947), pp. 180-190.

Saud, HRH Prince Torki M. Saud. "The Great Achievement: King 'Abd al-'Aziz and the Founding of the Third Su'udi State, 1902-1932." Ph.D. thesis, University of London, School of Oriental and African Studies, 1983.

Saudi Arabia. *Arbitration for the Settlement of the Territorial Dispute Between Muscat and Abu Dhabi on One Side and Saudi Arabia on the Other: Memorial*. Riyadh, 31 July 1955.

Sayyid, 'Isam Diya' al-Din al-. *'Asīr fī al-'alāqāt al-sīyāsīyah al-sa'ūdīyah al-yamanīyah (1338-1373/1919-1934)*. ("'Asir in Saudi-Yemeni Political Relations [1338-1373/1919-1934].") Cairo: Dār al-Zahrā', 1989.

Shamlan, Abdulrahman Rashid al-. "The Evolution of National Boundaries in the Southeastern Arabian Peninsula, 1934-1955." Ph.D. dissertation, University of Michigan, 1987.

Shamsi, Saeed Mohammad Al-. "The Al-Buraimi Dispute: A Case Study in Inter-Arab Politics." Ph.D. dissertation, American University, 1987.

Shebl, Abdlaziz S. "The Emergence and Demise of an Independent Arab State: The Kingdom of the Hejaz, 1916-1925." Ph.D. dissertation, University of California, Los Angeles, 1988.

Silverfarb, Daniel Nolan. "British Relations with Ibn Saud of Najd, 1914-1919." Ph.D. dissertation, University of Wisconsin, 1972.

―――. "The Anglo-Najd Treaty of December 1915." *Middle Eastern Studies*, Vol. 16, No. 3 (1980), pp. 167-177.

Soulié, G. Jean-Louis, and Lucien Champenois. *Le royaume d'Arabie Saoudite face à l'Islam révolutionnaire 1953-1964*. Paris: A. Colin, 1966.

Teitelbaum, Joshua. *The Rise and Fall of the Hashemite Kingdom of Arabia*. London: C. Hurst, for the Tel Aviv University Moshe Dayan Center, 2001.

―――. "Pilgrimage Politics: The Hajj and Saudi-Hashemite Rivalry, 1916-1925." In Asher Susser and Aryeh Shmuelevitz, eds., *The Hashemites in the Modern Arab World: A Festschrift in Honour of the Late Professor Uriel Dann* (London: Frank Cass, 1994), pp. 65-84.

―――. "Sharif Husayn ibn 'Ali and the Hashemite Vision of the Post-Ottoman Order: From Chieftaincy to Suzerainty." *Middle Eastern Studies*, Vol. 34, No. 1 (January 1998), pp. 103-122.

―――. "'Taking Back' the Caliphate: Sharif Husayn ibn 'Ali, Mustafa Kemal, and the Ottoman Caliphate." *Die Welt des Islams*, Vol. 40, No. 3 (2000), pp. 412-424.

Toulik, Suliman Ibrahim. "The Emergence of a National Identity in Saudi Arabia." Ph.D. dissertation, University of Idaho, 1985.

Troeller, Gary. *The Birth of Saudi Arabia: Britain and the Rise of the House of Sa'ud.* London: Frank Cass, 1976.

United Kingdom. Admiralty. Admiralty War Staff. Intelligence Division. *A Handbook of Arabia.* London: Prepared on behalf of the Admiralty and the War Office, Vol. 1: 1916, Vol. 2: 1917.

―――. Admiralty. Naval Intelligence Division. *Western Arabia and the Red Sea.* Oxford: HMSO, 1946. Geographical Handbook Series, B.R. 527.

Wasti, Syed Tanvir. "Muhammad Inshaullah and the Hijaz Railway." *Middle Eastern Studies*, Vol. 34, No. 2 (April 1998), pp. 60-73.

Yizraeli, Sarah. *The Remaking of Saudi Arabia: The Struggle Between King Sa'ud and Crown Prince Faysal, 1953-1962*. Tel Aviv: Tel Aviv University Moshe Dayan Center for Middle Eastern and African Studies, 1997. Moshe Dayan Center, No. 121.

Zaid, Abdulla S. "The Ikhwan Movement of Najd, Saudi Arabia, 1908-1930." Ph.D. dissertation, University of Chicago, 1989.

Zirkali, Khayr al-Din al-. *Shibh al-jazīrah fī 'ahd al-mālik 'abd al-'azīz.* ("The Arabian Peninsula in the Time of King 'Abd al-'Aziz.") 3rd ed.; Beirut: Dār al-'ilm lil-milāyīn, 1985. 2 vols.

BIOGRAPHY AND AUTOBIOGRAPHY

Algosaibi, Ghazi A. *Yes, (Saudi) Minister! A Life in Administration.* London: London Centre of Arab Studies, 1999. First published as *Hayah fīl-Idārah* (Beirut: Mu'assasah al-'Arabīyah lil-Dirāsat wal-Nashr, 1998). English ed. edited by William Facey, from a translation by Martin and Leila Asser of Arabic ed.

Almana, Mohammed. *Arabia Unified: A Portrait of Ibn Saud.* London: Hutchinson, Benham, 1980. Rev. ed., 1982.

Armstrong, Harold C. *Lord of Arabia: Ibn Saud, an Intimate Study of a King.* London: Penguin, 1938.

Barrett, William P. "I'm Not Finished Yet." *Forbes*, Vol. 142, No. 3 (8 August 1988), pp. 86ff.

Beckingham, Charles. "The Arabian Travels of Johann Wild." In G. Rex Smith, J. R. Smart, and B. R. Pridham, eds., *New Arabian Studies*, Vol. 3 (Exeter: University of Exeter Press, 1996), pp. 8-13.

Bidwell, Robin. "Non-Peninsular Arabs in the Service of Ibn Sa'ud." In André Gingrich et al., eds., *Studies in Oriental Culture and History: Festschrift for Walter Dostal* (Frankfurt: Peter Lang Verlag, 1993), pp. 222-241.

Bullard, Reader. *The Camels Must Go: An Autobiography.* London: Faber and Faber, 1961.

———. Ed. by E. C. Hodgkin. *Two Kings in Arabia: Sir Reader Bullard's Letters from Jeddah.* Reading: Ithaca Press, 1995.

Carmichael, Joel. "Prince of Arabs: Ibn Saud." *Foreign Affairs*, Vol. 20, No. 4 (1942), pp. 719-731.

Carter, J. R. L. *Leading Merchant Families of Saudi Arabia.* London: Scorpion Publications, 1979. 2nd ed., revised and updated as *Merchant Families of Saudi Arabia.* London: Scorpion Books, 1984.

de Gaury, Gerald. *Faisal: King of Saudi Arabia.* New York: Frederick A. Praeger, 1966; London: Arthur Barker, 1966.

Duguid, Stephen. "A Biographical Approach to the Study of Social Change in the Middle East: Abdullah Tariki as a New Man." *International Journal of Middle East Studies*, Vol. 1, No. 3 (July 1970), pp. 195-220.

Fandy, Mamoun. "Safar al-Hawali: Saudi Islamist or Saudi Nationalist?" *Islam and Christian-Muslim Relations*, Vol. 9, No. 1 (March 1998), pp. 5-23.

Goldberg, Jacob. "Captain Shakespear and Ibn Saud: A Balanced Reappraisal." *Middle Eastern Studies*, Vol. 22, No. 1 (January 1986), pp. 74-88.

———. "Philby as a Source for Early Twentieth-Century Saudi History: A Critical Examination." *Middle Eastern Studies*, Vol. 21, No. 2 (April 1985), pp. 223-243.

Howarth, David. *The Desert King: A Life of Ibn Saud.* London: Collins, 1964.

Kashmeeri, Bakor Omar. "Ibn Saud: The Arabian Nation-Builder." Ph.D. dissertation, Howard University, 1973.

Kelly, J. B. "Jeux sans frontieres: Philby's Travels in Southern Arabia." C. E. Bosworth et al., eds., *The Islamic World from Classical to Modern Times: Essays in Honor of Bernard Lewis* (Princeton, NJ: Darwin Press, 1988), pp. 701-732.

Kessler, Ronald. *The Richest Man in the World: The Story of Adnan Khashoggi.* New York: Warner, 1986.

Khadduri, Majid. *Arab Personalities in Politics.* Washington, DC: Middle East Institute, 1981.

Khaled Bin Sultan, HRH. *Desert Warrior.* London: HarperCollins, 1994.

Kortepeter, C. Max. "The Rise of King 'Abd al-'Aziz ibn Sa'ud During the Era of Ottoman Sultan 'Abd al-Hamid II (1876-1909)." In C. E. Bosworth et al., eds., *The Islamic World from Classical to Modern Times: Essays in Honor of Bernard Lewis* (Princeton, NJ: Darwin Press, 1988), pp. 733-770.

Lees, Brian. *Handbook of the Al Saud Ruling Family of Saudi Arabia.* London: Royal Genealogies, 1980.

McLoughlin, Leslie. *Ibn Saud: Founder of a Kingdom.* London: Macmillan Press for St. Antony's College, Oxford; New York: St. Martin's Press, 1993.

Monroe, Elizabeth. *Philby of Arabia.* London: Faber and Faber, 1973.

Osaimi, Mohammed 'Abd Al-Mohsen Al-. "The Persuasion of King Faisal Ibn 'Abd al-'Aziz: A Case Study in Contemporary Islamic Oratory." Ph.D. dissertation, Indiana University, 1990.

Peskes, Esther. *Muhammad b. 'Abdalwahhab (1703-92) in Widerstreit: Untersuchungen zur Reckonstruktion der Fruhgeschichte der Saudi-Arabien.* Stuttgart: Franz Steiner Verlag, 1993.

Philby, H. St. John. B. *Arabian Days.* London: Robert Hale, 1948.

———. *Forty Years in the Wilderness.* London: Robert Hale, 1957.

———. *A Pilgrim in Arabia.* London: Robert Hale, 1946.

Pollock, David. "Saudi Arabia's King Khaled and King Fahd." In Barbara Kellerman and Jeffrey Z. Rubin, eds., *Leadership and Negotiation in the Middle East* (New York: Praeger, in cooperation with Society for the Psychological Study of Social Issues, 1988), pp. 140-165.

Rentz, George S. "Muhammad ibn 'Abd al-Wahhab (1703/04-1792) and the Beginnings of the Unitarian Empire in Arabia." Ph.D. dissertation, University of California, Berkeley, 1948.

Rihani, Ameen Fares. *Ibn Saud of Arabia: His People and His Land.* London: Constable, 1928.

Royce, Knut. "Family Feud, Saudi Style." *The Nation,* Vol. 253, No. 23 (30 December 1991), pp. 844ff.

Shahid, Irfan. "Amin al-Rihani and King 'Abdul-'Aziz Ibn Sa'ud." In George N. Atiyeh and Ibrahim M. Oweiss, eds., *Arab Civilization: Challenges and Responses: Studies in Honor of Constantine K. Zurayk* (Albany: State University of New York Press, 1988), pp. 231-240.

Sheean, Vincent. *Faisal: The King and His Kingdom.* Tavistock, Devon: University Press of Arabia, 1975.

Sobh, Samir. "Arabie Saoudite: Les Seize Familles Qui Comptent." *Arabies,* No. 145 (January 1999), pp. 36-43.

Sullivan, R. Lee. "The World's Billionaires: Saudi Arabia." *Forbes,* Vol. 150, No. 2 (20 July 1992), pp. 214ff.

Uthaymin, Abd-Allah Salih al-. "Muhammad Ibn Abd-al-Wahhab: The Man and His Works." Ph.D. thesis, University of Edinburgh, 1972.

Williams, Kenneth. *Ibn Saud: The Puritan King of Arabia.* London: Jonathan Cape, 1933.

Yamani, Hani A. Z. *To Be a Saudi*. London: Janus, 1997.
Zirkali, Khayr al-Din al-. *Al-I'lām: qāmūs tarājim li-ashhar al-rijāl wa-nasā' min al-'arab wal-must 'arabin wal-mustasharaqūn*. ("al-I'lam [Personalities]: Biographical Dictionary of the Most Famous Arab, Arabist, and Orientalist Men and Women.") Beirut: Dār al-'ilm lil-malāyīn, 1984.

POLITICS AND GOVERNMENT

Aba-Namay, Rashed. "The New Saudi Representative Assembly." *Islamic Law and Society*, Vol. 5, No. 2 (June 1998), pp. 235-265.
Abir, Mordechai. *Saudi Arabia in the 1990s: Stability and Foreign Policy*. Jerusalem: Jerusalem Center for Public Affairs, 1 September 1997. Jerusalem Letters, No. 365. Online.
———. *Saudi Arabia in the Oil Era: Regimes and Élites—Conflict and Collaboration*. Boulder, CO: Westview Press, 1988. Revised as *Saudi Arabia: Government, Society and the Gulf Crises*. London: Routledge, 1993.
———. "The Consolidation of the Ruling Class and the New Elites in Saudi Arabia." *Middle Eastern Studies*, Vol. 23, No. 2 (April 1987), pp. 150-171.
Aburish, Said. *The Rise, Corruption and Coming Fall of the House of Saud*. London: Bloomsbury, 1994.
Abussund, Alawi Nuri. "Administrative Development and Planning in Saudi Arabia." Ph.D. dissertation, University of Maryland, 1979.
Ahrari, M. Ehsan. "The Future of Political Stability in Saudi Arabia." *Mediterranean Quarterly*, Vol. 8, No. 3 (Summer 1997), pp. 100-114.
Al Saud, Mashaal Abdullah Turki. "Permanence and Change: An Analysis of the Islamic Political Culture of Saudi Arabia As It Faces the Challenges of Development with Special Reference to the Royal Family." Ph.D. dissertation, Claremont Graduate School, 1982.
Alfaleh, Matrook. "The Impact of the Processes of Modernization and Social Mobilization on the Social and Political Structures of the Arab Countries with Special Emphasis on Saudi Arabia." Ph.D. dissertation, University of Kansas, 1987.
Amnesty International, USA. *Saudi Arabia: Detention Without Trial of Suspected Political Prisoners*. New York: January 1990.
Article 19. *Silent Kingdom: Freedom of Expression in Saudi Arabia*. London, October 1991. An Article 19 Country Report.
Awaji, Ibrahim al-. "Bureaucracy and Development in Saudi Arabia: The Case of Local Administration." In Joseph G. Jabbra, ed., *Bureaucracy and Development in the Arab World* (Kinderhook, NY: E. J. Brill, 1989; International Studies in Sociology and Social Anthropology, No. 51), pp. 49-61.
Awaji, Ibrahim Mohamed. "Bureaucracy and Society in Saudi Arabia." Ph.D. dissertation, University of Virginia, 1971.
Bahout, J. "Si l'Arabie doit rester séoudite..." *Les Cahiers de l'Orient*, Nos. 25-26 (1992), pp. 71-106.

Bin-Obaid, Ahmad Sulaiman. "Regional Development in Saudi Arabia: The Government's Role." Ph.D. dissertation, University of Nebraska, Lincoln, 1992.

Bligh, Alexander. *From Prince to King: Royal Succession in the House of Saud in the Twentieth Century.* New York: New York University Press, 1984.

———. "The Interplay Between Opposition Activity in Saudi Arabia and Recent Trends in the Arab World." In Robert W. Stookey, ed., *The Arabian Peninsula: Zone of Ferment* (Stanford, CA: Hoover Institution Press, 1984), pp. 65-78.

———. "The Saudi Religious Elite (Ulama) as Participants in the Political System of the Kingdom." *International Journal of Middle East Studies*, Vol. 17, No. 1 (February 1985), pp. 37-50.

Caesar, Judith. "Rumblings Under the Throne." *The Nation*, Vol. 251, No. 21 (17 December 1990), pp. 762-764.

Champion, Daryl. *The Paradoxical Kingdom: Saudi Arabia and the Momentum of Reform.* Abingdon, UK: Hurst, 2002.

———. "The Kingdom of Saudi Arabia: Elements of Instability Within Stability." *MERIA: Middle East Review of International Affairs*, Vol. 3, No. 4 (December 1999), online.

Chapman, Richard A. "Administrative Reform in Saudi Arabia." *Journal of Administration Overseas*, Vol. 13, No. 2 (April 1974), pp. 332-347.

Chubin, Shahram, ed. *Domestic Political Factors.* London: Gower, for the International Institute for Strategic Studies, 1981. Security in the Persian Gulf, No. 1.

Dekmejian, R. Hrair. "The Rise of Political Islamism in Saudi Arabia." *Middle East Journal*, Vol. 48, No. 4 (Autumn 1994), pp. 627-643.

———. "Saudi Arabia's Consultative Council." *Middle East Journal*, Vol. 52, No. 2 (Spring 1998), pp. 204-218.

Dunn, Michael Collins. "Is the Sky Falling? Saudi Arabia's Economic Problems and Political Stability." *Middle East Policy*, Vol. 3, No. 4 (1995), pp. 29-39.

Edens, David G. "The Anatomy of the Saudi Revolution." *International Journal of Middle East Studies*, Vol. 5, No. 1 (1974), pp. 50-64.

Edwards, Lynda. "A Royal Pain." *Regardie's Magazine*, Vol. 11, No. 7 (April-May 1991), pp. 40ff.

Eilts, Hermann Frederick. "Saudi Arabia: Traditionalism versus Modernism—A Royal Dilemma?" In Peter J. Chelkowski and Robert J. Pranger, eds., *Ideology and Power in the Middle East: Studies in Honor of George Lenczowski* (Durham, NC: Duke University Press, 1988), pp. 56-88.

———. "Social Revolution in Saudi Arabia." *Parameters, Journal of the Army War College.* Part I in Vol. 1, No. 1 (Spring 1971), pp. 4-18; Part II in Vol. 1, No. 2 (Fall 1971), pp. 22-33.

Entelis, John. "Oil Wealth and the Prospects for Democratization in the Arabian Peninsula: The Case of Saudi Arabia." In Naiem A. Sherbiny and Mark A. Tessler, eds., *Arab Oil: Impact on the Arab Countries and Global Implications* (New York: Praeger, 1976), pp. 77-101.

Faksh, Mahmud A. *The Future of Islam in the Middle East: Fundamentalism in Egypt, Algeria, and Saudi Arabia.* Westport, Conn: Praeger, 1997.

Fandy, Mamoun. *Saudi Arabia and the Politics of Dissent*. New York: St. Martin's Press; Basingstoke, UK: Macmillan, 1999.
———. "From Confrontation to Creative Resistance: The Shi'a Oppositional Discourse in Saudi Arabia." *Critique*, No. 9 (Fall 1996), pp. 1-27.
Farsy, Fouad al-. *Qadāya siyāsīyah mu'āsirah*. ("Contemporary Political Problems.") Jiddah: Tihama, 1982. al-Kitāb al-'arabī al-sa'ūdī, No. 61.
Feuillet, Claude. *Le système Saoud.* Lausanne: P.-M. Faure, 1983.
Fürtig, H. "Transformationsmodelle zum Kapitalismus: Revolution/Reform von oben in Iran and Saudi-Arabian." *Asia Africa-Lateinamerica*, Vol. 16, No. 2 (1988), pp. 264-272.
Ghamdi, Saleh Ahmed A. al-. "Leaders' Situational Control in the Public and Private Sectors in Saudi Arabia." Ph.D. dissertation, University of Denver, 1989.
Hamad, Turki Hamad Turki Al-. "Political Order in Changing Societies; Saudi Arabia: Modernization in a Traditional Context." Ph.D. dissertation, University of Southern California, 1985.
Harrington, Charles W. "The Saudi Arabian Council of Ministers." *Middle East Journal*, Vol. 12, No. 1 (1958), pp. 1-19.
Hazzaa, Sultan Mohammad al-. "Public Personnel Administration in the Civil Service of Saudi Arabia: Policies, Procedures and Practices." Ph.D. thesis, University of Exeter, 1992.
Hegelan, Abdelrahman Abdelaziz Al-. "Innovation in the Saudi Arabian Bureaucracy: A Survey Analysis of Senior Bureaucrats." Ph.D. dissertation, Florida State University, 1984.
Hegelan, Abdelrahman al-, and Monte Palmer. "Bureaucracy and Development in Saudi Arabia." *Middle East Journal*, Vol. 39, No. 1 (Winter 1985), pp. 48-68.
Heller, Mark, and Nadav Safran. *The New Middle Class and Regime Stability in Saudi Arabia.* Cambridge, MA: Harvard University, Center for Middle Eastern Studies, 1985. Harvard Middle East Papers, Modern Series, No. 3.
Henderson, Simon. *After King Fahd: Succession in Saudi Arabia.* Washington, DC: Washington Institute for Near East Policy, 1994. Washington Institute Policy Papers, No. 37.
Herb, Michael. *All in the Family: Absolutism, Revolution, and Democratic Prospects in the Middle Eastern Monarchies.* Albany: State University of New York Press, 1999.
Hersh, Seymour M. "King's Ransom." *New Yorker*, 22 October 2001, pp. 35-39.
Hiro, Dilip. "Saudi Dissenters Go Public." *The Nation*, Vol. 256, No. 25 (28 June 1993), pp. 906ff.
———. "Too Little and 32 Years Late." *The Nation*, Vol. 254, No. 14 (13 April 1992), pp. 484ff.
Huyette, Summer Scott. *Political Adaptation in Sa'udi Arabia: A Study of the Council of Ministers.* Boulder, CO: Westview Press, 1985. Westview Special Studies on the Middle East.
Islami, A. Reza S., and Rostam Mehraban Kavoussi. *The Political Economy of Saudi Arabia.* Seattle: University of Washington, 1984. Near Eastern Studies, No. 1.

Jerichow, Anders. *Saudi Arabia: Outside Global Law and Order; A Discussion Paper*. Richmond, UK: Curzon Press, 1997.

———. *The Saudi File: People, Power and Politics*. Richmond, UK: Curzon Press; New York: St. Martin's Press, 1997.

Jordan, Amos A., Jr. "Saudi Arabia: The Next Iran?" *Parameters: Journal of the US Army War College*, Vol. 9, No. 1 (March 1979), pp. 2-8.

Katz, Mark N. "Assessing Saudi Susceptibility to Revolution." In Joseph A. Kechichian, ed., *Iran, Iraq, and the Arab Gulf States* (New York: Palgrave, 2001), pp. 95-110.

Katzman, Kenneth. "How Stable Are Saudi Arabia and Kuwait?" *Middle East Quarterly*, Vol. 1, No. 3 (1994), pp. 21-29.

Kechichian, Joseph A. *Succession in Saudi Arabia*. New York: Palgrave, April 2001.

———. "Saudi Arabia's Will to Power." *Middle East Policy*, Vol. 7, No. 2 (February 2000), pp. 47-60.

———. "The Role of Al Saud in State Building." In *Saudi Arabia: One Hundred Years Later; Revised and Updated Proceedings of a Conference at the Center for Contemporary Arab Studies, 28 April 1999* (Washington, DC: Georgetown University Center for Contemporary Arab Studies, 1999), pp. 1-5.

Kelidar, A. R. "The Problem of Succession in Saudi Arabia." *Asian Affairs* (London), Vol. 65 (N. S. 9), Pt. 1 (February 1978), pp. 23-30.

Kern, Nathaniel. "Saudi Arabia Prepares for the 21st Century: New Institutions Ensure Public's Role in Government." *Middle East Insight*, Special Edition (1995), pp. 76-83.

Khairallah, N. "L'Arabie Séoudite: quelles perspectives pour quel futur?" *Cahiers de l'Orient*, No. 28 (1992), pp. 127-143.

Khashoggi, Hani Yousef. "Local Administration in Saudi Arabia." Ph.D. dissertation, Claremont Graduate School, 1979.

Kostiner, Joseph. "State, Islam, and Opposition in Saudi Arabia: The Post-Desert Storm Phase." *MERIA: Middle East Review of International Affairs*, No. 2 (1997), online. Reprinted as "State, Islam, and Opposition in Saudi Arabia: The Post-Desert Storm Phase." In Bruce Maddy-Weitzmann and Ephraim Inbar, eds., *Religious Radicalism in the Greater Middle East* (London: Frank Cass, 1997), pp. 75-89.

Koury, Enver M. *The Saudi Decision-Making Body*. Hyattsville, MD: Institute of Middle Eastern and North African Affairs, 1978.

Kramer, Martin. "Tragedy in Mecca." *Orbis*, Vol. 32, No. 2 (Spring 1988), pp. 231-247.

Lackner, Helen. *A House Built on Sand: A Political Economy of Saudi Arabia*. London: Ithaca Press, 1978.

Laswad, Said Ali. "Political Consciousness and Regime Longevity in the Middle East: A Comparative Analysis of the Monarchies of Libya and Saudi Arabia." Ph.D. dissertation, University of Idaho, 1993.

Levallois, A. "Arabie Séoudite: une royaume menacé?" *Cahiers de l'Orient*, No. 29 (1993), pp. 63-71.

Long, David Edwin. "The Board of Grievances in Saudi Arabia." *Middle East Journal*, Vol. 27, No. 1 (1973), pp. 71-76.

————. "Saudi Arabia in the 1990s: Plus ça Change." In Charles E. Doran and
     Stephen W. Buck, eds., *The Gulf, Energy, and Global Security: Political
     and Economic Issues* (Boulder, CO: Lynne Rienner, 1991), pp. 85-106.
McMillan, Joseph. "Saudi Arabia: Culture, Legitimacy, and Political Reform."
     Global Affairs, Vol. 7 (Spring 1992), pp. 56-75.
Mizjaji, Ahmad Dawood Al-. "The Public Attitudes Toward the Bureaucracy
     in Saudi Arabia." Ph.D. dissertation, Florida State University, 1982.
Mugren, Mohamed al-. "Field Administration in Saudi Arabia in Comparative
     Perspective: The Past and Present." Ph.D. thesis, University of Exeter, 1993?
Naba, R. "Arabie Séoudite: Perspectives au 2000." *Cahiers de l'Orient*, No. 29
     (1993), pp. 73-92.
Nazer, Hisham M. "Institution-Building in Developing Countries." In Ibrahim
     Ibrahim, ed., *Arab Resources: The Transformation of a Society* (Washington,
     DC: Georgetown University Center for Contemporary Arab Studies; London:
     Croom Helm, 1983), pp. 105-113.
Nehme, Michel G. "Political Development in Saudi Arabia: Empty Reforms from
     Above." *International Sociology*, Vol. 10, No. 2 (June 1995), pp. 155-171.
————. "The Shifting Sands of Political Participation in Saudi Arabia." *Orient*,
     Vol. 36, No. 1 (1995), pp. 45-60.
Nevo, Joseph. "The Saudi Royal Family: The Third Generation." *Jerusalem
     Quarterly*, No. 31 (Spring 1984), pp. 79-90.
Obaid, Nawaf. "The Power of Saudi Arabia's Islamic Leaders." *Middle East
     Quarterly*, Vol. 6, No. 3 (September 1999), pp. 51-58.
Okruhlik, Mary Gwenn. "Debating Profits and Political Power: Private Business
     and Government in Saudi Arabia." Ph.D. dissertation, University of Texas
     at Austin, 1992.
Otaibi, Saud al-. "Political Development, Bureaucracy, and Saudi Culture." Ph.D.
     dissertation, Florida State University, 1992.
Othman, Osama A. "Saudi Arabia: An Unprecedented Growth of Wealth With
     an Unparalleled Growth of Bureaucracy." *International Review of
     Administrative Sciences*, Vol. 45, No. 3 (1979), pp. 234-240.
Palmer, Monte, Abdelrahman al-Hegelan, Mohammed Bushara Abdelrahman,
     Ali Leila, and El Sayeed Yassin. "Bureaucratic Innovation and Economic
     Development in the Middle East: A Study of Egypt, Saudi Arabia, and the
     Sudan." In Joseph G. Jabbra, ed., *Bureaucracy and Development in the Arab
     World* (Kinderhook, NY: E. J. Brill, 1989; International Studies in Sociology
     and Social Anthropology, No. 51), pp. 12-27.
Paul, Jim. "Insurrection at Mecca." *MERIP Reports*, No. 91 (October 1980),
     pp. 3-4.
Peterson, J. E. "Saudi Arabia at the Threshold." In David Partington, ed., *The
     Middle East Annual: Issues and Events, Vol. 4—1984* (Boston: G. K. Hall,
     1985), pp. 53-82.
Pfaff, Richard. "The Kingdom of Saudi Arabia." In Tareq Y. Ismael and Jacqueline
     S. Ismael, eds., *Politics and Government in the Middle East and North Africa*
     (Miami: Florida International University Press, 1991), pp. 385-414.
"Pride and Prejudice in Saudi Arabia: Interview with Ahmad and Fatima Abdullah
     (pseud.)." *MERIP Middle East Report*, Vol. 23, No. 6 (1993), pp. 18-20.

Rasheed, Madawi al-. "God, the King and the Nation: Political Rhetoric in Saudi Arabia in the 1990s." *Middle East Journal*, Vol. 50, No. 3 (Summer 1996), pp. 360-371.
———. "Saudi Arabia's Islamic Opposition." *Current History*, Vol. 95, No. 597 (January 1996), pp. 16-22.
Rathmell, Andrew, and Mustafa Alani. "Saudi Arabia: The Threat from Within." *Jane's Intelligence Review*, Special Report No. 12 (1996).
Rawaf, Othman Y al-. "The Structure of the Saudi Government." *Middle East Insight*, Vol. 3, No. 1 (1983), pp. 28-32.
Rouleau, Eric. "Trouble in the Kingdom." *Foreign Affairs*, Vol. 81, No. 4 (July-August 2002), pp. 75-89.
Sadiq, Muhammad Tawfiq. *Taṭawwur al-ḥukm wal-idārah fī al-mamlakah al-'arabīyah al-sa'ūdīyah* ("Development of the Government and Administration in the Kingdom of Saudi Arabia.") Riyadh: Ma'had al-idārah al-'ammah, 1385/1965.
Salameh, Ghassane. "Political Power and the Saudi State." Tr. from the French by Vivian Steir. *MERIP Reports*, No. 91 (October 1980), pp. 5-22. Revised as "Political Power and the Saudi State." In Berch Berberoglu, ed., *Power and Stability in the Middle East* (London: Zed Books, 1989), pp. 70-89.
Saleh, Nassir A. "The Emergence of Saudi Arabian Administrative Areas: A Study in Political Geography." Ph.D. thesis, University of Durham, 1975.
Salem, Abdullah Abdulkareem al-. "A Case Study of the Organizational Culture of the Makkah Municipality in the Context of the Saudi Society." Ph.D. dissertation, Temple University, 1996.
Samore, Gary Samuel. "Royal Family Politics in Saudi Arabia (1953-1982)." Ph.D. dissertation, Harvard University, 1983.
Sankari, Farouk A. "Islam and Politics in Saudi Arabia." In Ali E. Hilal Dessouki, ed., *Islamic Resurgence in the Arab World* (New York: Praeger, 1982), pp. 178-193.
Seflan, Ali Mashhor Al-. "The Essence of Tribal Leaders' Participation, Responsibilities, and Decisions in Some Local Government Activities in Saudi Arabia: A Case Study of the Ghamid and Zahran Tribes." Ph.D. dissertation, Claremont Graduate School, 1980.
Shaked, Haim. "The Islamic Revolution—Is Saudi Arabia Next?" In George S. Wise and Charles Issawi, eds., *Middle East Perspectives: The Next Twenty Years* (Princeton, NJ: Darwin Press, 1981), pp. 141-146.
Shaker, Fatina Amin. "Modernization of the Developing Nations: The Case of Saudi Arabia." Ph.D. dissertation, Purdue University, 1972.
Shaw, John A. "Saudi Arabia Comes of Age." *Washington Quarterly*, Vol. 5, No. 2 (1982), pp. 151-156.
Shaw, John A., and David E. Long. *Saudi Arabian Modernization: The Impact of Change on Stability.* New York: Praeger, with the Georgetown University Center for Strategic and International Studies, 1982. Washington Papers, No. 89.
Shaykh, A. al-, S. al-Dakhil, and A. al-Zayr. *Intifāḍat al-mintaqah al-sharqīyah.* ("The Intifadah in the Eastern Province.") London, 1981.
Sheean, Vincent. "King Faisal's First Year." *Foreign Affairs*, Vol. 44, No. 2 (1966), pp. 304-313.

Siddiq, Mohammed H. *Why the Boom Went Bust: An Analysis of the Saudi Government*. Lincoln, NE: privately printed, 1995.
Simmons, Geoff. *Saudi Arabia: The Shape of a Client Feudalism*. New York: St. Martin's Press, 1998.
Sunari, Muhammad 'Abd al-'Al al-. *Al-qararāt al-idārīyah fī al-mamlakah al-'arabīyah al-sa 'ūdīyah*. ("Administrative Decisions in the Kingdom of Saudi Arabia.") Saudi Arabia: General Administration Institute, 1994.
Tahtinen, Dale R. *National Security Challenges to Saudi Arabia*. Washington, DC: American Enterprise Institute for Public Policy Research, 1978. AEI Studies, No. 194.
Tawail, Mohammed Abdulrahman al-. "Institute of Public Administration in Saudi Arabia: A Case Study in Institution Building." Ph.D. dissertation, West Virginia University, 1974.
Tawati, Ahmed Mohamed. "The Civil Service of Saudi Arabia: Problems and Prospects." Ph.D. dissertation, West Virginia University, 1976.
Tbeileh, Faisal. "The Political Economy of Legitimacy in Rentier States: A Comparative Study of Saudi Arabia and Libya." Ph.D. dissertation, University of California, Los Angeles, 1991.
Teitelbaum, Joshua. *Holier Than Thou: Saudi Arabia's Islamic Opposition*. Washington, DC: Washington Institute for Near East Policy, 2000.
Usmani, Abdulrazak Al-. "An Analytical Comparative Study of Television Systems and Decision-Making Processes in Four Arabian Gulf States (Saudi Arabia, Kuwait, Bahrain and Qatar)." Ph.D. dissertation, University of Wisconsin, Madison, 1984.
Viorst, Milton. "The Storm and the Citadel." *Foreign Affairs*, Vol. 75, No. 1 (January-February 1996), pp. 93-107.
Walsh, Elsa. "Louis Freeh's Last Case." *New Yorker Magazine* (14 May 2001), pp. 68ff.
Wenner, Manfred W. "Saudi Arabia: Survival of Traditional Elites." In Frank Tachau, ed., *Political Elites and Political Development in the Middle East* (New York: John Wiley, 1975), pp. 159-190.
Wilson, Peter W., and D. F. Graham. *Saudi Arabia: The Coming Storm*. London: M. E. Sharp, 1994.
Winder, Bayly. "Saudi Arabia: Sociopolitical Developments." *AEI Foreign Policy and Defense Review*, Vol. 2, Nos. 3-4 (1980), pp. 14-20.
Yamani, Mai. "Middle East Prospects – Saudi Arabia: Awakening." *The World Today*, Vol. 56, No. 12 (December 2000), pp. 21-22.
Yaphe, Judith S. *Saudi Arabia: Uncertain Stability; Persian Gulf Futures III*. Washington, DC: National Defense University, Institute for National Strategic Studies, 1997. Strategic Forum, No. 125.
Yassini, Ayman Al-. *Religion and State in the Kingdom of Saudi Arabia*. Boulder, CO: Westview Press, 1985.

LAW

Aba-Namay, Rashed. "Constitutional Reform: A Systemization of Saudi Politics." *Journal of South Asian and Middle Eastern Studies*, Vol. 16, No. 3 (Spring 1993), pp. 43-88.

————. "The Dynamics of Individual Rights and Their Prospective Development Under the New Constitution of Saudi Arabia." *Journal of South Asian and Middle Eastern Studies*, Vol. 18, No. 3 (Spring 1995), pp. 221-240.

Albaharna, Husain M. *The Arabian Gulf States: Their Legal and Political Status and Their International Problems.* 2nd rev. ed. Beirut: Librairie du Liban, 1975.

Ballantyne, W. M. "Legal Development in Arabia: A Selection of Articles and Addresses on the Arabian Gulf." London: Graham and Trotman, 1980.

Bodoh, Keith D. "The Routine Torture Practices of the Saudi Arabian Government as 'Commercial Activity' Within the Foreign Sovereign Immunities Act of 1976 in the Wake of Saudi Arabia v. Nelson, 113 S. Ct. 1471 (1993)." *Political Geography*, Vol. 13 (January 1994), pp. 559-580.

"Constitutional Reform: A Systemization of Saudi Politics." *Journal of South Asian and Middle Eastern Studies*, Vol. 16 (Spring 1993), pp. 43-88.

Ghadyan, A. A. al-. "The Judiciary in Saudi Arabia." *Arab Law Quarterly*, Vol. 13, No. 3 (1998), pp. 235-251.

Hakim, Ali A. El-. *The Middle Eastern States and the Law of the Sea.* Manchester: Manchester University Press; Syracuse: Syracuse University Press, 1979. Contemporary Issues in the Middle East.

Hamad, Hamad Sadun Al-. "The Legislative Process and the Development of Saudi Arabia." Ph.D. dissertation, University of Southern California, 1973.

Hamadi, Abdulkarim Mohamed. "Saudi Arabia's Territorial Limits: A Study in Law and Politics." Ph.D. dissertation, Indiana University, 1981.

Hamlin, Kristan, and L. Peters. "The Impact of Islamic Revivalism on Contract and Usury Law in Iran, Saudi Arabia, and Egypt." *Texas International Law Journal*, Vol. 22 (Spring-Summer 1987), pp. 351-381.

Karam, Nicola H. *Business Laws of Saudi Arabia.* London: Graham and Trotman, 1993.

Kishk, Muhammad Jalal. *Al-sa'ūdīyūn wal-hāl al-islāmī: maṣdar shar'īyah lil-nizām al-sa'ūdī.* ("The Saudis and the Islamic Solution: A Source of Legitimacy for the Sa'udi Regime.") Cairo: al-Maṭba'ah al-fannīyah, 1981. 2nd ed., 1984.

Lerrick, Alison, and Q. Javed Man. *Saudi Business and Labor Law.* London: Graham and Trotman, 1982.

Madani, Mohamed O. "The Relationship Between Saudi Arabian Domestic Law and International Law: A Study of the Oil Agreements with Foreign Companies." Ph.D. dissertation, George Washington University, 1970.

Mahassni, Hassan, and Neal F. Grenley. "Public Sector Dispute Resolution in Saudi Arabia: Procedures and Practices of Saudi Arabia's Administrative Court." *International Lawyer*, Vol. 21 (Summer 1987), pp. 827-844.

Nafissah, Motleb Abdullah. "Law and Social Change in Muslim Countries: The Concept of Islamic Law Held by the Hanbali School and the Saudi Arabian Legal System." S.J.D. dissertation, Harvard Law School, 1975.

Rahimi, Z. A. "Treatment of Offenders in the Saudi Criminal Justice System." *Journal of Muslim Minority Affairs*, Vol. 17, No. 1 (1997), pp. 189-193.
Saaty, Mohammed Amin. "The Constitutional Development in Saudi Arabia." Ph.D. dissertation, Claremont Graduate School, 1982.
"Saudi Arabia: The New Constitution." *Arab Law Quarterly*, Vol. 8, No. 3 (1993), pp. 258-270.
Sfeir, George N. "The Saudi Approach to Law Reform." *American Journal of Comparative Law*, Vol. 36 (Fall 1988), pp. 729-759.
Solaim, Soliman A. "Constitutional and Judicial Organization in Saudi Arabia." Ph.D. dissertation, Johns Hopkins University, 1970.
Stevenson, John Hart. "A License to Kill: A Look at Saudi Arabia v. Nelson." *Houston Journal of International Law*, Vol. 17 (Fall 1994), pp. 177-191.
Tarazi, A. Michael. "Saudi Arabia's New Basic Laws: The Struggle for Participatory Islamic Government." *Harvard International Law Journal*, Vol. 34 (1993), pp. 258-275.
Turck, Nancy. "Resolution of Disputes in Saudi Arabia." *Arab Law Quarterly*, Vol. 6, No. 1 (1991), pp. 3-32.
Vogel, Frank Edward. "Islamic Law and Legal System Studies of Saudi Arabia." Ph.D. dissertation, Harvard University, 1993.

FOREIGN AFFAIRS AND INTERNATIONAL RELATIONS

Foreign Policy and General

Abir, Mordechai. "Saudi-Soviet Relations and the Iran-Iraq War." *Middle East Review*, Vol. 22 (Fall 1989), pp. 10-16.
Algosaibi, Ghazi A. *The Gulf Crisis: An Attempt to Understand.* London: Kegan Paul International, 1993.
Ali, Sheikh Rustam. *Saudi Arabia and Oil Diplomacy.* New York: Praeger, 1976.
Anthony, John Duke. "Foreign Policy: The View From Riyadh." *Wilson Quarterly* (Winter 1979), pp. 73-91.
Bashir, Abdulaziz, and Stephen Wright. "Saudi Arabia: Foreign Policy After the Gulf War." *Middle East Policy*, Vol. l, No. 1 (1992), pp. 107-116.
Dawisha, Adeed. *Saudi Arabia's Search for Security.* London: International Institute for Strategic Studies, 1979-1980. Adelphi Papers, No. 158.
———. "Internal Values and External Threats: The Making of Saudi Foreign Policy." *Orbis*, Vol. 23, No. 1 (Spring 1979), pp. 129-143.
Dietl, Gulshan. "Foreign Policy of Saudi Arabia: Internal and External Contexts." *India Quarterly*, Vol. 41, Nos. 3-4 (1985), pp. 363-375.
Fayez, Abdul Aziz al-. "Saudi Foreign Policy." In *Saudi Arabia: One Hundred Years Later; Revised and Updated Proceedings of a Conference at the Center for Contemporary Arab Studies, 28 April 1999* (Washington, DC: Georgetown University Center for Contemporary Arab Studies, 1999), pp. 19-20.
Gause, Gregory, III. "Attempts to Understand Saudi Foreign Policies from Theoretical Prospects." In *Saudi Arabia: One Hundred Years Later; Revised*

and Updated Proceedings of a Conference at the Center for Contemporary Arab Studies, 28 April 1999 (Washington, DC: Georgetown University Center for Contemporary Arab Studies, 1999), pp. 21-22.

Goldberg, Jacob. "Saudi Arabia's Attitude Toward the USSR, 1977-80: Between Saudi Pragmatism and Islamic Conservatism." In Yaacov Ro'i, ed., *The USSR and the Muslim World: Issues in Domestic and Foreign Policy* (London: George Allen & Unwin, 1984), pp. 261-271.

Hussein, Abdulrahman Assad. "Alliance Behavior and the Foreign Policy of the Kingdom of Saudi Arabia, 1979-1991." Ph.D. dissertation, George Washington University, 1995.

Kabbaa, Abdullah Saud. "Saudi Arabia and the United Nations." Ph.D. dissertation, Southern Illinois University at Carbondale, 1979.

Katz, Mark N. *Russia and Arabia: Soviet Foreign Policy Toward the Arabian Peninsula.* Baltimore: Johns Hopkins University Press, 1986.

———. "Yemeni Unity and Saudi Security." *Middle East Policy*, Vol. 1, No. 1 (1992), pp. 117-135.

Kayal, Alawi Darweesh. "The Control of Oil: East-West Rivalry in the Persian Gulf." Ph.D. dissertation, University of Colorado, 1972.

Kurashi, Mohammed Farid Y. "The Social Responsibility of the Multinational Corporations Operating in Saudi Arabia." Ph.D. dissertation, Claremont Graduate School, 1984.

Madani, Nizar Obaid. "The Islamic Content of the Foreign Policy of Saudi Arabia: King Faisal's Call for Islamic Solidarity, 1965-1975." Ph.D. dissertation, American University, 1977.

Mani', Saleh A. al-. "The Politics of the GCC Dialogue with the European Community. *Journal of South Asian and Middle Eastern Studies*, Vol. 7, No. 4 (Summer 1989), pp. 57-74.

Mejcher, Helmut. "Die Wiederaufnahme der diplomatischen Beziehungen zwischen Deutschland und Saudi-Arabien nach dem Zweiten Weltkrieg." ("The Resumption of Diplomatic Relations Between West-Germany and Saudi Arabia After World War II.") *Orient*, Vol. 42, No. 3 (September 2001), pp. 469-484.

Moon, Chung In. "Korean Contractors in Saudi Arabia: Their Rise and Fall." *Middle East Journal*, Vol. 40, No. 4 (Autumn 1986), pp. 614-633.

Nonneman, Gerd. "Le relazione tra Arabia Saudita e l'Europa." In R. Aliboni and D. Pioppi, eds., *Arabia Saudita Cent'anni: Cooperazione, sicurezza, identita* (Rome: Franco Angeli for Istituto Affairi Internazionali, 2000), pp. 19-43.

———. "Saudi-European Relations 1902-2001: A Pragmatic Quest for Relative Autonomy." *International Affairs* (London), Vol. 77, No. 3 (July 2001), pp. 529-559.

Piscatori, James P. "Islamic Values and National Interest: The Foreign Policy of Saudi Arabia." In Adeed Dawisha, ed., *Islam in Foreign Policy* (Cambridge: Cambridge University Press, 1983; published in association with the Royal Institute of International Affairs), pp. 33-53.

Quandt, William B. *Saudi Arabia in the 1980s: Foreign Policy, Security, and Oil.* Washington, DC: Brookings Institution, 1981.

————. "Riyadh Between the Superpowers." *Foreign Policy*, No. 44 (1981), pp. 37-56.

Rawaf, Othman al-. "A View from the Gulf." In Sean McKnight, Neil Partrick, and Francis Toase, eds., *Gulf Security: Opportunities and Challenges for the New Generation* (London: Royal United Services Institute and Royal Military Academy Sandhurst, 2000), pp. 14-17.

Saeed, Sadiq Mehros. "Saudi Arabia as an Actor in World Affairs: A Study in the Political Role of Oil and Wealth in Saudi Arabian Foreign Relations Behavior, 1965-1984." Ph.D. dissertation, University of Southern California, 1985.

Semmari, Fahd Abdullah al-. "Saudi Arabian-German Political and Economic Relations 1926-1939." Ph.D. dissertation, University of California, Riverside, 1989.

Sowayel, Naila al-. "An Historical Analysis of Saudi Arabia's Foreign Policy in Time of Crisis: The October 1973 War and the Arab Oil Embargo." Ph.D. dissertation, Georgetown University, 1990.

Sugair, Khalid Ali al-. "The Foreign Aid Program of the Kingdom of Saudi Arabia, 1973-1990." Ph.D. dissertation, George Washington University, 1993.

Turner, Louis, and James Bedore. "Saudi Arabia: The Power of the Purse-Strings." *International Affairs* (London), Vol. 54, No. 3 (July 1978), pp. 405-420.

Whitehill, Robert. "The Sanctions That Never Were: Arab and Iranian Oil Sales to South Africa." *Middle East Review*, Vol. 19, No. 1 (Fall 1986), pp. 38-45.

Regional Relations

Abir, Mordechai. *Oil, Power and Politics: Conflict in Arabia, the Red Sea and the Gulf.* London: Frank Cass, 1974.

Ajami, Fouad. "Stress in the Arab Triangle." *Foreign Policy*, No. 29 (1977-78), pp. 90-108.

Ali, M. "Saudi-Iranian Relations: The Struggle for Religious or Political Leadership." *JIME Review*, No. 9 (1990), pp. 72-82.

Anthony, John Duke. "Saudi Arabian-Yemeni Relations: Implications for U. S. Policy." *Middle East Policy*, Vol. 7, No. 3 (June 2000), pp. 78-98.

Azhary, M. S. El. "Aspects of North Yemen's Relations with Saudi Arabia." In B. R. Pridham, ed., *Contemporary Yemen: Politics and Historical Background* (London: Croom Helm, for the University of Exeter Centre for Arab Gulf Studies, 1984), pp. 195-207.

Badeeb, Saeed M. *The Saudi-Egyptian Conflict Over North Yemen, 1962-1970.* Boulder, CO: Westview Press; Washington, DC: American-Arab Affairs Council, 1986.

Bahgat, Gawdat. "Iranian-Saudi Rapprochement: Prospects and Implications." *World Affairs*, Vol. 162, No. 3 (Winter 2000), pp. 108-115.

Bligh, Alexander. "Toward Israeli-Saudi Coexistence?" *Jerusalem Quarterly*, No. 35 (Spring 1985), pp. 24-35.

Chubin, Shahram, and Charles Tripp. *Iran-Saudi Arabia Relations and Regional Order.* Oxford: Oxford University Press for the International Institute of Strategic Studies, November 1996. Adelphi Papers, No. 304.

Dajani, Munther S., and Mohammed S. Daoudi. "New Frontiers in the Search for Peace: The Saudi Initiative." *International Studies*, Vol. 23 (January-March 1986), pp. 63-74.

Dawisha, Adeed. "Saudi Arabia and the Arab-Israeli Conflict: The Ups and Downs of Pragmatic Moderation." *International Journal*, Vol. 38, No. 4 (Autumn 1983), pp. 674-689.

Detalle, Renaud, ed. *Tensions in Arabia: The Saudi-Yemeni Faultline*. Baden-Baden: Nomos Verlagsgesellschaft, 2000. Conflict Prevention Network-Stiftung Wissenschaft und Politik.

Ehteshami, Anoushiravan, ed. *From the Gulf to Central Asia: Players in the New Great Game*. Exeter: University of Exeter Press, 1995.

Faksh, Mahmud A. "Saudi Arabia and Iran: The Challenge of an Insurgent Islam." *Journal of Arab Affairs*, Vol. 7, No. 2 (1988), pp. 121-144.

———. "Saudi Arabia and the Gulf Crisis: Foreign and Security Policy Dilemma." *Middle East Review*, Vol. 19 (Summer 1987), pp. 47-53.

Gause, F. Gregory, III. *Saudi-Yemeni Relations: Domestic Structures and Foreign Influence*. New York: Columbia University Press, 1990.

Goldberg, Jacob. "Saudi Arabia and the Egyptian-Israeli Peace Process, 1977-1981." *Middle East Review*, Vol. 18, No. 4 (1986), pp. 25-33.

———. "Saudi Arabia: The Bank Vault Next Door." In Amatzia Baram and Barry Rubin, eds., *Iraq's Road to War* (New York: St. Martin's Press, 1993), pp. 117-134.

Hartmann, Rainer. "Yemeni Exodus from Saudi Arabia: The Gulf Conflict and the Ceasing of the Workers' Emigration." *Journal of South Asian and Middle Eastern Studies*, Vol. 19, No. 2 (Winter 1995), pp. 38-52.

Hoppe, R. "Saudi-Arabiens Aussenpolitik als Versuch einer eigenstandigen kriseneindammenden Regional politik im Nahen Osten." *Orient*, Vol. 26, No. 2 (1985), pp. 205-217.

Jabber, Paul. "Oil, Arms, and Regional Diplomacy: Strategic Dimensions of the Saudi-Egyptian Relationship." In Malcolm H. Kerr and El Sayed Yassin, eds., *Rich and Poor States in the Middle East: Egypt and the New Arab Order* (Boulder, CO: Westview; Cairo: American University of Cairo Press, 1982), pp. 415-447.

Katz, Mark. "Yemeni Unity and Saudi Security." *Middle East Policy*, Vol. 1, No. 1 (1992), pp. 117-135.

Kostiner, Joseph. "Counterproductive Mediation: Saudi Arabia and the Iran Arms Deal." *Middle East Review*, Vol. 19 (Summer 1987), pp. 41-46.

Koszinowski, Thomas. "Yemeni Foreign Policy Since Unification and the Part Played by Saudi Arabia." In Rémy Leveau, Franck Mermier, and Udo Steinbach, eds., *Le Yémen Contemporain* (Paris: Éditions Karthala, 1999), pp. 61-77.

Leverrier, I. "L'Arabie saoudite, le pélerinage et l'Iran." *Cemoti*, No. 22 (1996), pp. 111-148.

Lucet, M. "Les rapatriés de la crise du Golfe au Yemen Hodeida quatre ans après." *Maghreb-Machrek*, No. 148 (1995), pp. 28-42.

Mani, Saleh al-. "The Ideological Dimension in Saudi-Iranian Relations." In Jamal S. al-Suwaidi, ed., *Iran and the Gulf: A Search for Stability* (London: I. B.

Tauris for the Emirates Centre for Strategic Studies and Research, 1996), pp. 158-174.

Mylroie, Laurie. "Regional Security After Empire: Saudi Arabia and the Gulf." Ph.D. dissertation, Harvard University, 1985.

Okruhlik, Gwenn, and Patrick Conge. "National Autonomy, Labor Migration and Political Crisis: Yemen and Saudi Arabia." *Middle East Journal*, Vol. 51, No. 4 (Autumn 1997), pp. 554-565.

Parrott, J. B. "The Response of Saudi Arabia to the Iran-Iraq War." *Journal of South Asian and Middle Eastern Studies*, Vol. 10, No. 2 (1986), pp. 42-56.

Rashid, Ahmed. "The Taliban: Exporting Extremism." *Foreign Affairs*, Vol. 78, No. 6 (November/December 1999), pp. 22-35.

Rieck, Andreas. "Iraq and Saudi Arabia: From Rivalry to Confrontation." In Derek Hopwood, Habib Ishow, and Thomas Koszinowki, eds., *Iraq: Power and Society* (Reading: Ithaca Press, 1995; St. Antony's Middle East Monographs Series, No. 29), pp. 319-339.

Roth, Katherine. *What Saudi and Yemeni Religious Authorities Had to Say About the Yemen War*. Hanover, NH: Institute of Current World Affairs, July 1994. Occasional Paper.

Sajedi, A. "Iran's Relations with Saudi Arabia." *India Quarterly*, Vol. 49, Nos. 1-2 (1993), pp. 75-96.

Shewaihy, Mohammed A. al-. "Historical Claim of Iraq Over Kuwait and the Position of the Kingdom of Saudi Arabia and Its Peaceful Solution." *Korean Journal of Middle East Studies*, No. 11 (1990), pp. 55-67.

Sours, Martin. "Saudi Arabia's Role in the Middle East: Regional Stability Within the New World Order." *Asian Affairs, an American Review*, Vol. 18, No. 1 (June 1991), pp. 43-51.

Stevenson, Thomas B. "Yemeni Migrants in the Wake of Desert Storm: A Research Report." *SACC Notes: Teaching Anthropology*, Spring/Summer 1993, pp. 12-13.

———. "Yemeni Workers Come Home: Reabsorbing One Million Migrants." *Middle East Report*, Vol. 23, No. 2 (March-April 1993), pp. 15-20.

Twinam, Joseph. "The Saudi Role in the New Middle East Order." In M. E. Ahrari and James H. Noyes, eds., *The Persian Gulf After the Cold War* (Westport, CT: Praeger, 1993), pp. 125-146.

Yamani, Mai. "Saudi Arabia and Central Asia: The Islamic Connection." In Anoushiravan Ehteshami, ed., *From the Gulf to Central Asia: Players in the New Great Game* (Exeter: University of Exeter Press, 1995), pp. 47-57.

Zabarah, Mohammed A. "Yemeni-Saudi Relations Gone Awry." In Joseph A. Kechichian, ed., *Iran, Iraq, and the Arab Gulf States* (New York: Palgrave, 2001), pp. 263-280.

Relations with the United States

Abu Khalil, As'ad. Bin Laden, Islam, and America's New "War on Terrorism." N.p.: Seven Stories Press, 2002.

Anderson, Irvine H. *Aramco, the United States and Saudi Arabia: A Study of the Dynamics of Foreign Oil Policy, 1933-1950*. Princeton, NJ: Princeton University Press, 1981.

Anti-Defamation League of B'nai B'rith. *The U. S.-Saudi Relationship*. New York: 1982. ADL Research Report.

Armstrong, Scott. "Eye of the Storm: The $200 Billion Reason We Had to Go to War in the Middle East." *Mother Jones*, November-December 1991, pp. 30-35, 75-76.

Awaji, Ibrahim Mohamed Al-. "U. S. Saudi Economic and Political Relations." *American-Arab Affairs*, No. 7 (Winter 1983-1984), pp. 55-59.

Bagour, Omar S. "Tête-à-Tête Is Always Best." *Middle East Insight*, Special Edition (1995), p. 37.

Binder, Leonard. "U. S. Policy in the Middle East: Towards a Pax Saudiana." *Current History*, Vol. 81, No. 471 (1982), pp. 1-4, 41-42, 48.

Casillas, Rex J. *Oil and Diplomacy: The Evolution of American Foreign Policy in Saudi Arabia, 1933-1945*. New York: Garland Publishing, 1988.

Citino, Nathan John. "Eisenhower, King Sa'ud, and the Politics of Arab Nationalism: United States-Saudi Relations, 1952-1960." Ph.D. dissertation, Ohio State University, 1999.

Cutler, Walter. "Continuity and Common Interest: A Conversation with Walter Cutler." *Middle East Insight*, Special Edition (1995), pp. 47-51.

Daher, Salim A. "From Crisis to Crisis: Saudi-American Relations, 1973-1979." Ph.D. dissertation, Harvard University, 1983.

Emerson, Steven. "America's House of Saud, Part I: The Petrodollar Connection." *New Republic*, 17 February 1982, pp. 18-25; "America's House of Saud, Part II: The ARAMCO Connection." *New Republic* (19 May 1982), pp. 11-16.

Farsy, Fouad A. Al-. "Contemporary Realities in Saudi-American Relations." *American-Arab Affairs*, No. 26 (Fall 1988), pp. 82-91.

————. "Saudi-American Relations in a Changing World." *American-Arab Affairs*, No. 19 (Winter 1986-1987), pp. 23-27.

Gause, F. Gregory, III. "From 'Over the Horizon' to 'Into the Backyard': The U. S.-Saudi Relationship and the Gulf War." In David W. Lesch, ed., *The Middle East and the United States: A Historical and Political Reassessment* (Boulder, CO: Westview Press, 1996), pp. 299-311.

Gormly, James L. "Keeping the Door Open in Saudi Arabia: The United States and the Dhahran Airfield, 1945-46." *Diplomatic History*, Vol. 4, No. 2 (1980), pp. 189-205.

Grayson, Benson Lee. *Saudi-American Relations*. Lanham, MD: University Press of America, 1982.

Harbinson, David K. "The US-Saudi Arabian Joint Commission on Economic Cooperation: A Critical Appraisal." *Middle East Journal*, Vol. 44, No. 2 (Spring 1990), pp. 269-283.

Kern, Nathaniel. "The US-Saudi Relationship Under a New Administration." *Middle East Insight*, Vol. 9, No. 1 (November-December 1992), pp. 16-21.

Kuniholm, Bruce R. "What the Saudis Really Want: A Primer for the Reagan Administration." *Orbis*, Vol. 25, No. 1 (1981), pp. 107-121.

Long, David E. *The United States and Saudi Arabia: Ambivalent Allies*. Boulder, CO: Westview Press, 1985. MERI Special Studies, No. 3.

————. "US-Saudi Relations: A Foundation of Mutual Needs." *American-Arab Affairs*, No. 4 (Spring 1983), pp. 12-22.

McLaurin, Ronald D. "Foundations of the Saudi-American Security Relationship." *Middle East Insight*, Vol. 8 (March-April 1992), pp. 36-42.

Marshall, J. "Saudi Arabia and the Reagan Doctrine." *MERIP Middle East Report*, Vol. 18, No. 6 (1988), pp. 13-17.

Mednicoff, David M. "The Maturing of the Saudi-American Relationship." *Middle East Review*, Vol. 12, No. 2 (Winter 1984-1985), pp. 33-41.

Mirkow, Frank J. "The Nature of Saudi Arabian Strategic Power: Implications for American Foreign Policy." *Fletcher Forum of World Affairs*, Vol. 17 (Winter 1993), pp. 157-165.

Morton, John F. "Saudi Arms Deal: Down, Not Out." *Defense & Diplomacy*, Vol. 9 (March-April 1991), pp. 12-22.

Murphy, Richard W. "Saudi Arabia: An American Diplomat Looks Back." *Middle East Insight*, Vol. 14, No. 3 (May-June 1999), pp. 71-74.

Nafjan, Fahad Mohammed al-. "The Origins of Saudi-American Relations: From Recognition to Diplomatic Representation (1931-1943)." Ph.D. dissertation, University of Kansas, 1989.

Peay, J. H. Binford, III. "A Commentary on Military Cooperation Between the United States and the Kingdom of Saudi Arabia." *Middle East Insight*, Special Edition (1995), pp. 52-56.

Peterson, J. E. "Saudi-American Relations After 11 September 2001." *Asian Affairs* (London), Vol. 33, Part 1 (February 2002), pp. 102-114.

Pounds, Bonnie. "The U. S. Saudi Arabian Joint Commission: A Model for Bilateral Economic Cooperation." *American-Arab Affairs*, No. 7 (Winter 1983-1984), pp. 60-68.

Prados, Alfred B. "Saudi Arabia: Post-War Issues and U. S. Relations." U. S. Library of Congress, Congressional Research Service, CRS Issue Brief IB93113, 1 November 2001.

Rustow, Dankwart A. "U. S. Saudi Relations and the Oil Crises of the 1980s." *Foreign Affairs*, Vol. 55, No. 3 (April 1977), pp. 494-516.

Shah, Shafqat Ali. "The Political and Strategic Foundations of International Arms Transfer: A Case Study of American Arms Supply to, and Purchase by, Iran and Saudi Arabia, 1968-76." Ph.D. dissertation, University of Virginia, 1977.

Telhami, Shibley. "US-Saudi Relations." In *Saudi Arabia: One Hundred Years Later; Revised and Updated Proceedings of a Conference at the Center for Contemporary Arab Studies, 28 April 1999* (Washington, DC: Georgetown University Center for Contemporary Arab Studies, 1999), pp. 23-25.

Turner, William O. "U. S. Arms Sales to Saudi Arabia: Implications for American Foreign Policy." Ph.D. dissertation, George Washington University, 1982.

Twinam, Joseph. "Controversial Arms Sales to Saudi Arabia: An American Tragedy in Possibly Four Acts." *American-Arab Affairs*, No. 29 (Summer 1989), pp. 47-55.

U. S. Congress. House of Representatives. Committee on Foreign Affairs. Subcommittee on Arms Control, International Security and Science; and Subcommittee on Europe and the Middle East. *Proposed Sale of F-15 Aircraft to Saudi Arabia and U. S.-Saudi Commercial Disputes*; Joint Hearings and Mark-Up, 23 September 1992. Washington, DC: USGPO, 1993.

————. *Proposed Sales to Saudi Arabia in Association with the Conduct of Operation Desert Storm*; Hearing, 31 October 1990. Washington, DC: USGPO, 1991.

————. *Proposed Tank Sale to Saudi Arabia*; Hearing, 7 November 1989. Washington, DC: USGPO, 1990.

U. S. Congress. House of Representatives. Committee on Foreign Affairs. Subcommittee on Europe and the Middle East. *Activities of the United States Army Corps of Engineers in Saudi Arabia*; Hearing, 25 June 1979. Washington, DC: USGPO, 1979.

————. *Developments in the Middle East*; Hearing, 1 October 1992. Washington, DC: USGPO, 1993.

————. *Developments in the Middle East, October 1993*; Hearing, 21 October 1993. Washington, DC: USGPO, 1993.

————. *Problems Confronting American Businessmen in Saudi Arabia.* Washington, DC: USGPO, 1987.

————. *Saudi Arabia and the United States: The New Context in an Evolving "Special Relationship"*; Report prepared by the Congressional Research Service. Washington, DC: USGPO, 1981.

U. S. Department of State. *U. S. Records on Saudi Affairs, 1945-1960.* Slough, UK: Archive Editions, 1996.

U. S. General Accounting Office. *How Military Sales Trust Funds Operate: Saudi Arabian and Iranian Funds Compared*; Report by the Comptroller General of the US. Washington, DC: GAO, 28 January 1980. FGMSD-80-26.

Vitalis, Robert. "The Closing of the Arabian Oil Frontier and the Future of Saudi-American Relations." *Middle East Report*, No. 204 (July-September 1997), pp. 15-21, 25.

Walt, Joseph William. "Saudi Arabia and the Americans." Ph.D. dissertation, Northwestern University, 1960.

Warwick, Graham. "Arming Arabia." *Flight International*, Vol. 134 (22 October 1988), pp. 30-32.

West, John C. "A Lasting Friendship Despite the Clash of Cultures." *Middle East Insight*, Special Edition (1995), pp. 32-36.

————. "US-Saudi Arabian Relations: Toward a New Parity." *Middle East Insight*, Vol. 7, Nos. 2 & 3 (1990), pp. 41-43.

Yakovei, Rehavia Uami. "Arms for Oil—Oil for Arms: An Analysis of President Carter's 1978 Planes 'Package Deal' Sales to Egypt, Israel and Saudi Arabia." Ph.D. dissertation, Claremont Graduate School, 1983.

NATIONAL AND REGIONAL SECURITY

Abir, Mordechai. "Saudi Security and Military Endeavor." *Jerusalem Quarterly*, No. 33 (Fall 1984), pp. 79-94.

————. "Saudi-Soviet Relations and the Iran-Iraq War." *Middle East Review*, Vol. 22 (Fall 1989), pp. 10-16.

Akins, James E. "Saudi Arabia, Soviet Activities, and Gulf Security." In Z. Michael Szaz, ed., *The Impact of the Iranian Events Upon Persian Gulf and United*

States Security (Washington, DC: American Foreign Policy Institute, 1979), pp. 89-110.

Algosaibi, Ghazi A. *The Gulf Crisis: An Attempt to Understand.* London: Kegan Paul International, 1993. First published in Arabic as *Azmat al-khalīj* (1991).

Cordesman, Anthony H. *The Gulf and the Search for Strategic Stability: Saudi Arabia, the Military Balance in the Gulf, and Trends in the Arab-Israeli Military Balance.* Boulder, CO: Westview Press; London: Mansell, 1984.

————. *Saudi Arabia, AWACS, and America's Search for Strategic Stability in the Near East.* Washington, DC: Smithsonian Institution, 1981. Woodrow Wilson Center for International Scholars.

————. "Saudi Military Forces and the Gulf." Washington, DC: Center for Strategic and International Studies, 4 February 1999, online.

————. *Saudi Arabia: Guarding the Desert Kingdom.* Boulder, CO: Westview Press, 1997. CSIS Middle East Dynamic Net Assessment.

————. *Western Strategic Interests in Saudi Arabia.* London: Croom Helm, 1987.

Dart, Jim. "USMTM: Point Guard on the Arabian Peninsula." *DISAM Journal* Vol. 14, No. 2 (Winter 1991-1992), pp. 1-12.

Dawisha, Adeed. "Saudi Arabia." In Samuel F. Wells, Jr., and Mark A. Bruzonsky, eds., *Security in the Middle East: Regional Change and Great Power Strategies* (Boulder, CO: Westview Press, 1987), pp. 89-100.

Faksh, Mahmud A., and Ramzi F. Faris. "The Saudi Conundrum: Squaring the Security-Stability Circle." *Third World Quarterly*, Vol. 14, No. 2 (1993), pp. 277-293.

Gause, F. Gregory, III. "Saudi Arabia: Desert Storm and After." In Robert O. Freedman, ed., *The Middle East After Iraq's Invasion of Kuwait* (Gainesville: University Press of Florida, 1993), pp. 207-234.

Goldberg, Jacob. "The Saudi Military Buildup: Strategy and Risks." *Middle East Review*, Vol. 21, No. 3 (Spring 1989), pp. 3-13.

Haass, Richard. "Saudi Arabia and Iran: The Twin Pillars in Revolutionary Times." In Hossein Amirsadeghi, ed., *The Security of the Persian Gulf* (London: Croom Helm; New York: St. Martin's Press, 1981), pp. 151-169.

Kechichian, Joseph A. "Trends in Saudi National Security." *Middle East Journal*, Vol. 53, No. 2 (Spring 1999), pp. 232-253.

Khalid, Zulfikar A. "Evolution of Saudi-Pakistan Strategic Relationship, 1947-1990: Military Security and Economic Factors." *Strategic Studies*, Vol. 13, No. 1 (1989), pp. 53-77.

Kostiner, Joseph. "Shi'i Unrest in the Gulf." In Martin Kramer, ed., *Shi'isrn, Resistance and Revolution* (Boulder, CO: Westview Press, 1987; Collected Papers, Dayan Center for Middle Eastern and African Studies), pp. 173-188.

Kumarasamy, P. "The Arabian Interpretation of Operation Desert Storm: An Analysis of Saudi Military Communiqués." *Strategic Analysis*, Vol. 14, No. 3 (1991), pp. 321-335.

McNaugher, Thomas L. *Arms and Oil: U. S. Military Strategy and the Persian Gulf.* Washington, DC: Brookings Institution, 1985.

————. *Pipelines and Power in the Gulf: Shifting Balances.* Cambridge, MA: Cambridge Energy Research Associates, December 1986. Private Report.

Mani, Saleh al-. "Of Security and Threat: Saudi Arabia's Perception." *Journal of South Asian and Middle Eastern Studies*, Vol. 20, No. 1 (Fall 1996), pp. 74-87.

Morton, John F. "Saudi Arms Deal: Down, Not Out." *Defense & Diplomacy*, Vol. 9 (March-April 1991), pp. 12-22.

Peterson, J. E. *Defending Arabia.* London: Croom Helm; New York: St. Martin's Press, 1986.

————. *Saudi Arabia and the Illusion of Security.* London: Oxford University Press, for the International Institute for Strategic Studies, 2002. Adelphi Paper, No. 348.

Rathmell, Andrew. "Saudi Arabia's Military Build-Up—An Extravagant Error?" *Jane's Intelligence Review*, Vol. 6, No. 11 (November 1994), pp. 500-505.

Record, Jeffrey. *Hollow Victory: A Contrary View of the Gulf War.* New York: Brassey's (US), 1993.

Safran, Nadav. *Saudi Arabia: The Ceaseless Quest for Security.* Cambridge, MA: Belknap Press of Harvard University Press, 1985.

Schichor, Yitzhak. *A Multiple Hit: China's Missiles Sale to Saudi Arabia.* Taiwan: Sun Yat-Sen Center for Policy Studies, 1991.

————. *East Wind Over Arabia: Origins and Implications of the Sino-Saudi Missile Deal.* Berkeley: University of California, Institute of East Asian Studies, Center for Chinese Studies, 1989. China Research Monograph, No. 35.

Tahir-Kheli, Shirin, and William O. Staudenmaier. "The Saudi-Pakistani Military Relationship: Implications for U. S. Policy." *Orbis*, Vol. 26, No. 1 (1982), pp. 155-171.

U. S. Congress. House of Representatives. Committee on Foreign Affairs. Subcommittee on Arms Control, International Security and Science, and Subcommittee on Europe and the Middle East. *Proposed Arms Sales to Saudi Arabia*; Hearing, 10 May 1988. Washington, DC: USGPO, 1988.

————. Subcommittee on Europe and the Middle East. *Presidential Certification on the Delivery of AWACS to Saudi Arabia*; Hearing, 15 July 1986. Washington, DC: USGPO, 1986.

————. Subcommittee on Europe and the Middle East. *Proposed Arms Sales to Saudi Arabia*; Hearing and Markup, 22-23 April 1986. Washington, DC: USGPO, 1986.

————. Subcommittees on International Security and Scientific Affairs, and on Europe and the Middle East. *Proposed U. S. Arms Sales to Saudi Arabia*; Hearing, 12 December 1979. Washington, DC: USGPO, 1980.

————. Subcommittees on Arms Control, International Security and Science, and on Europe and the Middle East. *Proposed Tank Sale Saudi Arabia*; Hearing, 7 November 1989. Washington, DC: USGPO, 1990.

————. *Proposed Sales and Upgrades of Major Defense Equipment to Saudi Arabia*; Hearing, 19 June 1990. Washington, DC: USGPO, 1991.

————. *Proposed Sales to Saudi Arabia in Association with the Conduct of Operation Desert Storm*; Hearing, 31 October 1990. Washington, DC: USGPO, 1991.

U. S. Congress. Senate. Committee on Appropriations. Subcommittee on Foreign
    Assistance and Related Programs. *Sales of Stinger Missiles to Saudi Arabia*;
    Hearing. Washington, DC: USGPO, 1984.
————. Committee on Foreign Relations. Subcommittee on Europe and the Middle
    East. *Arms Sales Package to Saudi Arabia, Part I*; Hearings, 1, 5, 6, 14,
    and 15 October 1981. Washington, DC: USGPO, 1981.
————. *Arms Sales Package to Saudi Arabia, Part II*; Hearings, 1, 5 , 6, 14, and
    15 October 1981. Washington, DC: USGPO, 1981.
————. *The Proposed AWACS/F-15 Enhancement Sale to Saudi Arabia*; Staff
    Report. Washington, DC: USGPO, 1981.

SOCIETY AND CULTURE

Abd al-Hay, Abdalkhalek A. Al-. "Contemporary Women's Participation in Public
    Activities: Differences Between Ideal Islam and Muslim Interpretation With
    Emphasis on Saudi Arabia." Ph.D. dissertation, University of Denver, 1983.
Abd-el Wassie, Abd-el Wahab. *Education in Saudi Arabia.* London: Macmillan,
    1970.
Abdul-Aziz, Moudi Mansour. *Settling the Tribes: The Role of the Bedouin in
    the Formation of the Saudi State.* London: Al Saqi, 1994.
Abdulkadar, Ali Abdulaziz Al-. "A Survey of the Contribution of Higher Education
    to the Development of Human Resources in the Kingdom of Saudi Arabia."
    Ph.D. dissertation, University of Kansas, 1978.
Akeel, Suleiman Abdullah al-. "The Impact of Modernization on Saudi Society:
    A Case Study of Saudi Students' Attitudes." Ph.D. dissertation, Mississippi
    State University, 1992.
Alafghani, Abdullah Sultan. "The Saudi House in the Past, Present and Future
    (A Study of Changes)." Ph.D. thesis, University of Glasgow, 1991.
Alghafis, A. N. *Universities in Saudi Arabia: Their Role in Science, Technology,
    and Development.* Lanham, MD: University Press of America, 1993.
Algosaibi, Ghazi A. *Arabian Essays.* London: Kegan Paul International, 1982.
Alireza, Marianne. "Women of Saudi Arabia." *National Geographic*, Vol. 172
    (October 1987), pp. 423-453.
Almana, Aisha Mohammed. "Economic Development and Its Impact on the Status
    of Women in Saudi Arabia." Ph.D. dissertation, University of Colorado at
    Boulder, 1981.
Altorki, Soraya. *Women in Saudi Arabia: Ideology and Behavior Among the
    Elite.* New York: Columbia University Press, 1986.
————. "The Anthropologist in the Field: A Case of 'Indigenous Authority' from
    Saudi Arabia." In Hussein Fahim, ed., *Indigenous Authority in Non-Western
    Countries* (Durham: University of North Carolina Press, 1982), pp. 167-175.
————. "The Ideology and Praxis of Female Employment in Saudi Arabia."
    Journal of South Asian and Middle Eastern Studies, Vol. 10 (Summer 1987),
    pp. 51-76.
Altorki, Soraya, and Donald P. Cole. *Arabian Oasis City: The Transformation
    of 'Unayzah.* Austin: University of Texas Press, 1989. Modern Middle East
    Series, No. 15.

————. "Unayzah, le Paris du Najd: le changement en Arabie saoudite." *Maghreb-Machrek*, No. 156 (1997), pp. 3-22.

Anderson, Gary. "Differential Urban Growth in the Eastern Province of Saudi Arabia: A Study of the Historical Interaction of Economic Development and Socio-Political Change." Ph.D. dissertation, Johns Hopkins University, 1985.

As'ad, Mohammed Ahmed. "The Possibility of Change in Bedouin Society: A Study of Current Development in Saudi Arabia." Ph.D. dissertation, Claremont Graduate School, 1981.

Asaly, Saif Mahyoub Al-. "Migration, Balance of Payments and Economic Growth: The Case of the Yemen Arab Republic." Ph.D. dissertation, University of South Carolina, 1990.

Attar, Eqbal Ahmed. "Major Personal and Social Problems Faced by Divorced Saudi Arabian Women." Ph.D. dissertation, University of San Francisco, 1987.

Baadi, Hamad Muhammad. "Social Change, Education, and the Roles of Women in Arabia." Ph.D. dissertation, Stanford University, 1982.

Bahry, Louay. "The New Saudi Woman: Modernizing in an Islamic Framework." *Middle East Journal*, Vol. 36, No. 4 (Autumn 1982), pp. 502-515.

Banyan, Abdullah Saleh Al-. *Saudi Students in the United States: A Study of Cross Cultural Education and Attitude Change.* London: Ithaca Press, 1980.

Barsalou, Judith Marie. "Foreign Labor in Saudi Arabia: The Creation of a Plural Society." Ph.D. dissertation, Columbia University, 1985.

Bogary, Hamza. *The Sheltered Quarter: A Tale of a Boyhood in Mecca.* Austin: University of Texas Center for Middle Eastern Studies, 1991. Modern Middle East Literatures in Translation Series.

Cole, Donald P. *Nomads of the Nomads: The Al Murrah Bedouin of the Empty Quarter.* Chicago: Aldine, 1975.

————. *Pastoral Nomads in a Rapidly Changing Economy: The Case of Saudi Arabia.* London: Overseas Development Institute, 1979. Pastoral Development Network Papers, No. 7e.

————. "The Bedouin and Social Change in Saudi Arabia." *Journal of Asian and African Affairs*, Vol. 16 (1981), pp. 128-149.

————. "Tribal and Non-Tribal Structures Among the Bedouin of Sa'udi Arabia." *al-Abhath*, Vol. 30 (1982), pp. 77-93.

Cole, Donald P., and S. E. Ibrahim. *Saudi Arabian Bedouin: An Assessment of Their Needs.* Cairo: American University in Cairo, 1978. Cairo Paper in Social Science, Monograph No. 5.

Cole, Donald P., and Soraya Altorki. "Production and Trade in North Central Arabia: Change and Development in 'Unayzah." In Martha Mundy and Basim Musallam, eds., *The Transformation of Nomadic Society in the Arab East* (Cambridge: Cambridge University Press, 2000), pp. 145-159.

De Jong, Olga Acosta. "The Perception of the Female Role in Saudi Arabian Society." Ph.D. dissertation, University of Arizona, 1987.

Dohaish, Abdullatif Abdullah. *History of Education in the Hijaz up to 1925 (Comparative and Critical Study).* Cairo: Dar al-Fikr al-Arabi, 1978.

Doumato, Eleanor A. "Arabian Women: Religion, Work and Cultural Identity in the Arabian Peninsula from the Nineteenth Century through the Age of 'Abd al-'Aziz." Ph.D. dissertation, Columbia University, 1989.
———. *Getting God's Ear: Women, Islam, and Healing in Saudi Arabia and the Gulf.* New York: Columbia University Press, 2000.
———. "Gender, Monarchy, and National Identity in Saudi Arabia." *British Journal of Middle Eastern Studies*, Vol. 19, No. 1 (1992), pp. 31-47.
———. "The Saudis and the Gulf War: Gender, Power and the Revival of the Religious Right." In Abbas Abdelkarim, ed., *Change and Development in the Gulf* (London: Macmillan, 1999), pp. 184-210.
———. "Women and the Stability of Saudi Arabia." *MERIP Middle East Report*, Vol. 21, No. 4 (1991), pp. 34-37.
Ebrahim, Mohammed Hossein Saleh. "Problem of Nomad Settlement in the Middle East With Special Reference to Saudi Arabia and the Haradh Project." Ph.D. dissertation, Cornell University, 1981.
Elmusa, Sharif S. "Faust without the Devil? The Interplay of Technology and Culture in Saudi Arabia." *Middle East Journal*, Vol. 51, No. 3 (Summer 1997), pp. 345-357.
Encyclopedia of Folklore of the Kingdom of Saudi Arabia. 12 vols. (in Arabic). N.p., Circle of Information, 2000.
Ende, W. "The Nakhawila: A Shi'ite Community in Medina, Past and Present." *Die Welt des Islams*, Vol. 37, No. 3 (1997), pp. 264-348.
Fabietti, Ugo. "Control and Alienation of Territory Among the Bedouin of Saudi Arabia." *Nomadic Peoples* (March 1986), pp. 33-39.
Fabietti, Ugo. "State Policies and Bedouin Adaptations in Saudi Arabia, 1900-1980." In Martha Mundy and Basim Musallam, eds., *The Transformation of Nomadic Society in the Arab East* (Cambridge: Cambridge University Press, 2000), pp. 82-89.
Facey, William. *Back to Earth: Adobe Building in Saudi Arabia.* London: I. B. Tauris, 1997. London Centre of Arab Studies.
Farra, Taha Osman M. El-. "The Effects of Detribalizing the Bedouins on the Internal Cohesion of an Emerging State: The Kingdom of Saudi Arabia." Ph.D. dissertation, University of Pittsburgh, 1973.
Fernea, Robert A. "Technological Innovation and Class Development Among the Beduwin of Hail, Saudi Arabia." In Byron Cannon, ed., *Terroirs et sociétés au Maghreb et au Moyen Orient* (Paris: Maison de l'Orient, 1987), pp. 389-405.
Fiar, Mohammed Hussein al-. "The Faisal Settlement Project at Haradh, Saudi Arabia: A Study in Nomad Attitudes Toward Sedentarization." Ph.D. dissertation, Michigan State University, 1977.
Ganoubi, Ahmed Ibrahim. "Irqah: A Village Community in Najd." Ph.D. thesis, University of Hull, 1976.
Hammad, Mohamed Abdulla. "The Educational System and Planning for Manpower Development in Saudi Arabia." Ph.D. dissertation, Indiana University, 1973.
Hazzaa, Abdulaziz Mohammed al-. "Scenario Projections for Women in Saudi Arabia: Their Changing Status, Educational and Employment Opportunities by the Year 2010." Ph.D. dissertation, University of Minnesota, 1993.

Helaissi, A. S. "The Bedouins and Tribal Life in Saudi Arabia." *International Social Science Journal*, Vol. 11, No. 4 (1959), pp. 532-538.

Hinai, Muhammad Talib al-. "Multinational Management and the Constraints of Culture, Law, and Economy: Experiences in Saudi Arabia and the Emirates." Ph.D. dissertation, US International University, 1978.

Ingham, Bruce. "Notes on the Dialect of the Al Murra of Eastern and Southern Arabia." *Bulletin of the School of Oriental and African Studies*, Vol. 49, Pt. 2 (1980), pp. 271-291.

Jasir, Hamad al-. *Mu'jam qabā'il al-mamlakah al-'arabīyah al-sa'ūdīyah.* ("Tribal Dictionary of the Kingdom of Saudi Arabia.") 2 vols. Riyadh: Manshūrāt dār al-yamāmah lil-baḥth wal-tarjimah wal-nashr, 1400/1980. Nuṣūṣ wa-abḥath tārīkhīyah wa-jughrāfīyah 'an jazīrat al-'arab, No. 23.

Jefri, Abdulrahim Houssain al-. "Relationships Between Traditional and Modern Values Held by Saudi Arabians and Perceptions of Life Satisfaction in Old Age." Ph.D. dissertation, University of Florida, 1985.

Juwayer, Ibrahim ibn Mubarak Al-. "Development and Family in Saudi Arabia: An Exploratory Study of the Views of University Students in Riyadh." Ph.D. dissertation, University of Florida, 1984.

Kaoud, Sanaa Abd El-Hamad. "Demographic Developments in Saudi Arabia During the Present Century." Ph.D. thesis, The City University, London, 1979.

Katakura, Motoko. *Bedouin Village: A Study of a Saudi Arabian People in Transition.* Tokyo: Tokyo University Press, 1977.

Khalaf, M. "Wajh: A Social Convention of East Qahtan Tribes in Saudi Arabia." (in Arabic) *al-Ma'thūrāt al-Sha'bīyah*, No. 26 (1992), pp. 7-23.

Khaldi, Abdullah Motad Al-. "Job Content and Context Factors Related to Satisfaction and Dissatisfaction in Three Occupational Levels of the Public Sector in Saudi Arabia." Ph.D. dissertation, Florida State University, 1983.

King, Geoffrey. *The Traditional Architecture of Saudi Arabia.* London: I. B. Tauris, 1997.

Kuhhalah, 'Umar Rida. *Mu'jam qabā'il al-'arab.* ("Dictionary of Arab Tribes.") 5 vols. 5th ed.; Beirut: Mu'assasat al-risālah, 1985.

Kurpershoek, P. Marcel. *Oral Poetry and Narratives From Central Arabia. Vol. III. Bedouin Poets of the Dawasir Tribe.* Studies in Arabic Literature, Suppl. to Journal of Arabic Literature. Leiden: E. J. Brill, 1999.

Lancaster, William. *The Rwala Bedouin Today.* Cambridge: Cambridge University Press, 1981.

Lewcock, R. "New Universities [in Saudi Arabia, Jordan, Bahrain, Iran, and Indonesia]." *Mimar: Architecture in Development*, No. 42 (1992), pp. 46-69.

Looney, Robert E. "Demographic Perspectives on Saudi Arabia's Development." *Population Bulletin of the United Nations Economic Commission for West Asia*, No. 26 (June 1985), pp. 93-111.

———. "Patterns of Human Resource Development in Saudi Arabia." *Middle Eastern Studies*, Vol. 27, No. 4 (1991), pp. 668-678.

Mahawi, Suha Mudrik al-. "Sedentarization and Social Change Among the Al Murrah Bedu in the Eastern Province of Saudi Arabia." Ph.D. thesis, Queen's University of Belfast, 1992.

Malik, Saleh Abdullah. "Rural Migration and Urban Growth in Riyadh, Saudi Arabia." PhD. dissertation, University of Michigan, 1973.

Manea, Azeezah A. al-. "History and Contemporary Policies of Women's Education in Saudi Arabia." Ph.D. dissertation, University of Michigan, 1984.

Mubarak, Faisal Abdul-Aziz M. "Urbanization, Urban Policy and City Form: Urban Development in Saudi Arabia." Ph.D. dissertation, University of Washington, 1992.

Mughram, A. A. "Assarah, Saudi Arabia: Change and Development in a Rural Context." Ph.D. thesis, University of Durham, 1973.

Munajjed, Mona al-. *Women in Saudi Arabia Today*. London: Macmillan; New York: St. Martin's Press, 1997.

Nimr, S. al-. "Attitudes of University Students Toward Work in Saudi Villages and the Countryside." (in Arabic) *al-Idārah al-'Amah*, No. 73 (1992), pp. 7-46.

Oshban, Abdulaziz Rashid al-. "'Al-Qabila': Inter-Group Relations, and the Environmental Context of Bani-Shiher in Southwestern Saudi Arabia. Ph.D. dissertation, Northwestern University, 1987.

Peterson, J. E. "The Political Status of Women in the Arab Gulf States." *Middle East Journal*, Vol. 43, No. 1 (Winter 1989), pp. 34-50.

Rasheed, Madawi al-. "The Shi'a of Saudi Arabia: A Minority in Search of Cultural Authenticity." *British Journal of Middle Eastern Studies*, Vol. 25, No. 1 (May 1998), pp. 121-138.

Rehemi, Madani Farai. "A Survey of the Attitudes of Saudi Men and Women Toward Saudi Female Participation in Saudi Arabian Development." Ph.D. dissertation, University of Colorado, Boulder, 1983.

Riar, Mohammed Hussein Al-. "The Faisal Settlement Project at Haradh, Saudi Arabia: A Study in Nomad Attitudes Toward Sedentarization." Ph.D. dissertation, Michigan State University, 1977.

Ritter, W. "A Note on the Sedentarization of Nomads in Eastern Saudi Arabia." In *Studien zur Allgemeinen und Regionalen Geographie* (Frankfurt?, 1977), pp. 409-433. Frankfurter Wirtschafts- und sozialgeographische Schriften, No. 26.

Roy, D. "Saudi Arabian Education: Development Policy." *Middle Eastern Studies*, Vol. 28, No. 3 (1992), pp. 477-508.

Rugh, William A. "Emergence of a New Middle Class in Saudi Arabia." *Middle East Journal*, Vol. 27, No. 1 (1973), pp. 7-20.

Said, Anwar Ghalib Abdul-Samie, al-. "Migrant Workers and Their Dependents in Kuwait, Saudi Arabia and the United Arab Emirates: Trends in Legal and Educational Provisions." Ed.D., Columbia University Teachers College, 1987.

Sanabary, Nagat el-. *The Saudi Arabian Model of Female Education and the Reproduction of Gender Divisions*. Los Angeles: UCLA, G. E. von Grunebaum Center for Near Eastern Studies, 1992. Working Paper, No. 16.

Seguin, J. "La 'stratégie nationale de peuplement' en Arabie Saoudite." *Peuples Mediterranéens*, Nos. 72-73 (1995), pp. 31-56.

Shahrani, Abullahseed M. al-. "Modernization in a Traditional Society: The Case of Saudi Arabia." Ph.D. dissertation, Clark Atlanta University, 1990.

Shamekh, Ahmed A. "Special Patterns of Bedouin Settlement in Al-Qasim Region, Saudi Arabia." Ph.D. dissertation, University of Kentucky, 1975.
Sheikh, Abdulaziz A. Al-. *Residential Mobility in Riyadh: A Study in Intraurban Migration.* Riyadh: University of Riyadh, 1980.
Shuaiby, Abdulla Mansour. "The Development of the Eastern Province, With Particular Reference to Urban Settlement and Evolution in Eastern Saudi Arabia." Ph.D. thesis, University of Durham, 1976.
Sofi, Jamil Yahya. "Responses of Rural Village Populations to Community Development in Saudi Arabia." Ph.D. dissertation, Case Western University, 1983.
Sudermann, Fredrick. "Saudi Teachers at Riyadh University: A Study in Manpower Development." *Public Administration,* No. 10 (July 1970), pp. 11-19.
Talib, Kaizer. "Squatter Settlement in Saudi Arabia." *International Journal of Housing Science and Its Applications,* Vol. 6, No. 4 (1982), pp. 343-360.
Uthaimeen, Yousef A. "The Welfare State in Saudi Arabia: Structure, Dynamics, and Function." Ph.D. dissertation, American University, 1986.
Vidal, Frederico S. *The Oasis of Al-Hasa.* New York: Arabian American Oil Company, 1955.
———. "Date Culture in the Oasis of Al-Hasa." *Middle East Journal,* Vol. 8, No. 4 (1954), pp. 417-428. Reprinted in Abdulla M. Lutfiyya, ed., *Readings in Arab Middle Eastern Societies and Cultures* (The Hague: Mouton, 1970), pp. 205-217.
Webster, Roger. "Bedouin Settlements in Eastern Arabia." Ph.D. thesis, University of Exeter, 1987.
Wynn, Lisa. "Youth Culture, Commodities and the Use of Public Space in Jiddah." *Middle East Report,* No. 204 (July-September 1997), pp. 30-31.
Yamani, Mai. *Changed Identities: The Challenges of the New Generation in Saudi Arabia.* London: Royal Institute of International Affairs, 1999.
———. "Changing the Habits of a Lifetime: The Adaptation of Hejazi Dress to the New Social Order." In Nancy Lindisfarne-Tapper and Bruce Ingham, eds., *Languages of Dress in the Middle East* (Richmond, UK: Curzon Press, 1997), pp. 55-66.
———. "Children of Oil." *The World Today,* Vol. 56, No. 3 (March 2000), pp. 22-23.
———. "The New Generation in the GCC: The Case of Saudi Arabia." In Rosemary Hollis, ed., *Oil and Regional Developments in the Gulf* (London: Royal Institute of International Affairs, Middle East Programme in association with Division of Research and Studies, Crown Prince Court of Abu Dhabi, 1998), pp. 136-148.
———. "The New Generation in Saudi Arabia: Cultural Change, Political Identity, and Regime Security." In Lawrence G. Potter and Gary G. Sick, eds., *Security in the Persian Gulf: Origins, Obstacles and the Search for Consensus* (New York: Palgrave, 2001), pp. 189-205.
———. "Some Observations on Women in Saudi Arabia." In Mai Yamani, ed., *Feminism and Islam: Legal and Literary Perspectives* (Reading: Ithaca Press, 1996), pp. 263-281.

Zahrani, Abdul-Razzaq Homoud al-. "Saudi Arabian Development: A Sociological Study of Its Relation to Islam and Its Impacts on Society." Ph.D. dissertation, Washington State University, 1986.

ISLAM

Algar, Hamid. *Wahhabism: A Critical Essay*. Oneonta, NY: Islamic Publications International, 2001.
Bill, James A. "Resurgent Islam in the Persian Gulf." *Foreign Affairs*, Vol. 63, No. 1 (Fall 1984), pp. 108-127.
Cook, Michael. "On the Origins of Wahhabism." *Journal of the Royal Asiatic Society*, 3rd Series, Vol. 2, Pt. 2 (July 1992), pp. 191-202.
Dallal, Ahmad. "The Origins and Objectives of Islamic Revivalist Thought, 1750-1850." *Journal of the American Oriental Society*, Vol. 113 (1993), pp. 341-359.
Goldberg, Jacob. "The Shi'i Minority in Saudi Arabia." In Juan R. I. Cole and Nikki R. Keddie, eds., *Shi'ism and Social Protest* (New Haven, CT: Yale University Press, 1986), pp. 230-246.
Humphrey, R. Stephen. "Islam and Political Values in Saudi Arabia, Egypt and Syria." *Middle East Journal*, Vol. 33, No. 1 (1979), pp. 1-19.
Kechichian, Joseph A. "Islamic Revivalism and Change in Saudi Arabia: Juhayman al-'Utaybi's 'Letters' to the Saudi People." *Muslim World*, Vol. 80, No. 1 (1990), pp. 1-16.
———. "The Role of the Ulama in the Politics of an Islamic State: The Case of Saudi Arabia." *International Journal of Middle East Studies*, Vol. 18, No. 1 (February 1986), pp. 53-71.
Long, David E. *The Hajj Today: A Survey of the Contemporary Pilgrimage*. Albany: State University of New York in cooperation with the Middle East Institute, 1979.
Peters, F. E. *The Hajj: The Muslim Pilgrimage to Mecca and the Holy Places*. Princeton, NJ: Princeton University Press, 1994.
Piscatori, James Paul. "Islam and the International Legal Order: The Case of Saudi Arabia." Ph.D. dissertation, University of Virginia, 1976.
———. "The Roles of Islam in Saudi Arabia's Political Development." In John L. Esposito, ed., *Islam and Development: Religion and Sociopolitical Change* (Syracuse, NY: Syracuse University Press, 1980), pp. 123-138.
Rentz, George. "Wahhabism and Saudi Arabia." In Derek Hopwood, ed., *The Arabian Peninsula: Society and Politics* (London: George Allen and Unwin, 1972), pp. 54-66.
Salamé, Ghassan. "Islam and Politics in Saudi Arabia." *Arab Studies Quarterly*, Vol. 9, No. 3 (Summer 1987), pp. 306-325.
Sardar, Ziauddin, and M. A. Zaki Badawi, eds. *Hajj Studies*. London: Croom Helm, for King Abdulaziz University, Hajj Research Centre, 1981.
Sirriyeh, Elizabeth. "Wahhabis, Unbelievers and the Problems of Exclusivism." *British Society for Middle Eastern Studies Bulletin*, Vol. 16, No. 2 (1989), pp. 123-132.

WEBSITES

Middle East Publications and Online News

Al-Bawaba.com – http://www.albawaba.com/main/index.ie.php3?lang=e
Arabic News.com for Arab News – http://www.arabicnews.com/
The Estimate – http://www.theestimate.com/html/current.html
MERIP - Middle East Research and Information Project –
    http://www.merip.org/
Middle East Economic Survey – http://www.mees.com/
Middle East Policy – http://www.mepc.org
Middle East Times – http://www.metimes.com/
Mideast Mirror – http://www.mideastmirror.com/
U.S. Report On The Middle East – http://www.usrom.com/

Middle East Guides and Resources

Almanach de Bruxelles (genealogies of royal families worldwide, including
    the Middle East) – http://www.almanach.be/search/index.htm
Arab Social Science Research (ASSR) – http://www.assr.org/index.html
Arab World Online - Country Information – http://www.awo.net/country/
ArabNet – http://www.arab.net/
Columbia University Library Resources on Middle East –
    http://web.columbia.edu/cu/lweb/indiv/mideast/cuvlm/
Council on Foreign Relations, Terrorism Questions and Answers –
    www.terrorismanswers.com/home
Dartmouth College, Middle East Maps – http://www.dartmouth.edu/~gov46/
    Gulf/2000 – http://gulf2000.columbia.edu/
National Security Archive – Sourcebook on Terrorism Attacks of 11 Sep-
    tember 2001 –
    http://www.gwu.edu/~nsarchiv/NSAEBB/NSAEBB55/index1.html
Operation Desert Storm Debriefing Book – http://www.leyden.com/gulfwar/
United States Government Documents Related to Terrorism Attacks of 11
    September 2001 – http://www.dartmouth.edu/~govdocs/9112001.htm
University of Texas, Middle East Network Information Center (MENIC) –
    http://link.lanic.utexas.edu/menic/

Organizations Focused on the Middle East

British Society for Middle Eastern Studies (BRISMES) –
    http://www.dur.ac.uk/brismes/
Institut du monde arabe (Paris) –
    http://www.imarabe.org/perm/mondearabe/pays/
Middle East Institute (Washington, DC) – http://www.mideasti.org/
Middle East Studies Association (MESA) – http://fp.arizona.edu/mesassoc
Middle East UK.com – Listing of UK centers and institutes for Middle East
    studies – http://www.middleeastuk.com/com/academic.htm

National Council on US-Arab Relations (Washington, DC) –
    http://www.ncusar.org

Islam

Hadith Search – http://db.islam.org:81/hadith/ssearch.htm
Islam, Introduction to (Middle East Institute) –
    http://www.mideasti.org/library/islam/introislam.htm
Islam (information, Qur'an, Pillars, Sunna, etc.) – http://www.iad.org/
al-Islam.com (comprehensive site for information & resources on Islam,
    including prayer times and date converter) –
    http://www.tohajj.com/eng/
Qur'an Search – http://db.islam.org:81/Quran/ssearch.htm

Government and Economic Sites Concerning the Middle East

Governments on the WWW – http://www.gksoft.com/govt/en/
Gulf Cooperation Council (GCC) – http://www.gcc-sg.org/index_e.html
United Kingdom Foreign and Commonwealth Office –
    http://www.fco.gov.uk
United Nations – http://www.un.org/
United States Central Intelligence Agency (CIA), Publications –
    http://www.odci.gov/cia/publications/pubs.html
United States Department of Defense –
    US Central Command (USCENTCOM) – http://www.centcom.mil/
    Fact File – http://www.defenselink.mil/sites/f.html
United States Government comprehensive search – http://first.gov.gov
United States Library of Congress, Congressional Research Service reports
    – http://www.house.gov/shays/resources/leginfo/crs.htm
United States National Security Council – http://www.whitehouse.gov/nsc/
United States State Department –
    International Information Programs, Near East & North Africa –
        http://usinfo.state.gov/regional/nea/
    Country Background Notes – http://www.state.gov/r/pa/bgn/
    Country Reports on Economic Practice and Trade Reports –
        http://www.state.gov/e/eb/rls/rpts/eptp/
University of Michigan Middle East & North Africa Governments Websites
    http://www.lib.umich.edu/govdocs/forme.html
World Bank Group – http://www.worldbank.org

Saudi Arabia Specific Sites

Datarabia.com (pay-for-information on Saudi royal family and businesses;
    formerly the Saudi Royals Database) – http://www.datarabia.com/
Saudi Arabia Country Study (United States Library of Congress) –
    http://lcweb2.loc.gov/frd/cs/satoc.html

Saudi Arabia Information Resource (a comprehensive database maintained by the Saudi Arabia Ministry of Information) – http://www.saudinf.com/main/index1.htm
Saudi Institute (an opposition organization in McLean, Virginia) – http://www.saudiinstitute.org/
Saudi Strategies – a business consultancy – http://www.saudistrategies.com/
United States Embassy, Riyadh – http://usembassy.state.gov/riyadh

Saudi Arabia Newspapers and Agencies

Arab News – http://www.arabnews.com/
Al-Hayat – http://www.alhayat.com/
Al-Jazirah – http://www.aljazirah.com/
Al-Riyadh – http://www.alriyadh-np.com
Saudi Press Agency – http://www.spa.gov.sa/
Al-Sharq al-Awsat – http://www.asharqalawsat.com/
'Ukaz (Okaz) – http://www.okaz.com.sa/
Al-Watan – http://www.alwatan.com.sa
Al-Yawm – http://www.alyaum.com.sa

Saudi Arabia Government Agencies

Majlis al-Shura (Consultative Council) – http://www.shura.gov.sa/
Ministry of Agriculture and Water – http://www.agrwat.gov.sa
Ministry of Finance and National Economy – http://www.mof.gov.sa/
Ministry of Foreign Affairs – http://www.mofa.gov.sa/
Ministry of Information – http://www.saudinf.com/
Ministry of Islamic Affairs, Awqaf, Da'wah, and Irshad – http://www.islam.org.sa/
Ministry of Labor and Social Affairs – http://www.mol.gov.sa
Ministry of Petroleum and Mineral Resources – http://www.mopm.gov.sa/
Ministry of Planning – http://www.planning.gov.sa/
Royal Commission for al-Jubayl and Yanbu' – http://www.rcjy.gov.sa/
Saudi Arabia Monetary Agency – http://www.sama-ksa.org/
Saudi Arabian Embassy, Washington, DC – http://www.saudiembassy.net/
Saudi Arabian Oil Company (Saudi ARAMCO) – http://www.saudiaramco.com

Saudi Arabia Universities and Institutes

Imam Muhammad b. Saud University – http://www.imamu.edu.sa/
Islamic University – http://www.iu.edu.sa/
King Abd al-Aziz Center for Science and Technology – http://www.kacst.edu.sa/
King Abd al-Aziz University – http://www.kaau.edu.sa/
King Abdulaziz Foundation for Research and Archives (ad-Darah) – http://www.darah.org.sa

King Fahd University of Petroleum and Minerals –
    http://www.kfupm.edu.sa/
King Faisal Foundation – http://www.kff.com/homepage.htm
King Faisal University – http://www.kfu.gov.sa/
King Khalid University – http://www.kku.gov.sa/
King Saud University – http://www.ksu.edu.sa/
Umm al-Qura University – http://www.uqu.edu.sa/

ABOUT THE AUTHOR

J. E. PETERSON most recently has served in the Office of the Deputy Prime Minister for Security and Defence in Muscat, Sultanate of Oman, where he wrote a history of the Sultan's Armed Forces, and at the International Institute for Strategic Studies, where he wrote an Adelphi Paper on *Saudi Arabia and the Illusion of Security* (July 2002). At present, he is affiliated with the Center for Middle Eastern Studies at the University of Arizona. He has travelled widely throughout the Middle East and has conducted extensive research in each of the Arabian Peninsula countries, including work on a number of occasions in Saudi Arabia.

Dr. Peterson received his Ph.D. from the Johns Hopkins University School of Advanced International Studies and has taught at Bowdoin College, the College of William and Mary, the University of Pennsylvania, and Portland State University. He has also been a Fellow at the Foreign Policy Research Institute (Philadelphia) and the Middle East Institute, and an Adjunct Fellow at the Center for Strategic and International Studies (Washington, D.C.), as well as the International Institute for Strategic Studies.

He is the author of more than three dozen scholarly articles, most recently on the historical pattern of Gulf security, succession in the Gulf, Saudi-American relations, recent reforms in Bahrain, and the economics of the United Arab Emirates. His previous books include: *Oman in the Twentieth Century* (1978), *Conflict in the Yemens and Superpower Involvement* (1981), *Yemen: The Search for a Modern State* (1982), *The Politics of Middle Eastern Oil* (editor, 1983), *Defending Arabia* (1986), *Cross-currents in the Gulf: Arab, Regional, and Global Interests* (coeditor, 1988), and *The Arab Gulf States: Steps Toward Political Participation* (1988).

Defending Oman: A History of the Sultan's Armed Forces and a revised edition of his annotated bibliography of Gulf security are forthcoming. Dr. Peterson is presently working on a comparative study of state-building in all the states of the Arabian Peninsula, a modern history of the Arabian Peninsula, a study of Oman since 1970, and a historical guide to Muscat. His website is www.JEPeterson.net.